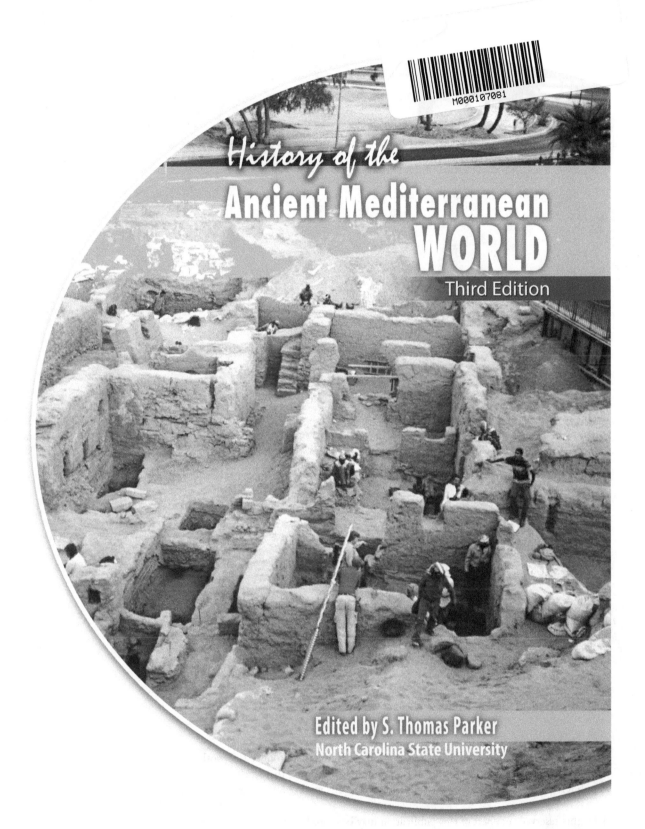

History of the
Ancient Mediterranean
WORLD

Third Edition

Edited by S. Thomas Parker
North Carolina State University

Kendall Hunt
publishing company

www.kendallhunt.com
Send all inquiries to:
4050 Westmark Drive
Dubuque, IA 52004-1840

Copyright © 2009, 2011, 2018 by S. Thomas Parker
Revised Printing 2013

ISBN 978-1-5249-4983-9

Contents

Dedication

To all my students in ancient history at
North Carolina State University. They have taught me so much.

Introduction

This book is intended to serve students studying the history of the ancient Mediterranean World. After a brief look at prehistory, which requires a broader geographical perspective, the book turns to the world that produced "Western civilization." The main focus is on three great civilizations, presented in more or less chronological order: the ancient Near East (including Mesopotamia, Egypt, Anatolia, and the Levant), ancient Greece, and ancient Rome. This is not to deny the great significance of other early centers of world civilization, such as India, China, sub-Saharan Africa, or Mesoamerica. But there is equally no denying the fundamental importance of the civilizations of the Mediterranean world in shaping subsequent human history.

This book consists of two main parts. The first is a series of **lecture outlines** that form the basis of our class lectures and discussions. It should be stressed that these are merely outlines and are not intended to be a substitute for detailed lecture notes. The second part of the book is a collection of **primary sources,** i.e. ancient documents produced by people from these civilizations. These primary sources have been translated from a variety of ancient languages (Akkadian, Egyptian, Hebrew, Greek, Latin, etc.) into English for your use. You will learn that the historian uses such primary sources, which are the "raw material" or evidence, in a critical fashion to write history. You will use such evidence while writing essays as part of the examinations for this class.

The study of each civilization begins with an analysis of its geography and environment. You will learn that all civilizations are to a greater or lesser degree products of their geography.

Finally, there is a traditional ancient history textbook for this class. The textbook contains much more detail about each ancient civilization, as well as useful images and a bibliography for additional reading.

When preparing for each class, students should first consult the syllabus and read over the lecture outline in this book. This will provide a rapid overview of the material. Students should next read the textbook assignment to gain more detailed knowledge. Finally, students should return to this book to read any primary sources assigned for that class. Reading the assignments in this order should enable students to learn the material most efficiently.

For this third edition I have revised several chapters to reflect new evidence or interpretations. I have also added a new introduction to the primary source readings and written new introductions to nearly all the individual primary sources.

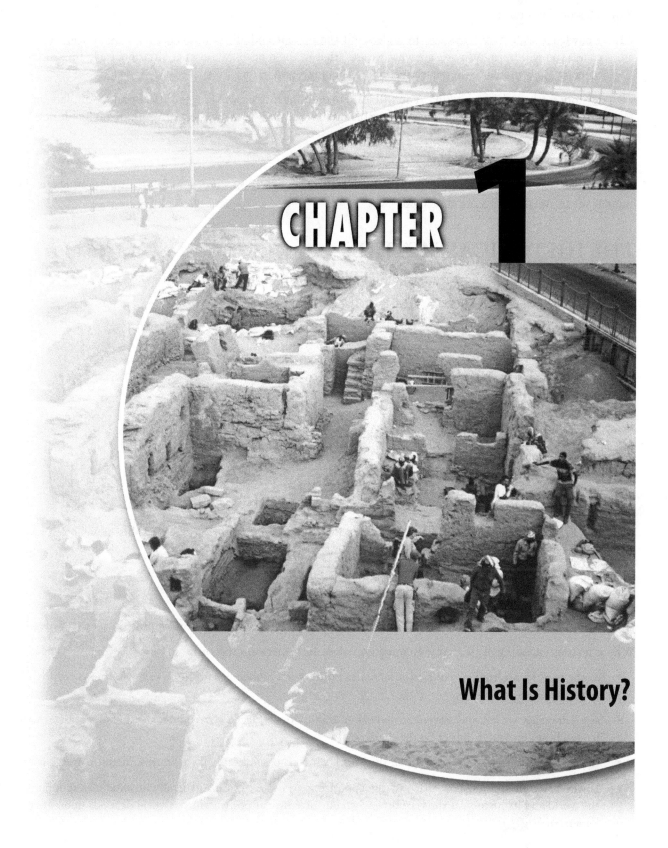

CHAPTER 1

What Is History?

History is a discipline that seeks to interpret the human past.

● Why is history important?   *Use it*

1. <u>Knowledge of history helps you to understand the present and all its problems and possibilities.</u> In this course you will learn "Why we are what we are," that is, the roots of Western civilization, including society, economy, government, religion, science and technology, and so on. ● *looking back on 1918 pandemic*

2. <u>History teaches critical thinking.</u> You will learn to examine historical evidence critically and formulate interpretations. The historical method is a valuable intellectual skill that will benefit you in many fields outside history. *Analyze / pose Q's*

● How is history written?

History is *not* just a lot of facts about the past. Rather, <u>the historian seeks answers to specific questions about the human past by use of the historical method.</u>

Primary Sources, artifacts, oral history

THE HISTORICAL METHOD

When posing a specific historical question, the historian proceeds by the following method:

a. Collect Primary Sources (relevant evidence or facts)

   1. written documents

   2. archaeological artifacts

Primary Source
- documents written by the ppl your studying
- artifacts

b. Analyze or Evaluate Primary Sources

   1. strengths/weaknesses

   2. reliability/bias (*all sources are biased*)

Secondary Source
- written work about the primary source

c. Interpretation/Synthesis   ● *rare to have everyone agree on one interpretation forever.*

   1. Well-organized/coherent argument or interpretation

   2. Supported by analysis of sources (e.g., an essay)

   3. Rarely, if ever, is there a single interpretation of any major historical question; historians often reach totally different interpretations about the same question

● In prehistory and ancient history, the task is much more difficult because:

- all participants are long dead
- 99+% of all sources (both written and archaeological) that once existed have disappeared over the millennia

organic materials don't survive / most arch sites haven't been uncovered

Why is an understanding of the past even <u>more important for Americans</u> than others?

- as the <u>world's preeminent</u> political, economic, military and cultural <u>power,</u> we have enormous worldwide responsibilities

- as a <u>democracy</u> we not only govern ourselves but as individuals elect a government that pursues policies with far-reaching, profound impact on the entire world

- therefore, our citizens must understand the world, which is possible only if we know something of its history

- however, recent studies show that just the opposite is true—<u>Americans</u> generally are woefully <u>ignorant</u> of the world and its history, at the very time when our preeminent position in the world depends upon greater understanding

PURPOSE OF ANCIENT HISTORY

ROOTS or "Why we are what we are?"

This class will:

- offer a brief look at prehistory (human origins) *5+ million yrs*

- explore origins of our civilization by studying three important ancient civilizations with enormous impact on our contemporary world: *3,300 yrs*

  1) Ancient Near East

  2) Ancient Greece

  3) Ancient Rome

We will examine each in terms of its geographic setting, economic basis, political and social organization, and an outline of its history.

What is History? —discipline that seeks to interpret the human past.
—ask Q's & seek answers

Part I

PREHISTORY

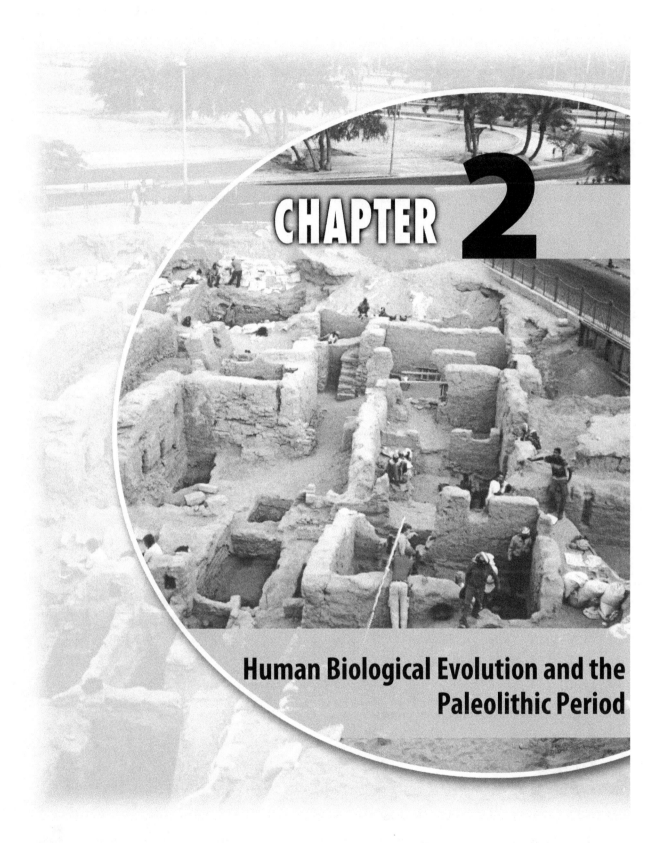

CHAPTER 2

Human Biological Evolution and the Paleolithic Period

Paleolithic — "old Stone Age"

PREHISTORY—covers over 99% of the human past (until ca. 3000 BC) *Until 5,000 yrs ago w/ invention of writing*

SOURCES—no written records, all knowledge of prehistory derived from archaeology (excavation of sites, analysis of artifacts) and sciences (geology, biology, genetics, etc.)

Charles Darwin—19th-century English naturalist who published *The Origin of Species* (1859) proposed "theory of evolution," based on two facts and two conclusions: *traveled around world / Beagle*

Facts: *w/n each species*

1. All organisms exhibit variability.

2. All organisms reproduce more offspring than can survive. *Ex: fish*

Conclusions: *Evidence for evolution = Fossils*

1. Natural selection—environment selects individuals best suited for survival, but individuals less well suited fail to reproduce.

2. Traits favored by natural selection that enhanced survival are then passed to next generation.

HUMAN BIOLOGICAL EVOLUTION: KEY QUESTIONS

1. When, where, and how did humans evolve?

2. What differentiates humans from other animals?

Earth—ca. 4.6 billion years old

Living organisms—appeared about 3.8 billion years ago

Mammals—appeared 160 million years ago, dominant after 65 million years ago (after extinction of dinosaurs)

- Primates—an order of mammals appeared 55 million years ago

Common characteristics of primates include:

1. Nails rather than claws on digits

2. Prehensile (grasping) hands and feet

3. One pair of mammary glands on thorax

4. Forward placement of eye orbits—reduced sense of smell but improved vision *for tree environment*

Four types of primates (in chronological order of appearance):

1. Prosimians (e.g., tarsiers and lemurs)

2. Monkeys *34 mya*

3. Apes (e.g., gorillas, chimpanzees) *23 mya / chimps closest living relative 96-98% genetically similar*

4. Humans
   • we didn't evolve from chimps but a common ancestor.

What distinguishes humans from other primates?

1. Bipedalism *- walking on 2 limbs*

2. Language *- only one w/ a true language*

3. Culture *(beliefs + customs passed through generations)* *Debatable*

MIOCENE (23–5 million years ago)—apes evolve in Africa

PALEOLITHIC—"old stone age" (5 million–10,000 BC)—end of Miocene witnessed dramatic change in climate and environment in East Africa, with extinction of many ape species; some apes who could adapt evolved into earliest *hominins* (proto-humans), who diverged from apes ca. 5 million years ago

• dense forrest turned to broken savannah - grasslands + some forrest
• dry

SOME KEY HOMININS

Ardipithecus · earliest certain hominid

(from "Ardi" meaning "ground" or "floor" in Afar language, "pithecus" meaning "ape"; 4.5–4.2 million years ago in Ethiopia in East Africa in a woodland environment)

 Best preserved Example

- "Ardi" was a female- 4'0" tall, 110 lbs
- cranial capacity 350 cc *cubic centimeters / size of chimp*
- very ape-like skull and face
- pelvis and other skeletal elements suggest a biped
- big toe splays out from foot like an ape's, thus partly arboreal
- teeth suggest diet of fruits, nuts, and other forest foods

Australopithecus   · very successful species

("Southern ape-man," 4–2 million years ago)—emerged in East Africa in a "broken savanna" environment

- several species known *found 1974*   *↓ Rare*
- *EX* "Lucy"—40% of fossilized female skeleton recovered: 3'6" tall, ca. 60 lbs, cranial capacity 450 cc
- males much larger: up to 5'0" tall, ca. 100 lbs *sexual dimorphism / size difference*
- skull and face very ape-like
- bipedal, despite stooped posture (partly arboreal?)
- largely vegetarian—fruit, nuts, seeds, tubers, perhaps insects

Explanations for evolution of bipedalism: *- slows us down / vulnerable to predators*

1. Freeing of hands for tools? *No known stone tools? Could've used organic materials (wood)*
2. Walking through and looking over savanna grass? *Avoid predators*
3. Provisioning females and young? *Males bringing food back to females bc they are pregnant & not as mobile. Higher birth rates bc mortality rate high. Evidence? No older than 40+*

Genus
Homo Habilis "Handy Man"

("Skillful man," 2.4–1.5 million years, in East Africa)

- males 5'0" tall, ca. 115 lbs; females 4'0" tall, ca. 70 lbs
- cranial capacity—650 cc
- flatter face, steeper forehead—much less ape-like skull
- primarily gathered wild plants and scavenged abandoned kills
- *1st tech advancement* first stone tools (marrow extraction while scavenging?) *chipped stone tools*

↳ protein rich - increase brain size?   *↳ the kills of large animal carcass killed by predators*

Homo Erectus

("Upright man," 1.8 million–300,000 years ago, originated in East Africa)

- males 5'10" tall, ca. 140 lbs; females 5'3", ca. 115 lbs

→ Humans don't ever get any taller (averagely)

- cranial capacity—1000 cc

• *1st to walk fully upright*

- first hominid to walk fully upright

- big-game hunters with better stone tools

1st • controlled use of fire (ca. 780,000 years ago in Palestine); uses of fire? ☆ *2nd biggest tch advancement*

• first hominid to migrate from Africa to Asia and Europe

↳ protection
cook food
preserve food (smoke it) Start of language ?
light   gather around fire

Homo Heidelbergensis *— During Ice Age on the Tundra*

("Archaic *Homo Sapiens*," 800,000–125,000 years ago; geographical origin disputed—attested in Africa, Asia, Europe)

- males 5'9", 140 lbs; females 5'2", 115 lbs

- cranial capacity—1200 cc.

- close to modern skull (e.g., less-pronounced brow ridges)

- hunted large game cooperatively with improved stone tools

Homo Neanderthalensis

(400,000–30,000 BC, in Europe and Middle East)

- first hominid ever found—Neander Valley in Germany (1856) *complete skeletons found*

- males 5'5", 185 lbs; females 5'1", 176 lbs—*short* stocky/powerfully built

- cranial capacity—1500 cc. (slightly more than modern average) *◦smaller part of the brain that controls reasoning / dsnt mean smarter*

- differs from modern humans in shape of skull, teeth, and brain

- big game hunters */killed large animals w/ weapons / consumed mostly meat >large animals*

- first evidence of intentional burial of dead (Shanidar, Iraq)—belief in afterlife and thus religion?

- evidence of art?   *↳ covered w/ flowers   stone tools (power)   ◦evidence of trauma & healing   meat   — cared for/nursed to neath*

- fate of Neanderthals? */couldn't compete w/ Homo sapiens*
or exterminated by↑
Interbreeding → Europeans now

Homo Sapiens

("Wise man," appeared 200,000 or earlier? years ago)

Origin debated—two main theories:

Consensus (1.) "Out of Africa"—based partly on genetic research, with later migration to other continents, replacing other humans - this is the current scholarly consensus *◦traced back to a single female in Africa*

2. "Multiregional"—modern humans evolved from archaic ancestors more or less simultaneously in several different regions
bow & arrow   *successful bc*

- gathered wild plants and hunted big game, armed with missile weapons   *◦adapted to various environments*

- migrated to Australia (60,000 BC) and Americas (after 20,000 BC)   *◦range of stone & bone tools*

- first art—cave paintings in Europe (ca. 30,000 BC at Chauvet Cave, France)   *◦gathered all food resources*
◦animals hunted   ◦sympathetic magic
◦not decorative   — drawn to increase success on a hunt

CONCLUSIONS

— moved in search of food

1. All Paleolithic humans were ***nomadic*** and ***food collectors*** (gatherers/hunters/scavengers) *@ mercy of environment*

2. Although basic outline of human evolution now clear, many questions remain (e.g., when did real language emerge?)

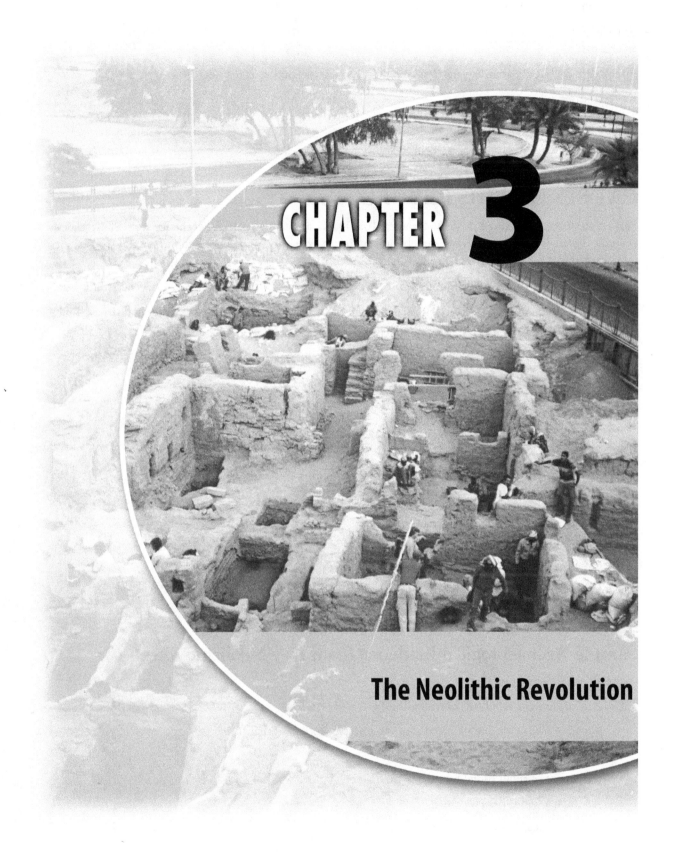

CHAPTER 3

The Neolithic Revolution

The final period of prehistory (10,000–3000 BC) and marked a fundamental "revolution" in human existence—its consequences profoundly shaped all subsequent human history and define our modern world.

Key transformation: Humans changed from being *food collectors* to *food producers* via domestication of animals and plants.

PRIMARY SOURCES: exclusively archaeological, no written sources available

• Analysis of ancient environ. site
• excavation of human habitation
• Regional surface survey
• Analysis of artifacts
• Analysis of organic remains (plants/animals)

Key questions:

1. How, when, where, and why did this happen?

2. What were the consequences of this revolution?

CAUSES OF THIS REVOLUTION

Earliest evidence from Near East (S.W. Asia) ca. 10,000 BC, associated with end of the Ice Age (Pleistocene), which brought dramatic worldwide changes in climate and mass extinction of many plant and animal species, including large mammals that had been key resources of late Paleolithic peoples

Causes debated but most explanations based on two main factors that necessitated new survival strategies:

? inter-related

1. Environmental factors—for the Near East, end of Ice Age witnessed a much hotter and drier climate (e.g., appearance of Sahara Desert in North Africa)

2. Demographic factors—population in some areas increased beyond the ability of a hunter/gatherer economy to support *• food supply threatened*

Current Scholarly Consensus *SW Asia (Near East)*

Domestication first occurred not in oases and river valleys but in **upland hill country** outside the river valleys (e.g., in Palestine, Syria, Iraq, and Iran)

Natufian culture (ca. 11,500–9,500 BC)—transitional lifestyle

- First discovered in caves on Mount Carmel (coast of Palestine)

- Spread widely throughout the Levant, especially exploiting forested regions

- Harvested *wild* grains and acorns

- Hunted gazelles with aid of *domesticated* dogs (from wolves) *auroch, cattle*

- Considered a late Paleolithic culture- still primarily food collectors

• lived in caves & temporary campsites
• Still H & G
• on threshold of being producers
1st wild animal domesticated

Sample Archaeological Evidence from Key Neolithic Sites

(Note all are *villages*): *Permanent settlements / producing food*   *• Still no agriculture*

1. Zawi Chemi (ca. 9500 BC northern Iraq):

- *possible* evidence for domesticated sheep but no evidence of agriculture   *evidence their smaller domesticated*

- hunting and gathering still key

- settlement of small round huts (ca. 5 m. diameter) *permanent*

2. Jericho (ca. 9400 BC Palestine):

- oasis in Jordan Valley   *• not in upland hill country*

- settlement of small circular huts

- cultivation of domesticated cereals & livestock (sheep, goat)

- hunting & wild grains still important food sources
- village fortified ca. 8300 B.C. with stone wall and tower *unique*

(ine) 3. Ain Ghazal (ca. 8300 BC central Jordan): *Storage holes in home*
- one of largest Neolithic villages (ca. 35 acres w/ estimated population ca. 3,000)
- settlement of rectangular houses w/ plaster floors */permanent*
- several apsidal structures interpreted as "temples" *"Temple"? —complex floor plan*
- domesticated wheat, barley, and legumes (lentils & peas)
- domesticated goats
- hunting (especially wild cattle) & wild grains still important food sources
- ca. 30 human statues made of plaster- buried under house floors & of enigmatic purpose (i.e., not displayed- ancestor worship? gods?) *skeletons* *Skull missing → plastered → put into homes*

earliest human statues (just plaster)
- early example of anthropogenic environmental catastrophe- overgrazing by domestic goats led to deforesta- tion, soil erosion, extinction of wildlife, & eventual abandonment of village *human caused*

Chatal Huieuke
4. Catal Huyuk (ca. 7500 BC, southern Turkey): *house packed together • move from house to house over the roof & got inside via ladder*
- one of largest Neolithic villages- estimated peak population of ca. 6,000
- densely pack houses of sun dried mud brick, accessed through roofs *Adobe*
- domesticated wheat, barley, legumes (peas)
- perhaps first evidence for domesticated cattle (from auroch- now extinct wild ancestor)
- cattle heads mounted on walls (ritual purpose?)
- early evidence of handmade pottery and plastered bins for storage/*cooking*
- many stone & ceramic figurines of females, possibly of religious significance

5. Jarmo (ca. 7000 BC, northern Iraq, foothills of Zagros Mountains):
- typical Neolithic village- 3-4 acres *100-150 ppl*
- domesticated wheat, barley, lentils
- domesticated sheep, goat, dogs, later pigs
- evidence for continued harvesting of wild grains & hunting- aurochs & onagers (wild asses)

Key characteristics of these villages:
- most in upland hill country
- nearly all unfortified
- ca. 5–40 acres
- population range from ca. 100 to ca. 6,000 (most near low end of this range)
- producing food from domestic plants and animals, supplemented by hunting & gathering

Key innovations at these villages:
1. Domestication of animals:
- for food, clothing, fertilizer (sheep/goat, cow, pig) *, meat & milk* *↓ Clothing*
- as work animals (dog, cat, cow, donkey) *hair & hides / bone / manure -fertilizer*
- horse and camel—appear only later, in Bronze Age (after 3000 BC)

plowing - cow
transport - donkey
security/hunting - dog
pest control - cat

Chapter Three—*The Neolithic Revolution*   **13**

2. Domestication of plants:

- grains (e.g., barley and wheat) first domesticated from wild grasses and became core of human diet

- legumes (beans, peas, etc.) *higher protein*

- by late Neolithic—variety of vegetables and fruits (olive and grape especially important) *Storage → fermented as wine + dried or eaten fresh*
  ↳ olive oil → food, light, medicine, cleaning self + nuts

3. First use of metals (ca. 8000 BC):

- copper first metal widely used—tools, weapons, containers, etc. *Soft/malleable*

- gold and silver exploited in late Neolithic

- bronze (ca. 3500 BC)—alloy of 90% copper + 10% tin heated together in furnace—stronger than either primary element

4. Pottery (ca. 6000 BC):

- enhanced storage capacity, especially of food

- many other uses—cooking, serving, lighting, construction material, etc.

- great importance for archaeologists as chronological marker—cheap, thus abundant, easily broken, and broken pieces ("pot sherds") virtually indestructible; pottery changes rapidly in style over time, thus closely datable

5. Wheel (ca. 3500 BC):

- land transport

- exploited in many other devices—potter's wheel, pulley, etc.

IMPACT OF NEOLITHIC REVOLUTION ON HUMAN LIFESTYLE?

1. Big increase in food supply—normally a surplus of food

2. Dramatic increase in population—food-producing economy could support much higher density population than food collecting

3. Sedentarization—villages (permanent food-producing settlements) with up to several thousand people in each

4. Specialized economy—small % of population could acquire food by trading their goods (e.g., potters, smiths, weavers) or services (e.g., warriors, priests, managers of people [i.e., politicians])

5. Beginnings of *social stratification*—less based on kinship but more on *occupation*—simple egalitarianism of Paleolithic era lost forever

Downside of Neolithic Life

- humans on average became smaller physically than late Paleolithic hunter/gatherers

- evidence for increased disease

Why?

- change in diet—decline in quantity of protein, less variety

- problems of sanitation posed by sedentary population

CONCLUSION

Changes in human society resulting from "Neolithic Revolution" were profound and far-reaching—we live with their consequences today

Part II

THE ANCIENT NEAR EAST

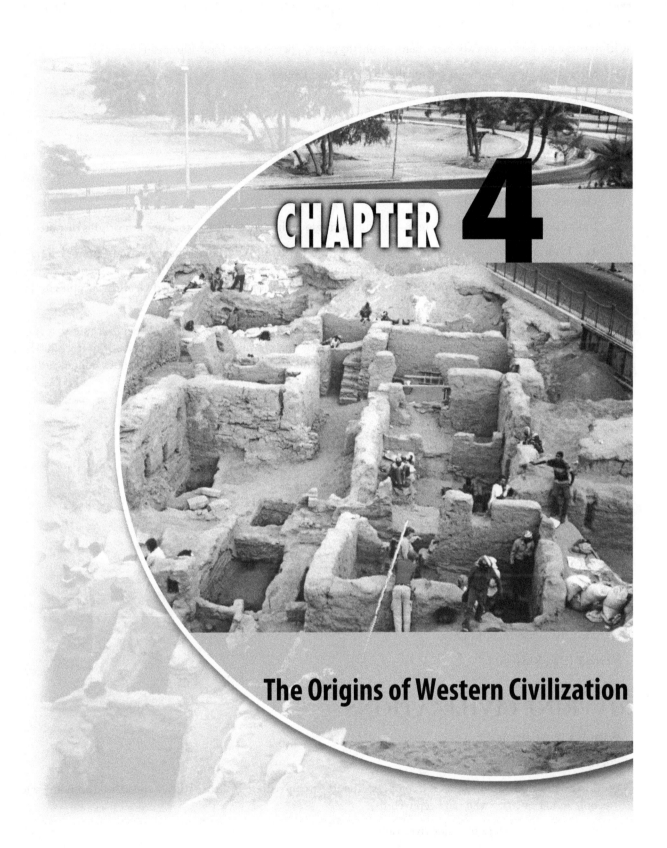

CHAPTER 4

The Origins of Western Civilization

<handwritten>Ethnocentric
near to europe</handwritten>

3 western religions

Ancient Near East and Mediterranean World as the cradle of Western Civilization; deeply influenced modern world—Judaism, Christianity, Islam, modern Western philosophy, Western law, architecture, language, literature, science all evolved from these cultures

Within this civilization are two major families of languages—Semitic and Indo-European

1. Semitic family of languages (originally from Arabian Peninsula) /arid / surrounded by water d to the North Fertile crescent

   Major Semitic language groups:

   East Semitic (e.g., Akkadian, Babylonian)

   NW Semitic (e.g., Hebrew, Canaanite, Aramaic, Arabic)

   South Semitic

   Hamitic (e.g., Egyptian)

2. Indo-European family of languages—all from a single prehistoric "mother-tongue" but origins disputed:

   1. Traditional view—a "mother-tongue" spoken in modern SW Russia, whence various groups migrated into Europe, Near East, and India beginning ca. 6000 BC; early Indo-European migrants viewed as "warrior-nomads" with metal-working technology who subjugated or expelled Neolithic peoples in their path

   2. Colin Renfrew, *Archaeology and Language: The Puzzle of Indo-European Origins* (1987)—argues that Indo-Europeans spread from original homeland in eastern Anatolia much earlier, early in Neolithic (ca. 8000 BC) as a result of agriculture, as more numerous peaceful farmers slowly replaced indigenous hunter-gatherer societies in their path

Controversial

Whatever their origin, groups of Indo-Europeans migrated into Europe, Near East, and India

   Major Indo-European language groups:

   Anatolian (e.g., Hittite)

   Indo-Iranian (e.g., Sanskrit, Persian)

   Armenian

   Greek

   Italic (e.g., Latin)

   Celtic (e.g., Irish, Scottish)

   Baltic (e.g., Lithuanian)

   Germanic (e.g., German, English)

   Slavonic (e.g., Russian)

RIVERINE CIVILIZATIONS 50% of English language comes from another Indo-European language

What is a "civilization"?

English word from Latin *civitas*—"city"

Working definition: "Civilization is a complex, literate, urban-centered culture" (i.e., a specialized economy with people living in cities who can keep records).

Earliest civilizations arose in major river valleys

Tigris/Euphrates (Mesopotamia)

Nile (Egypt)

Indus (Pakistan)

Yellow (China)

<u>Why</u> did earliest civilizations emerge in ~~rover~~ river valleys?

- rich alluvial soil offered potentially great agricultural surplus

- arid or semiarid climate required a complex system of irrigation *draw water from rivers to water fields*

- irrigation system mandated high degree of social organization to direct, protect, and redistribute economic surplus of the society (i.e., bureaucracy)

- bureaucracy required system of recordkeeping (i.e., literacy)

- earliest texts (in Mesopotamia, ca. 3400–3300 BC) are economic

<u>Origin of writing</u>: evolved in four stages:

1. pictograph *–draw picture of idea / can't draw abstract ideas*
2. ideograph *– 2 or more pictographs* *together to express an idea* *Bee + leaf picture = belief*
3. syllabic/phonetic *pictograph used to express ideas + sounds/syllables*

   First three stages completed by ca. 3000 B.C., but early writing systems required hundreds or thousands of characters; thus, literacy confined to tiny elite of highly trained scribes

   Mesopotamia—baked clay tablets inscribed in <u>cuneiform</u> ("wedge-shaped" characters) *symbols*

   Egypt—ink on papyrus ("hieroglyphics")

4. alphabetic script (ca. 1500 BC) invented by Canaanites in Syria—vastly simplified system, only <u>22 characters</u> (consonants only), expanded literacy beyond scribes but still confined to <u>tiny %</u> of population

<u>Significance of Literacy</u>: *Cananite Alphabet*
↳ borrowed by Phonecians & spread
to Greeks → had consonants & vowels
borrowed by Romans → Latin → what
we use now

Who was literate?
– only highly trained
Scribes / elite

- knowledge could be stored

- society could pass sum total of its knowledge to succeeding generations

- knowledge is power

Use of writing?
• economic records

Ex of cuneiform
   - Tablet recording allocation of beer
   - S, Iraq c. 3100 - 3000 B. C.
   - baked clay tablet when it was damp used a stylus to draw + then fire in a kiln
   - durable / thousands have survived
   - thousand diff symbols for their syllables
EX: The Flood Tablet, relating part of the Epic of Gilgamesh
   – Neo-Assyrian, 7th century BC from Nineveh, N. Iraq
   ⋈ Most famous cuneiform tablet from Mesopotamia

Mesopotamia - "land b/w rivers" Tigris & Euphrates, flow parallel
- Semi arid / dry hot - summer, cooler, some rain - winter
- river source of water, land rich bc ever of over flooding
  - floods could be catastrophic
  - flood fed by snow melt from mountains in N. Anatolia

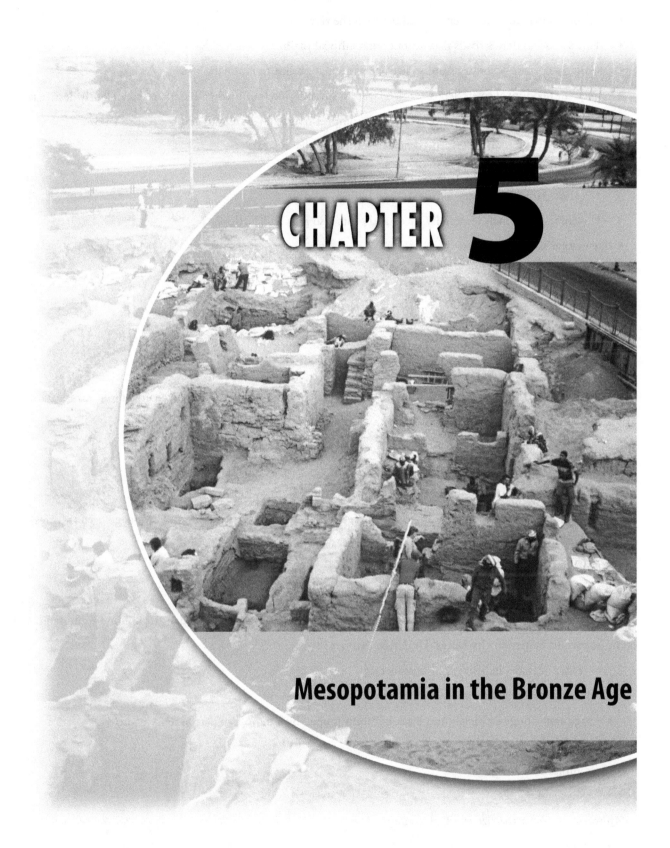

CHAPTER 5

Mesopotamia in the Bronze Age

GEOGRAPHY

- Mesopotamia (ancient Greek—"land between the rivers")
- Tigris and Euphrates rivers flow through flat alluvial plain
- semiarid climate—hot dry summers/cooler winters with limited rainfall
- frequent flooding of rivers deposited rich layers of silt, but floods unpredictable and often violently destructive
- rich potential for agriculture, but only with complex irrigation system to bring water to land
  - barley (key grain, tolerated salinity of soil better than wheat) *Core of economy — more resistant to the salt from river used for crops*
  - legumes (beans and peas)
  - fruits (especially dates and figs)
  - domestic animals (especially sheep and goats also pigs and cattle)
- few other natural resources:
  - reeds for weaving *no metal*
  - mud brick for most architecture
  - clay for pottery
  - fish and water fowl
- no forests, metals, nor stone—all key imports *How* ↓ *or take resources by force*
- necessity of trade—export agricultural surplus and manufactured products in exchange for key imports
- Mesopotamia wide open to invasion—unprotected by natural barriers
  repeated invasions + foreign conquests

THE SUMERIANS *"Sumer" southern*

Earliest known civilization arose in southern Mesopotamia ca. 3400–3200 BC

Origins obscure—Sumerian language appears completely unrelated to any other known language; two theories

1. Immigrant theory – *ppl themselves say they immigrated from Dilmun. No artificatual evidence of arrival of new ppl.*
2. Indigenous theory – *native as far back as 5000 B.C.*

Sumerians organized into many ***city-states***, each with its own king *city + rural area*

Definition: A city-state is an independent political unit composed of both a city and a surrounding hinterland.

Some important Sumerian city-states: Ur, Uruk, Nippur

City—center of trade, industry, and bureaucracy *high intercity warfare*

- heavily fortified with massive mudbrick walls
- ziggurat—huge artificial mud brick platform topped by a temple to patron deity of city *God* *Center of city*
- palace of king *housing of priest is larger than palace of King*
- temples to other gods
- shops and houses

Hinterland—about the size of a U.S. county

- farms
- villages

- pasture lands
- irrigation system

Sumerian class structure (in each city-state):

1. King   *"Big Man" in Sumerian*

- normally viewed as man—not worshipped, though *institution* of kingship of divine origin; king viewed as the chosen representative of the gods
- commander-in-chief of city-state's army   */military leader*
- chief judge
- high priest
- large landowner—royal lands

2. Royal bureaucracy (includes scribes)   *Administer justice, tax*

- oversaw maintenance of irrigation system
- taxation and redistribution of surplus production
- administered justice in name of king
- drew rations from king

3. Priests   */high power*

- intermediaries between gods and human society
- controlled large temple estates—thus, wealth and economic power   *, control farms outside city*
- principal educated class—dominated intellectual thought   *, only educated class*

4. Soldiers

- first professional armies in history
- frequent intercity warfare over land and water rights
- drew rations from king

Standard of Ur

5. Artisans and Merchants

- artisans (potters, weavers, metal-smiths)
- merchants conducted crucial import/export trade   *to get natural resources they lack*

6. Peasants

- vast bulk of population
- freeholders (owned land and paid taxes to king)
- tenants (worked king's land or temple estates as sharecroppers) *also pay taxes to king*

both common

7. Slaves numerous in Mesopotamia; sources: *, common*

- war captives
- debt slavery
- slave breeding

Victory Stele of Naram-Sin,
- Akkadian Dynasty
-reign of Naram-Sin
- bigger+higher up

Temple vs palace
priest vs king

OUTLINE OF MESOPOTAMIAN HISTORY (CA. 3200–2000 BC)

Early Dynastic Period (ca. 3200–2400 BC)

All Mesopotamia divided into independent city-states, often at war with each other—Sumerian city-states in south and Semitic city-states in north

Sargon of Akkad (ca. 2350 BC) *campaign of conquest*

- Semitic king of city-state of Akkad somewhere in central Mesopotamia (exact location unknown)

- name means "True King"

- rise to power problematic (*Legend of Sargon*) *claimed to be from another city, moved to Akkad & became king*

  How did Sargon become king?

- conquered all Mesopotamia and founded Akkadian Empire (2350–2200)

- first "empire-builder" in history *first to unify all of Mesopotamia under one king*

- ca. 2200 empire collapsed—Gutian invasions from Zagros Mountains and/or period of prolonged drought that affected entire Near East?

Ur III Period (ca. 2100–2000 BC) *reverted to city state*

- last period of Sumerian independence with Ur as the most powerful city-state under Third Dynasty of its kings

- Sumerian cultural renaissance

- *last* great flowering of Sumerian literature

MESOPOTAMIAN RELIGION

Pre-scientific Society */all ancient cultures*

- no understanding of natural causation

- nature viewed as controlled by powerful supernatural forces

- religion "explained the unexplainable" through **myths**

- gods could bring positive (bountiful harvests, birth of a healthy child) or negative (floods, illness, droughts) events to humans

- thus, it was crucial for society to maintain good relations with gods

- worship through prayer and sacrifice

- priests as intermediaries between humans and gods

- attempts to communicate with gods or learn their will through dream interpretation, omens, and magic

- emphasis on **fertility** (e.g., cultic prostitution as worship) *what life depended on. /fertility of crops /children* *sex w/ prostitute @ temple representing fertility gods have give something back in exchange*

- belief in afterlife: descent to vague underworld ("House of Dust" in Gilgamesh Epic) where human spirits existed but did not live *mesopotamia ↑*

Polytheism

- prevalent in Mesopotamia and nearly all other ancient societies—hundreds of deities, none with absolute power, all limited in some way
  • Some gods power only extends to geographic place
  • Certain aspect of life /fertility

- gods portrayed in anthropomorphic form with human-like personalities *Anger, lust, fear, etc.*   *Gods • super human powers • immortality*

- patron deity in each city-state with temple atop ziggurat but many other deities also worshipped

Major Mesopotamian Deities (Semitic Names)

Enlil—god of air and wind; patron god of Nippur; chief god by 2500 BC   *City*

Anu—sky god, father of gods

Ishtar—goddess of love and fertility/ *Most important female deity*

Tammuz—consort of Istar, dying and rising vegetation god / *climate ... drought died →rain+crops alive*

Shamash—god of sun and justice

Sin—moon god, wisdom

Marduk—god of storms and war; patron of god Babylon; replaced Enlil as chief Mesopotamian deity after ca. 1750 BC   *later*

Epic of Gilgamesh   *earliest piece of surviving literature anywhere*   *• still don't have entire epic*

- Sumerian epic poem—key primary source for Mesopotamian religion and many other aspects of this civilization

- epic rediscovered in 19th century; many fragments found but text of entire poem still not complete

- earliest surviving fragments date to ca. 2100 BC, but epic itself is much older in origin

Who was Gilgamesh?

- Sumerian king list mentions Gilgamesh as a king of Uruk in Early Dynastic Period (ca. 2600 BC)

- probably a historical figure but epic itself largely fictional   *why unpopular?*

- character of Gilgamesh—son of mortal father and goddess mother, yet clearly mortal—why?   *powerful*

- unpopular with people of Uruk, who call to gods for relief

- Enkidu—sent by gods to divert Gilgamesh and thus relieve his people; Enkidu—wild, naked, uncivilized, living with wild animals on steppe   *Equal in strength*   *Battle?*

- taming of Enkidu by prostitute

- after a brief conflict, Enkidu and Gilgamesh become friends ("brothers"), contrary to plans of the gods

- successful journey to Cedar Forest to slay the Huwawa (monster)

- failed attempt at seduction of Gilgamesh by Ishtar, infuriating goddess; "Bull of Heaven" sent to punish this insult but is killed by the two heroes   *• She promised wealth, power, fame*   *Why No?*

- gods decree "one must die"—Enkidu chosen, turning point in story—why?   *long death & Gilgamesh is helpless*

- Gilgamesh then begins **quest for immortality**—search for "Utnapishtim the Faraway" who (with wife) live in Dilmun and are only mortals ever granted immortality by gods *after the great flood*

- Gilgamesh has many adventures en route

- meets the barmaid Siduri, who urges him to abandon quest and instead enjoy what life he has remaining /   *Why angry? / later insertion*

- Gilgamesh reaches Dilmun and Utnapishtim, who then relates story of Great Flood as a flashback (close parallels with biblical story of Noah's Ark)   *Noah // Israelites borrowed this flood tale*

- reaction of gods to flood—terror, then regret; Utnapishtim and wife receive gift of immortality from gods after flood   *to then repopulate earth / the secret is a plant off coast*   *—reaction?*

   • Ishtar particularly upset bc she makes life & just killed all of life.

[handwritten top margin: • while asleep, a snake eats plants. // nation snakes live long life.]

- secret of immortality is a plant, which Gilgamesh obtains, then loses, returning to Uruk in failure as a tragic hero

Epic of Gilgamesh as a primary historical source

- not literally true, but contains wealth of cultural evidence about Mesopotamian civilization, for example:

[handwritten margin: Discussion]

1. Nature of Mesopotamian kingship

   Gilgamesh is strong, brave, capable of great love, but also fallible, mortal, and hated by his own people; he can occasionally ignore or even thwart the will of the gods

2. Mesopotamian religion */polytheism*

- portrait of gods—human form and personalities (display anger, jealousy, sexual lust, terror, remorse); limited power of each; differ from humans by superhuman powers and immortality

- view of afterlife ("House of Dust")—dark somber netherworld where all souls go, neither "heaven" nor "hell"
  [handwritten: – not reward/or punishment]

OUTLINE OF MESOPOTAMIAN HISTORY (CA. 2000–1200 BC)

[handwritten margin: – went back 2 mountain]

- prosperity and relative calm of Ur III period ended ca. 2000 BC with renewed invasions—Elamites and Amorites (Semites) from Arabia who became kings of various Mesopotamian city-states

- Sumerians now disappear—gradually absorbed by Semitic population of Mesopotamia

- Amorite dynasty of Babylon under its 6th king, Hammurabi (ca. 1750) achieved domination over entire region—Old Babylonian Empire *[handwritten: • united politically by force]*

- Marduk (patron god of Babylon) replaced Enlil as chief god

Law Code of Hammurabi *[handwritten: – justification?]*

- Hammurabi claimed Marduk chose him to rule and promulgate new law code

- code of 282 laws on black diorite stele—relief shows Hammurabi receiving commission from Shamash (god of justice) *[handwritten: complete   stolen by Susa]*

- oldest law code known when found in 1901; now fragments of earlier Sumerian law codes dating ca. 2400 BC

- many parallels with Israelite law in Hebrew Bible—both **Semitic** law

Basic structure: "if someone does so and so, the penalty is so and so"

Law recognizes several social and thus legal classes: */ different punishments by class ⟶ EX?*

1. Elite ("seigniors")—government officials, large landowners, etc.   *[handwritten: – women]*

2. Priests

3. Soldiers (sometimes officers distinguished from ordinary soldiers)

4. Freemen/commoners (peasants, artisans, merchants) */ largest group*

5. Women */ have rights but inequality*

6. Slaves (public [state-owned] and private)—have some limited rights (could own property)

Key elements of Law Code:

- difference in punishments based upon class distinctions

- guilt/innocence determined by king's agents, local city governments, or even divine judgment

[handwritten bottom margin: / Ex. if seignors sinks in river = guilty – land goes to other person. Float = innocent, gets land   river = a god]

- legal status of women (patriarchal society)
- responsibility of state towards individuals /if property will give back
- death penalty for many property offenses //no way to incarcerate ppl

Did law code also have political purpose? Did Hammurabi attempt to impose uniform laws throughout his empire to bind it together?

Value of law codes as primary sources to the historian?

- legal sources on criminal offenses and penalties
- great wealth of data about social organization (e.g., family relationships, inheritance, status of women and slaves, etc.)
- economic evidence (e.g., products and relative values—crops, animals, kinds of occupations, wages, interest rates)
- political evidence (e.g., use of city councils to administer local affairs)

Caution required of the historian when using this or any other law code as a primary source

- enforcement? dsn't mean each law equally/or actually enforced
- legal procedures? City council but how was a trial conducted? /investigation?
- effectiveness? did crime rate change?

Babylonian Empire declined after Hammurabi

- Babylon sacked by Hittites from Anatolia ca. 1600 BC, empire collapsed
- Mesopotamia invaded by Kassites from Armenia ca. 1550 who ruled southern Mesopotamia until ca. 1155 BC
- land empire difficult to maintain in Mesopotamia due to its openness to external invasion and tradition of independent city-states, who rebelled at times of imperial weakness

De Blois (1-5) (9-32)

7th century: Islam spread from Arabia into Mediterranean + Mid. East by creation of Caliphate empire

Christianity evolved from Judaism in Palestine/acquired organization structure in Roman empire, Islam has borrowed for Judaism, Christianity, Greek philosophy in W. rooted in Greek tradition

D Sn't mean antiquity exists today / history bias in translation

Source of info: inscriptions, papyri (letters/Egyptian paper) clay tablets, coins

Prehistory
- Stone Age, Bronze Age, Iron Age /beginning of historical times diffs b/w regions
  - much written evidence is not legible or limited info
  - reference to astronomical phenomena referenced in ancient texts helps us date

Mesopotamia
- used artifical irrigation bc flood season was only until Feb-April
- More productive than rainfall irrigation
- also more productive bc usage of sowing plough/minimized loss of seeds
- core of city - Temple - homed the states god, needs must be met by community
- transhumance - seasonal migration, remained in one area for short period then moved a few years later when they'd exhausted the soil; Agriculturists
- nomad & sedentary ppl @ odds - sedentary ppl afraid of being plundered by semi-nomads but two groups were dependent on one another for exchange of products
  - = popular theme in literature Ex: Bible, Abel Murdered by agriculturist, Cain [sheperd]

Early Bronze Age
Egypt, The old Kingdom
  - divided into 30 dynasties or 3 kingdoms > old, middle, New
Old Kingdom
  - unified under one ruler but distinction b/w Lower Egypt + Upper Egypt (South)
  - constructed pyramids, largest built during 4th dynasty, all stone, younger are mudbrick + smaller
  - ended bc governors had become so powerful w/ accumulation of generational land
    - also, famine, decrease floods

Middle Bronze Age
Egypt, Middle Kingdom + 2nd intermediate period
  - earliest mentions of towns like Jerusalem
  - Changed succession: one of their sons was co-regent during a kings life + after death became King
  - golden Age of Egyptian culture: literature
  - 1800-1550 Kings loose power, Hyksos in power
Mesopotamia
  - Birth of Assyria & Babylonia - rose to power due to its foreign ppl Amorites
  - N. Meso. City of Assur
  - S. Meso. Babylonian
    - culture laid out by king Hammurabi - conquered all of S. Mesopotamia / code of law

Late Bronze
  Stable balance of a group of great powers > Mitanni, Hittite, Assyrian, Babylonian
    - power based on new invention - war chariot - 2 wheel vehicle drawn by horses / reiues controlled
Egypt/New Kingdom
  Pharaoh Akhenaten - tried to change Polytheism - to one sun god Aten

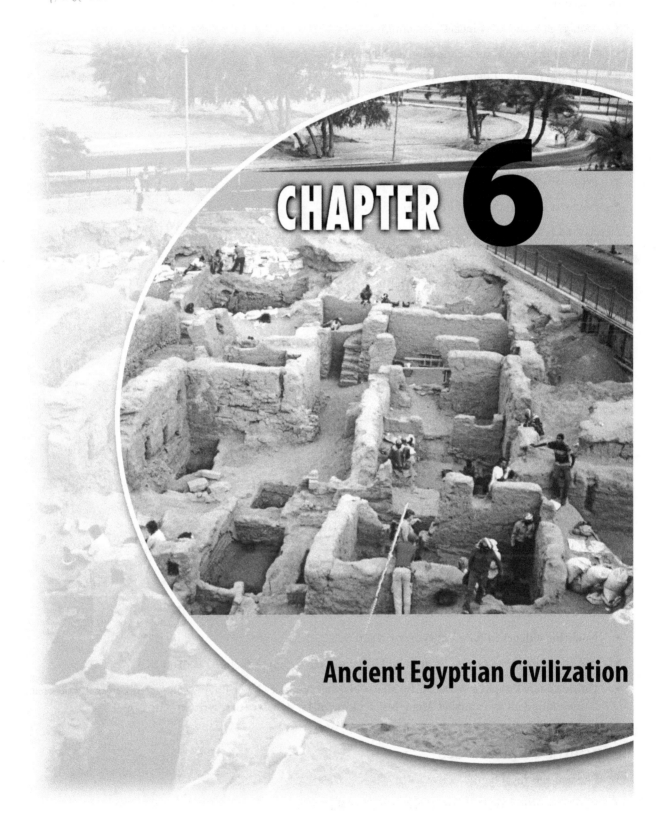

CHAPTER 6

Ancient Egyptian Civilization

GEOGRAPHY OF EGYPT
"father of history"

Herodotus (Greek historian, 5th century BC)—"Egypt is the gift of the Nile" —*worlds largest river*

- average rainfall—2–4 inches per annum *Egypt very arid, nile watersource*
- "natural irrigation" on a national scale by annual flood *, annually & predictable*
- flood also fertilized fields */soil*
- chief crop—wheat
- Egypt richest agricultural region of Mediterranean world
- food from Nile (fish, waterfowl, hippos)
- papyrus—chief writing material *, reed that grew along banks, layered to use as paper*
- Nile was chief highway of Egypt *, wind went from N → S*

Other natural resources in Nile Valley:

- stone for public monuments */ Pyramids*
- mud brick for most domestic architecture
- clay for pottery

Other key resources lacking:

This is Bronze Age

- no timber or metals in Nile valley */imported*
- key imports (wood from Lebanon, copper from Cyprus and Sinai, gold from Eastern Desert, etc.)
- Egyptian exports (wheat, papyrus, etc.)

Egypt divided into Upper Egypt and Lower Egypt (Delta)

(N) lower

(S) Upper

- Protected from invasion by formidable geographic barriers:
- deserts to east and west
- Mediterranean to north
- cataracts to south *, rapids & waterfalls / hard to navigate*
- Egypt not successfully invaded by foreigners for 1300 years

EMERGENCE OF EGYPTIAN CIVILIZATION

permanent / food producing

- Neolithic villages in Nile Valley by ca. 5500 B.C.
- two rival kingdoms eventually arose in Upper and Lower Egypt (before ca. 3100 BC)
- Unification of Egypt ca. 3100 BC by Menes/Narmer (king of Upper Egypt) conquered Lower Egypt; created unified kingdom w/ capital at Memphis; 1st king of 1st dynasty (first written sources)

@ Apex of Delta   *Pharaohs*

Egyptian Social Classes

1. Pharaoh and royal family *, Pharaoh- a living gods / unlike mesopotamia*
2. Landed nobility—top bureaucrats drawn from this class */ own farms*
3. Priests—great power
- intermediaries between people and gods

- controlled large temple estates (e.g., Amon-Re) *great economic power/ political influence*
- only educated class—dominated intellectual thought
4. Soldiers—relatively few—no internal conflicts and few external wars */unlike large mesopotamia military*
5. Artisans and merchants */ trade / products*
6. Free peasant farmers—vast bulk of population (tenants vs. freeholders) *→ owned their own small farm* *→ worked someone elses land*
7. Slaves—few until late in Egyptian history—why? *→ unlike mesopotamia — no wars, no source of slaves*

HISTORY OF EGYPT

Old Kingdom (3100–2200 BC) *I - VII*

(Early Dynastic: Dynasties I–II, ca. 3100–2600 and Dynasties III–VI, ca. 2600–2200)

- greatest period of Egyptian power and prosperity
- Egypt ruled as a single unified kingdom by pharaoh at Memphis
- pharaoh viewed as a god on earth (son of Amon-Re, sun-god and most important deity)
- highly centralized bureaucracy under Grand Vizier - *2nd most important person*
- kingdom divided into 42 nomes or provinces, each administered by nomarch or governor *– appointed by pharaoh*
- royal bureaucracy managed largely planned economy *, controls over irrigation, collection of taxes, + redistribution of surplus.*

Pyramids:

- largest structures ever created in the ancient world *•only surpassed by Eiffel Tower*
- royal tomb within a complex of structures
- to ensure happy afterlife for deceased kings *,*

Evolution:

1. Mastaba—low bench-like structure covered underground chamber */seen by pharaohs*
2. Step pyramid—by 3rd dynasty (by ca. 2700)—stacking mastabas *, getting smaller + smaller* *old kingdom*
3. True pyramid with sloping sides evolved by ca. 2600

Great Pyramid (ca. 2500) covers 13 acres and nearly 500 feet high; built just above flood plain during flood season by peasants

Each pyramid complex included:

• built by Egyptian peasants on a seasonal basis.

- valley temple on Nile with causeway leading to pyramid complex
- mortuary temple for regular offerings to "ka" (spirit) of pharaoh *- 4 months every year the peasants farm land under water.*
- pharaoh's pyramid
- smaller pyramids for royal family and chief officials *- paid w/ rations*

Egyptian view of afterlife: *Ka = Soul*

removed blood - pupped perfume organs removed - jars

- "ka" could live happily if physical body preserved, thus, mummification
- afterlife perceived much like former physical life on earth *- freely did it bc it was for their king*
- "ka" needed many items for afterlife (role of mortuary priests) *Food, Furniture, clay figurines of slaves*
- belief in possibility of afterlife gradually extended to all Egyptians

- rival view, Book of the Dead
Judgement by Osiris
Good deeds must outweigh bad → to go to afterlife

First Intermediate Period (ca. 2200–2050 BC) *lack written sources clear*

- causes for collapse of the Old Kingdom obscure
- no foreign invasion
- drought and/or series of low Niles? */climate change*

  both? ←
- rising power of landed nobility challenged the pharaohs? *elite under pharaoh rise in power?*
- evidence of civil unrest and internal political disintegration *for 200 yrs*

Egypt in the Middle Kingdom (ca. 2050–1670 BC)

- founded by new dynasty (XI) from south *, from Thebes, Upper Egypt*
- new capital at Thebes in Upper Egypt
- Middle Kingdom pharaohs (XI–XII dynasties) ruled in more decentralized fashion
- priestly and noble classes gained power at king's expense
- end of era of great pyramids suggests less wealth *, Evidence of less wealth of Pharaoh command*
- several pharaohs launched plundering expeditions into Syria ("Levant") and Nubia but no permanent conquests *raids, slaves, not controlling those territories*

  • First foreign conquest

Primary Source from the Middle Kingdom

Story of Sinuhe

peace & prosperity of middle Kingdom seen in primary source.

- court official (ca. 1960 BC) fled Egypt—why? *risk to his life*
- lived in exile in Syria for years
- pharaoh eventually welcomed Sinuhe home
- restored to a position as court official
- began arrangements for afterlife *— elaborate preparations?*

Story of Two Brothers (ca. 1200 BC, from New Kingdom)

- Anubis and Bata (both named after gods)   *• How does it illuminate peasant life?*
- mythological folktale */entertainment*   *• religion?*
- moral of the story?
- value of folktales as historical sources: rare look at peasants (vast bulk of Egyptian population) who are largely neglected in written sources

Second Intermediate Period (1670–1570 BC)   *• First successful conquest by a foreign power.*

- political unity of Middle Kingdom declined
- ca. 1670 BC Egypt successfully invaded by the Hyksos, "Rulers of Foreign Lands" (mostly Semites from Palestine)   *NE*
- Hyksos conquest aided by horse-drawn chariot *- technology unknown to Egypt b4*
- Hyksos ruled Delta directly and held indirect control over all Egypt *- shock for Egyptian national spirit*
- key turning point in Egyptian history *more fearful after this & aggressive*

horse & camel domesticated

New Kingdom Egypt (ca. 1570–1100 BC)

- national uprising against the Hyksos by XVII dynasty pharaohs from Thebes

- Hyksos expelled from Egypt and pursued into Palestine and Syria / *wanted to make sure they wouldn't return so they permanently occupied area*

- Egyptian Empire—Palestine, Syria, Nubia, and Libya *• first direct control outside of Nile valley*

- consequences of Empire:

  - vast wealth poured into Egypt *from various campaigns*

  - dramatic increase in slavery in Egypt

  - much wealth dedicated to gods as a thanksgiving *, pharaohs credited gods 4 success / gave offerings*

  - further increase in economic and political power of priests *, this wealth went to priests*

Primary Sources from New Kingdom   *Inscribed on walls of tomb*

Autobiography of Ahmose (ca. 1570 BC)

- traditional genre of tomb biographies—most of bureaucrats / *ppl who served pharaoh*

- Ahmose's is one of few military careers known

- one of few primary sources on expulsion of Hyksos, by eyewitness */ Bias?*

- origins—common soldier aboard an Egyptian naval vessel / *humble origins*

- distinguished service in battles against Hyksos, later in Nubia

- richly rewarded and died a wealthy landowner

- outstanding example of social mobility—how typical?

Asiatic Campaign of Thutmose III (ca. 1468 BC) *Intended audience are the gods, scribes made records on campaigns* / *Absent? list of casualties*

- one of many inscriptions on temple walls at Karnak near Thebes

- official royal account of military operations by pharaoh

- major victory at Megiddo over Canaanite confederation *A highway for conquering arms bc of geographical position*

- illustrates tremendous wealth obtained by Egypt from Empire / *pharaoh keeps a large part, some to soldiers, large amount to gods → given to priests*

- bias in such a source? *trust the #'s? Not too far from truth*

Amenhotep IV (ca. 1350 BC)

- elevation of Aton (sun disk god) to new prominence

- Amenhotep changed his name to Akhenaton ("Effective for the Aton")

- moved capital from Thebes to Akhetaton ("Horizon of the Aton")—modern / *All new buildings*

Tell el-Amarna *(modern name)*

- outlawed worship of all other gods, including Amon-Re *(chief god of Egypt)* *• closes temples for all other gods* *• reigned w/ wife Nefertiti*

- the first known monotheist? *Motives?* *—risky*

Hymn to the Aton

- inscribed on walls of several tombs at Amarna

- statement of theology of Atonism

- motives of Akhenaton?

- Akhenaton's religious reform failed

- after his death, priests reasserted their control

- priests dominated the young successor pharaoh, Tutankhamen, who renounced Atonism, returned capital to Thebes, and restored temples and lands to priestly class _son_

- Akhenaton's focus on religion resulted in neglect of Empire

- Egyptian Empire gradually lost to revolts and external attacks

- Egypt in decline after ca. 1300 BC _until 1952 gained independence_

What is Aton credited w/?
  - creation, fertility
  - described "o Sole God, whom there is no other"   _1st known monotheist in world?_

Pharaohs viewed as gods / did he renounced his own divinity?

Priests greatest threat
  → change to monotheism would decrease priests powers.

only reigned last 15yrs / not successful
  - mummy / tomb never found, overthrown?

King Tut
  - only pharaoh whose tomb has been found largely intact
  - Greatest archaeological discovery found
  - gold coffin

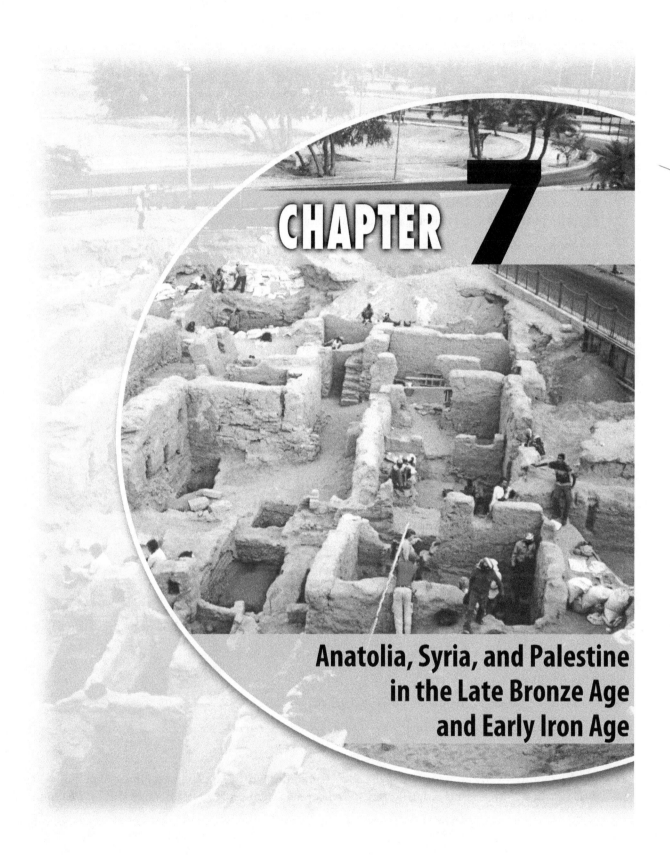

CHAPTER 7

Anatolia, Syria, and Palestine in the Late Bronze Age and Early Iron Age

HITTITES—1st Indo-European civilization

Scholars used knowledge of Akkadian to decipher Hittite (b/c) Indo/Euro)

- origins obscure but emerge in central Anatolia ca. 1750 BC

- developed unified kingdom *1400 B.C.*

- capital city—Hattusas (modern Boghaz-Koy)

- excavation of royal archives yielded many cuneiform tablets—some bilingual texts in Hittite and Akkadian (diplomatic language of Near East) permitted decipherment of Hittite language

- most important invention—iron-smelting (but iron remained luxury product) *•first to extract iron from iron ore •plentiful / tools widespread*

didn't have technology to mass produce iron tools
- Hittites transmitted key elements of Near Eastern culture to West, especially to Greeks of the Aegean in Late Bronze Age

- Hittite expansion into Syria in 14th century opposed by Egyptians; after some warfare, Hittite kings and Egyptian pharaohs reached a diplomatic accommodation

- Hittite power declined in 13th century BC */unknown why*

- Sea Peoples (ca. 1200 BC)—destroyed Hittite kingdom

SYRIA AND PALESTINE

- "Levant"—east coast of Mediterranean

- lacked huge agricultural surpluses of Mesopotamia and Egypt

- rarely produced great political powers

- highway for invading armies between Asia and Africa *•only land bridge b/w 2*

- usually dominated by major Near Eastern powers

Canaanites (Semites) *(NW)*

• predominant population
- inhabited most of Syria and Palestine in Bronze Age

• never politically unified
- economy based on agriculture, trade and industry

- independent city-states, each with its own king

Ebla (Tell Mardikh)

•used cuneiform script to write Canaanite language
- earliest Canaanite city-state (ca. 3000 BC–1600 BC), in northern Syria

- destroyed by Hittites ca. 1600 BC

- excavations yielded 15,000 cuneiform tablets (ca. 2250 BC), some written in Eblaite (Semitic language)

- Canaanite civilization emerged nearly as early as in Egypt and Mesopotamia

Ugarit (Ras Shamra)

- Canaanite city-state (ca. 1900–1200 BC) on north Syrian coast

- economy built on industry and commerce with Egypt, Cyprus, and Mesopotamia */on coast*

- destroyed by Sea Peoples ca. 1200 BC

- in 14th century—early evidence for 1st alphabet—simplified writing system for commercial purposes—two dozen characters (consonants only); literacy spread beyond scribes and priests although still limited to small minority

•passed to phoenicans, greeks, roman

Origin of the alphabet

•answered an economic need

EARLY IRON AGE (AFTER 1200 BC)

- beginning of widespread use of (iron)
- entire Near East shaken by major migrations and invasions /great conflict

"Sea Peoples"

created havaoc

- perhaps of mixed ethnic origins, including Indo-Europeans
- from Aegean? Balkans? Black Sea? NW /we dnt know
- ravaged most of eastern Mediterranean in several waves ca. 1200 BC
- destroyed Hittite Empire; sacked major Canaanite city-states on eastern Mediterranean coast; reached Egypt but defeated by Rameses III (ca. 1188); several surviving groups of Sea Peoples settled on Palestinian coast (e.g., Philistines)

Arameans (Semites)

- nomads from north Arabian desert—invaded Syria and Mesopotamia
- many were caravaneers, some eventually settled along desert fringe/ used camels in military
- Arameans eventually ruled many city-states of the Fertile Crescent, such as Damascus
- Aramaic language so widely spoken it became *lingua franca* of Near East in Iron Age (e.g., Jesus of Nazareth)
  - replaced others language
  - spoke Aramaic

Collapse or weakness of traditional regional powers (Hittites, Egyptians) ca. 1200 BC created **temporary power vacuum** in Syria/Palestine, allowing brief period of independence for small states in region

• no large empire could'nt dominate like they did in past

Philistines (Indo-Europeans)

- one element of the Sea Peoples
- occupied SW coast of Palestine (ca. 1200 BC)
- 5 major city-states (e.g., Gaza), each with its own king
- used knowledge of iron-working to dominate native Semites

Phoenicians (Semites) /W

great meriatime ppl

- direct descendants of Canaanites—flourished in Iron Age (after 1200 BC)
- central Syrian coast (modern Lebanon)
- organized into city-states, each with its own king—Byblos, Tyre, Sidon, each w/ own king
- economic system based on industry and commerce
- great seafarers of Near East; exported timber ("Cedars of Lebanon"), purple dye (murex), glass, metalwork (imported copper from Cyprus) /shipped to neighors /mesopotamia didn't have timber
  - rare/gland of mollusk/saved for royalty/purple
- established far-flung trading stations and colonies throughout Mediterranean (e.g., Carthage on N. African coast; 814 BC)
  - all of circumnavigated Africa
- transmitters of culture (e.g., passed Canaanite alphabet to Greeks)

Israelites (Semites) /\/\

- closely related to Canaanites, Phoenicians, and Aramaeans
- sources: Hebrew Bible/Old Testament, extra-biblical documents and archaeological excavations in Palestine

Who were the Israelites?

- claim of origin from a patriarch (Abraham) as Hebrews
- patriarchal narratives are collation of many different traditions unified and harmonized in later periods
- earliest portions of Hebrew Bible probably not written before ca. 1000 BC and Genesis probably not before ca. 550 BC

Some Explanations of Israelite Origins: /*what then believed about themselves*

1. Conquest (traditional Biblical account)

- Hebrews, enslaved in Egypt, escape (Exodus), led by Moses
- credited to intervention of their god—YHWH (Yahweh)
- Hebrew conquest of Canaan (Palestine)—13th century BC
- Joshua and Hebrew tribes wipe out Canaanites in well-coordinated invasion, beginning with capture of Heshbon, Jericho, and Ai

 dedicated them to the god

- after fall of each city, Yahweh commands Hebrews to massacre every living thing (book of Joshua) *from that city*
- archaeology casts doubt on historicity of some of these accounts, but lends possible support to other parts (e.g., Bethel, Hazor, and Lachish destroyed in 13th century) /*no evidence & destruction /or occupation*

2. Nomadic Infiltration /*rejects violent conquest*

- Hebrews originally pastoral nomads from desert (evidence?) *Cain & Abel*
- gradually infiltrated into Canaan, perhaps involving some warfare but also peaceful assimilation with sedentary population, eventually evolved into Israelites

3. Peasant Revolt /*most radical*   o*reject exodus*

- Israelite ancestors were indigenous peasant/pastoral population of Canaan
- oppressed by the wealthy urban elite of the Canaanite city-states
- peasants exploited regional turmoil ca. 1200 and revolted, threw off Canaanite urban elite, and forged new identity in the rural hill country of Palestine as Israelites

Whatever explanation is accepted, all agree that Israelites only partially occupied Palestine—central hill country; most productive land (coastal plain, Jordan Valley) remained under Philistines and Canaanites; non-Israelite pockets survived even in hill country (e.g. Jerusalem)

Outline of Israelite History

Period of Judges (ca. 1200–1025 BC)   /*·12 tribes*

- Israel as a loose tribal confederacy
- central tribal shrine at Shiloh (Ark of Covenant) *kept in a tent / 10 commandments*
- if nomadic in origin, period of transformation from nomadic herders to sedentary farmers
- constant threats to security (especially Philistines)
- occasional judges—temporary emergency military leaders (Samson, Samuel, Deborah—only female political leader of Israel) *successful*

United Monarchy (ca. 1025–925 BC)

- ineffectiveness of tribal confederacy against Philistines led Israelites to demand a king /Saul

Saul (ca. 1025–1005 BC)   ◦ glorified military leader

- 1st king of Israel, but king only in a limited sense (no real capital, royal bureaucracy, nor system of taxation)
- Saul and sons killed *army* at Mount Gilboa (ca. 1005) by Philistines—major disaster—Shiloh sacked, Ark captured /dark period

David (ca. 1005–965 BC) ◦ 2nd King / tough soldier   *exaggerated*

- defeated Philistines and allegedly conquered most of Palestine (but little mention of David outside Bible)
- seized Jerusalem—converted it into royal capital / Isrealitic city for 1st time   / warfare + expansion)
- organized professional army, royal bureaucracy, and system of taxation

Solomon (ca. 965–925 BC)

- David's son
- concentrated on internal development of kingdom
- system of public works (e.g., Temple of Yahweh in Jerusalem)
- encouraged trade and industry
- growing cost of army, public works, bureaucracy, court put great strain on Israelites; most refused to follow Solomon's heir   / end of united monarchy

Divided Monarchy (ca. 925–586 BC)

- 10 northern tribes broke away—formed Kingdom of Israel (capital at Samaria)
- 2 southern (Judah and Benjamin) tribes remained loyal to Solomon's heir as Kingdom of Judah (capital at Jerusalem)
- northern kingdom (Israel) destroyed by Assyrians in 722 BC, who deported political and religious elite ("10 lost tribes of Israel")
- southern kingdom (Judah) destroyed in 586 BC by Neo-Babylonians (Chaldeans), who exiled Jewish elite to Mesopotamia

Babylonian Captivity (586–539 BC)   ◦ had been exiled

- thousands of Jews settled in Mesopotamia
- assimilated Mesopotamian culture

Persian Empire (539–332 BC)

- Persian King Cyrus conquered Babylonian Empire
- allowed Jews to return to Palestine (some remained in Mesopotamia) / no return to political independence
- Jews now under Persian rule and cultural influence

Nothing special about political, economic, or social evolution of Israel, paralleled by other small states of Syria/Palestine in the early Iron Age; truly unique contribution of Israel is its religion

Israelite Religion   /No religion is static

Israelite religion *evolved* through a long historical process, strongly influenced by surrounding cultural environment

Critical examination of Hebrew Bible as a primary historical source suggests:

- theological document (not a historical or scientific document)
- written by many authors over long period (ca. 1000–160 BC)

- many different viewpoints
- two central themes:
    1) to demonstrate special relationship between Israelites and Yahweh
    2) to provide ethical guidelines for Israelite society

Israelite religion rooted in a perceived decisive historical event—

Exodus: deliverance of their ancestors (Hebrews) from bondage in Egypt by Yahweh and establishment of a special relationship ("covenant")

Origin of Yahweh unclear—perhaps from NW Arabia?

- god of storms who hurls thunder
- god of mountains (revealed to Moses on Mount Sinai)
- god of desert
- god of nomads (story of Cain and Able, ark of covenant in a tent)

Did Yahweh have a female consort?

- many biblical references to Asherah, Canaanite mother goddess /fertility goddess
- appears at Ugarit as consort of El—chief Canaanite god
- inscriptions from Sinai refer to "Yahweh and his Asherah"
- repeated biblical references refer to her image in the Temple of Yahweh in Jerusalem (e.g., 1 Kings 15:13; 2 Kings 21:7)
- repeated condemnations by biblical authors suggest widespread worship by Israelites of Asherah alongside Yahweh, even at times among Israelite royal family

Covenant between Israelites and Yahweh

- Yahweh saved Israelites from bondage and made them his chosen people
- Israelites would obey *Torah* (Yahweh's law)

Israelites perhaps originally *henotheists*—worship of one god while not denying existence of others— 1st commandment

Some key elements of the Torah: Gods Law

- believed to be of divine origin
- was principle of "eye for an eye" always adhered to? No
- were all equal before the law?
- patriarchal society
- slavery accepted as normal institution of life /common everywhere
- protection for widows, orphans, poor, and others seen as vulnerable
- usury (loans for interest) banned—why? Exploitation

Keeping the Covenant?

- demands of agricultural, sedentary life on Israelites
- exposure to sophisticated Canaanite polytheism—emphasis on fertility
- many Israelites worshipped other gods (e.g., Asherah, Baal, Astarte)

[handwritten margin notes: • early evidence of henotheism • used Asherah as an appeal to others bc of fertility]

Rise of the Prophets (Divided Monarchy)

- claimed to be mouthpiece of Yahweh /he spoke through Prophets   one & only
- emphasized ethical conduct and strict **monotheism** (no gods exist except Yahweh), but much resistance to monotheism among many Israelites
- Amos (mid-8th century)—criticized people of both kingdoms; rejected external practice of religion when belying internal moral condition
- Isaiah (late 8th century)—also strongly critical of Judah and even of Davidic monarchy
- 2nd Isaiah (Ch. 40–66 of Isaiah; in 6th century BC)—after fall of Jerusalem, destruction of Temple, and exile of Jewish elite (Babylonian Captivity);
- beginning of Messianic tradition (Messiah = "The Anointed One")

Impact of Babylonian Captivity (586–539 BC)

- Jews exposed to Mesopotamian religion (e.g., Garden of Eden, Great Flood, and other myths)
- much of Hebrew Bible written or drawn together in this period
- most Jews now fervent monotheists

Influence of Persian Zoroastrianism on Judaism (539–332 BC)

- Babylonian captivity ended in 539 BC
- some exiled Jews returned to Palestine but not to independence, Jews now subjects of Persian Empire
- Zoroaster—Persian prophet of 6th century BC (or much earlier?)
- dualistic faith (god of good vs. god of evil—concept of Satan)
- apocalyptic expectations
- belief in life after death first appears among *some* Jews (early belief in Sheol- where all souls go after death), but never accepted by many other Jews (even today)

Examples of Mesopotamian and Persian Influence on Judaism

- Satan (as a serpent) in story of Adam and Eve
- Noah's flood story borrowed from Sumerian flood story (Gilgamesh Epic)
- Creation stories—why two separate and somewhat contradictory stories back-to-back in Genesis 1–2?

Significance of Israelite Religion in Ancient Near East

1. High ethical tone expressed in Torah (Yahweh's law)
2. 1st people to embrace monotheism
3. Judaism would remain one of the important religions of the region
4. Christianity originated in Judaism and saw Hebrew Bible as word of god
5. Islam also accepted Hebrew Bible (and New Testament) as word of god

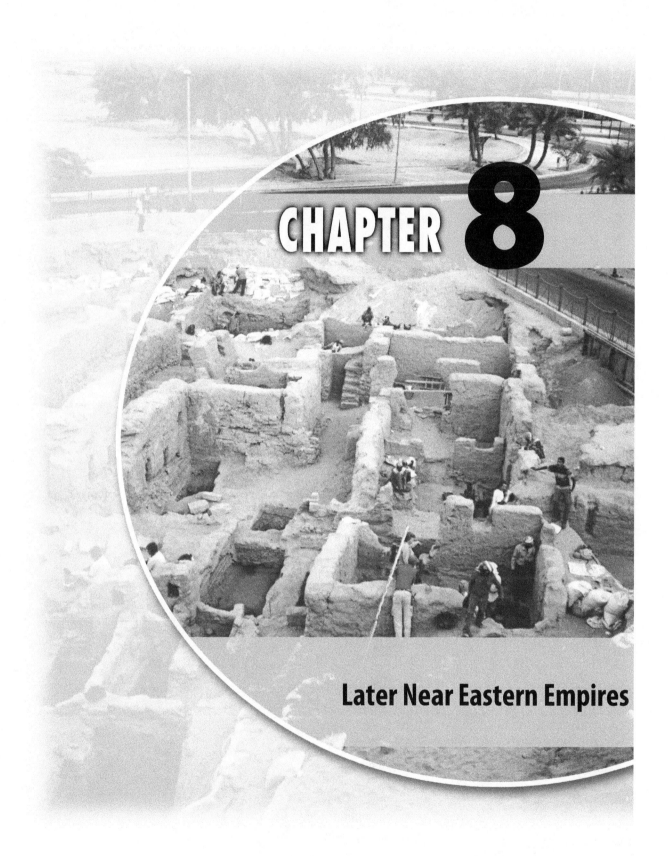

CHAPTER 8

Later Near Eastern Empires

Rise of new Mesopotamian empires after 750 BC ended both regional power vacuum and independence of small states in Syria/Palestine (e.g., Israel)

Assyrians (Semites)

- emerge on upper Tigris before 2000 BC

- rose to prominence after 1200 BC

- name from national god: Assur

- Assur/Asshur also name of their chief religious city

- Nineveh: political capital

Major Assyrian conquests after 750 BC:

- Mesopotamia

- Urartu (Armenia)

- Syria/Palestine

- Egypt

- empire reached greatest extent under King Asshurbanipal (668–626 BC)

Assyrian Empire

- ruled through a systematic program of terror

- Assyrians tough, disciplined, ruthless, excellent warriors

- army organized around chariots for open field battles

- sophisticated siege techniques to capture fortified cities

Excellent primary sources on Assyrians

- detailed written sources on military campaigns, civil administration, and political/diplomatic relations (e.g., Library of Asshurbanipal at Nineveh)

- archaeological evidence (e.g., sculptured reliefs w/ graphic images of army in action)

Annals of Assyrian kings—standard elements:

1. List of opponents (often w/ military strength)

2. Order of victories (thus route of king's march reconstructed)

3. Detailed list of booty

4. Thanks to gods

Annals provide evidence on techniques of Assyrian rule over conquered peoples (e.g., Samaria in 721 BC)

1. Assyrian military governor (and garrison)

2. Imposing tribute and taking hostages

3. Incorporate defeated soldiers into Assyrian army

4. Exile political/military elite

5. Forced settlement of foreign colonists among indigenous folk

Bias of *Annals*?

- (e.g., Sennacherib's siege of Jerusalem ca. 700 BC)

Decline of Assyria in late 7th century BC

- civil war among pretenders to Assyrian throne

- decline in native Assyrian population/increasing reliance on foreign troops

- resettlement of captive foreigners changed character of Assyrian homeland, increasingly Aramaic

- revolts in conquered regions—Egypt, Babylonia, and Media

- alliance of Medes and Babylonians sacked Nineveh (612 BC) and destroyed Assyrian power forever

Near Eastern Balance of Power (ca. 612–550 BC)

- balance of power among kingdoms of Egypt, Media, Lydia, and Neo-Babylonian Empire

- none strong enough to dominate entire Near East

Neo-Babylonian Empire

- ruled by Chaldean kings—dominated Mesopotamia

- Nebuchadnezzar (605–562 BC) conquered Syria and Palestine, sacked Jerusalem (586 BC) and took Jewish elite into "Babylonian captivity"

- Nabonidus (555–539 BC)—unpopular king who ignored Marduk (patron god of Babylon) in favor of Sin (moon god)

- disaffected population opened gates of Babylon in 539 to welcome Persian king Cyrus (posed as champion of Marduk)

Growth of Persian Empire (539–332 BC)

- Persians (Indo-Europeans—SW Iranian plateau)

- Cyrus the Great (560–530 BC)—founded Persian Empire, conquered:

  - 550—Media, SW of Caspian Sea

  - 547—Lydia, extended power to Aegean Sea

  - 539—Neo-Babylonian Empire (Mesopotamia and Syria/Palestine)

- Cambyses (530–522 BC) conquered Egypt in 525

- Darius I (521–486 BC) expanded into SE Europe and Indus Valley (modern Pakistan); Persian Empire now at its greatest extent

Administration of Persian Empire

- largest state world had ever seen

- Persian garrisons deployed at strategic points

- central government—4 capitals:

  - Persepolis (primary royal capital and treasury)

  - Susa (old Elamite capital)

  - Ecbatana (former Median capital)

  - Babylon

- provincial administration based on 20 provinces or satrapies (satrap = governor w/ civil authority; separate military command)

- local administration in hands of native dynasts or city-states

- Aramaic was chief administrative language of empire

- tribute collected in money (coins now circulating) or in kind

- efficient courier service for rapid communications

- major security problem—internal uprisings (e.g., Egypt)

A major Persian contribution to Near Eastern culture was Zoroastrianism (Ahuramazda vs. Ahriman)

Political unity of entire Near East by 500 BC

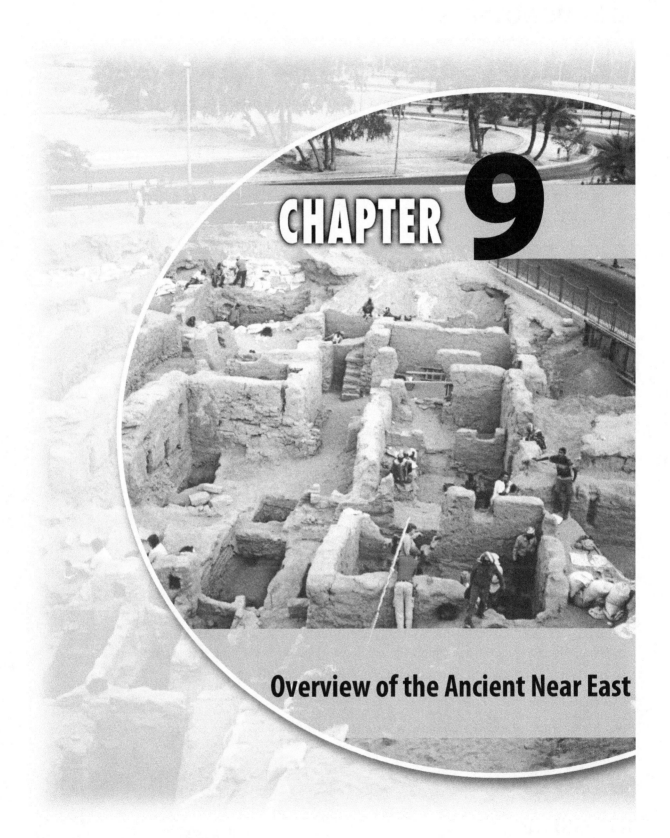

CHAPTER 9

Overview of the Ancient Near East

RELIGION: POLYTHEISM, HENOTHEISM, AND MONOTHEISM

Polytheism

- personification of natural forces as deities

- most deities anthropomorphic (but animal and human/animal hybrids in Egypt)

- kings often served as high priests but rarely worshipped (Egypt key exception)

- vital role for priests—intermediaries between gods and humans, great economic and (at times) political power, monopolized intellectual thought

- gods worshipped to ensure their favor for human survival (e.g., fertility) through prayer and sacrifice

Henotheism vs. Monotheism

- which was Atonism?

- Yahwehism evolved from henotheism into monotheism

- Zoroastrianism has elements of monotheism

Views about life after death vary greatly among these cultures.

ECONOMY AND SOCIETY

Economy

- overwhelmingly agricultural economy (crops and animals)

- land as principal source of wealth—largest holders: temple and palace

- redistribution economy to varying degrees—controlled by king and/or temple

- private land existed but amount unclear

- balance among peasants between tenants versus freeholders?

- means of payment—no money, so use of plots of land and rations

Trade

- most trade was local

- trade also critical for obtaining some key resources

- long-distance trade on land largely limited to luxury goods due to high cost of transport

- sea and river transport more cost-effective

Social Organization

- highly stratified societies (by birth, wealth, occupation)

- important distinction between slave and free

- limited evidence of social mobility

KINGSHIP

Nearly all societies ruled by monarchs ruling city-states, kingdoms or empires

King's main roles:

- military commander
- high priest
- dispenser of justice
- head of royal bureaucracy

Kings exercised regional control through provinces or vassal rulers; also permanent garrisons, punitive expeditions, tribute, transfers of population, etc.

Priests might pose as an alternative center of political power ("palace versus temple")

Rise of professional armies; widespread use of chariot after 1600 BC; enhanced siege warfare capability by early Iron Age

Part **III**

ANCIENT GREECE

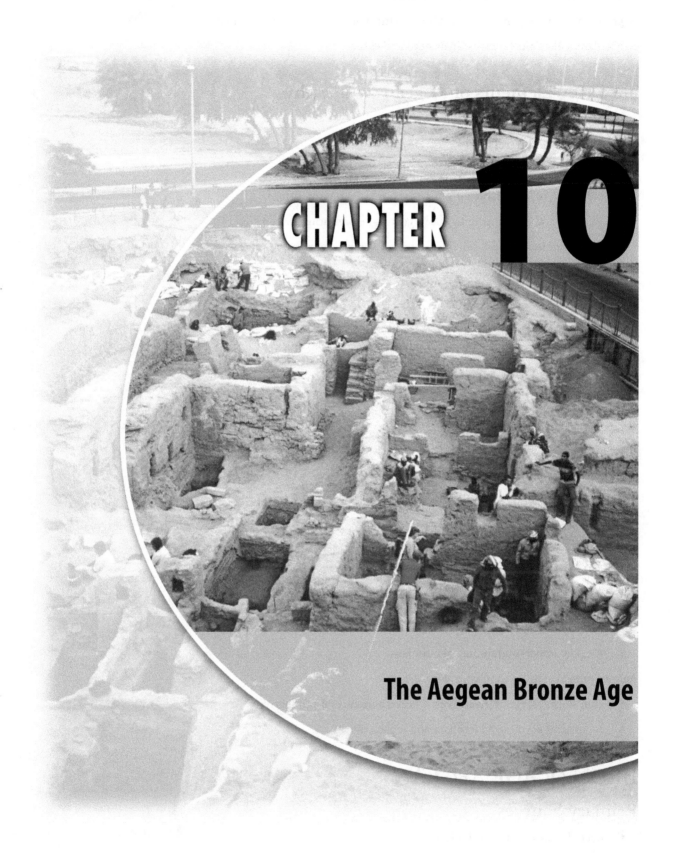

CHAPTER 10

The Aegean Bronze Age

GEOGRAPHICAL BACKGROUND

Aegean Sea—core region of ancient Greece with typical Mediterranean climate

Greeks later colonized extensive areas beyond Aegean

Two Key Elements of Aegean Geography

1. Mountains

- hindered land travel
- *compartmentalized* land into small isolated units
- only 10% of land arable for grain (thus, grain often imported)
- thin soil and overgrazing by sheep/goats—deforestation/soil erosion
- lower mountain slopes suitable for orchard crops—grapes and olives
- Aegean poor in metals (except silver)
- plenty of stone (including marble)
- good clay sources—pottery

2. The Sea

- Aegean filled with natural harbors
- transportation/commerce
- food
- piracy

Aegean economy based on:

- animal husbandry (especially sheep/goats)
- grain (grown in valleys)
- grapes and olives (on mountain slopes)—wine and oil
- pottery (containers for oil and wine; fine painted tableware)
- trade essential:
    - key exports: wine, oil, silver, pottery
    - key imports: grain, metals, timber

Aegean presents strong contrast to Near East

- thin soils/absence of great rivers limited agricultural productivity
- mountains encouraged localism and separatism

BRONZE AGE AEGEAN

Primary Sources

- overwhelmingly archaeological
- few written sources, most date after Bronze Age (e.g., Homer)

Prehistory

- Neolithic villages (i.e., sedentary food-producing settlements) emerge in Aegean ca. 7000 BC

- towns appear by beginning of Bronze Age ca. 3000 BC

The Two "Fathers" of Aegean Bronze Age Archaeology

1. Heinrich Schliemann (1822–1890)

- believed Homer had historical basis

- excavated Hissarlik (Troy?) in NE Aegean in 1871

- identified 7 superimposed levels—interpreted 2nd from bottom level as Homer's Troy

- later archaeologists recognized 9 levels

- Hissarlik now accepted as Troy w/ occupation back to 2900 BC

- Schliemann later excavated on Greek mainland (e.g., Mycenae)

- Schliemann proved civilization existed in Aegean far earlier than most previously believed

2. Arthur Evans (1851–1941)

- Greek myth—King Minos, Theseus, and the Minotaur

- began excavation of Knossos on Crete in 1900

- found a succession of superimposed palaces (ca. 2000–1450 BC), named "Palace of Minos"

- Evans dubbed new civilization "Minoan"

- other "Minoan" palaces on Crete—Phaestos, Malia, etc.

THE MINOANS

- Crete initially colonized ca. 7000 BC (from SW Asia Minor?)

- Minoan culture emerges ca. 3000 BC

- Minoan economy based on agriculture, pastoralism, hunting, fishing, but source of economic surplus was trade

- Crete lies between Egypt/Near East and Aegean

- Minoan exports: wool, oil, wine, pottery, finished metal products—established trading stations on Aegean islands and elsewhere in East Mediterranean

- Minoan civilization (i.e., urban, literate, complex culture) emerges by ca. 1900 BC

Primary Sources on Minoans

- Minoans developed pictographic and syllabic written script by ca. 1800 BC (dubbed "Linear A" by Evans)

- Linear A still not deciphered, but it is clearly NOT Greek (thus, Minoans were not Greeks)

- later myths and legends in Greek sources

- most evidence from archaeology

Minoan Palaces

- Knossos as type site—one of several palaces on Crete
- ca. 6 acres (surrounding city of ca. 185 acres with estimated pop. of 12,000)
- palace unfortified (as are all other Minoan palaces on Crete)
- built of stone, wood, mudbrick on four levels around large central courtyard
- ca. 1300 rooms- storerooms, workshops, domestic quarters, throne room, bathrooms with running water
- frescoes decorate palace walls w/ scenes from Minoan life
- Minoans depicted in sports ("bull-leaping") and dancing
- absence of military themes from art

Minoan palaces suggest a "redistribution economy," w/ bureaucracy collecting, storing, and redistributing surplus via ration system (like Near East)

Minoan Political Organization

- lack of contemporary documents leaves this unclear
- multiple unfortified palaces suggest monarchy of some kind
- one peripatetic king over entire island?
- independent city-states (each w/ its own king) living peacefully?

Evidence for a Minoan "thalassocracy" ("rule of the sea")?

- Theseus legend
- Minoan sea empire cited in later Greek sources (after ca. 400 BC)
- abundant Minoan artifacts throughout Aegean
- remains controversial

Minoan Religion

- remains obscure due to lack of texts and ambiguity of archaeological sources
- absence of great temples
- small shrines in palaces, private homes, and mountain caves where perhaps gods were thought to reside
- Minoan kings as high priests?
- Minoan religion seems dominated by female, earth deities (e.g., snake goddess, Great Mother goddess)
- Anatolian sky god (symbol—"labrys" = double axe in palaces; thus, "labryrinth" = "place of double axe")

Collapse of Minoan Civilization

- traditional view: Minoan Crete conquered ca. 1450 by Mycenean Greeks from mainland, who ruled Crete until end of Bronze Age (1100 BC)
- why were Minoans suddenly vulnerable to external conquest?
- catastrophic eruption of Thera, but now dated ca. 1620 BC, with clear evidence of Minoan continuity afterwards, but did it weaken Minoans?

THE MYCENEANS

ca. 2100 BC—widespread destruction of sites on Aegean mainland suggests arrival of new people—first Greeks (Indo-Europeans); modern name is "Myceneans," but probably called themselves "Acheans" (e.g., Homer)

Primary Sources

- Linear B (syllabic/phonetic script) tablets at several palaces

- deciphered by Michael Ventris (1952)

- early form of Greek (thus, Myceneans = first Greeks)

- only contemporary written sources

- Homer's *Iliad* and *Odyssey* (written after ca. 750 BC)—many problems as historical sources but offer some useful information

- archaeology furnishes most evidence about Myceneans

The Mycenean World

- centered in Peloponnesus

- many independent city-states, each with a king in a fortified hilltop citadel

- within citadel:

    - royal troops

    - royal bureaucrats

    - artisans and merchants

    - slaves

- outside citadel:

    - peasant/pastoral population

Mycenean Economy

- agriculture—grain, olives, grapes, and livestock

- trade—distribution of pottery and other artifacts suggest Myceneans traded widely, exporting oil, wine, and painted pottery throughout Aegean, Cyprus, Syria, Egypt, and Italy

- economic implications of Linear B Tablets:

    - palace at Pylos yielded ca. 4,000 tablets

    - mostly inventories, accounts, ration lists (no literature)

    - evidence for specialization of labor and industry within palace

    - tablets suggest a "redistribution economy"

Palace-citadel of Mycenae

Grave Circle A:

- excavated by Schliemann (1876)

- shaft tombs w/ human burials and rich grave offerings (e.g., gold foil masks)

- Schliemann's claim—"tomb of Agamemnon" (ca. 1250 BC)

- now dated much earlier (ca. 1550 century BC)

Tholos Tombs:

- new tomb design appeared ca. 1500 BC

- 9 at Mycenae, hundreds known throughout Aegean

- entered by unroofed passage (*dromos*) cut horizontally into hillside, leading to doorway accessing circular chamber with high domed roof (*tholos* proper)

- royal tombs, but visible and thus robbed in antiquity

Refortification of citadel of Mycenae (ca. 1350 BC):

- walls 23 feet thick and 60 feet high

- main entrance via: "Lion's Gate"

- royal palace on summit based on megaron-plan

Megaron:

- narrow, 3-room rectangular building

- typical form of Mycenean domestic architecture

- central focus and throne room of Mycenean palaces

- perhaps influenced later development of classical Greek temple

Mycenean Religion

- Myceneans originally worshipped Indo-European male sky gods

- assimilated Minoan female/earth deities

- result—Olympian pantheon of classical Greeks

- rich grave offerings from shaft tombs suggest belief in afterlife

Historical Outline

- ca. 1600 BC—Myceneans established in small cities dominated by fortified palace-citadels (e.g., Mycenae, Pylos, Tiryns, most in Peloponnesus)

- ca. 1450 (or 1375?) conquered Minoan Crete and dominated Aegean (until 1100 BC)

- ca. 13th century—Mycenean "feudal empire"? (Agamemnon as leader of alliance against Troy)

- ca. 1250—Trojan War: Mycenae-led confederation of Greek city-states against Troy, a non-Greek city near southern outlet of Hellespont

Cause of War?

- traditional explanation—Helen (Homer)

- commercial explanation—Troy controlled access through Hellespont linking Aegean and Black Seas

Collapse of Mycenean Civilization (12th Century BC)

Evidence:

- destruction of most major palace citadels by fire

- evidence of extensive depopulation in parts of European Greece

- Dorians (Indo-European, Greek-speaking folk) arrive from north

- beginning of the Iron Age

- key elements of civilization (urban centers, literacy, specialized economy) disappeared for 3 centuries (1100–800 BC)—Dark Age

Two Explanations:

1. External conquest by Dorians and/or Sea Peoples?

2. Internal collapse caused by climate change (Rhys Carpenter, *Discontinuity in Greek Civilization*, 1966)?

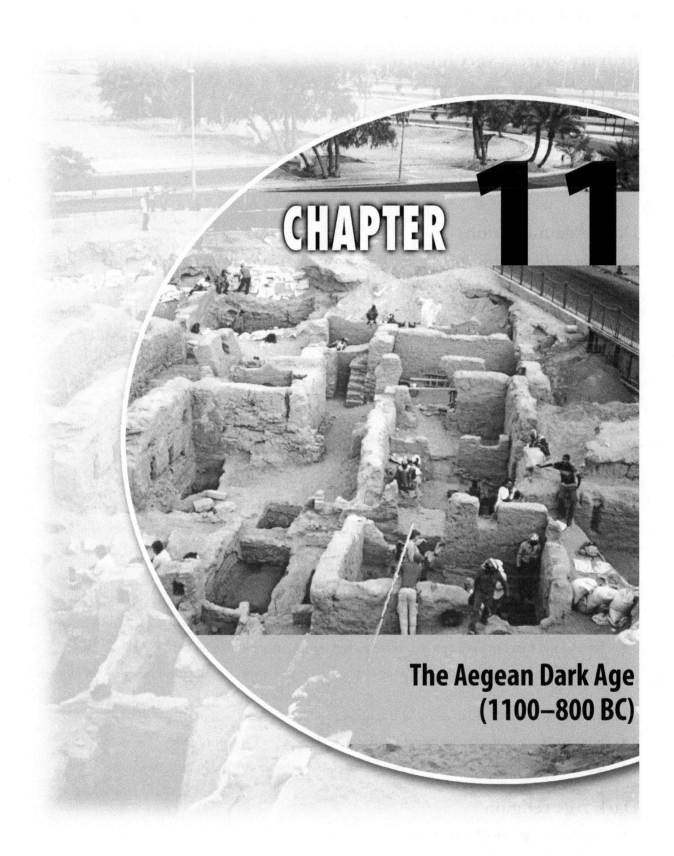

CHAPTER 11

The Aegean Dark Age (1100–800 BC)

Why a "Dark Age"?

Disappearance of civilization (urban centers, literacy, specialized economy)

Primary sources very limited

- no contemporary written sources
- later sources (e.g., Homer and other semilegendary accounts)
- archaeological record limited
- graves show iron now in widespread use
- thus, reconstruction of Dark Age tentative and speculative

Dark Age migrations

- many pre-Dorian Greeks migrated from Europe to Aegean islands and west coast of Anatolia—Ionian Greeks
- only major Ionian area left on European mainland: Attica (Athens)
- most of European mainland settled by Dorian Greeks, who expelled or subjugated earlier inhabitants
- Dorians and Ionians: two major groups of ancient Greeks based on their dialect (Doric and Ionic)

Economy in Dark Age

- near subsistence agriculture/animal herding
- little industry or commerce
- major source of wealth was land
- gradual accumulation of larger farms by a few landowners (*aristoi*—"the best men")

Political Organization in Dark Age

- many small polities ruled by petty "kings," each with limited powers (*primus inter pares*); each "king" chiefly a war leader, priest, judge
- *gerousia* (advisory council of elders): heads of leading families
- *ecclesia* (assembly): all adult males who could bear arms; called by king to ratify proposals (e.g., declaration of war)
- families and tribes retained much power (e.g., settling disputes and in religion)
- *aristoi* (landed aristocracy) stripped kings of most power and eventually abolished monarchy in most states by 800 BC
- king's powers transferred to executive magistrates from *aristoi* (e.g., "archons")
- many poorer citizens could no longer afford arms and lost right to sit in assembly
- government evolved from monarchy → aristocracy in most states by end of Dark Age

Dark Age religion

- polytheism based on Olympic Pantheon (headed by Zeus)
- Greek gods regarded as anthropomorphic (human form) and physically perfect, with immortality, humanlike personalities, but with superhuman powers

- sacred centers of Bronze Age remained sacred (e.g., Delphi with oracle to Apollo)
- no powerful priestly class arose in Greece
- gods thought to be near and no intermediaries needed
- gods could be contacted directly through prayer and sacrifice

End of Dark Age

- reintroduction of writing (ca. 800 BC)
- Greeks borrowed the Phoenician (i.e., Canaanite) alphabet
- Semitic consonants without phonetic value in Greek converted to vowels—1st alphabet with consonants and vowels
- new alphabet simpler and easier to learn than Linear B
- literacy still confined to a small elite

Homeric Question

- one of oldest issues in scholarship—who was Homer?
- current scholarly consensus: both *Iliad* and *Odyssey* composed in Ionia in mid-8th century by two different poets (essentially editors) after long period of oral transmission by traveling bards

Value of Homeric poems as historical sources?

- Poems reveal some knowledge about Mycenean world (Late Bronze Age):
  - location of main centers
  - great palaces filled with treasure (despite poverty of Dark Age)
  - use of bronze weapons and chariots
  - no Dorians appear

But many incongruities in poems:

- cremation of dead (Dark Age), not inhumation (Late Bronze Age)
- simple social system of Homer unlike complex, specialized palace economy of Myceneans
- power of petty Homeric kings and nobles based on land, with little focus on trade or industry (unlike Myceneans)

In short, Homeric poems retain a distant memory of Mycenean world, but better reflect conditions of Dark Age.

The Iliad

Single episode in 9th year of 10-year war—focus on feud between Agamemnon and Achilles

What does *Iliad* reveal about Dark Age society?

- kings seen as general and judge, but no palace bureaucracy and constant tension with only slightly less powerful nobles
- gods seen in human form and with human personalities, but with immortality and superhuman powers

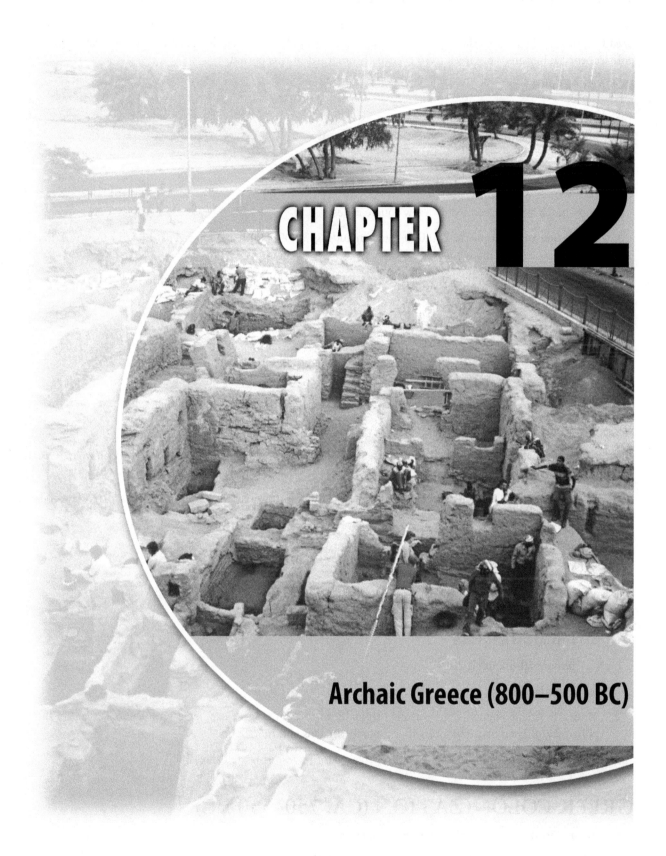

CHAPTER 12

Archaic Greece (800–500 BC)

EMERGENCE OF THE POLIS

polis = "city-state"; plural *poleis*—fundamental unit of Greek civilization *polis* emerged through process of *synoikismos* ("setting up house together"), that is, peasant and pastoral tribal societies coalesced in each valley to form a political entity; hundreds of Greek *poleis* eventually emerged in this period

Each *polis* included:

1. City—*acropolis* and *agora*

2. Hinterland—farms, villages, pastures, roads, etc.

Size of each *polis* varied greatly

- Athens (Attica) ca. 1,000 square miles

- most much smaller, some only a few square miles

- population varied from ca. 250,000 total (including 30,000 adult male citizens) in 5th century Athens to >1,000 citizens in many *poleis*

Polis encouraged frequent inter-city warfare, but also fostered a new concept of citizenship

Citizenship in each polis:

- a privilege, jealously guarded

- a matter of birth

- fostered intimacy among citizens and encouraged broad participation in local affairs

- reciprocal rights and obligations between citizen and state:

  - *polis* expected from each citizen: taxes, political loyalty, military service (as an *ephebe*), and participation in cultural life of city-state

  - *polis* promised to each citizen security, community, and protection under law (first written law codes in Greece from this period)

Three broad classes in each polis:

1. Citizens (held all political and military power, most land)

   a. aristocracy

   b. artisans and merchants

   c. peasants (bulk of citizens)

   d. poor, landless citizens

2. Metics (resident aliens)—free persons originally of foreign origin; had legal and economic rights but no political rights nor military obligation; mostly artisans and merchants

3. Slaves (common—from breeding, war captives, debt slaves, imported slaves)

GREEK COLONIZATION (CA. 750–550 BC)

- by ca. 750 BC many Greek states overpopulated

- colonization—safety valve to export surplus population

- most colonies founded on good farmland on Mediterranean and Black Sea coasts: Black Sea, Libya, Sicily, southern Italy, Corsica, southern France

- colonies usually established among less technologically advanced natives—why?

- who would join a new colony?

- once founded, each colony was a completely independent *polis* (retained cultural and commercial ties with mother city)

- colonies exported grain, timber, metals, and other raw materials to Greek homeland (Aegean) and imported wine, oil, pottery, and manufactured goods from Aegean

- expansion of trade aided by coinage (invented in Lydia ca. 700 BC)—first electrum, then gold and silver (originally bullion with standard weight and purity guaranteed by minting authority)

Economic Impact of Colonization

- economic stimulus to both colonies and mother *poleis*

- aristocracies had best land in both mother cities and colonies

- growing commercial class (artisans/merchants) of citizens and metics

- some peasants in mother cities prospered—switched to cash crops (e.g., olives and grapes) for export

- other peasants growing grain in mother cities fell into debt (could not compete against cheap imported grain from colonies)

Rise of Hoplite Tactics (ca. 650 BC)

- aristocracy had dominated warfare—cavalry and chariot tactics of Dark Age based on horses (kept only by elite—why?)

- rise of hoplites and phalanx revolutionized warfare

- all Greek *poleis* had to recruit all citizens who could provide their own armor into its phalanx

- these citizens eventually demanded greater political power from aristocracy

Age of Tyrants (ca. 650–550 BC)

- dictator (*tyrannos*), usually from aristocracy, seized power by extra-constitutional means

- *tyrannos* originally a neutral term

- tyrant overthrew aristocracy with support of lower-class citizens (artisans/merchants, peasants, laborers)

- pursued policies to aid his supporters

  - land redistribution

  - promotion of trade and industry

  - public works

  - written law codes

- tyranny usually only lasted 1–2 generations in most *poleis*

- most tyrants (or their sons) eventually expelled or killed—why?

After tyranny, most *poleis* took one of two paths:

1. Oligarchy/timocracy (alliance of aristocracy and commercial class)

2. Democracy (alliance of commercial and peasant classes)

By ca. 500 BC most Greek *poleis* had evolved politically as follows

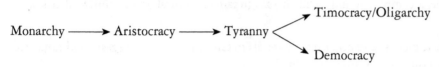

CHAPTER 13

Sparta

SOURCES

- one of the best known *poleis*
- abundant literary sources (e.g., Herodotus, Thucydides, Xenophon)
- some archaeological evidence

GEOGRAPHY

- city-state of Sparta in SE Peloponnesus
- Laconia (hinterland of Sparta) including Eurotas Valley
- larger and more fertile territory than most other *poleis*

EARLY HISTORY

- Mycenean Bronze Age—Spartan king Menelaus—key figure in Trojan war
- Collapse of Mycenean culture in 12th century BC
- Dorian settlement in 10th century BC
- Sparta emerges as Dorian city-state by ca. 750 (*synoikismos* of 6 villages)

Classes within Laconia

1. Spartiates (full citizens)
2. *Perioeci* (fellow Dorians who lived in villages around city of Sparta)
   - no political rights in Spartan government
   - local autonomy
   - obligated to serve in the Spartan army
3. Helots
   - descendants of pre-Dorian population of Laconia
   - agricultural serfs/slaves—owned by Spartan state

Conquest of Messenia

- although Laconia was large and fertile, by ca. 700 BC Spartans also under demographic pressure
- conquered polis of Messenia west of Laconia and converted all Messenians into helots
- no need for Sparta to join in colonization
- otherwise Sparta thus far was a relatively typical polis

The Transforming Crisis

- twin security threats simultaneously emerged ca. 670–630
  - internal: major helot revolt in Messenia

- external attack by Argos (traditional enemy in NE Peloponnesus)
- Sparta forced to totally revamp its society

"REFORMS OF LYCURGUS"

- radical political, economic, social reforms associated with semilegendary lawgiver of 7th century BC
- not complete until early 5th century, perhaps represents a compromise among Spartans
- adult male Spartiates (ca. 8,000) became professional military caste (ca. 8% of population) ruling over helot majority in Laconia and Messenia

Spartan Economy

- goal—maintain a self-sufficient agricultural economy to free all citizens for full-time military service
- Laconia was mostly privately held land
- in Messenia—most land was state-owned; farms assigned of equal size to each Spartiate
- state assigned helots (owned by state) to work each farm (whether publicly or privately owned)
- each farm produced food for common mess
- Spartiates prohibited from industry or trade
- limited needs in trade and industry handled by *perioeci*

Spartan Government

- 2 hereditary kings from 2 different families with limited powers
  - commanded Spartan army
  - religious duties
  - served on Gerousia
- Gerousia (council of elders)
  - 28 men over age 60 (+2 kings)
  - elected for life by assembly (*Apella*)
  - prepared business (e.g., legislation) for assembly
- Board of Ephors
  - 5 chief executive and judicial magistrates
  - elected annually by assembly
  - most powerful political organ in government—why?
- Apella (Assembly)
  - all adult male citizens over 30
  - legislature—passed all laws, treaties, declarations of war, etc.
  - elected Gerousia and board of ephors

- members could not themselves introduce, amend, or debate legislation presented by Gerousia
- voting by acclamation

How to characterize the Spartan government?

Spartan Social System

- Spartan boys at age 7 taken to live in barracks with older men
- severe physical training and military indoctrination
- at age 20 entered army and expected to marry; some assigned state-owned farm with state-owned helots as labor
- lived in barracks until age 30
- at age 30 joined Apella and could live at home with wife but still often ate in barracks and frequently absent for military campaigns or exercises
- focus on patriotism, fellowship, and egalitarianism among Spartiates
- close friendships (including sexual relationships) commonly formed between older and younger Spartan men
- liable for military service until age 60
- Spartan women in some sense were most free of any in Greece—why?
- Spartan girls educated and received separate physical training by state
- Spartan women could own property
- strong emphasis on health
- probably supervised farms

Spartan Foreign Policy

- generally nonaggressive—why?
- Peloponnesian League (formed ca. 550 BC)
  - defensive alliances between Sparta and neighboring *poleis*
  - created buffer states around Sparta
  - provided allies for league army—most powerful in Greece

Conclusions

Sparta was extremely conservative, stable, rigid society

Spartan soldiers were best in Greece

Sparta was most widely admired polis in Greece

Spartans had little cultural life and almost no freedom (lived in constant fear of helot revolts)

CHAPTER 14

Athens

SOURCES ON ATHENS

- best known by far of all Greek *poleis*
- abundant literary sources (e.g., Thucydides, Aristophanes, Plato)
- numerous inscriptions
- extraordinary archaeological evidence (e.g., architecture, sculpture, pottery, etc.)

GEOGRAPHY

- Ionian Greek *polis*
- sometimes hostile city-states to N (Thebes) and NW (Megara and Corinth)
- one of largest *poleis*—ca. 1,000 square miles (Attica)
- triangular peninsula with sea to E and W
- Attica—mountainous landscape, poorly suited for grain
- good deposits of clay (pottery)
- abundant stone, including marble
- some timber until end of 5th century
- silver mines in Laurium district

TYPICAL SOCIOECONOMIC STRUCTURE

- citizens subdivided into:
  - aristocracy/large landowners
  - artisans/merchants
  - peasants (owned small farms—bulk of population)
  - thetes (poor landless citizens)
- metics—free resident aliens (mostly artisans and merchants)—military obligation only in emergencies (*contra* de Blois)
- slaves—numerous and important in economy

Athenian Women

- even citizen women had no political power and few legal rights
- not formally educated
- girls married at 14–15
- must be represented in court by a male
- generally stayed at home for domestic work

HISTORICAL DEVELOPMENT

- original monarchy replaced by aristocracy (domination by large landowners) by end of Dark Age (800 BC)

- aristocrats controlled government as executive magistrates (archons)

- citizen assembly (legislature) based on property qualification

- by late 7th century Athens was overpopulated

- many citizens (mostly poorer peasants) fell into debt, even debt slavery—their small farms not economically viable

- many citizens now excluded from assembly due to property qualification—many poorer citizens demanded political, legal, and economic reforms

Reforms of Solon (Early 6th Century BC)

- member of aristocracy but trusted by most Athenians

- appointed as mediator with extraordinary powers to initiate broad political, economic, and legal reforms to forestall tyranny

1. abolished debt slavery among citizens and freed at public expense all citizens previously enslaved

2. recognized need for economic diversity through trade and industry

    - growing demand from colonization

    - encouraged development of olive oil as cash crop, pottery production (fine painted tableware), and other industries

    - rare offer of Athenian citizenship to foreigners who provided expertise (temporary measure)

3. New written law code

    - demanded by lower classes suffering from aristocracy's domination of courts

    - new code was less harsh

    - new court system with jurors drawn from wider body of citizens

4. Timocracy: Divided all citizens into 4 citizen classes based on wealth

    - aristocracy

    - commercial class

    - peasants

    - thetes

- Solon offered limited political rights to poorest citizens (thetes—could vote in assembly)

- executive magistracies limited to two highest classes—aristocrats and well-to-do merchants, who effectively controlled government

Impact of Solon's reforms

- began transformation of Athenian economy

- improved legal rights of all citizens

- staved off tyranny for a few decades

Tyranny of Peisistratus (546–527 BC)

- seized power with support of lower-class citizens and hired mercenaries
- classic example of a "good tyrant," that is, his policies served interests of his supporters:
1. Land redistribution from aristocracy to small farmers and thetes
2. Further encouraged trade and industry:
- introduced 1st Athenian coinage
- Athenian painted pottery drove Corinthian pottery from the market
3. Program of public works (e.g., new temple to Athena on Acropolis)—government contracts for artisans and jobs for thetes
4. Patron of arts and cultural activities (e.g., inaugurated drama contests during annual festival of Dionysus)

Tyranny of Hippias (527–510 BC)

- succeeded to power upon death of his father, Peisistratus
- less popular than father
- Athenians (with Spartan support) expelled Hippias in 510 BC

Establishment of Athenian Democracy (508 BC)

- *demokratia* = "rule by the *demos*"
- founded by Cleisthenes, an aristocrat
- divided all citizens into 10 tribes based on **_residence_** not kinship
- each tribe divided into "demes" ("precincts"); over 100 demes in all
- each tribe composed of demes scattered over Attica
- aimed to foster unity by breaking old bonds of kinship and regionalism

Organs of Athenian Democratic Government

1. *Ecclesia* (legislative assembly—all adult male citizens) held central position in government
2. *Boule* (Council of 500—50 members of each tribe selected annually by lot) proposed legislation to assembly and acted as a sitting government
3. Archons (9 executive magistrates, selected annually by lot from two highest property classes)—enforced laws
4. *Strategoi* (10 generals—1 annually elected by each tribe) commanded army and navy; could be reelected (e.g., Pericles in 461–429) and often had influence beyond military affairs
5. *dikasteria* (pool of 6,000 jurors selected annually by lot)—juries ranged from 201 to 1,001 chosen by lot to hear and decide specific cases

Key Elements of Athenian Democracy

1. Government by committee
2. Selection by lot

3. Pay for all public officials

4. All citizens equal before the law

Ostracism (1st attested in 488 BC)

- annual vote in assembly—"winner" exiled for 10 years from Athens but suffered no other penalty; could return and reenter politics after 10 years

By 480s Athens became the major sea power in Greece; by 470s Athens began creating a naval empire (Delian League); heavy reliance on naval forces increased political power of thetes and other lower-class citizens (who rowed the warships)

Some Issues about Athenian Democracy

1. Did class of "democrats" try to exclude wealthier citizens from power?

   Aristocrats still dominated board of 10 generals and remained influential in military and political affairs (e.g., Pericles)

2. Was democracy possible in Athens only because of imperialism—tribute from Delian League and leisure for citizens due to slavery?

   Democracy established in 508 BC, 30 years *before* creation of Delian League (477 BC)

3. Did Athenian democracy become "ochlocracy" ("mob-rule")?

- wide swings in policy

- proved inept in waging war and controlling Delian League, which was lost by end of 5th century

- yet democracy as government for city-state of Athens proved inherently stable and survived for centuries

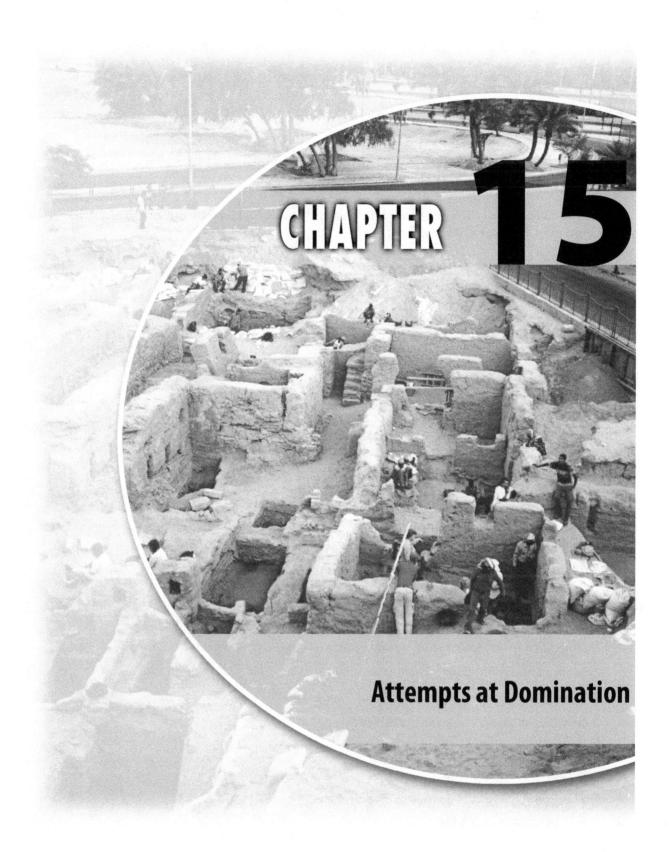

CHAPTER 15

Attempts at Domination

Marks beginning of the Classical Period (500–323 BC) of Greek history

The Persian Wars

Principal source—Herodotus (*Persian War*)

The Persian Empire

- by late 6th century BC Persia ruled entire Near East
- conquest of Lydia (546 BC) brought Ionian Greeks under Persian rule
- Persians established local Greek tyrants in Ionian cities, supervised by satrap (governor) at Sardis
- Persian rule relatively mild but Ionians chafed at loss of independence
- Persian King Darius I (520–485) extended Persian power into SE Europe (conquest of Thrace), leaving only Greek states of European mainland still free

Ionian Revolt (499–494 BC)

- began in Miletus, spread to other Ionian cities
- success possible only if European Greeks provided significant support
- Ionian embassies to Sparta and most other states failed
- only Athens and Eretria (both Ionian city-states) sent aid
- revolt initially successful (e.g., sack of Sardis)
- Persians eventually assembled overwhelming forces and crushed revolt, sacking Miletus and reconquering all Ionia

Persian Reprisals

- Darius launched punitive expedition against Eretria and Athens (490)
- Eretria fell after short siege and sacked
- Athens hoped for aid from Spartans, who promised help but arrived too late
- Persian fleet landed troops on plain of Marathon (east coast of Attica), along with Hippias, former tyrant of Athens
- Athenian army held high ground above plain and blocked land route over mountains
- Persians re-embarked troops to sail around Cape Sunion and attack Athens by sea from W
- Athenians attacked Persians on beach at Marathon
- Persians pushed into sea with loss of 6400 men and 7 ships
- bulk of Persian force escaped and headed for Athens
- Athenians warned in time by Phidippides (first "Marathon Man")

Significance of Marathon

- Greeks gained ten years to prepare for next invasion
- Athens gained self-confidence

Xerxes' Invasion of Greece

Developments during 480s:

- new deposits of silver at Laurium in Attica

- Themistocles urged Athenians to construct new fleet—200 triremes

- Athens now the leading naval power in Greece

- Death of Darius (485), new king Xerxes (485–464) faced internal revolts, which were eventually all crushed

- Xerxes' goal to conquer European Greece

- Xerxes assembled huge forces (ca. 100,000 men and 1200 warships?)

- Greeks formed Hellenic League, headed by Sparta

Battle of Thermopylae

- Greek advanced guard of 5,000 troops under Spartan King Leonidas to Thermopylae with fleet offshore to block Persian advance into central Greece

- Persians initially failed to break through pass and suffered heavy losses

- Persians, aided by treachery, eventually outflanked Greeks

Herodotus (ca. 484–425 BC)

- "Father of History" (1st historian)

- from Halicarnassus (Ionia)

- exiled from polis and traveled throughout eastern Mediterranean and Persian Empire

- *historie* ("inquiry") focused on great war between Greeks and Persians

- his sources?

- relatively impartial, even sympathetic towards non-Greeks

- use of historical method

Salamis and Platea

- Greek defeat at Thermopylae left central Greece open to invasion—Thebes surrendered, Athens evacuated

- Persians burned Athens

- Spartans wanted to withdraw to Peloponnesus

- Themistocles pressed for naval battle in Bay of Salamis

- Battle of Salamis (480)—decisive victory for Greeks

- Xerxes returned to Persia but left his army in central Greece

- united Greek armies (led by Sparta) routed Persian army at Platea (479)

- complete expulsion of Persians from Europe by 477

The Delian League

Formation

- Spartans withdrew from leadership of Greek counteroffensive (477)
- Greeks offered leadership to Athenians who, led by Themistocles, formed Delian League
- offensive and defensive alliance against Persia
- goal to drive Persians from Aegean and free all Greeks
- headquarters on island of Delos (treasury and congress of league)
- Athenians dominated military leadership and league treasurers from beginning
- league eventually numbered over 200 *poleis*
- each *polis* could choose to provide its own ships and crews or make financial contributions to pay for Athenian ships and crews—which choice did most city-states make and why?

History of Delian League

- league continued successful offensive, driving the Persians out of the Aegean (477–468)
- freed Greek city-states joined league
- after 468 some members wished to withdraw
- Athens kept these states within the league by force, crushing revolts
- Athenians had bigger ambitions (e.g., Cyprus, Egypt)
- after a military disaster in Egypt (454) league treasury moved from Delos to Athens
- henceforth Delian League essentially an ***Athenian Empire*** (naval empire) of tribute-paying subject allies
- Athenians controlled key subject states through *cleruchs*—Athenian military colonists serving as garrison forces
- Athenian navy used against major commercial rivals (e.g., Corinth) to exclude their commerce from league ports
- Athenian-style democracies were imposed in many League states
- Athenian coinage and commercial law imposed throughout Empire
- some evidence of great opposition to Athenian policies among many subject allies (especially local elites in many *poleis*)
- Other evidence suggests many lower-class citizens in these same *poleis* supported Athenians—why?
- Warfare between Athens and Persia ended by 449; Athens concentrated on domination of Greece

Internal Effects of Delian League on Athens

- Athenian Empire based on fleet manned by lower-class Athenians (thetes)—middle- and upper-class Athenians served as hoplites
- military service increased political power of thetes and led to further democratic reforms in Athenian government
- economic basis of Empire from two sources:
    1. Trade and industry of Athens (exported pottery, oil, wine, silver)
    2. Tribute from subject allies

- Pericles as dominant political leader (461–429) based on annual reelection to board of 10 generals

- Pericles promoted large navy and massive public works (e.g., Parthenon)

- naval service, service in government and public works provided jobs for lower-class citizens

- impressive cultural achievements of 5th century Athens subsidized by tribute of Delian League

- Athens now most powerful state in Aegean

- Was Pericles aiming for total domination of Greece?

PELOPONNESIAN WAR (431–404 BC)

Sparta and Peloponnesian League vs. Athens and Delian League

Primary Source

Thucydides (ca. 471–400) of Athens—contemporary eyewitness and participant

Causes

- expansion of Delian League caused fear among Greeks still free, especially Sparta and Peloponnesian League

- Corinth (key Spartan ally and major commercial rival to Athens) faced economic ruin—Athenians excluded Corinthians from traditional markets

- Sparta declared war on Athens

Strategy of Pericles

Based on assessment of both sides' strengths and weaknesses

Why was Athens defeated?

1. Plague hit Athens in 430—killed up to 1/3 of population (including Pericles)

2. Rise of demagogues (e.g., Alcibiades)

3. Expedition to Syracuse (415–413) urged by Alcibiades ended in total disaster—loss of two Athenian fleets and thousands of troops

4. Deceleia—Sparta established permanent fort within Attica on mountain top (413)—Athenians now confined to Long Walls year-round and more thorough destruction of Attica

5. Revolts of subject allies within Delian League

6. Persian financial support for Sparta and her allies allowed Spartans to challenge Athenian naval supremacy

7. Alcibiades returned to Athens (411 BC), won several battles and prolonged war (411–406)

8. Aegospotami (405)—decisive battle of war; Athens' last fleet destroyed in Hellespont; Peloponnesians blockaded Athens and starved Athenians into surrender (404)

Peace Terms Imposed on Athens

- Delian League disbanded

- Long Walls torn down

- democracy abolished
- "30 tyrants" (pro-Spartan oligarchy) installed in Athens and supported by Spartan garrison

Athenians soon expelled 30 tyrants and reestablished their traditional democracy (403 BC)

Thucydides Provides Two Different Views of Athens

1. Funeral Oration of Pericles (431 BC)—ideals of Athenian democracy
2. Melian Dialogue (416 BC)—reality of Athenian Empire

DOMINANCE OF SPARTA (404–371 BC)

- Spartan wartime propaganda—"freedom of Greeks"
- after Athenians defeat, Spartans attempt to dominate Aegean
- anti-Spartan alliance (394 BC)—included Thebes, Argos, Corinth, Athens with Persian financial support
- two alliances fought to near exhaustion
- "King's Peace" (387 BC)
  - Persians regained control of Ionian Greek cities
  - Sparta weakened but still the single most powerful polis
- Battle of Leuctra (371 BC)
  - first defeat of main Spartan field army in several centuries
  - won by Thebes under command of Epaminondas
  - new tactical formation—oblique phalanx
  - Epaminondas combined oblique phalanx, peltasts (light infantry) and cavalry
  - Sparta's citizen population nearly annihilated (ca. 8,000 adult males in ca. 480 reduced to ca. 1,500 just before Leuctra)
  - Messenians freed—reduced Sparta's territory and agricultural wealth
  - Sparta finished as a great power in Greece

ATTEMPTED DOMINATION BY THEBES (371–362 BC)

- other Greek *poleis* quickly imitated military innovations of Epaminondas
- death of Epaminondas (362 BC)
- rough balance of power among major Greek poleis (362–338 BC)

RESULTS OF FAILED ATTEMPTS AT DOMINATION

- nearly continuous warfare of 5th and early 4th centuries caused great loss of life and ravaged Greek economy
- undermined the system of independent city-states
- Greek city-states vulnerable to external conquest

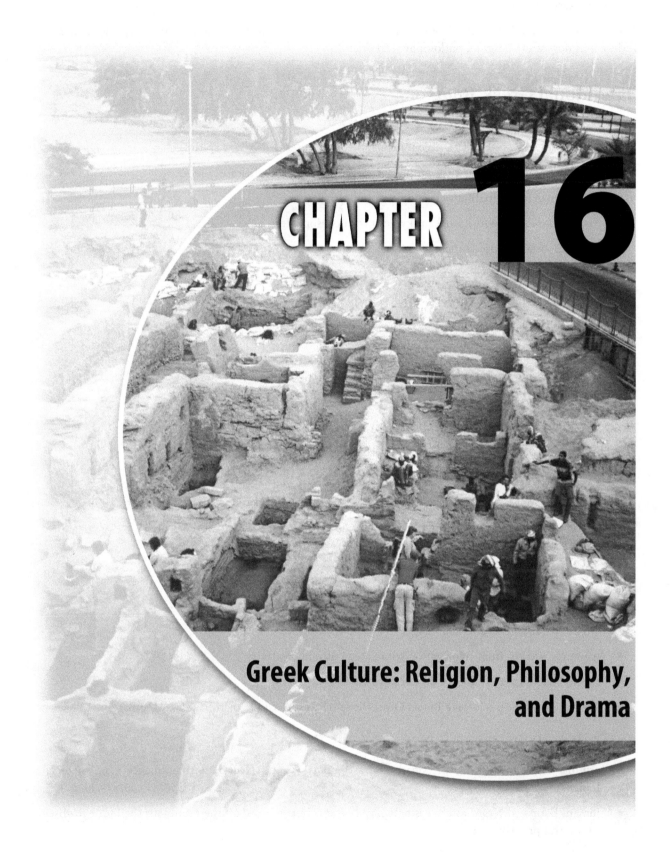

CHAPTER 16

Greek Culture: Religion, Philosophy, and Drama

Greek culture reached its height in 6th–4th centuries BC in many diverse fields, including architecture, sculpture, painted pottery, etc.

We have already sampled poetry (Homer's *Iliad*) and the creation of history as a discipline (Herodotus and Thucydides); will now study religion, philosophy, and drama

Traditional Greek Religion

In many ways similar to religion of the Ancient Near East:

- polytheism (e.g., in Homer)—Olympic pantheon + lesser deities and spirits
- gods portrayed in human form, imperfect, with human personalities
- superhuman (if limited) powers and immortality
- main god—Zeus (Indo-European sky god) with consort Hera
- other important gods—Athena, Dionysus, Apollo, etc.
- worship through prayer and sacrifice
- original concept of afterlife: descent of soul to Hades
- later belief in happy afterlife emerged via various *mystery cults*:
  - Demeter (goddess of grain, fertility)
  - Adonis (died but rose from the dead)
  - Dionysus (god of wine)
  - Orpheus (free soul from prison of body through pure, ascetic life)

One critically important difference between Greece and Near East:

- priests much less powerful and influential in Greece
- priests were not the only educated class and thus did not dominate intellectual thought
- more freedom of inquiry among educated Greeks

Greek Philosophy

Archaic Period (800–500 BC)

- Greek "renaissance" (after Dark Age)
- economic growth from colonization stimulated cultural creativity
- strong Near Eastern influence on Greek culture
- leading cultural centers were Ionian Greek cities on west coast of Anatolia (e.g., Miletus)

Ionian School (6th Century BC)

- original interest was scientific: math and astronomy (strong Near Eastern influence via Phoenicians to Ionians)
- Ionians borrowed Near Eastern cosmological *concepts* but stripped off their religious shell (due to absence of a powerful priestly class)
- Greek scientists and philosophers were *laymen, not* priests

- key contribution—search for natural (rather than supernatural) explanations to understand the cosmos: **Natural Causation** (i.e., rationalism)—use of reason and logic to analyze the world

Philosophers of the Ionian School (mostly 6th century BC)

1. Thales of Miletus

- predicted total solar eclipse in 585 BC

- water as primal element and was itself living; all else derived from water

- cosmology—cosmos was an enclosed sphere; earth was a flat disc floating in great bowl (Ocean) with inverted bowl forming roof of heavens; beyond sphere was primordial *aether* or fire; stars were holes in roof through which *aether* was seen

2. Anaximander of Miletus

- four primal elements—earth, air, fire, and water

- cosmos arose from separation and combination of opposites

- life began in water and later moved on to land

3. Heraclitus of Ephesus

- fire as chief catalyst to change one element into another

- continual flux or constant change

4. Pythagoras of Samos

- studied mathematics (but Pythogorean Theorem known in Near East at least 1000 years earlier)

- believed numbers had magical qualities

- transmigration of souls

5. Xenophanes of Colophon

- criticized "childish" nature of Homeric gods, mocked anthropomorphic notions of deity

- advocated monotheism with one god unlike humans

6. Democritus of Abdera

- atomic theory—all matter composed of indivisible particles (atoma)

- atoms cannot be created nor destroyed

- all matter in continual flux

- all events caused by recombinations of atoms

- no creation, no soul, no afterlife, no gods- atheism

Summary of Ionian School

- emphasized rationalism to understand the universe

- concerned with science—cosmology, astronomy, mathematics, and physics

- method based on observation and speculation (little experimentation)

Philosophy in the Classical Period (500–323 BC)

- change in focus (geographical and philosophical)

- destruction or decline of Ionian cities after Ionian Revolt (499–494)

- Athens new cultural leader of Greece thanks to its wealth, talent, freedom, and interested public
- new emphasis on personal ethics and skepticism of traditional beliefs

Sophists (late 5th century BC)

- originally teachers of rhetoric who sometimes became philosophers
- traveled widely to lecture to paying audiences on wide range of topics
- great orators, often with arrogant style
- sometimes claimed "universal knowledge"
- challenged conventional views on religion, customs, politics, and society

Socrates of Athens (469–399 BC)

- intellectual gadfly, sometimes accused of being a sophist
- questioned all in Athens about any subject (e.g., truth, justice, religion) via the Socratic method
- students (e.g., Alcibiades, Xenophon, Plato, and other young aristocrats)
- what was Socrates' own philosophy?
  - Socrates himself wrote nothing
  - sources contradictory (e.g., Plato vs. Xenophon)

Plato's *Apology* of Socrates (399 BC)

- trial of Socrates before 501 Athenian jurors
- how reliable is Plato's account?
- two formal charges:
1. Corruption of youth of Athens
2. Denial of old gods while inventing new false gods

Socrates distinguishes between formal charges and "more ancient" charges:

1. He was a natural philosopher and thus an atheist (like Democritus)
2. He "made the worse appear the better cause" (i.e., a sophist)

Why was Socrates so unpopular?

"Wisdom" of Socrates recognized by Apollo because "He is the wisest, who, like Socrates, knows that his wisdom is in truth worth nothing"

Socrates questioned his accusers to demonstrate foolishness of charges

Socrates likely acquitted if he promised to stop his past conduct, but refused—he must obey a higher law, of god

Jury voted to convict (280–221), then voted for death (360–141)

Does Socrates fear death?

Plato of Athens (429–347 BC)

- student of Socrates
- saw failure of democracy with defeat of Athens in Peloponnesian War

- witnessed execution of Socrates
- voluntary exile in 399
- returned to Athens in 387 to found the Academy
- distrusted knowledge based on sense experience; true knowledge from pure thought (inductive reasoning)
- world of ideas vs. world of forms ("Allegory of the Cave")

Plato's *Republic*

- presented as dialogue with Socrates as main speaker, but ideas are clearly Plato's
- model of ideal state—polis of special type
  - ruled by Philosopher-Kings
  - Guardians—trained elite to enforce laws and protect state
  - general body of citizens
  - status of women in ideal state?
- Plato's model for his ideal state?

Aristotle (384–322 BC)

- originally a student of Plato
- later broke with Plato and founded rival school (Lyceum) in Athens
- believed knowledge gained only through senses
- stressed observation over contemplation (i.e., deductive reasoning)
- organized and classified many fields of knowledge (e.g., logic, botany, zoology, physics, political science)

Greek philosophers laid foundations of Western thought by establishing concept of rationalism—search for natural causation and answer questions through reason and logic; also raised many basic moral and ethical questions (e.g., What is truth? What is a just society?)

GREEK DRAMA

Background

- origins associated with religion, especially Dionysus
- annual festival to god in Athens with song and dance by a chorus, who re-created episodes in life of Dionysus
- other themes from mythology gradually introduced
- leader of chorus became 1st actor, reacting to song and dance of chorus
- Peisistratus organized annual dramatic competitions in Athens
- by 5th century playwrights submitted a trilogy of tragedies + 1 satyr play
- judges selected work of three playwrights to present each year on three successive days, with prize to that judged best
- Greek theaters built into hillsides with excellent acoustics

- all actors were males and wore masks
- Theoric Fund in Athens allowed poor citizens to attend theater

Athenian Tragic Playwrights (5th Century BC)

1. Aeschylus—added 2nd actor; 1 trilogy (*Oresteia*) survives complete

2. Sophocles—added 3rd actor; most famous work—*Oedipus Rex*

3. Euripides—used mythological themes to comment on contemporary events (e.g., *The Trojan Women*—criticizing Athens' expedition against Melos)

Athenian Comedy

Aristophanes (ca. 450–385 BC)

- only comedic playwright of this era whose work survives
- 11 of 44 known plays survive
- comedy was topical, satirized prominent contemporary individuals and "stock types" of characters
- plays antidemocratic in tone (reflecting his aristocratic background)

His comedy, *The Lysistrata*, first performed in 411 BC

Scene: Athens, at foot of the Acropolis

Characters:

- Lysistrata—Athenian woman and heroine of play
- Kleonike—Athenian woman
- Myrrhine—Athenian woman
- Lampito—Spartan woman
- Kinesias—Athenian citizen and husband of Myrrhine
- Spartan envoy
- Baby—child of Myrrhine and Kinesias

Unusual feature is two choruses: of old men and of old women

Entire dialogue filled with sexual innuendo and double entendre; only some comes through in translation

Lysistrata as a primary historical source:

- play fictional, but what does it suggest about Athens in 411 BC?
- freedom of speech and artistic expression, even in war time?
- status of women in Athens?
- attitude towards sexuality?

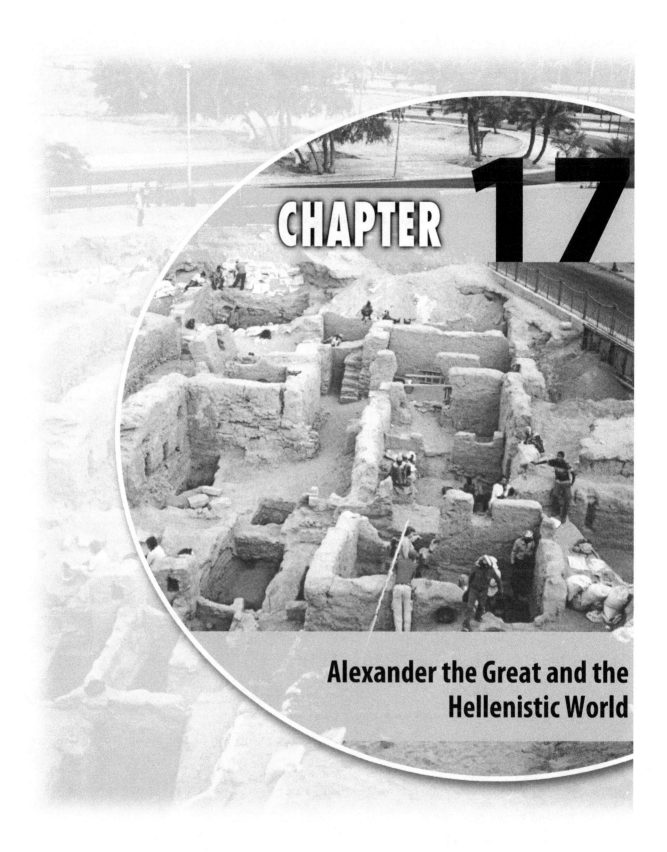

CHAPTER 17

Alexander the Great and the Hellenistic World

Macedonia

- large kingdom in NW Aegean but backward by Greek standards
- monarchy
- lacked urban centers—rural and tribal
- Macedonians officially viewed as Greeks but seen as "semi-barbarians"
- played a peripheral role in Greece until now

Philip II of Macedonia (359–336 BC)

- formerly a hostage at Thebes (era of Epaminondas)
- after becoming king, Philip reorganized Macedonian army
    - oblique phalanx (Macedonian peasants)
    - heavy cavalry (Macedonian aristocracy)
    - siege capability
- excellent general with great political cunning

Philip's Conquest of Greece

- exploited divisions among Greek *poleis*
- slowly expanded his power
- Demosthenes (Athenian politician) warned Greeks of this threat
- Battle of Chaeronea (338 BC)—Macedonia crushed Athens and Thebes and began long period of Macedonian domination of Greece

Philip's Pan-Hellenic Crusade Against Persia

- hoped a crusade against an old foreign enemy (Persians) would unify Greeks under his rule
- initial goal to free Ionian Greeks
- League of Corinth organized and led by Philip
- Philip assassinated in 336

Alexander III ("The Great" 336–323 BC)

- son of Philip, born in 356 BC
- tutored by Aristotle, who instilled great love of Greek culture
- long odds against him upon taking throne—age, lack of experience and money, major revolt in Greece, etc.
- key assets:
    1. Macedonian army (ca. 35,000) as reorganized by Philip
    2. military genius
- quickly crushed Greek revolt

- assumed leadership of League of Corinth (Greek allies)
- 334 BC—invaded Persian Empire

Initial strategy:

- threat posed by Persian fleet
- Alexander planned to defeat Persian fleet on land
- then invade Persian heartland
- 334—initial victory at Granicus
- liberated Ionian Greek city-states
- 333—Issus—defeated Darius III in northern Syria
- siege of Tyre—ingenious tactics
- 332—welcomed in Egypt—ended Persian naval threat
- founded new city of Alexandria with Greek and Macedonian veterans
- a dozen more "Alexandrias" founded as Greek cities along line of march
- served various purposes—held empire together, promoted trade, spread Greek culture throughout Near East
- Darius meanwhile prepared much larger army in Mesopotamia
- 331—Gaugamela—decisive battle of war—Mesopotamia and Iran fell
- Alexander now called himself "King of Asia" and successor to Persian kings
- 330–326—conquest of eastern Persian Empire
- conquest of Afghanistan
- invasion of India
- Macedonian troops mutinied in Indus Valley
- 325—Alexander returned to Babylon (new capital of new empire)
- 323—death of Alexander

Alexander and the "Great Man" View of History

- can single individuals fundamentally change history?
- modern views of Alexander vary considerably
- lack of contemporary primary sources (none before 1st century BC)
- Alexander spread Greek culture throughout Near East
- fusion of Greek + Near Eastern culture = "Hellenistic culture"

HELLENISTIC WORLD (323–30 BC)

- Alexander died without a clear successor
- civil war among top generals led to partition of empire (by 301 BC):
    1. Macedonia (dominated Greece) ruled by Antigonid dynasty from Pella

2. Seleucid Empire—Seleucid dynasty at Antioch ruled most of Asian parts of empire—Syria, Anatolia, Mesopotamia, Iran

3. Egypt—ruled by Ptolemies from Alexandria, plus Cyprus, Libya, Palestine

- rise of huge Hellenistic kingdoms meant end of Greek polis system

- most *poleis* now subject allies or local units of administration in these kingdoms

- in Greek homeland an alternative was leagues of *poleis* united for mutual defense (e.g., Achean League, Aetolian League):

  - each polis sent delegates to federal congress based on its size

  - unified military command with each polis providing troops

Greek leagues, Hellenistic kingdoms, and other states maintained balance of power until 2nd century BC, until expansion of Roman Empire

Social and Economic Structures of Hellenistic World

- many Greeks migrated to new kingdoms as mercenaries, administrators, and businessmen

- Alexander and successors liquidated huge bullion reserves of Persian kings by minting coins

- economic prosperity and growth of larger cities (Alexandria in Egypt—population ca. 500,000)

Ptolemaic Egypt

- best-known Hellenistic state from abundant papyri

- Ptolemies were god-kings (imitating pharaohs) and ruled absolutely

- small Greco-Macedonian elite ruled over Egyptian peasants

- highly centralized state with state-planned economy

- Ptolemies were great patrons of science and learning (e.g., Library of Alexandria)

Hellenistic Culture

- spread of Greek language throughout Near East

- Alexandria become leading center of science and learning

- Athens remained leader in Greek philosophy

- new philosophies appeared: Epicureanism & Stoicism (to be discussed later)

- these and other Greek philosophies all confined largely to elite of Hellenistic World; most continued to practice traditional polytheism

Science and the Hellenistic World

- several striking discoveries, many by scholars at Library of Alexandria

- Aristarchus of Samos (ca. 280) advanced heliocentric theory of cosmos (though rejected by most contemporaries)

- Eratosthenes (3rd century BC)—argued that earth was spherical and calculated circumference of earth correctly within 200 miles

Conclusion

- Hellenistic culture eventually extended from Spain to India—highly influential for later Western culture

- absorbed by Roman Empire—largely Hellenistic in culture

- e.g., Christianity—1st Christians were Near Eastern Jews whose sacred documents were written in Greek

Part IV

ANCIENT ROME

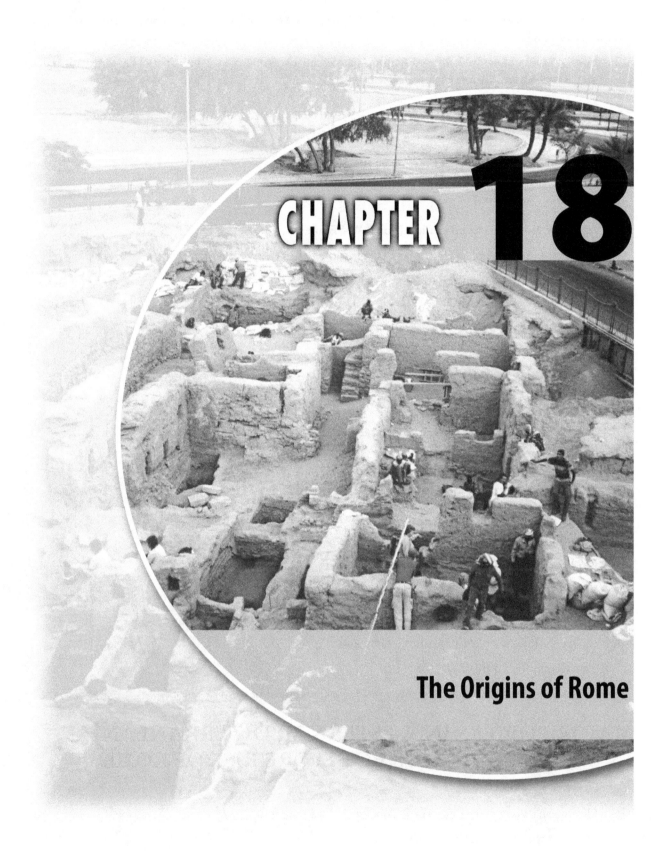

CHAPTER 18

The Origins of Rome

SIGNIFICANCE OF ANCIENT ROME

1. Many of our institutions and much of our culture borrowed from Rome (e.g., government, law, language, literature, religion, etc.)

2. Rome eventually evolved into an empire—successful experiment in a multinational, multicultural, and multiracial society with many lessons for us today

GEOGRAPHY OF ITALY AND ROME

Italy

- mountainous, boot-shaped peninsula

- Alps to N

- Apennine Mountains bisect peninsula on NW-SE line

- Po valley and coastal plains fertile—thus, self-sufficient in food production

- other resources—timber, stone, and minerals (e.g., iron)

Site of Rome

- in central Italy on Tiber River

- ca. 15 miles from mouth of Tiber at first easy crossing upstream from sea (Tiber island)

- access to salt pans at mouth of Tiber

- "Seven Hills" on E side of Tiber offered some protection

- region below hills fertile but marshy until drained

MAJOR PERIODS OF ROMAN HISTORY

1. Monarchy (753–509 BC)

- dates traditional; limited reliable evidence

- Rome emerges as a city-state

2. Roman Republic (509–30 BC)

- Rome grows from city-state to empire

- conquered Italy, then entire Mediterranean world

3. Roman Empire (30 BC–AD 476)

- series of emperors ruled entire Mediterranean world and most of western Europe

MAJOR POWERS IN WESTERN MEDITERRANEAN IN 8th–6th CENTURIES BC BEFORE RISE OF ROME

1. Carthage

- Phoenician colony founded in 814 BC on North African coast

- city-state with naval and commercial power

- ruled empire—much of North Africa, Sicily, Sardinia, Corsica, and Spain

2. Greek city-states of Sicily and southern Italy

- founded as colonies

- leading city-state was Syracuse in Sicily

- great influence on early Rome

3. Etruscans

- non-Indo-Europeans of obscure origins

  - most scholars now reject view of Etruscans as immigrants from Asia Minor to Italy in 9th century BC

  - probably an indigenous Italian people strongly influenced by Near East, adopted Greek alphabet by 700 BC

- developed independent city-states in Etruria (NW Italy)

- expanded N to Po Valley and S into Latium

- later weakened by political disunity and inter-city warfare

- expansion halted by Greeks in S and Celts (Gauls) in N

- greatly influenced early Rome

ORIGINS OF THE ROMANS

- Latins (Indo-Europeans) migrated to Italy in late 2nd millennium BC

- settled in Latium (W central Italy), including hills of Rome ca. 1000 BC

- Latins mostly peasant villagers- farmed and bred livestock

MONARCHY (753–509 BC)

- Latin villages coalesced into a city (Rome) in 7th and 6th centuries, under some Etruscan influence

- began drainage of Tiber marshes (forum)

- site fortified with walls

- first major temple (Capitoline Triad—Jupiter, Juno, and Minerva)

- succession of 7 kings—perhaps first 4 largely legendary; 2 of 3 later kings have Etruscan names

- Romans acknowledged debt to Etruscans in many areas, including art and religion, e.g.

  - divination—consulting gods (e.g., Romulus in Livy)

  - gladiatorial games

Government of Monarchy

- king (*rex*)—military commander, judge, priest (to consult gods)

- Senate (council of elders)—heads of leading families (patricians—aristocracy); purely advisory powers but great prestige

- *Comitia* (assembly of adult male citizens):

  - included both patricians and plebeians (lower-class citizens)

  - formally conferred power (*imperium*) on king

  - met to ratify decisions of king and Senate

Economy of Monarchy

- near subsistence agriculture focused on grain and livestock
- limited trade and industry

Social Structure of Monarchy

1. Patricians (landed aristocracy)—1st class citizens
2. Plebeians—2nd class citizens
- mostly peasants (some well-to-do, others poor)
- some artisans/merchants
- plebeians prohibited from holding public office, excluded from Senate, forbidden to intermarry with patricians
- most were *clientes* ("dependents") of patrician *patroni*
- obligated for military service, which was restricted to land-owning citizens
3. slaves (few in this period, most owned by patricians)

pater familias ("head of household")

- headed each Roman family
- life or death power over each member of household
- women passed upon marriage from control of *pater familias* of her family to *pater familias* of her husband's family

EARLY REPUBLIC (509–265 BC)

- last king expelled in 509 BC
- victory of aristocracy (patricians) who now dominated state
- king replaced by two chief executive magistrates (consuls) annually elected by assembly with same powers as king

External Conflicts

- Rome surrounded by hostile peoples (e.g., Etruscans and Samnites)
- Rome allied in 493 with fellow Latins (Latin League) for mutual defense
- in 390 Gauls invaded Italy and sacked Rome
- Rome recovered and reorganized its army—developed the "legion"
- Samnite Wars (341–290 BC)—Rome defeated Samnites and Etruscans and became dominant in central Italy
- Greek city-states of S Italy sought help from Pyrrhus, king of Epirus, who invaded Italy
- Romans with new "legion" vs. Greek phalanx of Pyrrhus
- Pyrrhus won "Pyrrhic victories" but forced to withdraw from Italy, Greek cities submitted
- 265 BC—Rome dominated entire peninsula of Italy

Roman Treatment of Conquered Peoples in Italy

- only ca. 15% of Italy ruled directly by Rome
- remainder under Rome's Italian allies

- retained local autonomy

- paid no taxes to Rome

- contributed troops to Roman army

- some allies, after years of loyal service to Rome, eventually awarded full Roman citizenship (1st to Latins, later others)

- treatment of Italians key to Rome's successful expansion—why?

Internal Conflict—Struggle of the Orders

- plebeians wanted legal and political equality with patricians

- *secessio*—forced patricians to compromise

- 494 BC—creation of tribunes—plebeian officials annually elected by plebs with right of *veto*

- 450 BC—XII Tables—written codification of Roman law

- 367 BC—plebs won eligibility for consulship, at least 1 of 2 consuls would be plebeian

- plebs won other rights: admission to Senate, to marry patricians, etc.

- victory of plebeians by 287 BC

- struggle of orders waged by nonviolent methods and resolved through peaceful compromise

GOVERNMENT OF ROMAN REPUBLIC (287 BC)

1. Assemblies (all adult male Roman citizens):

   Comitia Centuriata—Roman army meeting for political purpose: organized by centuries and heavily weighted towards wealth—declared war, ratified treaties, and elected all magistrates

   Comitia Tributa—organized into 30+ tribes (more democratic)—passed most legislation

2. Senate:

- advisory council of ca. 300 former magistrates (now with some leading plebeians)

- great prestige

- controlled foreign policy and state finances

3. Executive Branch—groups of annually elected magistrates:

- consuls—2 chief executive officials and military commanders

- praetors—judicial officials

- aediles—supervised public works, markets, and games

- quaestors—treasury officers

- tribunes—"protectors of plebeians"

Special Executive Officials

- censors—2 elected every 5 years to 18-month term to conduct census of citizens and property; also filled vacancies in Senate

- dictator—emergency office (e.g., Cincinnatus)

No magistracy paid a salary, thus all essentially open only to rich citizens (patrician or plebeian)

Roman Republic essentially an oligarchy dominated by aristocracy of large landowners, but with some democratic characteristics

Livy (59 BC–AD 17)—*History of Rome*

- from foundation of Rome (753 BC) to his own day

- problem of sources—no contemporary written sources until mid-5th century BC; relied on much later writers and oral testimony

- ideological bias—lived when Republic had collapsed after century of unrest and civil war

- purpose is didactic—to teach moral lessons

- theme of Rome's rise and decline

Several anecdotes illustrate this:

- Romulus and Remus

- Expulsion of Tarquin the Proud

- Titus Manlius

- Such anecdotes are at best legendary and semihistorical

- value to historian?

- reflects ideals and values of Romans (e.g., patriotism, discipline, obedience, courage, honor, family, disdain for wealth, etc.)

CHAPTER 19

Rome's Conquest of the Mediterranean

By 265 BC Rome controlled all Italy south of Po Valley

PUNIC WARS (264–146 BC)

- which great power would dominate the western Mediterranean: Carthage or Rome?
- no conflict between Rome and Carthage before 264 BC
- Carthage naval/commercial empire
- Rome land-based agricultural state confined to Italy

Carthage

- Phoenician city-state and empire—ruled by commercial oligarchy
- economy based on industry and trade plus rich agricultural hinterland in N Africa
- empire included W North Africa, W Sicily, Sardinia, Corsica, and Spain
- powerful navy manned by Carthaginian sailors protected its commerce
- army of mostly foreign mercenaries under Carthaginian officers

First Punic War (264–241)

- cause—Greek city-state of Messana in Sicily
- Rome forced to develop naval capability
- Romans copied design of captured Carthaginian warship
- development of *corvus*—kind of equalizer but problematic
- Rome finally won long war of attrition
- Peace Treaty (241 BC):
  - Rome gained Sicily (1st overseas province)
  - Carthage paid heavy indemnity to Rome

Mercenary War (241–238)

- Carthage vs. her own former mercenaries
- brutal conflict finally won by Carthage
- Rome opportunistically seized Corsica and Sardinia

Second Punic War (218–201)

- Carthage bent on revenge; built up forces in Spain
- led by one of the greatest generals of any age—Hannibal
- Hannibal's plan:
  - land invasion of Italy from Spain
  - defeat Romans in Italy

- encourage revolt among Rome's Italian allies
- force Rome to sue for peace
- Hannibal marched overland from Spain to Italy
- reached Po valley (218) and defeated Roman armies there
- for 15 years marched up and down Italy, repeatedly defeated Roman armies and devastated much of Italy
- Hannibal's strategy eventually failed
  - few Roman allies deserted
  - unable to take Rome—too heavily fortified
  - Scipio (later *Africanus*) conquered Spain, then invaded Africa
  - Hannibal forced to return to defend Carthage
  - Battle of Zama (202)—Hannibal decisively defeated

Peace treaty of 201:
- Spain ceded to Rome
- Carthaginian navy reduced to 10 ships
- Carthage paid heavy war indemnity over 50 years
- Carthage now a subject ally, promising never to make war without prior Roman permission, even if attacked
- Carthage finished as military power, but made quick economic recovery

ROME AND EASTERN MEDITERRANEAN (200–146)

- Hellenistic kingdoms had ruled region since Alexander the Great
- Rome exhausted from 1st and 2nd Punic Wars and not eager to intervene in East, but drawn in by pleas from Greek city-states to preserve independence from Hellenistic kingdoms
- Rome entered Greece—defeated Macedonian king Philip V (200–197)
- 196—Romans proclaimed "freedom of the Greeks"
- meaning of "freedom" to Greeks vs. Romans?
- with renewed warfare among Greeks, some Greek city-states invited Seleucid king Antiochus III to invade Greece
- Romans intervened again and defeated Antiochus (192–188)
- Romans again annexed no territory and withdrew from Greece
- another Macedonian war (171–168) led to suppression of Macedonian monarchy, but still no Roman annexation
- major anti-Roman revolt in both Macedonia and Greece (149–146); Romans crushed revolt, annexed Macedonia as Roman province and destroyed Corinth as object lesson to Greeks; by 146 Rome was dominant power throughout Mediterranean

THIRD PUNIC WAR (149–146)

- Carthage no longer a political or military power, but renewed economic strength worried some Romans (e.g., Cato—*"et Carthago delenda est!"*)

- pretext for war—Carthage defended itself from attack by African tribes without Roman permission

- siege of Carthage—heroic fierce defense, but city fell in 146

- population sold into slavery, city razed to ground

- hinterland of Carthage became new Roman province of Africa

Plutarch, *Life of Cato*

- Plutarch (AD 46–120)—most famous biographer of antiquity

- *Parallel Lives* (pairing one famous Greek with one famous Roman)

- great influence on subsequent Western literature (e.g., Shakespeare)

- Plutarch could consult written sources by and about Cato (234–149 BC)

- Cato as *novus homo*—rise to power from humble origins

- ultimately reached consulship, then censor

- hatred of Carthage pushed Rome towards 3rd Punic War

- frugal, thrifty, dedicated family man

- attitude towards Greek culture?

- became "ideal Roman" of Republic

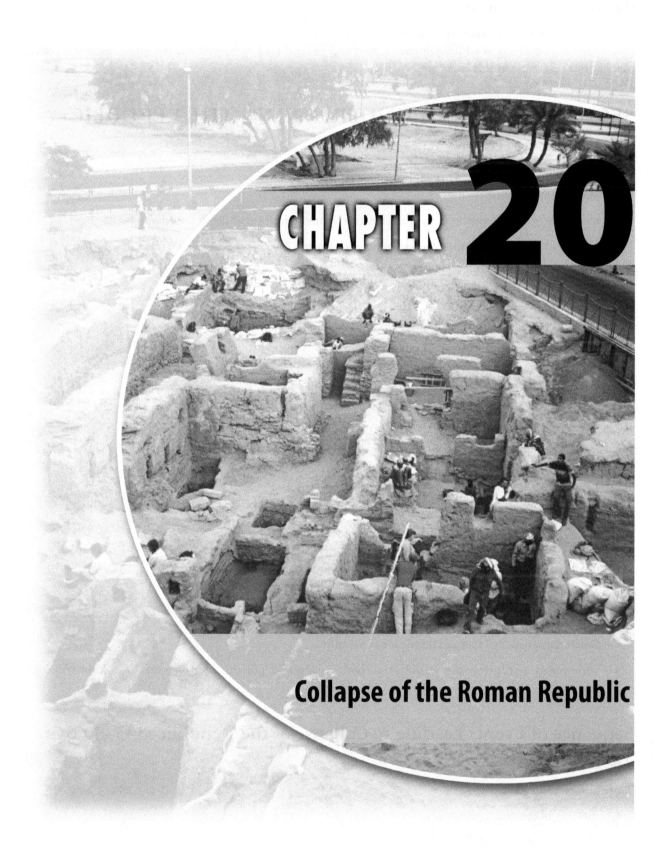

CHAPTER 20

Collapse of the Roman Republic

Backbone of the early Roman republic—most citizens were landowning peasants who paid taxes, voted in assemblies, and were conscripted into army for limited periods

Rome's unprecedented external expansion between 264–146 BC to domination of entire Mediterranean had enormous internal consequences on Roman government and society, leading to profound socioeconomic and political changes that undermined this backbone

SECULAR CHANGES UNDERMINING THE REPUBLIC

1. Impact of Second Punic War

- devastation of Italy

- many Romans killed

- many others served years in army, then returned home to find small farms wiped out

- many sold or abandoned their land to large landowners

- moved to Rome to seek jobs

- urban proletariat—often unemployed and at times unruly class of poor landless citizens

- peasant farmers declining rapidly in number

2. *latifundia* (sing. *latifundium*)—huge agricultural estates

- created by combining former peasant farms to existing estates

- *latifundia* produced cash crops (grapes/olives) or herds of livestock

- worked by imported slave labor

- many *latifundia* owned by senators who often appropriated abandoned land (legally part of the *ager publicus*—owned by Roman state)

3. rise of *equites*

- commercial class—2nd tier of Roman elite

- businessmen, bankers, contractors

- often served as tax-farmers (*publicani*) in newly conquered provinces

4. inadequacies of Republican government

- city-state now ruling a vast empire

- Senatorial oligarchy remained dominant politically

- widespread corruption and exploitation both in internal politics in Rome and in administration of empire

Sequence of Events Leading to Collapse of the Republic (133–30 BC)

The Gracchi

Tiberius Gracchus

- member of senatorial aristocracy

- elected tribune in 133 BC

- concerned by decline in number of landowning citizens

- proposed land reform law:
  - redistribution of publicly owned land in small plots to landless citizens
  - aimed to reduce urban proletariat and rebuild Roman peasantry
- land reform bill passed despite fierce senatorial opposition—why?
- commission began land redistribution
- Senate organized mob that killed Tiberius and 300 followers

Gaius Gracchus

- younger brother of Tiberius Gracchus
- elected tribune in 123 BC
- pushed more radical land bill and other measures
- opposition from Senate
- Gaius forced to commit suicide (121 BC) and 3,000 supporters killed in summary trials and in mob violence in Rome

Significance of the Gracchi:

- some land redistributed but not sufficient to reverse long-term trends
- first use of violence as political weapon in Rome

Rise of Gaius Marius

- crisis at end of 2nd century BC—major wars on 2 fronts:
  - protracted and difficult guerrilla war in North Africa
  - invasion of northern Italy by Germans
- result—military manpower shortage
- Marius elected consul for 106, enlisted many landless Romans into army, ignoring property qualification
- Marius won both wars, but
- two dangerous precedents established
  1) reelected consul 6 consecutive years
  2) created army of landless Romans more loyal to their own commander than to Roman state

Sulla

- first Roman general to lead his personal army on Rome (83 BC)—seized city, massacred thousands of political opponents
- proclaimed *dictator*; served 3 years until voluntary retirement in 79, died following year
- tried to reestablished power of Senatorial oligarchy but without success

First Triumvirate (60 BC)

- informal alliance of convenience by 3 former political rivals to control Roman state
- each brought assets to alliance and each wanted something in return

1. Crassus—wealthiest man in Rome; wanted consulship, then military command in provinces to establish a military reputation

2. Pompey—greatest general of the day; just back from victorious campaign in eastern Mediterranean; wanted land for his discharged veterans

3. Julius Caesar—*pontifex maximus* and brilliant orator; wanted consulship, then command in provinces to establish a military reputation

1st Triumvirate effectively controlled Rome (60–53 BC)

- Caesar, after consulship (59), conquered Gaul while forging a powerful personal army (58–49 BC)

- Crassus, after consulship (59), named governor of Syria as base to attack Parthian empire; but killed and army annihilated at Carrhae in N Mesopotamia (53 BC)

- Pompey got land for his vets and stayed in Rome

Civil War (49–48 BC)

- death of Crassus destabilized triumvirate

- Caesar invaded Italy (49 BC); Pompey withdrew to Greece

- Caesar defeated Pompey at Pharsalus in Greece (48 BC)

- Pompey later killed, leaving Caesar as supreme ruler of Roman world

Dictatorship of Caesar (48–44 BC)

- Caesar elected *dictator perpetuus*

- planned major reorganization of Roman state, e.g.

  - establishing colonies for vets and urban proletariat (e.g., Corinth)

  - reformed calendar by adding extra day every four years—"Leap Year" (Julian Calendar)

- assassinated on Ides of March, 44 BC by senators who hated monarchy and wanted to "restore the Republic"

Second Triumvirate (43–31 BC)

- formed by Caesar's supporters:

  - Mark Antony (Caesar's top subordinate commander)

  - Octavian (Caesar's gread-nephew and adopted heir)

  - Lepidus (another subordinate commander)

- hunted down Caesar's killers

- Lepidus soon exiled

- Octavian and Antony divided empire in two

- Antony ruled East and allied with Cleopatra VII, last Ptolemaic queen of Egypt

- Octavian ruled Italy and West

Final Phase of Civil War (31–30 BC)

- Octavian vs. Antony and Cleopatra

- Octavian won the decisive battle at Actium (31 BC) on west coast of Greece

- Antony and Cleopatra fled to Egypt and committed suicide (30 BC)

- Octavian annexed Egypt and now was sole ruler of Roman world

Having won the civil war, could Octavian now win the peace?

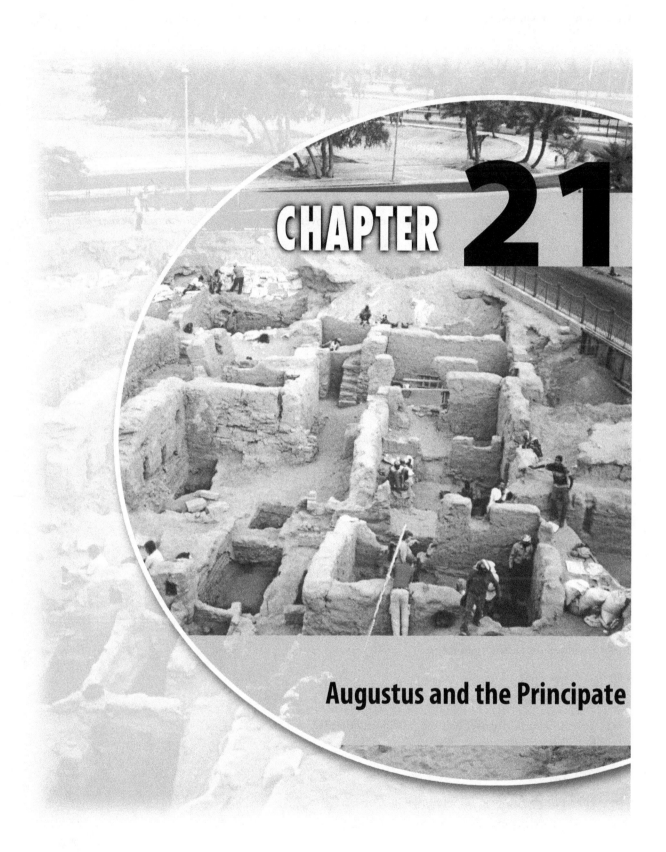

CHAPTER 21

Augustus and the Principate

Octavian's victory in 30 BC began a new era: Roman Empire

How could Octavian restore peace and stability after century of turmoil (133–30 BC)?

KEY FACTORS AT PLAY

- government of Republic inadequate to govern world empire
- various competing factions within Roman state
- his plan could not look like a monarchy—why not?

OCTAVIAN'S PLAN

- his program *superficially* left the old republican government unchanged but *actually created a monarchy*
- his program either satisfied or controlled all key factions within Roman state
- his propaganda proclaimed that he "restored the Republic"—how?

Official Titles, Powers, and Offices

- all voted to him by the Senate or the Roman people
- all voted to him over a period of many years during a long reign (30 BC–AD 14)
- all had republican precedents
- these explain both the nature of his program and his propaganda

Augustus ("revered one")

- title with enormous prestige
- now frequently called "Octavian Augustus" or simply "Augustus"

Princeps Senatus ("first citizen of the Senate")

- given to the leading or most distinguished senator (as *primus inter pares*)
- thus, the term "Principate" for early Roman Empire (30 BC–AD 284)

Tribunicia Potestas

- annually renewed by vote
- provided his authority in Rome

Imperium Proconsulare

- voted him this power at 5–10 year intervals
- gave him authority over half the provinces, other half left to Senate
- key is how provinces were divided: imperial vs. senatorial

Pontifex Maximus

- chief priest of Roman state religion
- authority over official religious establishment in Rome

Style of rule by Octavian Augustus also important

- acted the part of Roman senator—no crown, no palace, etc.
- helped to preserve the fiction of a restored Republic

How could Octavian Augustus claim to have restored the Republic?

Policies Towards Key Factions in Roman World

1. Senate

- now 1,000+ members
- source of potential opposition
- but also important pool of experienced talent needed to run the empire
- purges of senate—reduced to ca. 600 senators
- loyal senators could hold office and join in governing empire

2. *Equites*

- second tier of Roman elite: businessmen, bankers, contractors, tax-farmers
- Augustus largely abolished tax-farming in provinces
- benefited from massive public works program and general economic prosperity
- offered *equites* many posts in emerging imperial bureaucracy, e.g.
  - *Praefectus Annonae*
  - *Praefectus Vigilum*
  - *Praefectus Aegypti*
  - *Praefectus Praetorio*

3. Army

- how to control personal armies more loyal to own commanders than to Roman state?
- cut legions from 60 to 28—100,000+ discharged legionary veterans
- founded many colonies in both Italy and in the provinces to settle many vets
- later established *aerarium militare* to pay discharge bonuses to legionary vets
- reorganized professional, all-volunteer army of ca. 300,000 now composed of:
  - 28 legions of Roman citizens (heavy infantry)
  - *auxilia* of noncitizens (light infantry, cavalry, archers)
- new imperial army now looked to emperor for pay and benefits

4. Urban Proletariat

- often unemployed, sometimes unruly mob exploited for political violence in Rome
- some dispatched to new colonies
- massive program of public works to provide jobs in Rome
- maintained late Republican program of "bread and circuses"
- Night Watch (*Vigiles)* and Praetorian Guard to keep order

5. Provinces

- tax-farming largely abolished

- most taxes now collected by local elites as an unpaid public service of cities of empire (as local units of administration)—why would they agree to this?

- provinces benefited from *Pax Romana*—economic boom in 1st century AD

- increasing Romanization of provincials, especially elites who were eventually offered Roman citizenship

One unresolved problem: throne succession

- hereditary vs. adoptive principles attempted with varying success

- Julio-Claudian (30 BC–AD 68) and Flavian (AD 69–96) dynasties both used hereditary throne succession

- "Five Good Emperors" (AD 96–180)—used adoptive principle because all but last lacked a biological son

Octavian Augustus laid firm foundations for the next two centuries—golden age for Mediterranean World—peace, stability, and prosperity

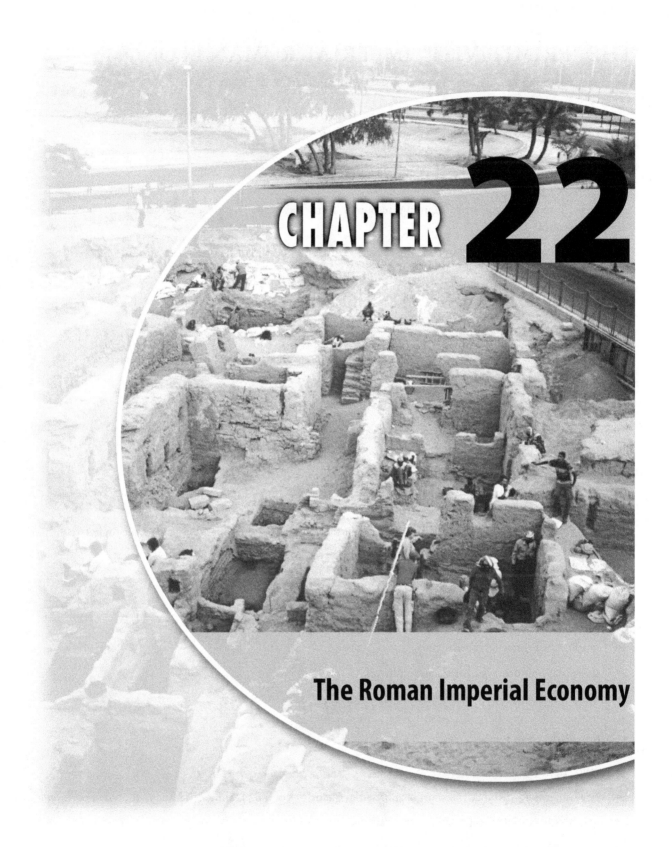

CHAPTER 22

The Roman Imperial Economy

Since the 1970s, debate has raged over the nature of the Roman Empire's economy; many scholars divided into two main camps: "Primitivist" vs "Modernist"

THE "PRIMITIVIST" IMPERIAL ROMAN ECONOMY

- overwhelming predominance of near-subsistence agriculture
- absence of mass markets
- trade limited in quantity, quality, and largely local
- long-distance trade mostly confined to luxuries
- trade and industry insignificant economically
- cities essentially parasitic, draining resources from local hinterlands but returning little of economic importance
- economy not monetarized but mostly barter—coinage largely restricted to cities and military bases

THE "MODERNIST" IMPERIAL ROMAN ECONOMY

- more complex economy
- greater agricultural surpluses
- existence of mass markets
- extensive long-distance trade in bulk commodities
- cities as significant centers of trade and industry
- economy as largely monetarized, with coins circulating widely even in rural areas

THE SOURCES

Lack of quantifiable economic data available for modern historical periods; apparent contradiction between literary and archaeological evidence

Literary Sources

- tend to support the "primitivist" view
- emphasize primacy of agriculture
- downplay importance of trade and industry
- these reflect strong senatorial bias for agriculture and disdain for trade and industry

Archaeological Sources

- lend support to "modernist" view
- document long-distance transport of substantial quantities of bulk commodities (e.g., oil, wine, pottery, glass)
- imply substantial surpluses and mass markets
- excavated cities reveal evidence for extensive trade and substantial industries
- but are all these artifacts merely exceptions?

PORT OF AILA AS A CASE STUDY ABOUT THE ROMAN ECONOMY

- located on northern end of Gulf of Aqaba (northern arm of Red Sea)—a coastal oasis in Arabian desert

- founded by Nabataean Arabs (Roman clients) in late 1st century BC as transshipment point between ships and camel caravans crossing narrow land bridge between Red Sea and Mediterranean

- literary sources describe this as traffic in luxury goods, especially frankincense and myrrh

- direct Roman control of Aila began in AD 106, when Nabataea annexed to Roman Empire as province as Arabia

- major Roman road between Aila and Syria completed in AD 114

- Roman legion later garrisoned at Aila

- continued as a major international port for centuries

Roman Aqaba Project

- NCSU archaeological project (1994–2002) aimed to reconstruct economy of Aila from 1st century BC to 7th century AD

- project's regional survey revealed no agricultural hinterland to support the city; thus, most supplies were imported to Aila from great distances

- excavation revealed major parts of ancient Aila, including domestic complexes, city wall, cemeteries, and an early Christian church

- excavation also produced huge quantities of artifacts (including pottery, glass, metal, and stone artifacts)

- suggests the movement of significant amounts of bulk commodities through the port

- excavation revealed that Aila hosted several industries, such as pottery production, metalworking, etc.

Conclusion

Aila was not simply a transfer point for trade in luxury items, but also participated in long-distance trade of large quantities of bulk commodities and hosted several industries (in line with the "modernist" view)

Excavation of other ports around the Roman Empire have yielded evidence similar to that from Aila, supporting the "modernist" view, but debate continues

Major unresolved problem is lack of sufficient evidence from rural sites; that is, did peasants (whether tenants or freeholders) have sufficient surplus income to afford many nonessential imports (e.g., wine, olive oil, fine tableware pottery, glass, etc.)?

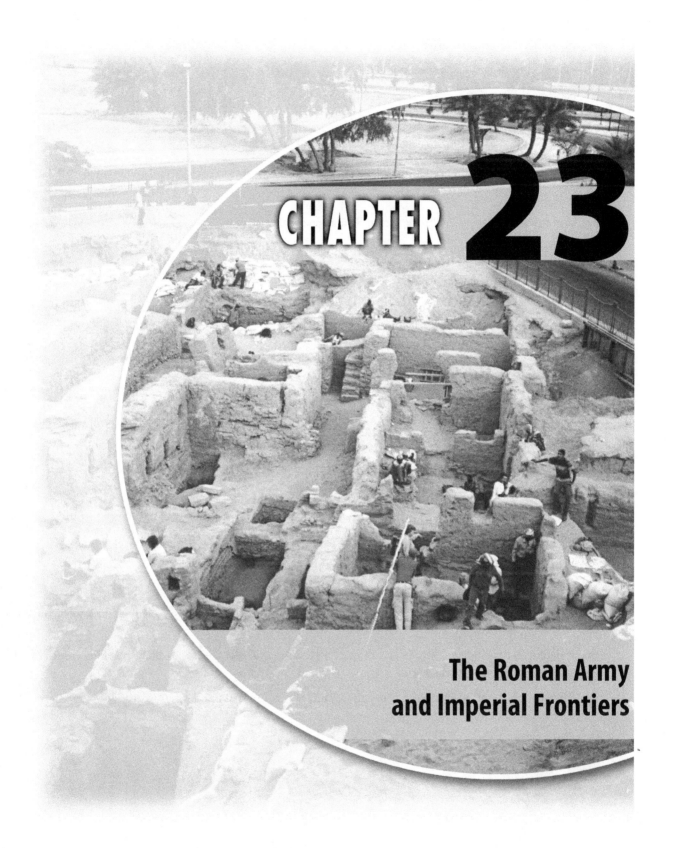

CHAPTER 23

The Roman Army and Imperial Frontiers

ARMY AS A KEY INSTITUTION IN ROMAN EMPIRE

- Security Role:
    - maintained internal security
    - defended frontiers against external threats
    - occasional wars of conquest to expand empire
- Economic Impact:
    - by far the biggest single portion of imperial budget
    - as an enormous consumer, it stimulated demand for wide variety of agricultural and manufactured goods
- Social Impact:
    - major avenue of social mobility within Roman society
    - major influence in "romanizing" provincials, especially in western empire
- Political Power:
    - support of army critical for any emperor to remain in power
    - army could sometimes make (and unmake) emperors

ORGANIZATION OF THE ARMY

- all-volunteer army of well-paid, long-serving professionals
- ca. 28 legions of 5,000 men each, all Roman citizens (heavy infantry), enlisted for 20 years, then eligible for discharge bonus
- *auxilia* of noncitizens (light infantry, cavalry, archers) recruited from provinces, enlisted for 25 years, then they and their children received Roman citizenship
- Roman navy patrolled Mediterranean—suppressed piracy and transported troops and supplies
- Total strength—ca. 300,000–400,000 troops

MISSION OF THE ARMY

- largely deployed along frontiers of empire both to prevent external attacks and to launch occasional wars of conquest (e.g., Britain)
- major deployments along the Rhine and Danube Rivers (against the Germans) along northern frontier and on eastern frontier (against the Pathians)
- some Roman units garrisoned within the empire to suppress internal uprisings (e.g., the Jews in Palestine)

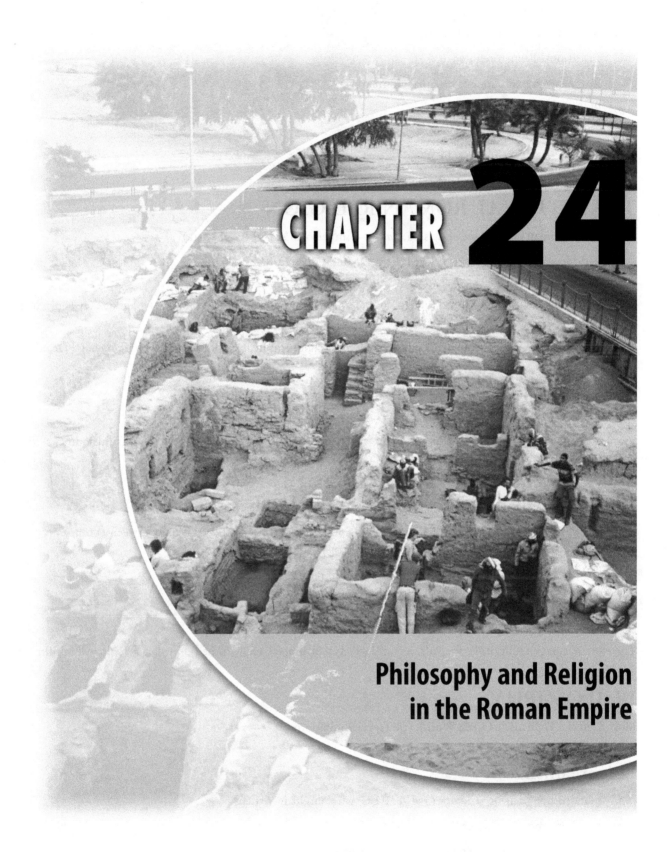

CHAPTER 24

Philosophy and Religion in the Roman Empire

Diversity of cultures within Empire reflected in diversity of its religions; Empire was a religious "melting pot" that spawned Christianity

This chapter will review and analyze

1. Traditional Roman religion

2. Reasons why many sought spiritual alternatives

3. Philosophy in Empire

4. Mystery religions

5. Origins of Christianity

TRADITIONAL ROMAN RELIGION

- oldest Roman deities—*numina* (sing. *numen*)—impersonal spirits (e.g., Vesta)

- anthropomorphic deities introduced (Etruscan and Greek influence)—Jupiter, Juno, Minerva, Mars—much like Greek gods

- Romans generally receptive to foreign gods (e.g., Greek Apollo), especially if perceived that they could help Rome (e.g., Magna Mater)

- Romans generally practiced religious toleration throughout empire; rarely outlawed any religion (e.g., Druidism in Gaul)

SEARCH FOR SPIRITUAL ALTERNATIVES

Empire provided peace, security, and economic well-being for many, yet clear evidence of disillusionment with traditional gods of Rome and other official city-state cults of Empire

Sources of Disillusionment with Official Religion

- most were highly ritualistic; chief goal to maintain *pax deorum*—good relations between community and gods, but some had evolved into empty formalism

- most permitted only passive observance by worshippers—no participation

- most essentially nonethical, emphasizing ritual over morality

- most did not focus on personal salvation or life after death

Therefore, although traditional state gods were still widely worshipped, many turned elsewhere for spiritual fulfillment

PHILOSOPHY

Most from the Hellenistic Greek World; two especially important:

Epicureanism

- founded by Epicurus of Samos (341–270 BC) who taught in Athens

- based on atomic theory of Democritus

- essentially atheistic—no gods or afterlife to worry about

- "death was eternal and painless sleep"

- happiness through pursuit of moderate pleasures/avoidance of pain
- achieved by withdrawal from world

Lucretius (ca. 96–55 BC), *De Rerum Natura*

- Roman of senatorial aristocracy who embraced Epicureanism
- goal to reject superstition, fear of supernatural, fear of death, etc.
- by what means? *demythologize* world, i.e., use reason to understand that world governed by *natural* phenomena
- atomic theory permits one to free oneself from shackles of religion, which was born from ignorance and has caused great suffering

Stoicism

- founded by Zeno (335–263 B.C.) who taught in Athens on a *stoa* (covered porch)
- tended towards monotheism—based on belief in Divine Reason as creator of entire cosmos
- every human has spark of Divine Reason within as their soul
- "brotherhood/sisterhood of humanity"
- upon death spark (soul) would return to its creator (kind of immortality)
- happiness through *virtue*, by performance of *duty* to god, family, state, profession, which required *participation* in life
- stressed control over emotions

Marcus Aurelius (Roman emperor, reigned AD 161–180), *Thoughts* (*Meditations*)

- most famous Stoic of Roman Empire
- *Thoughts*—kind of philosophical diary written on campaign
- duty liberates man by allowing right reason
- uncertainty about what lies beyond death

Such Greek philosophies were practiced throughout Roman Empire but their appeal strictly limited to elite—why?

MYSTERY RELIGIONS

- appealed to all classes of empire
- dozens attested but most little known in detail
- three important examples:
    1) Dionysus
    2) Isis and Osiris
    3) Mithra (Taurobolium)
- common characteristics of mysteries:
    - promised mystical knowledge to initiates
    - gained admission by initiation ritual

- entered fellowship of believers

- promised adherence to strict moral code

- mystical union with god, often a dying and rising deity

- promise of personal salvation or afterlife

Was Christianity in origin a mystery religion?

ORIGINS OF CHRISTIANITY

Sources on the Historical Jesus

- Jesus himself wrote nothing

- no contemporary sources discuss Jesus (anticipation of *Parousia*)

- first Gospels not written until late 1st century AD (ca. AD 65/70–100)

Non-Christian Sources:

- brief mention in a few Roman writers (e.g., Tacitus, Josephus)

- Jewish Talmud—many references, most very negative about Jesus

- confirm some details in Gospels (e.g., Pontius Pilate)

Non-canonical Christian Sources:

- non-canonical Gospels (e.g., Gospel of Peter, Gospel of Thomas, etc.)

- might preserve some authentic sayings of Jesus

- much apparently bogus material, especially about childhood of Jesus

Four Canonical Gospels:

- various problems as historical sources:

    - language (Greek translation of Aramaic)

    - authorship

    - date—written 2–3 generations later (after oral transmission)

    - none a real biography of Jesus (e.g., childhood)

    - clear bias—to "evangelize" (propagandistic purpose)

- Synoptic Gospels:

    - Mark (ca. AD 65–70)—focus on "passion"

    - Matthew and Luke (ca. AD 80–90)—possibly used Mark, a "sayings source" ("Q" = German *Quelle*, e.g., Sermon on the Mount) and some unique material (infancy narratives)

    - all three focus on Jesus as "Messiah" ("the anointed one")

- Gospel of John:

    - latest in date (ca. AD 90–100)

    - Hellenization of Jesus in Greek philosophical terms

    - Jesus as God incarnate

From critical analysis of all primary sources, who was the historical Jesus?

All or most sources agree that Jesus was

- a Jew
- baptized by John the Baptist
- a teacher who preached to a broad spectrum of Jewish society
- gathered followers, including women (even prostitutes)
- was crucified by Roman governor of Judaea, Pontius Pilate

Both Jewish and Christian sources assert that he performed what were perceived as "miracles" or "magic"

Much more uncertainty about *message* of Jesus—to what degree do Gospels preserve authentic sayings?

- "Jesus Seminar"—ca. 20% of sayings in New Testament likely authentic
- other scholars argue for more authenticity

Some possible themes of message:

- personal ethics: inner goodness vs. external practice
- demands higher ethical standard than Jewish law
- pacifism
- strong bias against material wealth (Mark 10:17–31)
- against capital punishment (John 7:53–8:11)

Why was Jesus crucified?

1. Gospels blame Jewish religious establishment, who accused Jesus of blasphemy and pressured Pontius Pilate to order execution
2. Many modern scholars believe that Romans, not Jews, were primarily responsible, fearing Jesus as a political revolutionary—why?

- Messianic claims—"Kingdom of God is at hand"
- at least some disciples armed
- Simon the "Zealot"
- Jesus expelled moneychangers from temple
- insurrection had occurred in Jerusalem at time of his arrest (Mark 15:7)
- placard above cross with formal charge against him—"This is Jesus, the King of the Jews" (Matthew 27:37)

This view argues that Jesus was executed by Romans on charge of *treason*, not blasphemy. If so, why would Gospels try to shift blame to Jews?

Was Jesus in fact a political revolutionary, dedicated to violent overthrew of Roman rule in Judea, as Romans apparently believed?

Jesus stressed nonviolence, even pacifism (Luke 20:25)

Early Spread of Christianity

Sources

- Epistles (Letters) of Paul (ca. 45–65)
- Acts (ca. 80–90)

Reaction to Christian message

- most Jews rejected message and claims of Jesus
- Paul of Tarsus and other apostles turned to Gentiles (non-Jews)
- earliest Christians primarily urban lower classes, including slaves and women, in eastern empire

Primitive Christian Church

- baptism as initial ritual
- worship centered around consuming body and blood of Christ
- strong bonds of fellowship
- communism of property—why?
- strongly patriarchal—why?

Was Christianity to some degree a mystery religion of Roman Empire?

Why was Christianity quickly outlawed by Roman government?

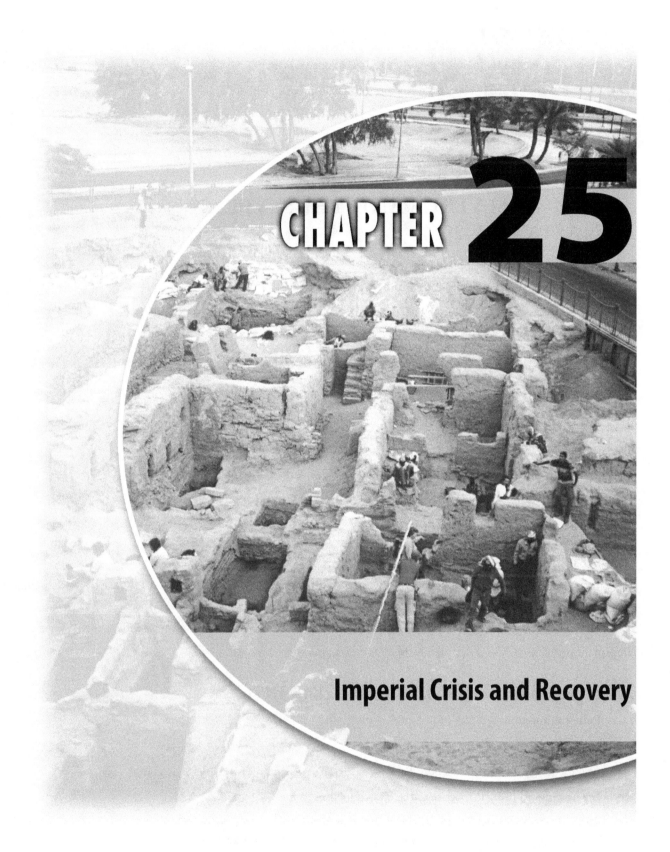

CHAPTER 25

Imperial Crisis and Recovery

Late 1st and 2nd centuries (AD 70–192) marked long period of stability and economic prosperity

"5 GOOD EMPERORS" (96–180)

- all but last lacked biological son and thus used adoptive principle of throne succession

- Marcus Aurelius (161–180) had a natural son—Commodus (180–192)

- youth of 18 unfit to rule

- his assassination led to civil war (193–197)

- victor was Septimius Severus (193–211)

SEPTIMIUS SEVERUS AND THE SEVERAN DYNASTY (193–235)

- Septimius was a senator and provincial governor of African origin

- relied more nakedly on army for political support

- increased size of army to deal with greater threats on frontiers

- increased army pay and privileges

- favored the class of *equites* over senators, who began to be excluded from military commands and as governors of provinces

- Severans kept empire together for two more decades

CRISIS OF THIRD CENTURY (235–284)

1. Civil War—ca. 24 "legitimate" emperors in 50 years; many more pretenders

2. External Invasion (e.g., Germans on northern frontiers and Sassanian Persians on eastern frontier; deep penetrations ravaged the provinces)

3. Depopulation—plagues (began in late 2nd century), civil wars, external invasion, famine, etc.; killed millions but no precise figures

4. Economic Decline—steep fall in agricultural production, trade and industry, exacerbated by warfare and depopulation; debasement of silver coinage led to rampant inflation

5. Parts of Empire (Gaul and Britain in West, Syria in East) temporarily broke away as independent states

Empire might have collapsed completely, but Diocletian saved the empire

REFORMS OF DIOCLETIAN (284–305)

1. Political Reforms:

- ideology of Principate now bankrupt

- new ideology: Dominate (*dominus et deus*)—autocratic theocracy with emperor as god on earth

- Senate reduced to little more than the city council of Rome

- Tetrarchy created to deal with problems of throne succession and internal revolts—2 Augusti (senior emperors) and 2 Caesars (junior emperors)—adoptive principle of throne succession

- Tetrarchy crushed all pretenders, defeated all invaders and reunited the empire

2. Administrative Reforms:

- number of provinces nearly doubled from ca. 50 to 96

- each province with 2 governors: *praeses* (civil governor) and *dux* (military governor)

- given cost of increased bureaucracy, what was the perceived benefit of this reform?

3. Military Reforms:

- more manpower obtained by conscription and hereditary military service

- reorganized army into:

    - *comitatenses* (mobile field army based behind the frontiers)

    - *limitanei* (manned *limes* {pl. *limites*} or frontiers)

- refortification of frontiers

- did Diocletian greatly increase the size of the army?

4. Economic Reforms:

- new system of taxation—now paid largely in kind—why?

- many compulsory services imposed on civilians

- key jobs made hereditary (e.g., peasants bound to land as *coloni*—origins of medieval serfdom)

- Edict on Prices (301)—to combat inflation—set maximum prices for thousands of goods and services; all violations punishable by death—how effective?

5. Religious Policy:

- emperor worship demanded by new theocracy

- most viewed this as essentially political

- many Christians refused

- Christians already viewed with suspicion as a "cult" and had already been outlawed in 1st century AD

- common charges against Christians (what was their basis?):

    - incest

    - atheism

    - cannibalism

    - treason

- empire-wide persecutions began in mid-3rd century when Christians, as a widely disliked minority, were convenient scapegoats

- Diocletian viewed Christians as a "state within a state" and launched the "Great Persecution" (303–311):

    - edict required all Romans to sacrifice to emperors as gods

    - any who refused subject to arrest, exile, and/or execution

    - many churches destroyed, clergy imprisoned or killed

    - several thousand Christians killed

    - many more recanted

    - impact of persecutions?

Consequences of Diocletian's Reforms:

- saved Empire—restored peace, stability, and some economic recovery

- but imperial system now more centralized and autocratic

- enlarged bureaucracy required more taxes from shrunken tax base

- thus, higher taxes, more compulsion and oppression

Diocletian and his senior partner abdicated in 305 as planned; but soon civil war broke out and the Tetrarchy collapsed

CONSTANTINE (306–337)

- son of Constantius, member of Tetrarchy

- during civil war (312) Constantine had a dream or vision, credited his victory at Battle of the Milvian Bridge outside Rome to the Christian god, then converted to Christianity

- ended persecution of Christianity and began supporting it

- in late 4th century now Christian emperors outlawed polytheism ("paganism") and Christians began persecuting pagans

Why did Christianity prevail over other spiritual alternatives?

1. Philosophy appealed only to educated elite

2. Christianity open to all, regardless of class, sex, ethnicity, etc. some mystery religions restricted membership (e.g., Mithraism)

3. Unlike mysteries, Christianity was a *historical* religion

4. Christianity was an *exclusive* religion

5. Conversion of Constantine—all but one of the subsequent emperors were Christians, used resources of government to support church

6. Christianity assimilated much of paganism, easing conversion

Constantine founded Constantinople (330) as new capital of Empire on site of old Greek city of Byzantium on Bosporus (strategic position)

EPILOGUE

1. After death of Constantine (337) empire split in two—Western Empire with capital at Rome, Eastern Empire with capital at Constantinople

2. West collapsed in 5th century with German barbarian invasions, but Eastern Empire ("Byzantine Empire") survived for 1,000 years until 1453 as a leading state in the Middle Ages

Introduction to the Primary Sources

The following sections contain written documents from the Ancient Near East, ancient Greek, and ancient Roman civilizations, translated from the original ancient languages (Sumerian, Akkadian, Babylonian, Egyptian, Hebrew, Greek, Latin, etc.) into English. It is important to stress that, although literacy emerged about 5,000 years ago in ancient Mesopotamia, these past fifty centuries represent only a tiny fraction (less than 0.01%) of all the time humans have inhabited the earth. The invention of literacy seems initially to have been a response to economic needs, i.e. for keeping accurate records. But it was soon adapted to many other purposes, serving various political, religious, and social purposes.

Literacy truly represented a fundamental revolution in human existence since knowledge could now be stored. The sum total of knowledge from one generation could be passed to the next. Further, it is a commonplace that "knowledge is power". Those who controlled literacy, usually but not invariably the elite in society, could exploit literacy for specific political, economic, social, or ideological needs. The vast remainder of the population, the so-called "Silent Peoples of Antiquity", usually only appears through the lens of these mostly elite sources. But they can also be approached through archaeological evidence.

The level of literacy in ancient Mediterranean societies is much debated. The complex writing systems of the Bronze Age Near East and Aegean meant that literacy was almost entirely confined to highly trained scribes and some priests, who were the only educated classes. The invention of the alphabet by the Canaanites near the end of the Bronze Age and its wide dissemination in the early Iron Age provided a vastly simplified system of writing. Thus literacy expanded somewhat more widely in later Near Eastern, Greek and Roman societies. Although precise levels remain unknown, it is likely that literacy never exceeded more than about 10% of the population of the Roman Empire, perhaps the peak of literacy in the ancient Mediterranean world. Therefore, it must be remembered that most documents were written by the elite, about the elite, and for the elite.

The selected excerpts in the following sections represent a wide range of documentary sources, including myths and legends, law codes, folk tales, biographies, royal inscriptions, religious texts, histories, philosophical tracts, and a comedic play. Remember that these are the "raw material" exploited by all modern historians when writing history.

When reading these sources, always keep the following questions in mind. Who actually wrote each source? When was the source actually written? Who was the intended audience? Remember that all sources are biased, i.e., there is no such thing as an unbiased source. There are many forms of bias: political, social, ideological, ethnic, religious, etc. Also remember that all these sources derive from "prescientific societies", lacking modern science. Thus supernatural forces and myths were used to "explain the unexplainable". This is not to deny some historical value of all such documents but only to emphasize that they can never be taken by the historian at face value. All must be evaluated from a critical perspective, even while keeping our own biases in mind!

Part V

PRIMARY SOURCES FROM THE ANCIENT NEAR EAST

THE LEGEND OF SARGON

Known as the "first empire-builder of history", Sargon became king of the Semitic city-state of Akkad (or "Agade", precise location unknown but somewhere in central Mesopotamia) ca. 2340 B.C. Sargon proved to be a successful warrior, eventually conquering all the city-states of Mesopotamia and some neighboring territories, known as the Akkadian Empire. After a reign of over 50 years he passed power to his descendants, creating a dynasty. This empire proved to be short-lived however. The Akkadian Empire collapsed ca. 2200 B.C. due to the invasion of the rather mysterious Gutians from the Zagros Mountains and/or a major drought.

The "Legend of Sargon" purports to be an autobiographical account of his rise to power and the conquests which created the Akkadian Empire. But the two surviving copies, both fragmentary, date much later, to the early 1st millennium. Note that the reference to the "black-headed people" appears to refer to the Sumerians of southern Mesopotamia.

Sargon, the mighty king, king of Agade, am I.
My mother was a high priestess, my father I knew not.
The brother(s) of my father *loved* the hills.
My city is Azupiranu, which is situated on the banks of the Euphrates.
My mother, the high priestess, conceived me, in secret she bore me.
She set me in a basket of rushes, with bitumen she sealed my lid.
She cast me into the river which rose not (over) me.
The river bore me up and carried me to Akki, the drawer of water.
Akki, the drawer of water lifted me out as he dipped his e[w]er.
Akki, the drawer of water, [took me] as his son (and) reared me.   (10)
Akki, the drawer of water, appointed me as his gardener.
While I was a gardener, Ishtar granted me (her) love,
And for four and [. . .] years I exercised kingship.
The black-headed [people] I ruled, I gov[erned];
Mighty [moun]tains with chip-axes of bronze I conquered,
The upper ranges I scaled,
The lower ranges I [trav]ersed,
The sea [*lan*]*ds* three times I circled.
Dilmun my [hand] cap[tured],
[To] the great Der I [went up], I [. . .],   (20)
[K]azallu I destroyed and [. . . . . .].
Whatever king may come up after me, [. . .],
Let him r[ule, let him govern] the black-headed [peo]ple;
[Let him conquer] mighty [mountains] with chip-axe[s of bronze],
[Let] him scale the upper ranges,

[Let him traverse the lower ranges],
Let him circle the sea [*lan*]*ds* three times!
[Dilmun let his hand capture],
Let him go up [to] the great Der and [. . .]!   (30)
[. . .] from my city, Aga[de . . .]
[. . .] . . . [. . .].
(Remainder broken away. The remains of column ii, as extant in Text B, and *CT* 46, 46 are too fragmentary for translation.)

THE EPIC OF GILGAMESH:

note religion

The Sumerian Heroic Age

This epic poem from ancient Mesopotamia may be the earliest surviving work of literature. Originally composed more than 4,000 years ago, it was lost for nearly 2,000 years until the discovery in 1853 of inscribed clay tablets preserving portions of the epic in Iraq. Some of the best preserved fragments were recovered from excavations of the 7th century B.C. Library of Ashurbanipal at Nineveh, capital of the Assyrian Empire. Since then many more fragments, written in various languages, have appeared although the entire text is still not complete. The earliest fragments date to ca. 2100 B.C. but the epic is clearly far older, probably dating to the Early Dynastic Period (3200-2400).

A separate source, "The Sumerian King List", names Gilgamesh as the fifth king of the city-state of Uruk, who possibly reigned about 2600 B.C. This suggests that Gilgamesh was an actual historical figure, although the epic itself clearly contains much mythical and supernatural content.

Note that although Gilgamesh is the hero of the epic, portrayed as strong, brave, and capable of great love (as shown for his friend Enkidu), he is also pictured as a rather flawed ruler, actually hated by many of his own subjects. In addition to evidence of ancient Mesopotamian conceptions of kingship, the epic is a rich source of evidence about many aspect of ancient Mesopotamian culture, including its religion, including notions of the gods and afterlife.

The Sumerians were the first people to produce epic tales of semi-legendary heroes, the most famous of whom was Gilgamesh, ruler of the city-state of Uruk (or Erech) about 2600 B.C. About 2000 B.C., or somewhat later, an unknown Babylonian collected some of the Gilgamesh stories, together with other tales, and wove them into a new whole. The following selections are from this Babylonian *Epic of Gilgamesh.*

The theme which gives unity to the varied heroic adventures described in the *Epic of Gilgamesh* is that of death—the sudden realization that death will cut short the glorious career of the great hero and the frantic but unsuccessful search for some means of living forever. The story opens with an account of the friction between Gilgamesh and the nobles of Uruk, who claim that their ruler is acting tyrannically. (Their complaint that Gilgamesh drafted their sons to serve in his army is described in a separate epic tale; their charge in the tale below that he mistreated their wives and daughters is probably pure propaganda.) The nobles appeal to the gods for aid, with the result that Enkidu is created by Aruru, the mother goddess, to check Gilgamesh's "arrogance." Gilgamesh sends a temple prostitute to tame Enkidu's barbarous nature before he is brought to Uruk, where the two heroes fight to a draw and thereafter become fast friends. Together they set out on dangerous adventures, slaying the terrible monster Huwawa who guards the Cedar Forest for the storm-god Enlil, insulting the goddess Ishtar who falls in love with Gilgamesh—love that here, as elsewhere in the epic, contains no romantic element—and destroying the awesome Bull of Heaven sent by the angered Ishtar to kill Gilgamesh. When next Enkidu dies as the result of Enlil's displeasure over the slaying of Huwawa, Gilgamesh is panic-stricken by the sudden realization of the stark reality of death. His life is henceforth dominated by the one aim of finding everlasting life. This leads him to search out Utnapishtim, the one man to whom the gods have granted immortality, in order to learn from him the secret of eternal life. The remainder of the epic incorporates the story of the Flood (next selection), which originally existed as an independent tale. Utnapishtim relates how he obtained eternal life as a reward for the deeds he performed at the time of the Flood. But this unique event cannot be duplicated. As a parting gift to the dejected Gilgamesh, Utnapishtim tells him of the Plant of Life that grows on the bottom of the sea and renews the life of him who eats it. But once again Gilgamesh's hopes are ended when the Plant of

Life is stolen from him by a snake. The epic ends with Gilgamesh's bitter lament over the failure of his quest; though snakes may hereafter slough off their old skins and eternally renew their youth, the sad lot of man is old age and death.

> He who saw everything to the ends of the land,
> Who all things experienced, considered all! . . .
> Two-thirds of him is god, one third of him is human. . . .
> The onslaught of his weapons verily has no equal.
> By the drum are aroused his companions.

Gilgamesh's despotic behavior leads to the creation of Enkidu.

> The nobles of Uruk are gloomy in their chambers:
> "Gilgamesh leaves not the son to his father;
> Day and night is unbridled his arrogance.
> Yet this is Gilgamesh, the shepherd of Uruk.
>
> He should be our shepherd: strong, stately, and wise!
> Gilgamesh leaves not the maid to her mother,
> The warrior's daughter, the noble's spouse!"
> The gods hearkened to their plaint,
> The gods of heaven, Uruk's lords . . .
> The great Aruru they called:
> "Thou, Aruru, didst create Gilgamesh;
> Create now his double;
> His stormy heart let him match.
> Let them contend, that Uruk may have peace!" . . .
> Aruru washed her hands,
> Pinched off clay and cast it on the steppe.
> On the steppe she created valiant Enkidu, . . .
> Shaggy with hair is his whole body,
> He is endowed with head hair like a woman. . . .
> He knows neither people nor land; . . .
> With the gazelles he feeds on grass,
> With the wild beasts he jostles at the watering-place,
> With the teeming creatures his heart delights in water. . . .

Having heard of the animal-like Enkidu, Gilgamesh sends a harlot to civilize him by means of the unromantic, purely physical love found in heroic-age epic tales, Enkidu performs heroically.

> The lass beheld him, the savage-man,
> The barbarous fellow from the depths of the steppe: . . .
> The lass freed her breasts, bared her bosom,
> And he possessed her ripeness.
> She was not bashful as she welcomed his ardor.
> She laid aside her cloth and he rested upon her.
> She treated him, the savage, to a woman's task,
> As his love was drawn unto her.
> For six days and seven nights Enkidu comes forth,
> Mating with the lass.
> After he had had his fill of her charms,
> He set his face toward his wild beasts.
> On seeing him, Enkidu, the gazelles ran off,
> The wild beasts of the steppe drew away from his body.
> Startled was Enkidu, as his body became taut,

His knees were motionless—for his wild beasts had gone.
Enkidu had to slacken his pace—it was not as before;
But he now had wisdom, broader understanding.
Returning, he sat at the feet of the harlot.
He looks up at the face of the harlot,
His ears attentive, as the harlot speaks;
The harlot says to him, to Enkidu:
"Thou art wise, Enkidu, art become like a god!
Why with the wild creatures dost thou roam over the steppe?
Come, let me lead thee to ramparted Uruk,
To the holy temple, abode of Anu and Ishtar,
Where lives Gilgamesh, accomplished in strength,
And like a wild ox lords it over the folk."
As she speaks to him, her words find favor,
His heart enlightened, he yearns for a friend. . . .
Enkidu says to her, to the harlot:
"Up, lass, escort thou me,
To the pure sacred temple, abode of Anu and Ishtar,
Where lives Gilgamesh, accomplished in strength,
And like a wild ox lords it over the folk.
I will challenge him and will boldly address him,
I will shout in Uruk: 'I am he who is mighty! . . .'"
The nobles rejoiced:
"A hero has appeared
For the man of proper mien!
For Gilgamesh, the godlike,
His equal has come forth." . . .

Enkidu and Gilgamesh meet and battle to a draw.

They met in the Market-of-the-Land.
Enkidu barred the gate with his foot,
Not allowing Gilgamesh to enter.
They grappled each other, butting like bulls,
They shattered the doorpost, as the wall shook.
As Gilgamesh bent the knee—his foot on the ground—
His fury abated and he turned away. . . .
They kissed each other
And formed a friendship. . . .

Enkidu quails at the prospect of fighting the monstrous Huwawa, guardian of the Cedar Forest, and Gilgamesh reassures him with a reminder of the heroic meaning of life.

Gilgamesh opened his mouth, saying to Enkidu:
"In the forest resides fierce Huwawa.
Let us, me and thee, slay him,
That all evil from the land we may banish! [. . .]
Enkidu opened his mouth, saying to Gilgamesh:
"I found it out, my friend, in the hills,
As I was roaming with the wild beasts.
For ten thousand leagues extends the forest.
Who is there that would go down into it?

Part Five—*Primary Sources from the Ancient Near East*   **143**

Huwawa—his roaring is the flood-storm,
His mouth is fire, his breath is death!
Why dost thou desire to do this thing?
An unequal struggle is rangling with Huwawa." . . .
Gilgamesh opened his mouth, saying to Enkidu:
"Who, my friend, is superior to death?
Only the gods live forever in the sun.
As for mankind, numbered are their days;
Whatever they achieve is but the wind!
Even here thou art afraid of death.
What of thy heroic might?
Let me go then before thee,
Let thy voice call to me, 'Advance, fear not!?
Should I fall, I shall have made me a name:
'Gilgamesh'—they will say—'against fierce Huwawa
Has fallen!' Long after
My offspring has been born in my house, [. . .]
Thus calling to me, thou hast grieved my heart.
My hand I will poise and will fell the cedars.
A name that endures I will make for me! . . ."

After slaying Huwawa, Gilgamesh next rejects the goddess Ishtar's request for love ("Come, Gilgamesh, be thou my lover/Do but grant me of thy fruit."), and she forces the gods to create the Bull of Heaven to punish his insolence.

Ishtar was enraged and mounted to heaven.
Forth went Ishtar before Anu, her father,
To Antum, her mother, she went and said:
"My father, Gilgamesh has heaped insults upon me! . . ."
Anu opened his mouth to speak,
Saying to glorious Ishtar:
"But surely thou didst invite [. . .]."
Ishtar opened her mouth to speak,
Saying to Anu, her father:
"My father, make me the Bull of Heaven that he smite Gilgamesh. . . .
If thou dost not make me the Bull of Heaven,
I will smash the doors of the nether world,
I will [. . .],
I will raise up the dead caring and alive,
So that the dead shall outnumber the living!" . . .

The heroes slay the Bull of Heaven and again insult Ishtar.

Up leaped Enkidu, seizing the Bull of Heaven by the horns,
The Bull of Heaven hurled his foam in his face,
Brushed him with the back of his tail. . . .
Between neck and horns he thrust his sword.
When they had slain the Bull, they tore out his heart,
Placing it before Shamash.
They drew back and did homage before Shamash.
The two brothers sat down.

Then Ishtar mounted the wall of ramparted Uruk,
Sprang on the battlements, uttering a curse:
"Woe unto Gilgamesh because he insulted me
By slaying the Bull of Heaven!"
When Enkidu heard this speech of Ishtar,
He tore loose the right thigh of the Bull of Heaven
And tossed it in her face:
"Could I but get thee, like unto him
I would do unto thee.
His entrails I would hang at thy side!" . . .
In the Euphrates they washed their hands,
They embraced each other as they went on,
Riding through the market street of Uruk,
The people of Uruk are gathered to gaze upon them.
Gilgamesh to the lyre maidens of Uruk
Says these words:
"Who is most splendid among the heroes?
Who is most glorious among men?"
"Gilgamesh is most splendid among the heroes,
Gilgamesh is most glorious among men."

By means of a dream, Enkidu learns two things; that the gods have decided he must die as punishment for the insolent behavior of the two heroes, and that the land of the dead is a most dismal place.

Gilgamesh in his palace holds a celebration.
Down lie the heroes on their beds of night.
Also Enkidu lies down, a dream beholding.
Up rose Enkidu to relate his dream,
Saying to his friend:
"My friend, why are the great gods in council? . . .
My friend, I saw a dream this night;
The heavens moaned, the earth responded;
[. . .] I stood alone.
[. . .] his face was darkened. . . .
Looking at me, he leads me to the House of Darkness,
The abode of Irkalla,
To the house which none leave who have entered it,
On the road from which there is no way back,
To the house wherein the dwellers are bereft of light,
Where dust is their fare and clay their food.
They are clothed like birds, with wings for garments,
And see no light, residing in darkness.
In the House of Dust, which I entered,
I looked at rulers, their crowns put away:
I saw princes, those born to the crown,
Who ruled the land from the days of yore. . . ."

Enkidu dies, and the reality of death as the common lot of all mankind—even fearless heroes—strikes home to Gilgamesh. The remainder of the epic deals with his attempt to find everlasting life, a quest that all tell him is hopeless. In the following selection, Gilgamesh is talking to a barmaid who gives him sage advice.

"He who with me underwent all hardships—
Enkidu, whom I loved dearly,
Who with me underwent all hardships—
Has now gone to the fate of mankind!
Day and night I have wept over him.
I would not give him up for burial—
In case my friend should rise at my plaint—
Seven days and seven nights,
Until a worm fell out of his nose.
Since his passing I have not found life,
I have roamed like a hunter in the midst of the steppe.
O ale-wife, now that I have seen thy face,
Let me not see the death which I ever dread."
The ale-wife said to him, to Gilgamesh:
"Gilgamesh, whither rovest thou?
The life thou pursueth, thou shalt not find.
When the gods created mankind,
Death for mankind they set aside,
Life in their own hands retaining.
Thou, Gilgamesh, let full be thy belly,
Make thou merry by day and by night.
Of each day make thou a feast of rejoicing,
Day and night dance thou and play!
Let thy garments be sparkling fresh,
Thy head be washed; bathe thou in water.
Pay heed to the little one that holds on to thy hand,
Let thy spouse delight in thy bosom!
For this is the task of mankind!" . . .

Gilgamesh next searches out Utnapishtim, the immortal hero of the Flood (Selection 2), who also cannot help him. The dejected Gilgamesh is about to depart when he is told of the Plant of Life—his last and most disappointing hope.

His spouse says to him, to Utnapishtim the Faraway:
"Gilgamesh has come hither, toiling and straining.
What wilt thou give him that he may return to his land?"
At that he, Gilgamesh, raised up his pole,
To bring the boat nigh to the shore.
Utnapishtim says to him, to Gilgamesh:
"Gilgamesh, thou hast come hither, toiling and straining.
What shall I give thee that thou mayest return to thy land?
I will disclose, O Gilgamesh, a hidden thing,
And about a plant I will tell thee:
This plant, like the buckthorn is [. . .].
Its thorns will prick thy hands just as does the rose.
If thy hands obtain the plant, thou wilt attain [eternal] life."
No sooner had Gilgamesh heard this, . . .
He tied heavy stones to his feet.
They pulled him down into the deep and he saw the plant.
He took the plant, though it pricked his hands.

He cut the heavy stones from his feet.
The sea cast him up upon its shore.
Gilgamesh says to him, to Urshanabi, the boatman:
"Urshanabi, this plant is a plant apart,
Whereby a man may regain his life's breath.
I will take it to ramparted Uruk. . . .
Its name shall be 'Man Becomes Young in Old Age.'
I myself shall eat it
And thus return to the state of my youth."
After twenty leagues they broke off a morsel,
After thirty more leagues they prepared for the night.
Gilgamesh saw a well whose water was cool.
He went down into it to bathe in the water.
A serpent snuffed the fragrance of the plant;
It came up from the water and carried off the plant,
Going back it shed its slough.
Thereupon Gilgamesh sits down and weeps,
His tears running down over his face.
He took the hand of Urshanabi, the boatman:
"For whom, Urshanabi, have my hands toiled?
For whom is being spent the blood of my heart?
I have not obtained a boon for myself.
For the serpent have I effected a boon!"

THE EPIC OF THE FLOOD

The Babylonian Noah

Archaeologists have discovered evidence of great floods in the Tigris-Euphrates valley, one of which left a deposit of sediment eight feet deep. Undoubtedly one such disastrous flood became the historical basis for a Sumerian flood epic, fragments of which have survived. It told how a Sumerian Noah, Ziusudra, warned beforehand by the god Ea of the intention of the gods "to destroy the seed of mankind" by a flood, built a ship and embarked upon it with his household, his possessions, and all types of living things. Because Ziusudra had thus "perceived the secret of the gods," they decided to give him "life like a god" and so made him one with themselves.

The later Babylonians incorporated the flood story into their composite version of the Epic of Gilgamesh. When the yearning for everlasting life takes hold of Gilgamesh after the death of his friend Enkidu, he searches out Ziusudra, whom the Babylonians called Utnapishtim, to gain from him the secret of eternal life. Utnapishtim tells him his story, and it is this more complete Babylonian version that is given in part below. The striking similarities with the later Hebrew story (The Bible: The Old Testament) are quite evident, but the great gulf between them needs to be emphasized: the Hebrew version has been completely moralized. In the Hebrew account the Flood is sent because of sin, and the hero is saved because he is righteous. In the Sumero-Babylonian version the hero is saved out of mere favoritism and the gods send the Flood, as we learn from a separate account, because their sleep has been disturbed: "oppressive has become the clamor of mankind, by their uproar they prevent sleep." Above all, the one supreme righteous God of the Hebrews contrasts with the gang of weak, quarrelsome, greedy gods who "cowered like dogs" in the presence of the Flood and who later "like flies gathered around the sacrificer."

Gilgamesh speaks to him, to Utnapishtim, the far-removed:
"I gaze at thee, Utnapishtim!
Thy appearance is not different. As I am, so art thou. . . .
Tell me how thou didst enter into the assembly of the gods and secure [eternal] life."
Utnapishtim said to him, to Gilgamesh:
"I will reveal to thee, Gilgamesh, a secret story,
And the decision of the gods I will tell thee.
The city Shuruppak, a city which thou knowest,
The one that lies on the Euphrates,
That city was old, as were the gods thereof,
When the great gods decided to bring a flood over it. . . .

The God Ea Warns Utnapishtim

"The lord of brilliant vision, Ea, was with them.
He repeated their decision to the reed-hut.
'Reed-hut, reed-hut, wall, wall,
Reed-hut, hear! Wall, give ear!
O man of Shuruppak, son of Ubara-Tutu,

Break up this house, build a ship,
Abandon your property, seek life!
Bring into the ship seed of all living things!
The ship that thou shalt build,
Let its dimension be measured, so that
Its breadth and length be made to correspond.
On a level with the deep, provide it with a covering.'
I understood and spoke to Ea, my lord:
'The command of my lord which thou hast commanded,
As I have understood it, I will carry out.
But what shall I answer the city—the people and the elders?'
Ea opened his mouth and spoke:
'As answer thus speak to them:
Know that Enlil {god who rules all Sumer} has conceived hatred towards me,
So that I can no longer dwell in your city.
On Enlil's territory I dare no longer set my face.
Therefore, I go to the Deep to dwell with Ea, my lord.
Over you he will cause blessings to rain down.' . . .

The Ship is Built and Loaded

"On the fifth day, I designed its outline.
Its walls were ten *gar* {180 feet} high;
Ten *gar* the measure of its width.
I determined its shape and drew it.
I gave it six decks.
I divided (the superstructure?) into seven parts.
Its interior I divided into nine sections.
Water-plugs I constructed in the interior.
I selected a punting-pole and added accessories.
Six measures of asphalt I poured on the outer wall.
Three measures of pitch I poured on the inner wall. . . .
All that I had I loaded on her.
All that I had of silver I loaded on her.
All that I had of gold I loaded on her.
All that I had of living beings of all kinds I loaded on her.
I brought to the ship all my family and household;
Cattle of the field, beasts of the field, all the workmen I brought on board. . . .

The Flood

"As morning dawned,
There arose on the firmament of heaven black clouds;
Adad thundered therein; . . .
Adad's roar reaches to heaven,
All light is changed to darkness. . . .
For one day the hurricane raged,
Storming furiously, . . .
Coming like a combat over men.
Brother sees not brother,
And from heaven people cannot be recognized.

"The Gods are Terrified"

"The gods are terrified by the deluge,
They flee and mount to the heaven of Anu;
The gods cowered like dogs in an enclosure.
Ishtar cried aloud like one in birth throes,
The mistress of the gods howls aloud:
'The former days are turned to clay. . . .
My people are like fish, they fill the sea.'
All of the Anunnaki gods weep with her;
The gods sit down, depressed and weeping. . . .

The Flood Subsides

"Six days and nights
The storm and flood continued to sweep over the land.
When the seventh day approached, the storm and flood ceased the combat,
After having fought like warriors. . . .
I looked at the day and the roar had quieted down,
And all mankind had returned to clay.
The landscape was level as a flat roof.
I opened a window and light fell on my face,
I bowed down and sat and wept,
Tears flowed over my face.
I looked in all directions of the sea.
At a distance of twelve miles an island appeared.
On Mount Nisir the ship stood still.
Mount Nisir held the ship so that it could not move.
One day, two days, Mount Nisir held the ship fast. . . .
When the seventh day arrived,
I sent forth a dove, letting it free.
The dove went hither and thither;
Not finding a resting place, it came back.
I sent forth a swallow, letting it free.
The swallow went hither and thither.
Not finding a resting place, it came back.
I sent forth a raven, letting it free.
The raven went and saw the decrease of the waters.
It ate, croaked, but did not turn back.
Then I let all out to the four regions and brought an offering.
I brought a sacrifice on the mountain top.
Seven and seven cult jars I arranged.
Beneath them I strewed reeds, cedarwood and myrtle.
The gods smelled the odor,
The gods smelled the sweet odor.
The gods like flies gathered around the sacrificer.

The Gods Quarrel

"As soon as [Ishtar] the mistress of the gods arrived, . . .
[she cried out:]
'Ye gods . . . I will remember these days—never to forget them.
Let the gods come to the sacrifice,
But let not Enlil come to the sacrifice,
Because without reflection he brought on the flood,

And decreed destruction for my people.'
As soon as Enlil arrived,
He saw the ship, and Enlil was enraged,
Filled with anger at the gods.
'Who now has escaped with his life?
No man was to survive the destruction!'
Ninib opened his mouth and spoke,
Spoke to the warrior Enlil,
'Who except Ea can plan any affair?
Ea indeed knows every order.'
Ea opened his mouth and spoke,
Spoke to the warrior Enlil:
'Thou art the leader and warrior of the gods.
But why didst thou, without reflection, bring on the flood?
On the sinner impose his sin,
On the transgressor impose his transgression,
But be merciful not to root out completely, be considerate not to destroy altogether! . . .
I did not reveal the secret of the great gods,
I sent Utnapishtim a dream and he understood the secret of the gods.
Now take counsel for him.'

Utnapishtim is Granted Eternal Life

"Enlil mounted the ship,
Took hold of my hand and led me up,
Led me up and caused my wife to kneel at my side,
Touched our foreheads, stepped between us and blessed us.
'Hitherto Utnapishtim was a man;
Now Utnapishtim and his wife shall be on a level with the gods.
Utnapishtim shall dwell in the distance, at the mouth of the rivers.'
Then they took me and settled me at the mouth of the rivers."

THE LAWS OF HAMMURABI

King Hammurabi of Babylon (ruled ca. 1792–1750 BC) promulgated one of the world's oldest written codes of law. The laws were inscribed on a basalt stele, probably at Sippar, a city in Mesopotamia and sacred to the sun god Shamash. Centuries later the stele was taken as booty by the Elamites to their capital at Susa in southwestern Iran, where it was discovered by archaeologists in 1901. Although fragments of earlier Sumerian law codes, some dating as early as 2100 B.C., have since appeared, Hammurabi's law code is still the earliest that survives nearly complete. Its 282 laws were written in the Semitic Akkadian language in the cuneiform script. A relief at the top of the monument depicts a standing Hammurabi facing the seated god Shamash, the god of justice, who is offering the laws to the king.

Hammurabi was the sixth king of the city-state of Babylon who eventually conquered all of Mesopotamia, founding the "Old Babylonian Empire". Thus the law code appears to have been intended not just for his capital city of Babylon but for the entire empire. The code is essentially divided into three parts:

1. An historical prologue describing the selection of Hammurabi as chosen by the gods to be "the shepherd" and thus protector of his people and the construction of his empire.
2. The corpus of 282 laws
3. An epilogue which summarizes how his laws will protect and bring justice to his people.

The laws follow a predictable pattern, constructed in a similar manner. Each law sets out a conditional problem with a response in the future tense, outlining the penalty for person judged guilty and/or a settlement. In other words, "If someone does such a thing, the penalty will be this." The laws are grouped into chapters and include both civil and criminal law. They primarily concern laws about the family, slavery, agriculture, commerce, and the professions.

The law code thus comprises an extraordinary source of information about the social structure, economy, religion, and political organization of Mesopotamia in this period.

Prologue

When the lofty Anu, king of the Anunnaki gods, and Enlil, lord of heaven and earth, he who determines the destiny of the land, committed the rule of all mankind to Marduk, the chief son of Ea; when they made him great among the Igigi gods; when they pronounced the lofty name of Babylon; when they made it famous among the quarters of the world and in its midst eastablished an everlasting kingdom whose foundations were firm as heaven and earth—at the time, Anu and Enlil named me, Hammurabi, the exalted prince, the worshiper of the gods, to cause justice to prevail in the land, to destroy the wicked and the evil, to prevent the strong from oppressing the weak, to go forth like the sun over the black-headed people, to enlighten the land and to further the welfare of the people. Hammurabi, the shepherd named by Enlil, am I, who brought about plenty and abundance; . . . obedient to the mighty Shamash; . . . who rebuilt [the temple] Ebabbar for Shamash, his helper; . . . the powerful king, the sun of Babylon, who caused light to go forth over the lands of Sumer and Akkad; the king who caused the four quarters of the world to render obedience; the favorite of Ishtar, am I.

When Marduk sent me to rule the people and to bring help to the country, I established law and justice in the language of the land and promoted the welfare of the people. At that time (I decreed):

The Administration of Justice

1. If a man brings an accusation against another man, charging him with murder, but cannot prove it, the accuser shall be put to death.

3. If a man bears false witness in a case, or does not establish the testimony that he has given, if that case is a case involving life, that man shall be put to death.

4. If he bears (false) witness concerning grain or money, he shall himself bear the penalty imposed in that case.

5. If a judge pronounces a judgment, renders a decision, delivers a verdict duly signed and sealed, and afterward alters his judgment, they shall call that judge to account for the alteration of the judgment which he has pronounced, and he shall pay twelve-fold the penalty in that judgment; and, in the assembly, they shall expel him from his seat of judgment, and with the judges in a case he shall not take his seat.

Property

9. If a man who has lost anything finds that which was lost in the possession of (another) man, and the man in whose possession the lost property is found says, "It was sold to me, I purchased it in the presence of witnesses"; and the owner of the lost property says, "I will bring witnesses to identify my lost property"; if the purchaser produces the seller who has sold it to him and the witnesses in whose presence he purchased it, and the owner of the lost property produces witnesses to identify his lost property, the judges shall consider their evidence. The witnesses in whose presence the purchase was made and the witnesses to identify the lost property shall give their testimony in the presence of god. The seller shall be put to death as a thief; the owner of the lost property shall recover his loss; the purchaser shall recover from the estate of the seller the money which he paid out.

10. If the purchaser does not produce the seller who sold it to him and the witnesses in whose presence he purchased it, and if the owner of the lost property produces witnesses to identify his lost property, the purchaser shall be put to death as a thief. The owner of the lost property shall recover his lost property.

11. If the (alleged) owner of the lost property does not produce witnesses to identify his lost property, he has attempted fraud, he has stirred up strife, he shall be put to death.

22. If a man practices robbery and is captured, that man shall be put to death.

23. If the robber is not captured, the man who has been robbed shall, in the presence of god, make an itemized statement of his loss, and the city and the governor in whose province and jurisdiction the robbery was committed shall compensate him for whatever was lost.

24. If it is a life (that is lost), the city and governor shall pay one mina {about one pound} of silver to his heirs.

Irrigation

53. If a man neglects to maintain his dike and does not strengthen it, and a break is made in his dike and the water carries away the farmland, the man in whose dike the break has been made shall replace the grain which has been damaged.

54. If he is not able to replace the grain, the shall sell him and his goods and the farmers whose grain the water has carried away shall divide (the results of the sale).

55. If a man opens his canal for irrigation and neglects it and the water carries away an adjacent field, he shall pay out grain on the basis of the adjacent field.

56. If a man opens up the water and the water carries away the improvements of an adjacent field, he shall pay out ten *gur* of grain per *bur* {of damaged land}.

Loans and Interest

88. If a merchant lends grain at interest, for one *gur* {300 *sila*} he shall receive one hundred *sila* as interest {33$\frac{1}{3}$ per cent}; if he lends money at interest, for one shekel of silver he shall receive one-fifth of a shekel as interest {20 per cent}.

90. If a merchant increases the interest on grain above one hundred *sila* for one *gur,* or the interest on silver above one-fifth of a shekel (per shekel), and takes this interest, he shall forfeit whatever he lent.

94. If a merchant lends grain or silver at interest and when he lends it at interest he gives silver by the small weight and grain by the small measure but when he gets it back he gets silver by the large weight and grain by the large measure, the merchant shall forfeit whatever he lent.

Regulation of Trade

104. If a merchant gives to an agent grain, wool, oil, or goods of any kind with which to trade, the agent shall write down the value and return (the money) to the merchant. The agent shall take a sealed receipt for the money which he gives to the merchant.

105. If the agent is careless and does not take a receipt for the money which he has given to the merchant, the money not receipted for shall not be placed to his account.

108. If a wine seller does not take grain for the price of a drink but takes money by the large weight, or if she makes the measure of drink smaller than the measure of grain, they shall call that wine seller to account and throw her into the water.

109. If bad characters gather in the house of a wine seller and she does not arrest those bad characters and bring them to the palace, that wine seller shall be put to death.

110. If a priestess who is not living in a convent opens a wine shop or enters a wine shop for a drink, they shall burn that woman.

Debt Slavery

117. If a man is in debt and sells his wife, son, or daughter, or binds them over to service, for three years they shall work in the house of their purchaser or master; in the fourth year they shall be given their freedom.

118. If he binds over to service a male or female slave and lets the time (of redemption) expire and the merchant transfers or sells such slave, there is no cause for complaint.

Marriage and the Family

128. If a man takes a wife and does not arrange a contract for her, that woman is not a wife.

129. If the wife of a man is caught lying with another man, they shall bind them and throw them into the water. If the husband of the woman wishes to spare his wife, then the king shall spare his servant.

131. If a man has accused his wife but she has not been caught lying with another man, she shall take an oath in the name of god and return to her house.

136. If a man deserts his city and flees and afterwards his wife enters into another house, if that man returns and wishes to take back his wife, the wife of the fugitive shall not return to her husband because he hated his city and fled.

138. If a man wishes to divorce his wife who has not borne him children, he shall give her money to the amount of her marriage price and he shall make good to her the dowry which she brought from her father's house and then he may divorce her.

141. If the wife of a man who is living in his house sets her face to go out and plays the part of a fool, neglecting her house and belittling her husband, they shall call her to account; and if her husband says, "I divorce her," he may let her go. On her departure nothing shall be given to her for her divorce. If her husband says, "I will not divorce her," her husband may marry another woman. The first woman shall dwell in the house of her husband as a maidservant.

142. If a woman hates her husband and says, "You may not possess me," the city council shall inquire into her case; and if she has been careful and without reproach and her husband has been going about and greatly belittling her, that woman has no blame. She may take her dowry and go to her father's house.

143. If she has not been careful but has gadded about, neglecting her house and belittling her husband, they shall throw that woman into the water.

145. If a man takes a wife and she does not present him with children and he sets his face to take a concubine, that man may take a concubine and bring her into his house. That concubine shall not rank with his wife.

146. If a man takes a wife and she gives a maidservant to her husband, and that maidservant bears children and afterwards claims equal rank with her mistress because she borne children, her mistress may not sell her, but she may reduce her to bondage and count her among the slaves.

148. If a man has married a wife and a disease has seized her, if he is determined to marry a second wife, he shall marry her. He shall not divorce the wife whom the disease has seized. In the home they made together she shall dwell, and he shall maintain her as long as she lives.

150. If a man gives to his wife a field, garden, house, or goods and delivers to her a sealed deed, after (the death of) her husband her children cannot enter a claim against her. The mother may will her estate to her son whom she loves, but to an outsider she may not.

159. If a man, who has brought a gift to the house of his father-in-law and has paid the marriage price, looks with longing upon another woman and says to his father-in-law, "I will not marry your daughter," the father of the daughter shall take to himself whatever was brought to him.

160. If a man has brought a gift to the house of his father-in-law and has paid the marriage price and the father of the daughter says, "I will not give you my daughter," he shall double the amount that was brought to him and return it.

162. If a man takes a wife and she bears him children and that woman dies, her father may not lay claim to her dowry. Her dowry belongs to her children.

165. If a man presents a field, garden, or house to his favorite son and writes for him a sealed deed, after the father dies, when the brothers divide (the estate), he shall take the present which the father gave him, but otherwise they shall divide the goods of the father's estate equally.

168. If a man sets his face to disinherit his son and says to the judges, "I will disinherit my son," the judges shall inquire into his record, and if the son has not committed a crime sufficiently grave to cut him off from sonship, the father may not cut off his son from sonship.

170. If a man's wife bears him children and his maidservant bears him children, and the father during his lifetime says to the children which the maidservant bore him, "My children," and reckons them with the children of his wife, after the father dies the children of the wife and the children of the maidservant shall divide the goods of the father's estate equally. The son of the wife shall have the right of choice at the division.

Adoption

185. If a man takes in his own name a young boy as a son and rears him, one may not bring claim for that adopted son.

191. If a man, who has taken a young boy as a son and reared him, establishes his own house and acquires children, and sets his face to cut off the adopted son, that son shall not go off empty-handed. The father who reared him shall give to him of his goods one-third the portion of a son and then he shall go. He may not give to him (any portion) of field, garden, or house.

Personal Injury and Manslaughter

195. If a son strikes his father, they shall cut off his hand.

196. If a man destroys the eye of another man, they shall destroy his eye.

197. If he breaks another man's bone, they shall break his bone.

198. If he destroys the eye of a client or breaks the bone of a client, he shall pay one mina of silver.

199. If he destroys the eye of a man's slave or breaks a bone of a man's slave, he shall pay one-half his price.

200. If a man knocks out a tooth of a man of his own rank, they shall knock out his tooth.

201. If he knocks out a tooth of a client, he shall pay one-third mina of silver.

206. If a man strikes another man in a quarrel and wounds him, he shall swear, "I struck him without intent," and he shall pay for the physician.

207. If he dies as the result of the blow, he shall swear (as above), and if the man was a free man, he shall pay one-half mina of silver.

208. If he was a client, he shall pay one-third mina of silver.

Physician's Fees and Malpractice

(handwritten note: Gets more money working on upper class but consequences are worse)

215. If a physician operates on a man for a severe wound with a bronze lancet and saves the man's life, or if he opens an abscess (in the eye) of a man with a bronze lancet and saves that man's eye, he shall receive ten shekels of silver.
216. If he is a client, he shall receive five shekels.
217. If he is a man's slave, the owner of the slave shall give two shekels of silver to the physician.
218. If a physician operates on a man for a severe wound with a bronze lancet and causes the man's death, or opens an abscess (in the eye) of a man with a bronze lancet and destroys the man's eye, they shall cut off his hand.
219. If a physician operates on a slave of a client for a severe wound with a bronze lancet and causes his death, he shall restore a slave of equal value.
221. If a physician sets a broken bone for a man or cures a sprained tendon, the patient shall give five shekels of silver to the physician.
222. If he is a client, he shall give three shekels of silver.
223. If he is a man's slave, the owner shall give two shekels of silver to the physician.

Building Regulations

228. If a builder builds a house for a man and completes it, he shall give him two shekels of silver per *sar* of house as his fee.
229. If a builder builds a house for a man and does not make its construction sound, and the house which he has built collapses and causes the death of the owner of the house, the builder shall be put to death.
233. If a builder builds a house for a man and does not make its construction sound, and a wall cracks, that builder shall strengthen that wall at his own expense.

Wage Regulations

257. If a man hires a field laborer, he shall pay him eight *gur* of grain per year.
258. If a man hires a herdsman, he shall pay him six *gur* of grain per year.
268. If a man hires an ox to thresh, twenty *sila* of grain is its [daily] hire.
269. If a man hires an ass to thresh, ten *sila* of grain is its hire.
271. If a man hires oxen, a wagon, and a driver, he shall pay 180 *sila* of grain per day.
273. If a man hires a laborer, from the beginning of the year until the fifth month he shall pay six *she* of silver per day; from the sixth month till the end of the year he shall pay five *she* of silver per day.
274. If a man hires an artisan, the [daily] wage of a [potter?] is five *she* of silver; the wage of a bricklayer is five *she* of silver; the wage of a tailor is five *she* of silver; the wage of a stonecutter is [. . .] *she* of silver; the wage of a jeweler is [. . .] *she* of silver; the wage of a smith is [. . .] *she* of silver; the wage of a carpenter is four *she* of silver; the wage of a leather worker is [. . .] *she* of silver; the wage of a basketmaker is [. . .] *she* of silver; the wage of a builder is [. . .] *she* of silver.

Epilogue

(These are) the just laws which Hammurabi, the wise king, established and by which he gave the land stable support and good government. Hammurabi, the perfect king, am I. I was not careless, nor was I neglectful of the black-headed people, whose rule Enlil presented and Marduk delivered to me. . . .

The great gods called me, and I am the guardian shepherd whose scepter is just and whose beneficent shadow is spread over my city. In my bosom I carried the people of the land of Sumer and Akkad; under my protection they prospered; I governed them in peace; in my wisdom I sheltered them.

In order that the strong might not oppress the weak, that justice be given to the orphan and the widow, in Babylon, the city whose turrets Anu and Enlil raised, in Esagila, the temple whose foundations are firm as heaven and earth, for the pronouncing of judgments in the land, for the rendering of decisions for the land, and to give justice to the oppressed, my weighty words I have written upon my monument, and in the presence of my image as king of justice have I established it.

The king who is preeminent among kings am I. My words are precious, my wisdom is unrivaled. By the command of Shamash, the great judge of heaven and earth, may I make justice to shine forth on the land. By the order of Marduk, my lord, may no one scorn my statutes, may my name be remembered with favor in Esagila forever.

Let any oppressed man, who has a cause, come before my image as king of justice! Let him read the inscription on my monument! Let him give heed to my weighty words! And may my monument enlighten him as to his cause and may he understand his case! May he set his heart at ease! (and he will exclaim): "Hammurabi indeed is a ruler who is like a real father to his people; he has given reverence to the words of Marduk, his lord; he has obtained victory for Marduk in north and south; he has made glad the heart of Marduk, his lord; he has established prosperity for the people for all time and given good government to the land." . . .

In the days that are yet to come, for all future time, may the king who is in the land observe the words of justice which I have written upon my monument! May he not alter the judgments of the land which I have pronounced, or the decisions of the country which I have rendered! May he not scorn my statutes! If that man have wisdom, if he wish to give his land good government, let him give attention to the words which I have written upon my monument! And may this monument enlighten him as to procedure and administration, the judgments which I have pronounced, and the decisions which I have rendered for the land! And let him rightly rule his black-headed people; let him pronounce judgments for them and render for them decisions! Let him root out the wicked and the evil from his land! Let him promote the welfare of his people!

Hammurabi, the king of justice [*misharum*], to whom Shamash has committed truth [*kittum*], am I. My words are weighty; my deeds are unrivaled; only to the fool are they vain; to the wise they are worthy of every praise.

THE STORY OF SINUHE

This purportedly autobiographical account describes the life and career of Sinuhe, an Egyptian court official of the Middle Kingdom (ca. 2000-1670 BC). According to the story, ca. 1960 B.C. Sinuhe was serving as an attendant to the pharaoh's daughter, who was married to the heir to the throne, Sen-Usert. When the story opens Sinuhe is outside Egypt, on campaign in Libya (west of Egypt) with an Egyptian army under the command of Sen-Usert. Upon hearing of the death of the pharaoh, Sinuhe, at great risk to his life, decides to flee and ultimately reaches Syria, where he lives for many years in exile. Eventually he is allowed to return to Egypt, restored to his position at the pharaoh's court, and prepare for his afterlife.

The popularity of the story is suggested by the large number of surviving manuscripts, the earliest dating from the Middle Kingdom. Although most of the details of the story cannot be independently confirmed, the names of the rulers and the cultural milieu it presents seem quite authentic. Some scholars have suggested that this story was actually copied from the walls of a tomb biography, which were common in Egypt. The source not only provides much insight into Egypt itself (especially the royal court) but also includes precious insights into Syria at the turn of the 2nd millennium B.C., a period for which we otherwise have few literary sources for that region. Also note the descriptions of Sinuhe's elaborate preparations for his afterlife at the end of the story, underscoring its importance in Egyptian culture.

(R1) THE HEREDITARY PRINCE AND COUNT, Judge and District Overseer of the domains of the Sovereign in the lands of the Asiatics, real acquaintance of the king, his beloved, the Attendant Si-nuhe. He says:

I was an attendant who followed his lord, a servant of the royal harem (and of) the Hereditary Princess, the great of favor, the wife of King Sen-Usert in (the pyramid town) Khenem-sut, the daughter of King Amenem-het (R5) in (the pyramid town) Qa-nefru, Nefru, the lady of reverence.[1]

YEAR 30, THIRD MONTH OF THE FIRST SEASON, DAY 7.[2] The god ascended to his horizon; the King of Upper and Lower Egypt: Sehetep-ib-Re was taken up to heaven and united with the sun disc. The body of the god merged with him who made him.[3] The Residence City was in silence, hearts were in mourning, the Great Double Doors were sealed shut. (R10) The courtiers (sat) head on lap, and the people were in grief.

Now his majesty had sent an army to the land of the Temeh-Libyans, with his eldest son as the commander thereof, the good god Sen-Usert, (R15) and even now he was returning and had carried off living captives of the Tehenu-Libyans and all (kinds of) cattle without number.

The courtiers of the palace sent to the western border to let the King's Son know the events which had taken place at the court. The messengers met him on the road, (R20) and they reached him in the evening time. He did not delay a moment; the falcon[4] flew away with his attendants, without letting his army know it. Now the royal children who had been following him in this army had been sent for, (B1) and one of them was summoned. While I was standing (near by) I heard his voice as he was speaking and I was a little way off. My heart was distraught, my arms spread out (in dismay), trembling fell upon all my limbs.[5] I removed myself *by leaps and bounds* to seek a hiding place for myself. I placed (5) myself between two bushes, in order to *cut (myself) off from* the road and its *travel.*

---

[1] Si-nuhe's service was to Nefru, the daughter of Amen-em-het I and wife of Sen-Usert I.

[2] Around 1960 B.C., the date of Amen-em-het I's death, as given here, would have fallen early in March.

[3] The pharaoh was the "Son of Re," the sun-god. At death he was taken back into the body of his creator and father.

[4] The new king Sen-Usert I. Although he had been coregent with his father for ten years, he had to go immediately to the capital before word of his father's death became widely known. See the next note.

[5] We are never directly told the reason for Si-nuhe's sudden fright and voluntary exile. Later both he and the king protest his innocence. He may have been legally guiltless, but the transition between kings was a dangerous time for one who was not fully identified with the new king. Si-nuhe's official loyalty was to the princess. The Instruction of King Amen-em-het acquaints us with a palace conspiracy, perhaps a harem conspiracy, at or near the end of that king's reign. We must assume that Si-nuhe had adequate reason for his sudden and furtive departure and his long stay in Asia.

---

*I set out southward, (but) I did not plan to reach this Residence City, (for) I thought that there would be civil disorder, and I did not expect to live after him. I crossed Lake Ma'aty near Sycamore, and I came to Snefru Island. I spent the day there on the *edge* of (10) the fields. I *came into the open* light, while it was *(still)* day, and I met a man standing near by. He stood in awe of me, for he was afraid. When the time of the evening meal came, I drew near to Ox-town. I crossed over in a barge without a rudder, by aid of the west wind.[6] I passed by the east of the quarry (15) above Mistress-of-the-Red-Mountain.[7] I gave (free) road to my feet going northward, and I came up to the Wall-of-the-Ruler,[8] made to oppose the Asiatics and to crush the Sand-Crossers. I took a crouching position in a bush, for fear lest the watchmen upon the wall where their day's (duty) was might see me.

I set out (20) at evening time, and when day broke I reached Peten. I halted at the Island of Kem-wer.[9] An attack of thirst overtook me. I was parched, and my throat was dusty. I said: "This is the taste of death!" (But then) I lifted up my heart and collected myself, for I had heard the sound of the lowing of cattle, (25) and I spied Asiatics. The sheikh among them, who had been in Egypt, recognized me. Then he gave me water while he boiled milk for me. I went with him to his tribe. What they did (for me) was good.

One foreign country gave me to another. I set off for Byblos and approached Qedem,[10] and spent (30) a year and a half there. Ammi-enshi[11]—he was a ruler of Upper Retenu[12]—took me and said to me: "Thou wilt do well with me, and thou wilt hear the speech of Egypt." He said this, for he knew my character, he had heard of my wisdom, and the people of Egypt who were there with him[13] had borne witness for me.

Then he said to me: (35) "Why hast thou come hither? Has something happened in the Residence City?" Then I said to him: "The King of Upper and Lower Egypt: Sehetep-ib-Re is departed to the horizon, and no one knows what might happen because of it." But I said equivocally: "I had come from an expedition to the land of Temeh, when report was made to me. My heart quailed; it carried (40) me off on the way of *flight*. (Yet) no one had gossiped about me; no one had spat in my face; not a belittling word had been heard, nor had my name been heard in the mouth of the herald. I do not know what brought me to this country. It was as though it might be a god."

Then he said to me: "Well, what will that land be like without him, that beneficent god, the fear of whom pervaded (45) foreign countries like (the fear of) Sekhmet in a year of pestilence?"[14] I spoke to him that I might answer him: "Well, of course, his son has entered into the palace and has taken the inheritance of his father. Moreover, he is a god without his peer. There is no other who surpasses him. He is a master of understanding, effective in plans and beneficent of decrees. Going forth and coming back are in conformance with (50) his command. He it was who subdued the foreign countries while his father was in his palace, and he reported to him that what had been charged to him had been carried out. . . .[15] How joyful is this land which he has ruled! (71) He is one who extends its frontiers. He will carry off the lands of the south, and he will not consider the northern countries (seriously), (for) he was made to smite the Asiatics and to crush the Sand-Crossers. Send to him! Let him know thy name! Do not utter a curse against his majesty. He will not fail to do (75) good to the country which shall be loyal to him!"

Then he said to me: "Well, really, Egypt is happy that it knows that he is flourishing. Now thou art here. Thou shalt stay with me. What I shall do for thee is good."

He set me at the head of his children. He married me to his eldest daughter. He let me choose for myself of his country, (80) of the choicest of that which was with him on his frontier with another country. It was a good land,

---

[6]Apparently Si-nuhe went southeast along the edge of the cultivated land, to avoid the peopled stretches of the Delta, and crossed the Nile where it is a single stream, somewhere near modern Cairo.

[7]Gebel el-Ahmar, east of Cairo.

[8]The fortresses at the eastern frontier, along the general line of the present Suez Canal.

[9]The area of the Bitter Lakes.

[10]Semitic for "the East" generally. A vague term, either in the writer's ignorance of Asiatic geography or intentionally vague for a wide nomadic area.

[11]An Amorite name. It was unfamiliar to one Egyptian scribe, who tried to egyptianize it to "Amu's son Enshi."

[12]Highland country, probably including northern Palestine, southern and central Syria. See A. H. Gardiner, *Ancient Egyptian Onomastica* (London, 1947), 1, 142* ff. Si-nuhe's Asiatic home of Yaa cannot be located any more definitely than this. It may be noted that it is agricultural, with herds, but within reasonable distance of desert hunting, and that it is close enough to some main road that Si-nuhe may entertain Egyptian couriers. Since he apparently went east from Byblos, a location in the valley between the Lebanon and Anti-lebanon is a possibility, but it would be wrong to push the evidence so closely. As it stands, the story gives a picture of Syria-Palestine in the patriarchal period.

[13]Other exiles like Si-nuhe? He is in a land of refuge from Egypt. From the nature of this land it seems unlikely that there would have been many Egyptian merchants.

[14]The goddess Sekhmet had to do with disease.

[15]This translation omits some of the fulsome praise.

named Yaa. Figs were in it, and grapes. It had more wine than water. Plentiful was its honey, abundant its olives. Every (kind of) fruit was on its trees. Barley was there, and emmer. There was no limit to any (king of) cattle. (85) Moreover, great was that which accrued to me as a result of the love of me. He made me ruler of a tribe of the choicest of his country. Bread was made for me as daily fare, wine as daily provision, cooked meat and roast fowl, beside the wild beasts of the desert, for they hunted (90) for me and laid before me, beside the catch of my (own) hounds. Many . . . were made for me, and milk in every (kind of) cooking.

I spent many years, and my children grew up to be strong men, each man as the restrainer of his (own) tribe. The messenger who went north or who went south to the Residence City (95) stopped over with me, (for) I used to make everybody stop over. I gave water to the thirsty. I put him who had strayed (back) on the road. I rescued him who had been robbed. When the Asiatics became so bold as to oppose the rulers of foreign countries,[16] I counseled their movements. This ruler of (100) (Re)tenu had me spend many years as commander of his army. Every foreign country against which I went forth, when I had made my attack on it, was driven away from its pasturage and its wells. I plundered its cattle, carried off its inhabitants, took away their food, and slew people in it (105) by my strong arm, by my bow, by my movements, and by my successful plans. I found favor in his heart, he loved me, he recognized my valor, and he placed me at the head of his children, when he saw how my arms flourished.

A mighty man of Retenu came, that he might challenge me (110) in my (own) camp. He was a hero without his peer, and he had repelled all of it.[17] He said that he would fight me, he intended to despoil me, and he planned to plunder my cattle, on the advice of his tribe. That prince discussed (it) with me, and I said: "I do not know him. Certainly I am no confederate of his, (115) so that I might move freely in his encampment. Is it the case that I have (ever) opened his *door* or overthrown his fences? (Rather), it is hostility because he sees me carrying out thy commissions. I am really like a stray bull in the midst of another herd, and a bull of (these) cattle attacks him. . . ."[18]

During the night I strung my bow and shot my arrows,[19] I gave free play to my dagger, and polished my weapons. When day broke, (Re)tenu was come. (130) It had *whipped up* its tribes and collected the countries of a (good) half of it. It had thought (only) of this fight. Then he came to me as I was waiting, (for) I had placed myself near him. Every heart burned for me; women and men groaned. Every heart was sick for me. They said: "Is there another strong man who could fight against him?" Then (*he took*) his shield, his battle-axe, (135) and his *armful of javelins. Now* after I had let his weapons issue forth, I made his arrows pass by me uselessly, one close to another. He charged me, and I shot him, my arrow sticking in his neck. He cried out and fell on his nose. (140) I felled him with his (own) battle-axe and raised my cry of victory over his back, while every Asiatic roared. I gave praise to Montu,[20] while his adherents were mourning for him. This ruler Ammi-enshi took me into his embrace. Then I carried off his goods and plundered his cattle. What he had planned to do (145) to me I did to him. I took what was in his tent and stripped his encampment. I became great thereby, I became extensive in my wealth, I became abundant in my cattle.

Thus did god to show mercy to him upon whom he had *laid blame,* whom he had led astray to another country. (But) today his heart is assuaged.[21] . . .

Now when the majesty of the King of Upper and Lower Egypt: Kheper-ka-Re, the justified,[22] was told about this situation in which I was, then his majesty kept sending (175) to me with presentations from the royal presence, that he might gladden the heart of this servant[23] like the ruler of any foreign country. The royal children in his palace let me hear their commissions.[24]

COPY OF THE DECREE WHICH WAS BROUGHT TO THIS SERVANT ABOUT BRINGING HIM (BACK) TO EGYPT.

---

[16]*Heqau-khasut* probably simply "the rulers of (other) foreign countries," but it is worth noting that these Egyptian words were the probable origin of the term "Hyksos." We may have here an early reference to restless peoples who were later to participate in the invasion of Egypt. cf. pp. 229, n.9; 247, n.56.
[17]He had beaten every one of the land of Retenu.
[18]Si-nuhe goes on to state that he accepts the challenge, which has come to him because he is an outsider in the Asiatic scene.
[19]In practice.
[20]The Egyptian god of war.
[21]It is not clear how Si-nuhe expiated his sins, except by being a successful Egyptian in another country. This translation omits in the following text a poetical statement of homesickness for Egypt.
[22]Sen-Usert I. The manuscript incorrectly writes Kheper-kau-Re.
[23]"This servant" = me.
[24]They also wrote to Si-nuhe.

"The Horus: Living in Births; the Two Goddesses: Living in Births; the King of Upper and Lower Egypt: Kheper-ka-Re; the Son of Re: (180) Amen-em-het,[25] living forever and ever. Royal decree to the Attendant Si-nuhe. Behold, this decree of the king is brought to thee to let thee know that:

"Thou hast traversed the foreign countries, starting from Qedem to (Re)tenu. One country gave thee to another, under the advice of thy (own) heart to thee. What hast thou done that anything should be done to thee? Thou hast not cursed, that thy word should be punished. Thou hast not spoken against the counsel of the nobles, that thy speeches should be opposed. (185) This plan (simply) carried away thy heart. It was in n) heart against thee. This thy heaven which is in the palace[26] is firm and steadfast today. Her head *is covered* with the kingship of the land.[27] Her children are in the court.

"MAYEST THOU LAY UP TREASURES WHICH THEY MAY GIVE THEE; MAYEST THOU LIVE ON THEIR BOUNTY. Do thou return to Egypt, that thou mayest see the home in which thou didst grow up and kiss the ground at the Great Double Door and join with the courtiers. For today, surely, (190) thou hast begun to grow old; thou hast lost (thy) virility. Recall thou the day of burial, the passing to a revered state, when the evening is set aside for thee with ointments and wrappings from the hands of Tait.[28] A funeral procession is made for thee on the day of inter-ment, a mummy case of gold, with head of lapis lazuli, with the heaven above thee,[29] as thou art placed upon a sledge, oxen dragging thee and singers in front of thee, when the dance (195) of the *muu* is performed at the door of thy tomb,[30] when the requirements of the offering table are summoned for thee and there is sacrifice beside thy offering stones, thy pillars being hewn of white stone in the midst of (the tombs of) the royal children. It should not be that thou shouldst die in a foreign country. Asiatics should not escort thee. Thou shouldst not be placed in a sheepskin when thy wall is made. This is (too) long to be roaming the earth. Give heed to *sickness,* that thou mayest return."[31]

"THIS DECREE REACHED ME AS I WAS STANDING (200) IN THE MIDST OF MY TRIBE. It was read to me. I put myself upon my belly; I touched the ground; I scattered it upon my hair. I went about my encampment rejoicing and saying: "How can this be done for a servant whom his heart led astray to barbarous countries? But the indulgence which saved me from death is really good! Thy *ka* will let me effect the end of my body at home!"

"*COPY OF THE ANSWER TO THIS DECREE. THE SERVANT OF *THE PALACE* SI-NUHE (205) says:

"In very good peace! This flight which this servant made in his ignorance is known by thy *ka,* O good god, Lord of the Two Lands, whom Re loves and whom Montu, Lord of Thebes, favors! . . .[32]

"This is the prayer of this servant to his Lord, the saviour in the West: THE LORD OF PERCEPTION, WHO PERCEIVES PEOPLE, MAY HE PERCEIVE (215) in the majesty of the palace that this servant was afraid to say it. It is (still) like some-thing (too) big to repeat.[33] . . . FURTHER, MAY THY MAJESTY COMMAND THAT THERE BE BROUGHT Maki from Qedem, (220) Khenti-iaush from Khent-*keshu,* and Menus from the lands of the Fenkhu.[34] They are *men exact* and reliable, *young men* who grew up in the love of thee—not to mention (Re)tenu: it is thine, like thy (own) hounds.

"Now this flight which the servant made, it was not planned, it was not in my heart, I had not worried about it. I do not know what severed me from (my) place. It was after (225) the manner of a dream, as if A MAN OF THE DELTA were to see himself IN ELEPHANTINE, or a man of the (northern) marshes in Nubia. I had not been afraid. No one had run after me. I had not heard a belittling word. My name had not been heard in the mouth of the herald. And yet—my body *shuddered,* my feet were *trembling,* my heart led me on, and the god who ordained this flight (230) drew me away. I was not at all stiff-backed *formerly.* A man who knows his land should be afraid, (for) Re has set the fear of thee throughout the earth, and the dread of thee in every foreign country. Whether I am at home or whether I am in this place, thou art he who covers this horizon, the sun disc rises at thy pleasure, the water in the

---

[25]*Sic,* but read "Sen-Usert."
[26]The Queen.
[27]She wears the insignia of rule?
[28]The goddess of weaving—here for mummy wrappings.
[29]The canopy over the hearse.
[30]An old funerary dance.
[31]It may be all right to roam about when you are young, but now you must think that a sickness might carry you off and deprive you of a proper burial in Egypt.
[32]This translation omits good wishes for the king.
[33]Si-nuhe feels that his case is so delicate that he must sidle into it.
[34]Fenkhu perhaps Phoenicia. These Asiatics were recommended as reliable character witnesses or hostages or escort for Si-nuhe.

River is drunk as thou wishest, and the air in the sky is breathed as thou biddest. This servant will hand over (235) THE VIZIERSHIP WHICH THIS SERVANT HAS EXERCISED IN THIS PLACE."[35]

Then they came for this servant. . . . I was permitted to spend a day in Yaa handing over my property to my children, my eldest son being responsible for my tribe. (240) My tribe and all my property were in his charge: my serfs, all my cattle, my fruit, and every pleasant tree of mine.

Then this servant came southward. I halted at the "Ways of Horus."[36] The commander there who was responsible for the patrol sent a message to the Residence to make (it) known. Then his majesty sent a capable overseer of peasants of the palace, with loaded ships in his train, (245) carrying presentations from the royal presence FOR THE ASIATICS WHO HAD FOLLOWED ME, ESCORTING ME TO THE "WAYS OF HORUS." I called each of them by his name.[37] Every butler was (busy) at his duties. When I started and set sail, the kneading and straining (of beer) was carried on beside me, until I had reached the town of Lisht.[38]

When day had broken, very early, they came and summoned me, ten men coming and ten men going to usher me to the palace.[39] I put my brow to the ground between the sphinxes, (250) while the royal children were waiting in a recess to meet me. The courtiers who usher into the audience hall set me on the way to the private chambers. I found his majesty upon the Great Throne in a recess of fine gold. When I was stretched out upon my belly, I knew not myself in his presence, (although) this god greeted me pleasantly. I was like a man caught in the dark: (255) my soul departed, my body was powerless, my heart was not in my body, that I might know life from death.

THEN HIS MAJESTY SAID TO ONE OF THESE COURTIERS: "Lift him up. Let him speak to me." Then his majesty said: "Behold, thou art come. Thou hast trodden the foreign countries *and made a flight*. (But now) elderliness has attacked thee; thou hast reached old age. It is no small matter that thy corpse be (properly) buried; thou shouldst not be interred by bowmen.[40] Do not, do not act thus any longer: (for) thou dost not speak (260) when thy name is pronounced!" Yet (I) was afraid to respond, and I answered it with the answer of one afraid: "What is it that my lord says to me? I should answer it, (but) there is nothing that I can do: it is really the hand of a god. It is a terror that is in my belly like that which produced the fated flight. BEHOLD, I AM BEFORE THEE. THINE IS LIFE. MAY THY MAJESTY DO AS HE PLEASES."

THEREUPON the royal children WERE ushered in. Then his majesty said to the Queen: "Here is Si-nuhe, (265) come as a Bedu, (in) *the guise* of the Asiatics." She gave a very great cry, and the royal children clamored all together. Then they said to his majesty: "It is not really he, O Sovereign, my lord!" Then his majesty said: "It is really he!" Now when they had brought with them their bead-necklaces, their rattles, and their sistra, then they presented them to his majesty. ". . . Loose the horn of thy bow and relax thy arrow! (275) Give breath to him that was stifled! Give us our goodly gift in this sheikh Si-Mehit,[41] a bowman born in Egypt. He made a flight through fear of thee; he left the land through terror of thee. (But) the face of him who beholds thy face shall not *blanch*; the eye which looks at thee shall not be afraid!"

Then his majesty said: "He shall not fear. (280) He has no *title* to be in dread. He shall be a courtier among the nobles. He shall be put in the ranks of the courtiers. Proceed ye to the inner chambers of the *morning (toilet)*, in order to make his position."[42]

So I went forth from the midst of the inner chambers, with the royal children giving me their hands. (285) Thereafter we went to the Great Double Door. I was put into the house of a royal son, in which were splendid things. A cool room was in it, and images of the horizon.[43] Costly things of the Treasury were in it. Clothing of royal linen, myrrh, and prime oil of the king and of the nobles whom he loves were in every room. (290) Every butler was (busy) at his duties. Years were made to pass away from my body. I was *plucked*, and my hair was combed. A load (of dirt) was given to the desert, and my clothes (to) the Sand-Crossers. I was clad in fine linen and anointed with prime oil. I slept on a bed. I gave up the sand to them who are in it, (295) and wood oil to him who is anointed with it. I was

---

[35]He maintains the flattering fiction that he has been ruling his part of Asia on behalf of the pharaoh.

[36]The Egyptian frontier station facing Sinai, probably near modern Kantarah. cf. pp. 416, 478.

[37]He introduced the Asiatics to the Egyptians.

[38]The capital in the Faiyum. Si-nuhe traveled on a boat with its own kitchen.

[39]Ten were assigned to summon him and ten to escort him.

[40]Foreigners.

[41]A playful designation of Si-nuhe, on his return from Asia, as "Son of the North Wind."

[42]Si-nuhe's new rank is to be established by a change of dress in a properly designated place.

[43]Painted decorations. "Cool room" may have been either a bathroom or a cellar for preserving foods.

given a house *which had a garden,* which had been in the possession of a courtier. Many *craftsmen* built it, and all its wood (work) was newly restored. Meals were brought to me from the palace three or four times a day, apart from that which the royal children gave, without ceasing a moment.

(300) There was constructed for me a pyramid-tomb of stone in the midst of the pyramid-tombs. The stone-masons who hew a pyramid-tomb took over its ground-area. The outline-draftsmen designed in it; the chief sculptors carved in it; and the overseers of works who are in the necropolis made it their concern. (305) Its necessary materials were made from all the outfittings which are placed at a tomb-shaft. Mortuary priests were given to me. There was made for me a necropolis garden, with fields in it *formerly (extending)* as far as the town, like that which is done for a chief courtier. My statue was overlaid with gold, and its skirt was of fine gold. It was his majesty who had it made. There is no poor man for whom the like has been done.

(So) I was under (310) the favor of the king's presence until the day of mooring had come.[44]

IT HAS COME (TO ITS END), FROM BEGINNING TO END AS IT HAD BEEN FOUND IN WRITING.

---

[44]Until the day of death. Gardiner has pointed out that the story resembles an autobiography prepared for a tomb wall, and "its nucleus may be derived from the tomb of a real Sinuhe, who led a life of adventure in Palestine and was subsequently buried at Lisht" (*Notes on the Story of Sinuhe,* 168).

THE STORY OF TWO BROTHERS

The vast majority of ancient written sources were composed by the elite, about the elite, and for the elite. But sources such as folk tales provide rare but precious glimpses into the lives of the so-called "silent peoples of antiquity", the vast majority of who were peasants. This folk tale concerns a peasant family from ancient Egypt consisting of two brothers (Aubis and Bata) and the wife of the elder brother (Anubis). The names of the two brothers are also the names of two Egyptian gods and the story clearly has many mythological and supernatural elements. Yet the setting also provides many interesting details about Egyptian peasant life, such as cultivating grain and raising cattle, which have the ring of truth. Such folk tales, which likely were also recounted orally, clearly had value as entertainment for their audience but also often offered moral teaching.

The plot has often been compared to the Biblical story of Joseph and Potiphar's wife, also placed in Egypt, in the book of Genesis.

The earliest surviving manuscript dates to the New Kingdom (ca. 1200 B.C.) but the original date of composition and its author are unknown.

NOW THEY SAY THAT (ONCE) THERE WERE two brothers of one mother and one father. Anubis was the name of the elder, and Bata[1] was the name of the younger. Now, as for Anubis, he {had} a house and had a wife, {and} his younger brother (lived) with him as a sort of minor. He was the one who made clothes for him and went to the fields driving his cattle. He was the one who did the plowing and who harvested for him. He was the one who did all (kinds of) work for him which are in the fields. Really, his younger {brother} was a good (grown) man. There was no one like him in the entire land. Why, the strength of a god was in him.

{NOW} AFTER MANY DAYS AFTER THIS,[2] his younger brother (5) {was tending} his cattle in his custom of every {day}, and he {left off} (to go) to his house every evening, loaded {with} all (kinds of) plants of the field, {with} milk, with wood, and {with} every {good thing of} the fields, and he laid them in front of his {elder brother}, who was sitting with his wife. And he drank and he ate, and {he *went out to sleep* in} his stable among his cattle {*by himself*}.

NOW WHEN IT WAS DAWN AND A SECOND DAY HAD COME, {he *prepared food*}, which was cooked, and laid it before his elder brother. {And he} gave him bread for the fields. And he drove his cattle out to let them feed in the fields. He went along after his cattle, {and} they would say to him: "The grass {of} such-and-such a place is good," and he would understand whatever they said and would take them to the place (ii I) of good grass which they wanted. So the cattle which were before him became very, very fine. They doubled their calving very, very much.

NOW AT THE TIME OF plowing his {elder} brother said to him: "Get a yoke {*of oxen*} ready for us for plowing, for the fields have come out, and it is fine for plowing. Also come to the fields with seed, for we shall be busy (with) plowing {in} the morning." So he spoke to him. THEN {his} (5) younger brother did all the things which his elder brother had told him to {do}.

NOW WHEN IT WAS DAWN {AND A SECOND} DAY HAD COME, they went to the fields with their {seed}, and they were busy {with} plowing, and {their hearts} were very, very pleased with their activity at the beginning of {their} work.

---

[1]On the god Bata, see V. Vikentiev, in *JEA*, XVII (1931), 71–80.
[2]The unthinking formula of a storyteller making a transition in his narrative.

Now [after] many [days] after this,[2] they were in the fields and ran short of seed. Then he sent his younger brother, saying: "Go and fetch us seed from the village." And his younger brother found the wife of his elder brother sitting and doing her hair. Then he said to her: "Get up and give me (some) seed, (iii I) for my younger[3] brother is waiting for me. Don't delay!" Then she said to him: "Go and open the bin and take what you want! Don't make me leave my combing unfinished!" Then the lad went into his stable, and he took a big jar, for he wanted to carry off a lot of seed. So he loaded himself with barley and emmer and came out carrying them.

Then she said to him: "How much (is it) that is on your shoulder?" [And he] said to her: (5) "Three sacks of emmer, two sacks of barley, five in all, is what is on your shoulder."[4] So he spoke to her. Then she [talked with] him, saying "There is [great] strength in you! Now I see your energies every day!" And she wanted to know him as one knows a man.

Then she stood up and took hold of him and said to him: "Come, let's spend an [hour] sleeping (together)! This will do you good, because I shall make fine clothes for you!" Then the lad [became] like a leopard with [great] rage at the wicked suggestion which she had made to him, and she was very, very much frightened. Then he argued with her, saying: "See here—you are like a mother to me, and your husband is like a father to me! Because—being older than I—he was the one who brought me up. What (iv I) is this great crime which you have said to me? Don't say it to me again! And I won't tell it to a single person, nor will I let it out of my mouth to any man!" And he lifted up his load, and he went to the fields. Then he reached his elder brother, and they were busy with activity (at) their work.

Now at the [time] of evening, then his elder brother left off (to go) to his house. And his younger brother tended his cattle, and [he] loaded himself with everything of the fields, and he took his cattle (5) in front of him, to let them sleep (in) their stable which was in the village.

But the wife of his elder brother was afraid (because of) the suggestion which she had made. Then she took fat and grease,[5] and she became like one who has been criminally beaten, wanting to tell her husband: "It was your younger brother who did the beating!" And her husband left off in the evening, after his custom of everyday, and he reached his house, and he found his wife lying down, terribly sick. She did not put water on his hands, after his custom, nor had she lit a light before him, and his house was in darkness, and she lay (there) vomiting. So her husband said to her: "Who has been talking with you?" Then she said to him: "Not one person has been talking with me except your (v I) younger brother. But when he came [to] take the seed to you he found me sitting alone, and he said to me 'Come, let's spend an hour sleeping (together)! Put on your curls!'[6] So he spoke to me. But I wouldn't listen to him: 'Aren't I your mother?—for your elder brother is like a father to you!' So I spoke to him. But he was afraid, and he beat (me), so as not to let me tell you. Now, if you let him live, I'll kill myself! Look, when he comes, *don't [let him speak]*, for, if I accuse (him of) this wicked suggestion, he will be ready to do it *tomorrow (again)*!"

Then his elder brother became (5) like a leopard, and he made his lance sharp, and he put it in his hand. Then his elder (brother) stood behind the door (of) his stable to kill his younger brother when he came back in the evening to put his cattle in the stable.

Now when the sun was setting, he loaded himself (with) all plants of the fields, according to his custom of every day, and he came back. When the first cow came into the stable, she said to her herdsman: "Here your elder brother waiting before you, carrying his lance to kill you! Run away from him!" Then he understood what his first cow had said. And (vi I) another went in and she said the same. So he looked under the door his stable, and he saw the feet of [his] elder brother, as he was waiting behind the door, with his lance in his hand. So he laid his load on the ground, and he started to run away and escape. And his elder brother went after him, carrying his lance.

Then his younger brother prayed to the Re-Har-akhti, (5) saying: "O my good lord, thou art he who judges the wicked from the just!" Thereupon the Re heard all his pleas, and the Re made a great (body of) water appear between him and his elder (brother), and it was full of crocodiles. So one of them came to be on one side and the other on the other. And his elder brother struck his hand twice because of his not killing him. Then his younger brother called to him from the (other) side, saying: "Wait here until dawn. When the sun disc rises, I shall (vii I) be

[3]*Sic,* but read "elder."
[4]*Sic,* but read "my shoulder." He was carrying more than 11 bushels.
[5]It has been suggested that these were to make her vomit.
[6]The wig of her festive attire.

judged with you in his presence, and he will turn the wicked over to the just, for I won't be with you ever [*again*]; I won't be in a place where you are—I shall go to the Valley of the Cedar!"[7]

Now WHEN IT WAS DAWN AND A SECOND DAY HAD COME, the Re-Har-akhti arose, and one of them saw the other. THEN the lad argued with his elder brother, saying: "What do you (mean by) coming after me to kill (me) falsely, when you wouldn't listen to what I had to say? Now I am still your younger brother, and (5) you are like a father to me, and your wife is like a mother to me! Isn't it so? When I was sent to fetch us (some) seed, your wife said to me: 'Come, let's spend an hour sleeping (together)!' But, look, it is twisted for you into something else!" THEN HE let him know all that had happened to him and his wife. THEN HE swore to the Re-Har-akhti, saying "As for your killing (me) falsely, you carried your lance on the word of a filthy whore!" And he took a reed-knife, and he cut off his phallus, and he threw it into the water. And the shad swallowed (it).[8] And he (viii I) was faint and became weak. And his elder brother's heart was very, very sad, and he stood weeping aloud for him. He could not cross over to where his younger brother was because of the crocodiles. . . .

THEN (the younger brother) went (7) off to the Valley of the Cedar, and his elder brother went off to his house, with his hand laid upon his head, and he was smeared with dust.[9] So he reached his house, and he killed his wife, and he threw her out (to) the dogs. And he sat in mourning for his younger brother. . . .

The story continues with a number of episodes.

---

[7]In the poem on Ramses II's battle at Kadesh on the Orontes, the Valley of the Cedar appears to be in or near the Lebanon. cf. p. 256 below. cf. JEA, XIX (1933), 128.

[8]The mutilation was a self-imposed ordeal to support his oath to the sun-god. There was a familiar element in the swallowing of the phallus by the fish. In the Plutarch account of the Osiris myths, it is related that Seth dismembered Osiris and scattered the pieces. Then Isis went about and buried each piece as she found it. However, she could not find the phallus, which had been thrown into the river and eaten by certain fishes, which thereby became forbidden food.

[9]Thus showing his grief.

THE EXPULSION OF THE HYKSOS

The Hyksos ("the rulers of foreign lands") were largely Semites from the Levant. They had migrated into Egypt during the Second Intermediate Period (whether by invasion and/or gradual infiltration). For the next century (after ca. 1670 B.C.) the Hyksos ruled much of the Nile valley from their capital at Avaris in the eastern Delta. Their power was based in part on newly imported military technology, such as the horse-drawn chariot, which they introduced into Egypt.

Beginning about 1570 B.C. native Egyptian pharaohs of the XVII dynasty from Thebes in Upper Egypt began driving the Hyksos out of Egypt. One of the few contemporary sources for these events is the autobiography of Ahmose, who served as a soldier in the Egyptian army. Many such tomb biographies are known from Egypt but most describes the lives of civilian bureaucrats. The story of Ahmose is one of the few military biographies now extant. The son of a soldier, Ahmose rose in the ranks from a common soldier (a kind of marine serving aboard an Egyptian naval vessel) to be a ship captain. He eventually died as a wealthy landowner and thus able to afford such a tomb inscribed with his autobiography in his hometown in Upper Egypt.

The historical value of this autobiography is clear. It offers a detailed account by an eyewitness and participant to these events. But also think carefully about the potential bias in any such autobiographical sources.

The commander of a crew, Ah-mose, son of Eben, the triumphant, says:

I speak to you, all mankind, that I may let you know the favors which have come to me. I have been awarded gold seven times in the presence of the entire land, and male and female slaves in like manner, and I have been vested with very many fields.[1] The reputation of a valiant man is from what he has done, not being destroyed in this land forever.[2]

He speaks thus:

I had my upbringing in the town of el-Kab, my father being a soldier of the King of Upper and Lower Egypt: Seqnen-Re, the triumphant,[3] his name being Bebe, (5) the son of (the woman) Ro-onet. Then I served as soldier in his place in the ship, "The Wild Bull," in the time of the Lord of the Two Lands: Neb-pehti-Re, the triumphant,[4] when I was (still) a boy, before I had taken a wife, (but) while I was (still) sleeping in a *net hammock*.[5]

But after I had set up a household, then I was taken on the ship, "Northern," because I was valiant. Thus I used to accompany the Sovereign—life, prosperity, health!—on foot, following his excursions in his chariot.[6] When the town of Avaris was besieged,[7] then I showed valor on foot in the presence of his majesty. Thereupon I was appointed to the ship, "Appearing in Memphis." Then there was fighting on the water in *the canal PaDjedku* of Avaris. Thereupon I made a capture, (10) and I carried away a hand.[8] It was reported to the king's herald. Then the Gold of Valor

---

[1]In his tomb, Ah-mose gives a list of 9 male and 10 female slaves which were his booty; see n.11 below. His grants of land from the king came to something like 70 acres.

[2]As B. Gunn has pointed out (*JEA*, XII [1926], 283), this is a proverb which occurs three times in 18th dynasty inscriptions.

[3]One of the pharaohs named Seqnen-Re in the 17th dynasty.

[4]Ah-mose I.

[5]Perhaps: "I was (still) sleeping with the phallic sheath attached"? So B. Grdseloff, in *ASAE*, XLIII (1943), 357.

[6]Note the first use of the horse and chariot by the Egyptians. The Hyksos had introduced this war force into Egypt.

[7]"When one sat down at the town of Avaris." We are abruptly confronted with a curt statement that the Egyptians attacked the Hyksos in the latter's capital in the eastern Delta. It is significant that the following sentence names a boat as "He Who Has (Ceremonial) Appearance in Memphis," suggesting that Memphis had already been recaptured by the Egyptians.

[8]It was an Egyptian army custom to cut off the hand of a dead enemy as a proof of killing.

---

was given to me. There-upon there was fighting again in this place. Then I made a capture again there and brought away a hand. Then the Gold of Valor was given to me over again.

Then there was fighting in the Egypt which is south of this town.[9] Thereupon I carried off a man (as) living prisoner. I went down into the water—now he was taken captive on the side of the town[10]—and crossed over the water carrying him. Report was made to the king's herald. Thereupon I was awarded gold another time.

Then Avaris was despoiled. Then I carried off spoil from there: one man, three women, a total of four persons. Then his majesty gave them to me to be slaves.[11]

Then (15) Sharuhen was besieged for three years.[12] Then his majesty despoiled it. Thereupon I carried off spoil from there: two women and a hand. Then the Gold of Valor was given to me, *and* my spoil was given to me to be slaves.

Now after his majesty had killed the Asiatics, then he sailed southward to Khenti-hen-nefer, to destroy the Nubian nomads. . . .[13]

After this (Thut-mose I) went forth to Retenu,[14] to assuage his heart throughout the foreign countries. His majesty reached Naharin,[15] (37) and his majesty—life, prosperity, health!—found that enemy[16] while he was mar-shaling the battle array. Then his majesty made a great slaughter among them. There was no number to the living prisoners whom his majesty carried off by his victory. Now I was in the van of our army,[17] and his majesty saw how valiant I was. I carried off a chariot, its horse, and him who was in it as a living prisoner. They were presented to his majesty. Then I was awarded gold another time. . . .[18]

[9]South of Avaris. This looks like a temporary retirement by the Egyptians.

[10]Beside the town, but across a body of water from the Egyptian army.

[11]In Ah-mose's "list of the male and female slaves of the spoil," most of the 19 names are good Egyptian. However, there appear a pa-'Aam, "The Asiatic," a T'amutj, which is a feminine name similar to Amos, and an Ishtar-ummi, "Ishtar is My Mother."

[12]"Then one sat down at Sharuhen in three years." Sharuhen (Josh. 19:6) lay in the extreme southwestern corner of the land of Canaan, in the territory of the tribe of Simeon. Perhaps it was modern Tell el-Fâr'ah. It seems that it was the first stronghold of the Hyksos on their departure from Egypt. "In three years" is a little strange and may mean in three successive campaigning seasons, rather than an unbroken siege.

[13]This translation omits the account of campaigns in Nubia under Ahmose I, Amen-hotep I, and Thut-mose I, and resumes with the record of an Asiatic campaign under Thut-mose I, when Ah-mose must have been a relatively old man.

[14]Syria-Palestine in general.

[15]"The Two Rivers," the area of the Euphrates bend.

[16]"That fallen one," a frequent designation of a major enemy.

[17]It has been pointed out that only in the stretch of patriotic enthusiasm of the first century of the 18th dynasty did the Egyptians speak of "our army," instead of ascribing the troops to the pharaoh.

[18]Two more documents may be cited on Ah-mose I's campaigning in Asia. In the tomb of a certain Ah-mose called Pen-Nekhbet at el-Kab (Sethe, *op.cit.,* 35; Breasted, *op.cit.,* §20), a notation runs: "I followed the King of Upper and Lower Egypt: Neb-pehti-Re, the triumphant. I took booty for him in Djahi: I person and I hand." In a text of Ah-mose I's 22nd year in the quarries of Maâsara, south of Cairo (Sethe, *op.cit.,* 25; Breasted, *op.cit.,* §27), there is a record of the reopening of the quarries for stone to be used in certain temples. Part of the inscription runs: "The stone was dragged by the cattle which his [*victories*] throughout the lands of the Fenkhu had carried off." The accompanying scene shows Asiatics driving the cattle. Djahi and Fenkhu apply to the Phoenician coast running down into Palestine and including the hinterland—further north than southern Palestine.

THE ASIATIC CAMPAIGNS OF THUTMOSE III

The First Campaign:
The Battle of Megiddo

Thutmose III (reigned ca. 1479-1425 B.C.) was one of the greatest pharaohs of the New Kingdom. He was the sixth king of the XVIII dynasty. A mere boy at his ascension, he shared power with his stepmother and his father's principal queen, Hatshepsut, who actually ruled Egypt as pharaoh during the first twenty-two years of his reign. Upon her death Thutmose assumed full power and launched the first of many campaigns seeking to expand Egyptian power outside the Nile Valley. He conquered an extensive empire, extending from northern Syria deep into Nubia to the south of Egypt.

The following is an "official account" of his first campaign, providing a detailed narrative. The first portion was inscribed on a granite stela, found in Upper Egypt. The second and much longer account was inscribed on the walls of the great temple of Amon-Re (the chief god of Egypt and often described as the father of the pharaoh) at Karnak, in Upper Egypt near Thebes, the royal capital. The campaign culminates in a decisive battle between the Egyptians and a Canaanite army formed by an alliance of city-states, centered on the strategic city of Megiddo in northern Palestine. This is the first of several significant battles fought near this site over the millennia.

When analyzing any such an "official" account, consider the intended audience for whom it was written. Further, although the inscriptions contain many specific details, also consider what kind of information is missing from this account.

A. The Armant Stela

A red granite stela, broken and reused in later constructions, was found at Armant in Upper Egypt. Here only the material of the first campaign is translated.

Live the Horus: Mighty Bull, Appearing in Thebes; the Two Goddesses: Enduring of Kingship, like Re in Heaven; the Horus of Gold: Majestic of Appearances, Mighty of Strength; the King of Upper and Lower Egypt, Lord of the Two Lands, Lord of Making Offerings: Men-kheper-Re; the Son of Re, of his Body: Thut-mose Heqa-Maat, beloved of Montu, Lord of Thebes, Residing in Hermonthis,[1] living forever.

Year 22, 2nd month of the second season, day 10.[2] Summary of the deeds of valor and victory which this good god performed, being every effective deed of heroism, beginning from the first generation; that which the Lord of the Gods, the Lord of Hermonthis, did for him: the magnification of his victories, to cause that his deeds of valor

---

[1]Hermonthis is modern Armant.

[2]For the first twenty-two years of his reign, Thut-mose III had been over shadowed by the queen Hat-shepsut. Then he seized power with some show of violence and indulged his desire for military activity almost immediately. The present date is two and a half months earlier than Thut-mose's departure from the Egyptian frontier (n.9 below), Drower, *op.cit.,* 183 n. *b*, suggests that the present date may be the beginning of his sole reign.

---

be related for millions of years to come, apart from the deeds of heroism which his majesty did at all times. If (they) were to be related all together by their names, they would be (too) numerous to put them into writing. . . .

His majesty made no delay in proceeding to the land of (10) Djahi,[3] to kill the treacherous ones who were in it and to give things to those who were loyal to him; *witness, indeed, {their} names, each {country} according to its time.* His majesty returned on each occasion, when his attack had been effected in valor and victory, so that he caused Egypt to be in its condition as (it was) when Re was in it as king. [*Year 22, 4th month of the second season, day . . . Proceeding*] from Memphis,[4] to slay the countries of the wretched Retenu, on the first occasion of victory. It was his majesty who opened its roads and forced its every way for his army after *it had made {rebellion, gathered in Megiddo.* His majesty entered upon that road which becomes very narrow,[5] as the first of his entire army, while every country had gathered, standing prepared at its mouth. . . . The enemy quailed, fleeing headlong to their town, together with the prince who was in . . . (15) . . . to them, beseeching [*breath*], their goods upon their backs. His majesty returned in gladness of heart, with this entire land as vassal . . . [*Asia*]*tics, coming at one time, bearing [their] tribute . . .*

B. The Annals in Karnak

The "Annals" of Thut-mose III's military campaigns are carved on the walls of the Temple of Karnak, in recognition of the fact that the god Amon-Re had given victory.

The Horus: Mighty Bull, Appearing in Thebes; . . . (Thut-mose III).[6]

His majesty commanded that [the victories which his father Amon had given to him] should be established [upon] a monument in the temple which his majesty had made for [his father Amon, in order to set down] (5) each individual campaign,[7] together with the booty which [his majesty] carried [off from it, *and the dues of*] every [*foreign country*] which his father Re had given to him.

Year 22, 4th month of the second season, day 25.[8] [*His majesty passed the fortress of*] Sile,[9] on the first campaign of victory [*which his majesty made to extend*] the frontiers of Egypt, in valor, [in victory, in power, and in justification]. Now this was a [long] time in years . . . (10) plunder, while every man *was [tributary]* before . . .[10] But it happened in later times[11] that the garrison which was there was in the town of Sharuhen,[12] while from Iursa to the outer ends of the earth[13] had become rebellious against his majesty.[14]

Year 23, 1st month of the third season, day 4, the day of the feast of the king's coronation—as far as the town of "That-Which-the-Ruler-Seized," [*of which the Syrian name is*] Gaza.[15]

---

[3]Centrally Phoenicia, but here Syria-Palestine.

[4]The formal departure from Memphis must have preceded the passing of the Egyptian frontier (n.9 below).

[5]The pass through the Carmel range leading to Megiddo; cf. n.20 below.

[6]The royal titulary, much as translated above for the Armant Stela.

[7]"An expedition by its name." cf. n.39 below.

[8]Tentatively, April 16, 1468 B.C., accepting, for this translation, the date for the battle of Megiddo (n.35 below), as given by L. Borchardt, *Die Mittel zur zeitlichen Festlegung von Punkten der ägyptischen Geschichte* (*Quellen und Forschungen zur ägyptischen Geschichte*, II, Cairo, 1935), 120. The precise date will depend upon an establishment of what the ancient Egyptians meant by a "new moon."

[9]Or Tjaru, the Egyptian frontier post, at or near modern Kantarah.

[10]Sethe (see his justification in *ZÄeS,* XLVII [1910], 74–84) restores a context referring to the Hyksos rule in Egypt, as a forerunner of the present "revolt" in Palestine: "Now it was a [long] time in years [that they had ruled this land, which had been] plundered, while every man was [tributary] before [their princes, who were in Avaris]." This is too specific for a restoration. See n.15 below.

[11]"In the times of other (persons)."

[12]In southwestern Canaan; see p. 233b, n.12, above.

[13]From southern Palestine to northern Syria.

[14]Sethe's restoration (n.II above) assumes three steps: (a) the Hyksos ruled Egypt from Avaris; (b) they were driven by Ah-mose I to Sharuhen in Palestine; (c) now, a century later, Asia is in revolt against Thut-mose III—that is, the enemies are these same Hyksos. B. Gunn and A. H. Gardiner, in *JEA,* V (1918), 54, n.2, reject Sethe's restoration as assuming too much. They translate the last sentence: "But it happened in other times that the garrison which was there (i.e. in Palestine) was in Sharühen, when from *Yrḏ* to the ends of the earth had fallen into rebellion against His Majesty." This would take the Hyksos out of the context and would assume that an Asiatic rebellion had pushed back an Egyptian garrison from a northern town (like Megiddo) to Sharuhen at the extreme south of Palestine.

[15]Instead of the above translation, one may render: "as far as a town of the holding of the Ruler, [of which the name was] Gaza . . ." On Borchardt's reckoning, the Egyptians reached Gaza on April 25, 1468, having traveled at the respectable rate of 150 miles in 9 or 10 days. As this date was the anniversary of Thut-mose III's coronation, the year number changed from 22 to 23.

[Year 23,] (15) 1st month of the third season, day 5—departure from this place, in valor, [in victory,] in power, and in justification, in order to overthrow that wretched enemy,[16] and to extend the frontiers of Egypt, according to the command of his father Amon-Re, the [valiant] and victorious, that he should capture.

Year 23, 1st month of the third season, day 16[17]—as far as the town of Yehem. [His majesty] ordered a conference with his victorious army, speaking as follows: "That [wretched] enemy (20) of Kadesh has come and has entered into Megiddo. He is [there] at this moment. He has gathered to him the princes of [every] foreign country [which had been] loyal to Egypt, as well as (those) as far as Naharin and M [itanni], them of Hurru, them of Kode, their horses, their armies, [and their people], for he says—so it is reported—'I shall wait [here] (25) in Megiddo [to fight against his majesty].' Will ye tell me [what is in your hearts]?"[18]

They said in the presence of his majesty: "What is it like to go [on] this [road] which becomes (so) narrow? It is [reported] that the foe is there, waiting on [the outside, while they are] becoming (more) numerous. Will not horse (have to) go after [horse, and the army] (30) and the people similarly? Will the vanguard of us be fighting while the [rear guard] is waiting here in Aruna, unable to fight?[19] Now two (other) roads are here. One of the roads—behold, it is [to the east of] us, so that it comes out at Taanach. The other—behold, it is to the (35) north side of Djefti, and we will come out to the north of Megiddo.[20] Let our victorious lord proceed on the one of [them] which is [satisfactory to] his heart, (but) do not make us go on that difficult road!"

Then messages [were brought in *about that wretched enemy, and discussion was continued*] of [that] problem on which they had previously spoken. That which was said in the majesty of the Court—life, prosperity, health![21]—"I [swear], (40) as Re loves me, as my father Amon favors me, as my [nostrils] are rejuvenated with life and satisfaction, my majesty shall proceed upon this Aruna road! Let him of you who wishes go upon these roads of which you speak, and let him of you who wishes come in the following of my majesty! 'Behold,' they will say, these (45) enemies whom Re abominates, 'has his majesty set out on another road because he has become afraid of us?'—so they will speak."

They said in the presence of his majesty: "May thy father Amon, Lord of the Thrones of the Two Lands, Presiding over Karnak, act [*according to thy desire*]! Behold, we are following thy majesty everywhere that [thy majesty] goes, for a servant will be after [his] lord."

[*Then* his majesty *laid a charge*] (50) upon the entire army: "[Ye] shall [*hold fast to the stride of your victorious lord on*] that road which becomes (so) na[rrow. Behold, his majesty has taken] an oath, saying: 'I will not let [my victorious army] go forth ahead of my majesty in [this place!'" *Now his majesty had laid it in his heart*] that he himself should go forth at the head of his army. [Every man] was made aware (55) of his order of march, horse following horse, while [his majesty] was at the head of his army.

Year 23, 1st month of the third season, day 19[22]—the awakening in [life] in the tent of life, prosperity, and health, at the town of Aruna.[23] Proceeding northward by my majesty, carrying my father Amon-Re, Lord of the Thrones of the Two Lands, [that he might open the ways] before me,[24] while Har-akhti established [*the heart of my victorious army*] (60) and my father Amon strengthened the arm [of my majesty]. . . .

Then [his] majesty issued forth[25] [at the head of] his [army], which was [prepared] in many ranks. [He had not met] a single [enemy. Their] southern wing[26] was in Taanach, [while their] nothern wing was on the south

---

[16]Not yet specified by name or title. The Prince of Kadesh—probably Kadesh on the Orontes—was the leader of the coalition against Egypt. See n.19 below.

[17]May 7, 1468 (Borchardt). After leaving the Egyptian-held city of Gaza, the army's rate was notably slower through territory which was actually or potentially rebellious. Perhaps 80 miles were covered in 11 or 12 days. Yehem (possibly Jahmai or similar) is tentatively located by Nelson at Yemma on the south side of the Carmel ridge.

[18]It is probable from the nature of this coalition and from Thut-mose's subsequent campaigns that this Kadesh was the city on the Orontes. The Barkal Stela (p. 238) gives the coalition as 330 princes, i.e. rulers of city states. Naharin and Mitanni (restoration not certain) were at the bend of the Euphrates. Hurru (or Kharu) was generally Syria-Palestine, and Kode the coast of north Syria and of Cilicia.

[19]Nelson's topographic reconstruction gives the situation confronting the Egyptians. If they went straight ahead on the narrow track debouching just south of Megiddo, they had to go in single file and would be particularly vulnerable. Aruna, perhaps modern Tell 'Ără in the pass, was not "here" at Yehem, since it was a few miles further north. It was "here" on the southern side of the mountain range.

[20]Two safer mountain tracks were offered as alternatives, one debouching at Taanach, 4 or 5 miles southeast of Megiddo, and one debouching at an unknown point north (west) of Megiddo.

[21]That is, the voice from the throne. The Court moved with the pharaoh.

[22]Three days after the arrival in Yehem. See n.18 above, n.35 below.

[23]An impersonal expression for the beginning of the day with the king's awaking.

[24]The standard of Amon led the way. See it thus leading the way in the time of Ramses III, in the Epigraphic Survey, *Medinet Habu, I. The Earlier Historical Records of Ramses III* (OIP, VIII, Chicago, 1930), Pl. 17.

[25]From the pass on to the Megiddo plain.

[26]"Horn." This was the Asiatic wing. Why they were drawn up opposite the mouth of the pass and yet had not held the pass against the thin Egyptian line is inexplicable.

side [of *the Qina Valley.*[27] Then] (65) his majesty *rallied them saying*: ". . . ! They are fallen![28] While that [wretched] enemy . . . [*May*] ye [*give praise*] to (70) [*him; may ye extol the might of*] his majesty, because his arm is greater than (that of) [*any king. It has indeed protected the rear of*] his majesty's army in Aruna!"

Now while the rear of his majesty's victorious army was (still) at [the town] of Aruna, the vanguard had come out into the [Qi]na Valley, and they filled the mouth of this valley.

Then they said to his majesty—life, prosperity, health!—(75) "Behold, his majesty has come forth with his victorious army, and they have filled the valley. Let our victorious lord listen to us this time, and let our lord await for us the rear of his army and his people. When the rear of the army comes forth for us into the open, then we shall fight against these foreigners, then we shall not trouble our hearts [about] the rear of (80) our army."

A halt was made by his majesty outside, [*seated*] there and awaiting the rear of his victorious army. Now the [*leaders*] had just finished coming forth on this road when the shadow turned.[29] His majesty reached the south of Megiddo on the bank of the Qina brook, when the seventh hour was in (its) course in the day.[30]

Then a camp was pitched there for his majesty, and a charge was laid upon the entire army, [saying]: "Prepare ye! Make your weapons ready, since one[31] will engage in combat with that wretched enemy in the morning, because one is . . .!"

Resting in the enclosure of life, prosperity, and health.[32] Providing for the officials. *Issuing rations* to the retinue. Posting the sentries of the army. Saying to them: "Be steadfast, be steadfast! Be vigilant, be vigilant!" Awakening in life in the tent of life, prosperity, and health. They came to tell his majesty: "The desert is well,[33] and the garrisons of the south and north also!"

Year 23, 1st month of the third season, day 21, the day of the feast of the *true* new moon.[34] Appearance of the king at dawn. Now a charge was laid upon the entire army to *pass by* . . . (85) His majesty set forth in a chariot of fine gold, adorned with his accoutrements of combat, like Horus, the Mighty of Arm, a lord of action like Montu, the Theban, while his father Amon made strong his arms. The southern wing of his majesty's army was at a hill south of [the] Qina [*brook*], and the northern wing was to the northwest of Megiddo, while his majesty was in their center, Amon being the protection of his person (in) the melee and the strength of [*Seth pervading*] his members.

Thereupon his majesty prevailed over them at the head of his army. Then they saw his majesty prevailing over them, and they fled headlong [to] Megiddo with faces of fear. They abandoned their horses and their chariots of gold and silver, so that someone might draw them (up) into this town by *hoisting* on their garments. Now the people had shut this town against them, (but) they [let down] garments to *hoist* them up into this town. Now, if only his majesty's army had not given up their hearts to capturing the possessions of the enemy, they would [have captured] Megiddo at this time, while the wretched enemy of Kadesh and the wretched enemy of this town were being dragged (up) *hastily* to get them into their town, for the fear of his majesty entered [their bodies], their arms were weak, [*for*] his serpent-diadem had overpowered them.

Then their horses and their chariots of gold and silver were captured as an easy [prey.[35] *Ranks*] of them were lying stretched out on their backs, like fish in the *bight of a net,* while his majesty's victorious army counted up their possessions. Now there was captured [that] wretched [enemy's] tent, which was worked [with *silver*], . . .

Then the entire army rejoiced and gave praise to Amon [because of the victory] which he had given to his son on [this day. They *lauded*] his majesty and extolled his victories. Then they presented the plunder which they had taken: hands,[36] living prisoners, horses, and chariots of gold and silver and of *painted work.* (90). . . .

---

[27]The Qina is still represented by a brook flowing south of Megiddo.

[28]The preceding verb means "summon," rather than "cry out." Therefore, we should have Thut-mose's rallying cry to his army behind him. When he said: "They are fallen!" he was anticipating the fall of the Asiatics, because they had failed to guard the pass.

[29]It was noon, and the shadow clock should be turned around. The Egyptian van thus reached the Megiddo plain seven hours (see the next note) before the rear of the army emerged and Thut-mose could go into camp.

[30]Presumably seven hours after the turning of the sun, although this is not certain.

[31]Pharaoh.

[32]These brief notations, without true sentence form, probably derive from the army's daybook. The royal enclosure was doubtless an elaborate pavilion such as that shown in scenes of Ramses II's campaigns, e.g. A. Erman and H. Ranke, *Aegypten* (Tübingen, 1923), 635.

[33]Faulkner suggests that this is the equivalent of "The coast is clear."

[34]Borchardt's date for the battle is May 12, 1468. However, this rests on his understanding of "the true(?) new moon." In addition, Faulkner points out that "day 20" seems to have dropped out since the departure from Aruna (n.23 above).

[35]"As a go-[and-take]."

[36]Cut off from the fallen foe as tokens of battle accomplishment.

[Then his majesty commanded] his army with the words: "Capture ye [effectively, my] victorious [army]! Behold, [*all foreign countries*] have been put [*in this town by* the command] of Re on this day, inasmuch as every prince of every [northern] country is shut up within it, for the capturing of Megiddo is the capturing of a thousand towns! Capture ye firmly, firmly! . . ."

[*Orders were issued to* the com]manders of the troops to *pro*[*vide for their divisions and to inform*] each [man] *of* his place. They measured [this] city, which was corralled with a moat and enclosed with fresh timbers of all their pleasant trees, while his majesty himself was in a fortress east of this town, [being] watchful . . . . . . [enclosed] with a girdle wall, . . . *by* its girdle wall. Its name was called "Men-kheper-Re-is-the-Corraller-of-the-Asiatics." People were appointed as sentries at the enclosure of his majesty, and they were told: "Be steadfast, be steadfast! Be vigilant, [be vigilant]!" . . . his majesty. . . . [Not one] of them [was permitted to go] outside from behind this wall, except to come out *at a knock* on the door of their fortress.[37]

Now everything which his majesty did to this town and to that wretched enemy and his wretched army is set down by the individual day, by the individual expedition, and by the individual [troop] commanders.[38] . . . They [are] set down on a roll of leather in the temple of Amon today.

Now the princes of this foreign country came on their bellies to kiss the ground to the glory of his majesty and to beg breath for their nostrils, because his arm was (so) great, because the prowess of Amon was (so) great [over (95) every] foreign [country][39] . . . [all] the princes whom the prowess of his majesty carried off, bearing their tribute of silver, gold, lapis lazuli, and turquoise, and carrying grain, wine, and large and small cattle for the army of his majesty, with one gang of them bearing tribute southward.[40] Then his majesty appointed princes anew for [*every town*]. . . .

[List of the booty which his majesty's army carried off from the town of] Megiddo: 340 living prisoners and 83 hands; 2,041 horses, 191 foals, 6 stallions, and . . . colts; 1 chariot worked with gold, with a *body* of gold, belonging to that enemy, [*I*] fine chariot worked with gold belonging to the Prince of [*Megiddo*] . . . , and 892 chariots of his wretched army—total: 924; I fine bronze coat of mail belonging to that enemy, [*I*] fine bronze coat of mail belonging to the Prince of Meg[iddo, and] 200 [*leather*] coats of mail belonging to his wretched army; 502 bows; and 7 poles of *meru*-wood, worked with silver, of the tent of that enemy.

Now the army [of his majesty] carried off [*cattle*] . . . : 387 . . . , 1,929 cows, 2,000 goats, and 20,500 sheep.

List of what was carried off afterward by the king from the household goods of that enemy, who [was in] Yanoam, Nuges, and Herenkeru,[41] together with the property of those towns which had made themselves subject to him . . . : . . . ; 38 [*maryanu*] belonging to them,[42] 84 children of that enemy and of the princes who were with him, 5 *maryanu* belonging to them, 1,796 male and female slaves, as well as their children, and 103 pardoned persons, who had come out from that enemy because of hunger—total: 2,503—apart from bowls of costly stone and gold, various vessels, (100) . . . , a large *akunu*-jar in Syrian work, jars, bowls, *plates,* various drinking vessels, large kettles, [*x* +] 17 knives—making 1,784 *deben;*[43] gold in discs, found in the process of being worked, as well as abundant silver in discs—966 *deben* and I *kidet;*[44] a silver statue *in the form of* . . . , [*a statue*] . . . , with head of

---

[37]The besieged Asiatics were permitted only to appear if Egyptians called them out? Alternatively: "except to come out to surrender(?) at the door of their fortress." The siege lasted seven months (Barkal Stela, p. 238 below). Further information on the siege is given on a stela from the Ptah Temple at Karnak (Sethe, *op.cit.,* 767): "My majesty returned from the foreign country of Retenu on the first occasion of the victories which my father Amon gave to me, when he gave me all the countries of Djahi, gathered together and shut up in a single town. The fear of my majesty pervaded their hearts; they were fallen and powerless when I reached them. There was no lack of runaways among them. I corralled them in a single town. I built a girdle wall around it, to cut them off from the breath of life."

[38]"On the day in its name, in the name of the journey, and in the names of the commanders of [troops]." In the Theban tomb biography of "the Army Scribe" Tjaneni, who served under Thut-mose III (Sethe, *op.cit.,* 1004), we read: "I was the one who set down the victories which he achieved over every foreign country, put into writing as it was done."

[39]On the surrender, see also the Barkal Stela (p. 238).

[40]Toward Egypt.

[41]Elsewhere in the Temple of Karnak (Sethe, *op.cit.,* 744), Thut-mose III states that he presented to Amon "three towns in Upper Retenu—Nuges the name of one, Yanoam the name of another, and Herenkeru the name of another—taxed with annual dues for the divine offerings of my father Amon." "Upper Retenu" properly stands for the mountain territory of north Palestine and southern Syria, and Yanoam seems to have been in the Lake Huleh area. The three towns would then be somewhere in that area. See A. H. Gardiner, *Ancient Egyptian Onomastica* (London, 1947), 1, 168* ff. We do not know what is meant by "that enemy" being in these towns. The dedicatory inscriptions translated under D below suggest that Thut-mose had time for a campaign in the Lebanon while Megiddo was under siege.

[42]The *maryanu* were the warrior or officer class in Asia at this time. cf. p. 22, n.2. "Belonging to them" refers to listed individuals in the lost context above (474 are missing from the total), and probably includes the women of the Asiatic princes.

[43]About 435 lb. Troy of metal value (probably reckoned in silver) in the listed pieces.

[44]About 235 lb. Troy. Uncertain whether of silver only, or of the combined value of gold and silver.

gold; 3 walking sticks with human heads; 6 carrying-chairs of that enemy, of ivory, ebony, and *carob*-wood, worked with gold, and the 6 footstools belonging to them; 6 large tables of ivory and *carob*-wood; I bed belonging to that enemy, of *carob*-wood, worked with gold and with every (kind of) costly stone, in the manner of a *kerker*,[45] completely worked in gold; a statue of that enemy which was there, of ebony worked with gold, its head of lapis [lazuli] . . . ; bronze vessels, and much clothing of that enemy.

Now the fields were made into arable plots and assigned to inspectors of the palace—life, prosperity, health!—in order to reap their harvest. List of the harvest which his majesty carried off from the Megiddo acres: 207,300 [+ x] sacks of wheat,[46] apart from what was cut as forage by his majesty's army, . . .

[45] An unknown object of wood.
[46] Something like 450,000 bushels.

THE HYMN TO THE ATON

Egyptian religion was polytheistic from its origins and remained so for many centuries thereafter. The chief god was Amon-Re, a solar deity. Pharaohs were viewed as sons of Amon-Re. However, the ascension of Amenhotep IV as pharaoh (reigned ca. 1350-1334 B.C.) inaugurated a radical religious change in favor of a different solar god, the Aton, or sun disk god. This pharaoh changed his name to Akhenaton (possibly meaning "he who is of service to the Aton"), abandoned the royal capital at Thebes, and constructed an entirely new capital on a virgin site far down the Nile called Akhetaton ("Horizon of the Aton", modern site of Tell e-Amarna). More radically, the pharaoh eventually denied the existence of all other gods and may possibly be the first known monotheist in history. As might be expected his attempted religious reform was bitterly opposed by most Egyptians who understandably did not wish to abandon their traditional religion. After the end of his reign (the circumstances of which are unclear) the cult of Aten fell out of favor under his successors. Akhetaton was abandoned and the royal capital returned to Thebes.

The career of Akhenaton and the cult of Atonism are known primarily from inscriptions, particularly from tombs, of royal officials from Akhetaton. Several of these tombs preserve various versions of hymns to the Aton, which represent a kind of theology of Atonism. The following is the so-called "long hymn". It has often been compared to passages in Psalm 104 in the Hebrew Bible (Old Testament).

Praise of Re Har-akhti, Rejoicing on the Horizon, in His Name as Shu Who Is in the Aton-disc,[1] living forever and ever; the living great Aton who is in jubilee, lord of all that the Aton encircles, lord of heaven, lord of earth, lord of the House of Aton in Akhet-Aton;[2] (and praise of) the King of Upper and Lower Egypt, who lives on truth, the Lord of the Two Lands: Nefer-kheperu-Re Wa-en-Re; the Son of Re, who lives on truth, the Lord of Diadems: Akh-en-Aton, long in his lifetime; (and praise of) the Chief Wife of the King, his beloved, the Lady of the Two Lands: Nefer-neferu-Aton Nefert-iti, living, healthy, and youthful forever and ever; (by) the Fan-Bearer on the Right Hand of the King . . . Eye. He says:

> Thou appearest beautifully on the horizon of heaven,
>> Thou living Aton, the beginning of life!
> When thou art risen on the eastern horizon,
>> Thou hast filled every land with thy beauty.
> Thou art gracious, great, glistening, and high over every land;
> Thy rays encompass the lands to the limit of all that thou hast made:
>> As thou art Re, thou reachest to the end of them;[3]
>> (Thou) subduest them (for) thy beloved son.[4]
> Though thou art far away, thy rays are on earth;
> Though thou art in *their* faces, *no one knows thy* going.
>
> When thou settest in the western horizon,
> The land is in darkness, in the manner of death.
> They sleep in a room, with heads wrapped up,
>> Nor sees one eye the other.
> All their goods which are under their heads might be stolen,

[1]The Aton had a dogmatic name written within a royal cartouche and including the three old solar deities, Re, Har-of-the-Horizon, and Shu.

[2]Akhet-Aton was the name of the capital at Tell el-Amarna.

[3]Pun: *Ra* "Re," and *er-ra* "to the end."

[4]Akh-en-Aton.

(But) they would not perceive (it).
Every lion is come forth from his den;
All creeping things, they sting.
Darkness *is a shroud,* and the earth is in stillness,
For he who made them rests in his horizon.[5]

At daybreak, when thou arisest on the horizon,
When thou shinest as the Aton by day,
Thou drivest away the darkness and givest thy rays.
The Two Lands are in festivity *every day,*
Awake and standing upon (their) feet,
For thou hast raised them up.
Washing their bodies, taking (their) clothing,
Their arms are (raised) in praise at thy appearance.
All the world, they do their work.[6]

All beasts are content with their pasturage;
Trees and plants are flourishing.
The birds which fly from their nests,
Their wings are (stretched out) in praise to thy *ka.*
All beasts spring upon (their) feet.
Whatever flies and alights,
They live when thou hast risen (for) them.[7]
The ships are sailing north and south as well,
For every way is open at thy appearance.
The fish in the river dart before thy face;
Thy rays are in the midst of the great green sea.[8]

Creator of seed in women,
Thou who makest fluid into man,
Who maintainest the son in the womb of his mother,
Who soothest him with that which stills his weeping,
Thou nurse (even) in the womb,
Who givest breath to sustain all that he has made!
When he descends from the womb to *breathe*
On the day when he is born,
Thou openest his mouth completely,
Thou suppliest his necessities.
When the chick in the egg speaks within the shell,
Thou givest him breath within it to maintain him.
When thou hast made him his fulfillment within the egg, to break it,
He comes forth from the egg to speak at his completed (time);
He walks upon his legs when he comes forth from it.

How manifold it is, what thou hast made!
They are hidden from the face (of man).
O sole god, like whom there is no other!
Thou didst create the world according to thy desire,
Whilst thou wert alone:[9]
All men, cattle, and wild beasts,

[5]cf. Ps. 104:20–21.
[6]cf. Ps. 104:22–23.
[7]cf. Ps. 104:11–14.
[8]cf. Ps. 104:25–26.
[9]cf. Ps. 104:24.

(5)

Whatever is on earth, going upon (its) feet,
And what is on high, flying with its wings.

The countries of Syria and Nubia, the *land* of Egypt,
Thou settest every man in his place,
Thou suppliest their necessities:
Everyone has his food, and his time of life is reckoned.[10]
Their tongues are separate in speech,
And their natures as well;
Their skins are distinguished,
As thou distinguishest the foreign peoples.
Thou makest a Nile in the underworld,
Thou bringest it forth as thou desirest
To maintain the people (of Egypt)[11]
According as thou madest them for thyself,
The lord of all of them, wearying (himself) with them,
The lord of every land, rising for them,
The Aton of the day, great of majesty.
All distant foreign countries, thou makest their life (also),
For thou hast set a Nile in heaven,
That it may descend for them and make waves upon the mountains,[12]   (10)
Like the great green sea,
To water their fields in their towns.[13]
How effective they are, thy plans, O lord of eternity!
The Nile in heaven, it is for the foreign peoples
And for the beasts of every desert that go upon (their) feet;
(While the true) Nile comes from the underworld for Egypt.

Thy rays suckle every meadow.
When thou risest, they live, they grow for thee.
Thou makest the seasons in order to rear all that thou hast made,
The winter to cool them,
And the heat that *they* may taste thee.
Thou hast made the distant sky in order to rise therein,
In order to see all that thou dost make.
Whilst thou wert alone,
Rising in thy form as the living Aton,
Appearing, shining, *withdrawing or approaching,*
Thou madest millions of forms of thyself alone.
Cities, towns, fields, road, and river—
Every eye beholds thee over against them,
For thou art the Aton of the day over *the earth.* . . .

Thou art in my heart,
And there is no other that knows thee
Save thy son Nefer-kheperu-Re Wa-en-Re,[14]
For thou hast made him well-versed in thy plans and in thy strength.[15]

[10]cf. Ps. 104:27.
[11]The Egyptians believed that their Nile came from the waters under the earth, called by them Nun.
[12]cf. Ps. 104:6, 10.
[13]The rain of foreign countries is like the Nile of rainless Egypt.
[14]Even though the hymn was recited by the official Eye, he states that Akh-en-Aton alone knows the Aton.
[15]Pharaoh was the official intermediary between the Egyptians and their gods. The Amarna religion did not change this dogma.

The world came into being by thy hand,
According as thou hast made them.
When thou hast risen they live,
When thou settest they die.
Thou art lifetime thy own self,
For one lives (only) through thee.
Eyes are (fixed) on beauty until thou settest.
All work is laid aside when thou settest in the west.
(But) when (thou) risest (again),
[*Everything is*] made to flourish for the king, . . .
Since thou didst found the earth
And raise them up for thy son,
Who came forth from thy body:

the King of Upper and Lower Egypt, . . . Akh-en-Aton, . . . and the Chief Wife of the King . . . Nefert-iti, living and youthful forever and ever.

THE BIBLE: OLD TESTAMENT

The Hebrew Bible, called by Christians the Old Testament, was accepted by both Jews and Christians as the divinely inspired word of God (Yahweh). It is the product of many different authors writing over many centuries and thus understandably contains different viewpoints. Nevertheless, the central themes are clear, including providing ethical guidelines for the Jewish people and to demonstrate their special relationship with Yahweh. Many Biblical scholars believe that some portions of the Hebrew Bible may date as early as 1000 B.C. while others were probably not composed until the 2nd century B.C. The main collation and editing appears to have occurred in the 6th century B.C., during the so-called "Babylonian Captivity", although with later additions and revisions. The influence of Mesopotamian religion and culture during this period can clearly be discerned in such books as Genesis.

The first five books of the Bible are known as the Torah (law). The first book, Genesis, begins with two back-to-back creation stories which interestingly differ in significant ways from one another. The story of Adam and Eve explains the origin of evil (the original sin). Yahweh's punishment of sin is portrayed in the Great Flood narrative, which is clearly drawn from the much earlier Mesopotamian flood story from the Epic of Gilgamesh. The salvation of the Hebrews from bondage in Egypt sets the stage for the Covenant between Yahweh and his chosen people. In exchange for their deliverance and selection as the chosen people, the Hebrews will obey Yahweh's Torah or Law, the core of which is delivered to Moses as the Ten Commandments in the book of Exodus. Later passages in this book lay out the law in more detail and reflect a largely agricultural society. Note that the laws reflect a strongly patriarchal society in which slavery is an accepted and normal institution.

Another major portion of the Hebrew Bible/Old Testament is devoted to the books of the prophets, all living after the appearance of the Israelites (the descendants of the Hebrews) in Canaan (ancient Palestine). The prophets were viewed by many Israelites as the mouthpiece of Yahweh. They were strongly critical of the Israelites' failure to follow the Torah and thus the Israelites were guilty of breaking the Covenant. Such prophets as Amos (8th century B.C.) criticized the corruption and hypocrisy they saw among the Israelites, above all the worship of other gods besides Yahweh. In consequence, they predicted future divine punishment of the Israelites, to be delivered by foreign powers. Thus the northern Kingdom of Israel was destroyed by the Assyrians in 721 B.C. and the southern Kingdom of Judah was conquered by the Neo-Babylonians in 586 B.C. This latter event resulted in the destruction of Yahweh's temple in Jerusalem and the exile of several thousand Jews (as the people of Judah were called) to Mesopotamia to endure the "Babylonian Captivity" (586-539 B.C.).

The fortunes of the Jews were now at their nadir. But the so-called Second Isaiah emerged as a prophet in the 6th century B.C. who preached a message of new hope and renewal for the Jews through a "Suffering Servant". Interpretations of this otherwise unnamed "Suffering Servant" vary. It may be describing the Jewish people collectively or it may a prophesize a forthcoming Messiah ("Anointed One"). Centuries later, Christians would interpret this passage as a prediction of the coming of Jesus Christ.

Genesis[1]

The Beginnings of History

1:1–4:16

In the beginning God created the heavens and the earth. The earth was without form and void, and darkness was upon the face of the deep; and the Spirit of God was moving over the face of the waters.

And God said, "Let there be light"; and there was light. And God saw that the light was good; and God separated the light from the darkness. God called the light Day, and the darkness he called Night. And there was evening and there was morning, one day.

And God said, "Let there be a firmament in the midst of the waters, and let it separate the waters from the waters." And God made the firmament and separated the waters which were under the firmament from the waters which were above the firmament. And it was so.[2] And God called the firmament Heaven. And there was evening and there was morning, a second day.

And God said, "Let the waters under the heavens be gathered together into one place, and let the dry land appear." And it was so. God called the dry land Earth, and the waters that were gathered together he called Seas. And God saw that it was good. And God said, "Let the earth put forth vegetation, plants yielding seed, and fruit trees bearing fruit in which is their seed, each according to its kind, upon the earth." And it was so. The earth brought forth vegetation, plants yielding seed according to their own kinds, and trees bearing fruit in which is their seed, each according to its kind. And God saw that it was good. And there was evening and there was morning, a third day.

And God said, "Let there be lights in the firmament of the heavens to separate the day from the night; and let them be for signs and for seasons and for days and years, and let them be lights in the firmament of the heavens to give light upon the earth." And it was so. And God made the two great lights, the greater light to rule the day, and the lesser light to rule the night; he made the stars also. And God set them in the firmament of the heavens to give light upon the earth, to rule over the day and over the night, and to separate the light from the darkness. And God saw that it was good. And there was evening and there was morning, a fourth day.

And God said, "Let the waters bring forth swarms of living creatures, and let birds fly above the earth across the firmament of the heavens." So God created the great sea monsters and every living creature that moves, with which the waters swarm, according to their kinds, and every winged bird according to its kind. And God saw that it was good. And God blessed them, saying, "Be fruitful and multiply and fill the waters in the seas, and let birds multiply on the earth." And there was evening and there was morning, a fifth day.

And God said, "Let the earth bring forth living creatures according to their kinds: cattle[3] and creeping things and beasts of the earth according to their kinds." And it was so. And God made the beasts of the earth according to their kinds and the cattle according to their kinds, and everything that creeps upon the ground according to its kind. And God saw that it was good.

Then God said, "Let us make man in our image, after our likeness; and let them have dominion over the fish of the sea, and over the birds of the air, and over the cattle, and over all the earth, and over every creeping thing that creeps upon the earth."

So God created man in his own image, in the image of God he created him; male and female he created them. And God blessed them, and God said to them, "Be fruitful and multiply, and fill the earth and subdue it; and have dominion over the fish of the sea and over the birds of the air and over every living thing that moves upon the earth." And God said, "Behold, I have given you every plant yielding seed which is upon the face of all the earth, and every tree with seed in its fruit; you shall have them for food. And to every beast of the earth, and to every bird

---

[1]A Greek word meaning "origin" or "birth." Genesis is the first book of the Bible and begins with two versions of the Creation story. It then tells about the expulsion of the first humans from Eden, the first murder, the flood, and the Hebrew founders down to the settling of some of their people in Egypt. Genesis thus introduces the ancestry of the Israelites (Hebrews)—first, like all humanity, from Adam, and then, more particularly, from "Father" Abraham. The book also describes the special relationship and *covenant* (agreement) that God established with Noah, and later with Abraham and his descendants.

[2]This description of God's creative action on the second day rests upon the belief that the world was created out of a watery chaos. The "firmament" was imagined as a sort of solid dome, which separated the "waters above" from the "waters under."

[3]All domestic animals.

of the air, and to everything that creeps on the earth, everything that has the breath of life, I have given every green plant for food." And it was so. And God saw everything that he had made, and behold, it was very good. And there was evening and there was morning, a sixth day.

Thus the heavens and the earth were finished, and all the host of them. And on the seventh day God finished his work which he had done, and he rested on the seventh day from all his work which he had done. So God blessed the seventh day and hallowed it, because on it God rested from all his work which he had done in creation.

These are the generations of the heavens and the earth when they were created.[4]

In the day that the Lord God made the earth and the heavens, when no plant of the field was yet in the earth and no herb of the field had yet sprung up—for the Lord God had not caused it to rain upon the earth, and there was no man to till the ground; but a mist went up from the earth and watered the whole face of the ground—then the Lord God formed man of dust from the ground, and breathed into his nostrils the breath of life; and man became a living being. And the Lord God planted a garden in Eden, in the east; and there he put the man whom he had formed. And out of the ground the Lord God made to grow every tree that is pleasant to the sight and good for food, the tree of life also in the midst of the garden, and the tree of the knowledge of good and evil.

A river flowed out of Eden to water the garden, and there it divided and became four rivers. The name of the first is Pishon; it is the one which flows around the whole land of Hav'ilah, where there is gold; and the gold of that land is good; bdellium and onyx stone are there. The name of the second river is Gihon; it is the one which flows around the whole land of Cush. And the name of the third river is Tigris, which flows east of Assyria. And the fourth river is the Euphra'tes.

The Lord God took the man and put him in the garden of Eden to till it and keep it. And the Lord God commanded the man, saying, "You may freely eat of every tree of the garden; but of the tree of the knowledge of good and evil you shall not eat, for in the day that you eat of it you shall die."

Then the Lord God said, "It is not good that the man should be alone; I will make him a helper fit for him. So out of the ground the Lord God formed every beast of the field and every bird of the air, and brought them to the man to see what he would call them; and whatever the man called every living creature, that was its name. The man gave names to all cattle, and to the birds of the air, and to every beast of the field; but for the man there was not found a helper fit for him. So the Lord God caused a deep sleep to fall upon the man, and while he slept took one of his ribs and closed up its place with flesh; and the rib which the Lord God had taken from the man he made into a woman and brought her to the man. Then the man said,

> "This at last is bone of my bones
> and flesh of my flesh;
> she shall be called Woman,
> because she was taken out of Man."[5]

Therefore a man leaves his father and his mother and cleaves to his wife, and they become one flesh. And the man and his wife were both naked, and were not ashamed.

Now the serpent was more subtle than any other wild creature that the Lord God had made. He said to the woman, "Did God say, 'You shall not eat of any tree of the garden'?" And the woman said to the serpent, "We may eat of the fruit of the trees of the garden; but God said, 'You shall not eat of the fruit of the tree which is in the midst of the garden, neither shall you touch it, lest you die.'" But the serpent said to the woman, "You will not die. For God knows that when you eat of it your eyes will be opened, and you will be like God, knowing good and evil." So when the woman saw that the tree was good for food, and that it was a delight to the eyes, and that the tree was to be desired to make one wise, she took of its fruit and ate; and she also gave some to her husband, and he ate. Then the eyes of both were opened, and they knew that they were naked; and they sewed fig leaves together and made themselves aprons.

And they heard the sound of the Lord God walking in the garden in the cool of the day, and the man and his wife hid themselves from the presence of the Lord God among the trees of the garden. But the Lord God called to the man, and said to him, "Where are you?" And he said, "I heard the sound of thee in the garden, and I was afraid, because I was naked; and I hid myself." He said, "Who told you that you were naked?

---

[4]This sentence begins a second version of the creation; it differs in some significant ways from the first.
[5]In Hebrew, a word for "man" is *ish*; for "woman," *ishshah*.

Have you eaten of the tree of which I commanded you not to eat? The man said, "The woman whom thou gavest to be with me, he gave me the fruit of the tree, and I ate." Then the Lord God said to the woman, "What is this that you have done?" The woman said, "The serpent beguiled me, and I ate." The Lord God said to the serpent,

> "Because you have done this,
> cursed are you above all cattle,
> and above all wild animals;
> upon your belly you shall go,
> and dust you shall eat
> all the days of your life.
> I will put enmity between you and the woman,
> and between your seed [descendants] and her seed;
> he shall bruise your head,
> and you shall bruise his heel."

To the woman he said,

> "I will greatly multiply your pain in childbearing;
> in pain you shall bring forth children,
> yet your desire shall be for your husband,
> and he shall rule over you."

And to Adam[6] he said,

> "Because you have listened to the voice of your wife,
> and have eaten of the tree
> of which I commanded you,
> 'You shall not eat of it,'
> cursed is the ground because of you;
> in toil you shall eat of it all the days of your life;
> thorns and thistles it shall bring forth to you;
> and you shall eat the plants of the field.
> In the sweat of your face
> you shall eat bread
> till you return to the ground,
> for out of it you were taken;
> you are dust,
> and to dust you shall return."

The man called his wife's name Eve, because she was the mother of all living.[7] And the Lord God made for Adam and for his wife garments of skins, and clothed them.

Then the Lord God said, "Behold, the man has become like one of us, knowing good and evil; and now, lest he put forth his hand and take also of the tree of life, and eat, and live for ever"—therefore the Lord God sent him forth from the garden of Eden, to till the ground from which he was taken. He drove out the man; and at the east of the garden of Eden he placed the cherubim,[8] and a flaming sword which turned every way, to guard the way to the tree of life.

Now Adam knew[9] Eve his wife, and she conceived and bore Cain saying, "I have gotten a man with the help of the Lord." And again she bore his brother Abel. Now Abel was a keeper of sheep, and Cain a tiller of the ground. In the course of time Cain brought to the Lord an offering of the fruit of the ground, and Abel brought of the first-ling of his flock and of their fat portions. And the Lord had regard for Abel and his offering, but for Cain and his

[6]Another Hebrew word for "man" or "mankind" is *adam*.
[7]Eve's name, in Hebrew, resembles the word for "living."
[8]Winged, semi-divine creatures who served as guardians of sacred areas.
[9]That is, had sexual intercourse.

offering he had no regard.[10] So Cain was very angry, and his countenance fell. The Lord said to Cain "Why are you angry, and why has your countenance fallen? If you do well, will you not be accepted? And if you do not do well, sin is couching at the door; its desire is for you, but you must master it."

Cain said to Abel his brother, "Let us go out to the field." And when they were in the field, Cain rose up against his brother Abel, and killed him. Then the Lord said to Cain, "Where is Abel your brother?" He said, "I do not know; am I my brother's keeper?" And the Lord said, "What have you done? The voice of your brother's blood is crying to me from the ground. And now you are cursed from the ground, which has opened its mouth to receive your brother's blood from your hand. When you till the ground, it shall no longer yield to you its strength; you shall be a fugitive and a wanderer on the earth." Cain said to the Lord, "My punishment is greater than I can bear. Behold, thou hast driven me this day away from the ground; and from thy face I shall be hidden; and I shall be a fugitive and a wanderer on the earth, and whoever finds me will slay me." Then the Lord said to him, "Not so! if anyone slays Cain, vengeance shall be taken on him sevenfold." And the Lord put a mark[11] on Cain, lest any who came upon him should kill him. Then Cain went away from the presence of the Lord, and dwelt in the land of Nod, east of Eden.

The Flood

6:1–22

When men began to multiply on the face of the ground, and daughters were born to them, the sons of God saw that the daughters of men were fair; and they took to wife such of them as they chose. Then the Lord said, "My spirit shall not abide in man for ever, for he is flesh, but his days shall be a hundred and twenty years." The Nephilim [giants] were on the earth in those days, and also afterward, when the sons of God came in to the daughters of men, and they bore children to them.[12] These were the mighty men that were of old, the men of renown.

The Lord saw that the wickedness of man was great in the earth, and that every imagination of the thoughts of his heart was only evil continually. And the Lord was sorry that he had made man on the earth, and it grieved him to his heart. So the Lord said, "I will blot out man whom I have created from the face of the ground, man and beast and creeping things and birds of the air, for I am sorry that I have made them." But Noah found favor in the eyes of the Lord.

These are the generations of Noah. Noah was a righteous man, blameless in his generation; Noah walked with God. And Noah had three sons, Shem, Ham, and Japheth.

Now the earth was corrupt in God's sight, and the earth was filled with violence. And God saw the earth, and behold, it was corrupt; for all flesh had corrupted their way upon the earth. And God said to Noah, "I have determined to make an end of all flesh; for the earth is filled with violence through them; behold, I will destroy them with the earth. Make yourself an ark of gopher wood; make rooms in the ark, and cover it inside and out with pitch. This is how you are to make it: the length of the ark three hundred cubits,[13] its breadth fifty cubits, and its height thirty cubits. Make a roof for the ark, and finish it to a cubit above; and set the door of the ark in its side; make it with lower, second, and third decks. For behold, I will bring a flood of waters upon the earth, to destroy all flesh in which is the breath of life from under heaven; everything that is on the earth shall die. But I will establish my covenant with you; and you shall come into the ark, you your sons, your wife, and your sons' wives with you. And of every living thing of all flesh, you shall bring two of every sort into the ark to keep them alive with you; they shall be male and female. Of the birds according to their kinds, and of the animals according to their kinds, of every creeping thing of the ground according to its kind, two of every sort shall come in to you, to keep them alive. Also take with you every sort of food that is eaten, and store it up; and it shall serve as food for you and for them." Noah did this; he did all that God commanded him.[14]

---

[10]The Cain and Abel story may personify a social conflict between settled farmers and seminomadic shepherds. No reason is given for the Lord's acceptance only of Abel's offering.

[11]A protective mark, perhaps a tattoo.

[12]This story of the mating of "the sons of God" with "the daughters of men" reveals the survival of an earlier, non-Hebrew mythology. Unlike those earlier myths, however, this biblical account of a divine parent does not grant semi-divine status to the offspring. The story attempts, rather, to explain the origin of a legendary race of giants.

[13]A cubit is an ancient unit of measurement based on the length of a man's forearm, usually about eighteen inches.

[14]God then sends the great flood as a punishment for human wickedness. (Many details of the biblical flood story resemble the account in the earlier *Epic of Gilgamesh*, with the essential difference that the biblical flood represents a single, divine moral judgment—not the whims of many gods.) God's mercy will be shown by his saving of a "righteous remnant" (Noah and his family), by whom humanity can begin anew. Through Noah, God will make a covenant with all humanity that "never again shall there be a flood to destroy the earth."

Exodus[15]

The Covenant

19:1–20:21

On the third new moon after the people of Israel had gone forth out of the land of Egypt, on that day they came into the wilderness of Sinai. And when they set out from Reph'idim and came into the wilderness of Sinai, they encamped in the wilderness; and there Israel encamped before the mountain. And Moses went up to God, and the Lord called to him out of the mountain, saying, "Thus you shall say to the house of Jacob, and tell the people of Israel: You have seen what I did to the Egyptians, and how I bore you on eagles' wings and brought you to myself. Now therefore, if you will obey my voice and keep my covenant, you shall be my own possession among all peoples; for all the earth is mine, and you shall be to me a kingdom of priests and a holy nation.[16] These are the words which you shall speak to the children of Israel."

So Moses came and called the elders of the people, and set before them all these words which the Lord had commanded him. And all the people answered together and said, "All that the Lord has spoken we will do." And Moses reported the words of the people to the Lord. And the Lord said to Moses, "Lo, I am coming to you in a thick cloud, that the people may hear when I speak with you, and may also believe you for ever."

Then Moses told the words of the people to the Lord. And the Lord said to Moses, "Go to the people and consecrate them today and tomorrow, and let them wash their garments, and be ready by the third day; for on the third day the Lord will come down upon Mount Sinai in the sight of all the people. And you shall set bounds for the people round about saying, 'Take heed that you do not go up into the mountain or touch the border of it; whoever touches the mountain shall be put to death; no hand shall touch him, but he shall be stoned or shot; whether beast or man, he shall not live.' When the trumpet sounds a long blast, they shall come up to the mountain." So Moses went down from the mountain to the people, and consecrated the people; and they washed their garments. And he said to the people, "Be ready by the third day; do not go near a woman."

On the morning of the third day there were thunders and lightnings, and a thick cloud upon the mountain, and a very loud trumpet blast, so that it all the people who were in the camp trembled. Then Moses brought the people out of the camp to meet God; and they took their stand at the foot of the mountain. And Mount Sinai was wrapped in smoke, because the Lord descended upon it in fire; and the smoke of it went up like the smoke of a kiln, and the whole mountain quaked greatly. And as the sound of the trumpet grew louder and louder Moses spoke, and God answered him in thunder. And the Lord Came down upon Mount Sinai, to the top of the mountain; and the Lord called Moses to the top of the mountain, and Moses went up. And the Lord said to Moses, "Go down and warn the people, lest they break through to the Lord to gaze and many of them perish. And also let the priests who come near to the Lord consecrate themselves, lest the Lord break out upon them." And Moses said to the Lord, "The people cannot come up to Mount Sinai; for thou thyself didst charge us saying, 'Set bounds about the mountain, and consecrate it.'" And the Lord said to him, "Go down, and come up bringing Aaron [Moses brother] with you; but do not let the priests and the people break through to come up to the Lord, lest he break out against them." So Moses went down to the people and told them.

And God spoke all these words, saying,[17]

"I am the Lord your God, who brought you out of the
land of Egypt, out of the house of bondage.

"You shall have no other gods before me. — henotheism

---

[15]A Greek word meaning "a going out." The book of Exodus tells of the departure, under hostile circumstances (*ca.* 1300 B.C.), of an oppressed community of Hebrews from Egypt. It begins the story of their forty years journey through the desert back to the land of their ancestors—Abraham, his son Isaac, and Isaac's son Jacob (also called Israel). Their religious and political leader is Moses. The book's climactic event is God's reassertion of his covenant with the Hebrew people through his giving of the Law to Moses at Mount Sinai. With the establishment of this law, the *Jewish religion* assumes a clear identity.

[16]The first part of this sentence identifies the Hebrews as God's chosen people or "own possession"—on the condition that they follow God's law. The second part emphasizes that their God is also the God of the whole universe and that they are "a holy nation" in the sense of being the consecrated carrier of God's word.

[17]The following "Ten Commandments" state the essence of Jewish duties to God and to the rest of humanity. The Commandments are given as the basic requirements if the Hebrews are to enter into covenant with God and become his "holy nation."

"You shall not make for yourself a graven image,[18] or any
likeness of anything that is in heaven above, or that is in the
earth beneath, or that is in the water under the earth; you shall
not bow down to them or serve them; for I the Lord your God
am a jealous God, visiting the iniquity of the fathers upon the
children to the third and fourth generation of those who hate me,
but showing steadfast love to thousands of those
who love me and keep my commandments.

"You shall not take the name of the Lord your God in vain;
for the Lord will not hold him guiltless who takes his name in vain.

"Remember the sabbath day, to keep it holy. Six days you
shall labor, and do all your work; but the seventh day is a
sabbath to the Lord your God; in it you shall not do any work,
you, or your son, or your daughter, your manservant, or your maidservant, or
your cattle, or the sojourner who is within
your gates; for in six days the Lord made heaven and earth, the
sea, and all that is in them, and rested the seventh day; therefore
the Lord blessed the sabbath day and hallowed it.

"Honor your father and your mother, that your days may be
long in the land which the Lord your God gives you.

"You shall not kill.[19]

"You shall not commit adultery.

"You shall not steal.

"You shall not bear false witness against your neighbor.

"You shall not covet your neighbor's house; you shall not
covet your neighbor's wife, or his manservant, or his maidservant,
or his ox, or his ass, or anything that is your neighbor's."

Now when all the people perceived the thunderings and the lightings and the sound of the trumpet and the mountain smoking, the people were afraid and trembled; and they stood afar off, and said to Moses, "You speak to us, and we will hear; but let not God speak to us, lest we die." And Moses said to the people, "Do not fear; for God has come to prove you, and that the fear of him may be before your eyes, that you may not sin."

And the people stood afar off, while Moses drew near to the thick darkness where God was.

The Torah, or Law[20]

20:22–23:33

And the Lord said to Moses, "Thus you shall say to the people of Israel: 'You have seen for yourselves that I have talked with you from heaven. You shall not make gods of silver to be with me, nor shall you make yourselves gods of gold. An altar of earth you shall make for me and sacrifice on it your burnt offerings and your peace offerings, your sheep and your oxen; in every place where I cause my name to be remembered I will come to you and bless you. And if you make me an altar of stone, you shall not build it of hewn stones; for if you wield your tool upon it you profane it. And you shall not go up by steps to my altar, that your nakedness be not exposed on it.'

[18]The second commandment, prohibiting worship of any "graven image" (carved statue), was unique in the ancient world.

[19]The sixth commandment is sometimes translated, "You shall not commit murder." (Capital punishment for crimes, and war, are *not* absolutely forbidden in the Old Testament.)

[20]In addition to the basic principles established in the Ten Commandments, the Old Testament lists 603 other commandments. They regulate many details in the daily lives of the faithful. Some of these regulations can be seen in the following passage. Many are taken from neighboring societies, but reflect distinctive ethical and ritual practices of the Hebrews.

"Now these are the ordinances which you shall set before them. When you buy a Hebrew slave, he shall serve six years, and in the seventh he shall go out free, for nothing. If he comes in single, he shall go out single; if he comes in married, then his wife shall go out with him. If his master gives him a wife and she bears him sons or daughters, the wife and her children shall be her master's and he shall go out alone. But if the slave plainly says, 'I love my master, my wife, and my children; I will not go out free,' then his master shall bring him to God and he shall bring him to the door or the doorpost; and his master shall bore his ear through with an awl; and he shall serve him for life.

"When a man sells his daughter as a slave, she shall not go out as the male slaves do. If she does not please her master, who has designated her for himself, then he shall let her be redeemed; he shall have no right to sell her to a foreign people, since he has dealt faithlessly with her. If he designates her for his son, he shall deal with her as with a daughter. If he takes another wife to himself, he shall not diminish her food, her clothing, or her marital rights. And if he does not do these three thing for her, she shall go out for nothing, without payment of money.

"Whoever strikes a man so that he dies shall be put to death. But if he did not lie in wait for him, but God let him fall into his hand, then I will appoint for you a place to which he may flee. But if a man willfully attacks another to kill him treacherously, you shall take him from my altar, that he may die.

"Whoever strikes his father or his mother shall be put to death.

"Whoever steals a man, whether he sells him or is found in possession of him, shall be put to death.

"Whoever curses his father or his mother shall be put to death.

"When men quarrel and one strikes the other with a stone or with his fist and the man does not die but keeps his bed, then if the man rises again and walks abroad with his staff, he that struck him shall be clear; only he shall pay for the loss of his time, and shall have him thoroughly healed.

"When a man strikes his slave, male or female, with a rod and the slave dies under his hand, he shall be punished. But if the slave survives a day or two, he is not to be punished; for the slave is his money.

"When men strive together, and hurt a woman with child, so that there is a miscarriage, and yet no harm follows, the one who hurt her shall be fined, according as the woman's husband shall lay upon him; and he shall pay as the judges determine. If any harm follows, then you shall give life for life, eye for eye, tooth for tooth, hand for hand, foot for foot, burn for burn, wound for wound, stripe for stripe.

"When a man strikes the eye of his slave, male or female, and destroys it, he shall let the slave go free for the eye's sake. If he knocks out the tooth of his slave, male or female, he shall let the slave go free or the tooth's sake.

"When an ox gores a man or woman to death, the ox shall be stoned, and its flesh shall not be eaten; but the owner of the ox shall be clear. But if the ox has been acustomed to gore in the past, and its owner has been warned but has not kept it in, and it kills a man or a woman, the ox shall be stoned, and its owner also shall be put to death. If a ransom is laid on him, then he shall give for the redemption of his life whatever is laid upon him. If it gores a man's son or daughter, he shall be dealt with according to the same rule. If the ox gores a slave, male or female, the owner shall give to their master thirty shekels of silver, and the ox shall be stoned.

"When a man leaves a pit open, or when a man digs a pit and does not cover it, and an ox or an ass falls into it, the owner of the pit shall make it good; he shall give money to its owner, and the dead beast shall be his.

"When one man's ox hurts another's, so that it dies, then they shall sell the live ox and divide the price of it; and the dead beast also they shall divide. Or if it is known that the ox has been accustomed to gore in the past, and its owner has not kept it in, he shall pay ox for ox, and the dead beast shall be his.

"If a man steals an ox or a sheep, and kills it or sells it, he shall pay five oxen for an ox, and four sheep for a sheep. He shall make restitution; if he has nothing, then he shall be sold for his theft. If the stolen beast is found alive in his possession, whether it is an ox or an ass or a sheep, he shall pay double.

"If a thief is found breaking in, and is struck so that he dies, there shall be no bloodguilt for him; but if the sun has risen upon him, there shall be bloodguilt for him.

"When a man causes a field or vineyard to be grazed over, or lets his beast loose and it feeds in another man's field, he shall make restitution from the best in his own field and in his own vineyard.

"When fire breaks out and catches in thorns so that the stacked grain or the standing grain or the field is consumed, he that kindled the fire shall make full restitution.

"If a man delivers to his neighbor money or goods to keep, and it is stolen out of the man's house, then, if the thief is found, he shall pay double. If the thief is not found, the owner of the house shall come near to God, to show whether or not he has put his hand to his neighbor's goods.

"For every breach of trust, whether it is for ox, for ass, for sheep, for clothing, or for any kind of lost thing, of which one says, 'This is it,' the case of both parties shall come before God; he whom God shall condemn shall pay double to his neighbor.

"If a man delivers to his neighbor an ass or an ox or a sheep or any beast to keep, and it dies or is hurt or is driven away, without any one seeing it, an oath by the Lord shall be between them both to see whether he has not put his hand to his neighbor's property; and the owner shall accept the oath, and he shall not make restitution. But if it is stolen from him, he shall make restitution to its owner. If it is torn by beasts, let him bring it as evidence; he shall not make restitution for what has been torn.

"If a man borrows anything of his neighbor, and it is hurt or dies the owner not being with it, he shall make full restitution. If the owner was with it, he shall not make restitution; if it was hired, it came for its hire.

"If a man seduces a virgin who is not bethrothed, and lies with her, he shall give the marriage present for her, and make her his wife. If her father utterly refuses to give her to him, he shall pay money equivalent to the marriage present for virgins.

"You shall not permit a sorceress to live.

"Whoever lies with a beast shall be put to death.

"Whoever sacrifices to any god, save to the Lord only, shall be utterly destroyed.

"You shall not wrong a stranger or oppress him, for you were strangers in the land of Egypt. You shall not afflict any widow or orphan. If you do afflict them, and they cry out to me, I will surely hear their cry; and my wrath will burn, and I will kill you with the sword, and your wives shall become widows and your children fatherless.

"If you lend money to any of my people with you who is poor, you shall not be to him as a creditor, and you shall not exact interest from him. If ever you take your neighbor's garment in pledge, you shall restore it to him before the sun goes down; for that is his only covering, it is his mantle for his body; in what else shall he sleep? And if he cries to me, I will hear, for I am compassionate.

"You shall not revile God, nor curse a ruler of your people.

"You shall not delay to offer from the fulness of your harvest and from the outflow of your presses.

"The first-born of your sons you shall give to me. You shall do likewise with your oxen and with your sheep: seven days it shall be with its dam; on the eighth day you shall give it to me.[21]

"You shall be men consecrated to me; therefore you shall not eat any flesh that is torn by beasts in the field; you shall cast it to the dogs.

"You shall not utter a false report. You shall not join hands with a wicked man, to be a malicious witness. You shall not follow a multitude to do evil; nor shall you bear witness in a suit, turning aside after a multitude, so as to pervert justice; nor shall you be partial to a poor man in his suit.

"If you meet your enemy's ox or his ass going astray, you shall bring it back to him. If you see the ass of one who hates you lying under its burden, you shall refrain from leaving him with it, you shall help him to lift it up.

"You shall not pervert the justice due to your poor in his suit. Keep far from a false charge, and do not slay the innocent and righteous, for I will not acquit the wicked. And you shall take no bribe, for a bribe blinds the officials, and subverts the cause of those who are in the right.

"You shall not oppress a stranger; you know the heart of a stranger, for you were strangers in the land of Egypt.

"For six years you shall sow your land and gather in its yield; but the seventh year you shall let it rest and lie fallow, that the poor of your people may eat; and what they leave the wild beasts may eat. You shall do likewise with your vineyard, and with your olive orchard.

"Six days you shall do your work, but on the seventh day you shall rest; that your ox and your ass may have rest, and the son of your bondmaid, and the alien, may be refreshed. Take heed to all that I have said to you; and make no mention of the names of other gods, nor let such be heard out of your mouth.

"Three times in the year you shall keep a feast to me. You shall keep the feast of unleavened bread; as I commanded you, you shall eat unleavened bread for seven days at the appointed time in the month of Abib, for in it you came out of Egypt. None shall appear before me empty-handed. You shall keep the feast of harvest, of the first fruits

---

[21]In many ancient cultures the first-born male offspring had a special value. Some religious groups, neighbors of the Hebrews, actually sacrificed their children, but that was never a part of the Jewish religion. This passage states that the first-born male oxen and sheep would be part of a sacrificial meal. The sons would be consecrated to God's service. Shortly afterwards, in the biblical narrative (in the book of Numbers), the Jewish tribe of Levites assumed the priestly duties in place of all the other Hebrew first-born males.

of your labor, of what you sow in the field. You shall keep the feast of ingathering at the end of the year, when you gather in from the field the fruit of your labor. Three times in the year shall all your males appear before the Lord God.

"You shall not offer the blood of my sacrifice with leavened bread, or let the fat of my feast remain until the morning.

"The first of the first fruits of your ground you shall bring into the house of the Lord your God.

"You shall not boil a kid in its mother's milk.

"Behold, I send an angel before you, to guard you on the way and to bring you to the place which I have prepared. Give heed to him and hearken to his voice, do not rebel against him, for he will not pardon your transgression; for my name is in him.

"But if you hearken attentively to his voice and do all that I say, then I will be an enemy to your enemies and an adversary to your adversaries.

"When my angel goes before you, and brings you in to the Amorites, and the Hittites, and the Per'izzites, and the Canaanites, the Hivites, and the Jeb'usites, and I blot them out, you shall not bow down to their gods, nor serve them, nor do according to their works, but you shall utterly overthrow them and break their pillars in pieces. You shall serve the Lord your God, and I will bless your bread and your water; and I will take sickness away from the midst of you. None shall cast her young or be barren in your land; I will fulfill the number of your days. I will send my terror before you, and will throw into confusion all the people against whom you shall come, and I will make all your enemies turn their backs to you. And I will send hornets before you, which shall drive out Hivite, Canaanite, and Hittite from before you. I will not drive them out from before you in one year, lest the land became desolate and the wild beasts multiply against you. Little by little I will drive them out from before you, until you are increased and possess the land. And I will set your bounds from the Red Sea to the sea of the Philistines, and from the wilderness to the Euphra'tes; or I will deliver the inhabitants of the land into your hand, and you shall drive them out before you. You shall make no covenant with them or with their gods. They shall not dwell in your land lest they make you sin against me; for if you serve their gods, it will surely be a snare to you."

Amos[22]

The Prophecy

1–2; 2:4–3:8; 5:14–27; 7:10–8:10; 9:1–4, 8–15

The words of Amos, who was among the shepherds of Teko'a, which he saw concerning Israel in the days of Uzzi'ah king of Judah and in the days of Jerobo'am the son of Jo'ash, king of Israel, two years before the earthquake. And he said:

> The LORD roars from Zion,
> and utters his voice from Jerusalem;
> the pastures of the shepherds mourn,
> and the top of [Mount] Carmel withers."

• • •

Thus says the LORD:

> For three transgressions of Judah,
> and for four, I will not revoke the punishment;
> because they have rejected the law of the LORD,
> and have not kept his statutes,

---

[22]The earliest of the "writing" prophets after the Exodus from Egypt. The Hebrew nation had divided into the northern kingdom of Israel and the southern kingdom of Judah, which included Jerusalem. Amos was an eighth-century B.C. shepherd from Tekoa, in Judah, who first preached at a festival in the town of Bethel, in Israel. He blasted the luxurious living and corrupt morals of the rich, their exploitation of the poor, and religious observance based only on outward ritual. The local priest, Amaziah, then reported him to Jeroboam, king of Israel. Amos prophesied the destruction of that kingdom (which would fall to the Assyrians in 721 B.C.), but also stated that a remnant of the Jews would "rebuild the ruined cities and inhabit them." God judges all nations, Amos preached, but his special covenant with the Jews makes special moral demands upon them.

but their lies have led them astray,
after which their fathers walked.
So I will send a fire upon Judah,
and it shall devour the strongholds of Jerusalem."

Thus says the LORD:

"For three transgressions of Israel,
and for four, I will not revoke the punishment;
because they sell the righteous for silver,
and the needy for a pair of shoes—
they that trample the head of the poor into the dust of the earth,
and turn aside the way of the afflicted;
a man and his father go in to the same maiden,
so that my holy name is profaned;
they lay themselves down beside every altar
upon garments taken in pledge;
and in the house of their God they drink
the wine of those who have been fined.

"Yet I destroyed the Amorite[23] before them,
whose height was like the height of the cedars,
and who was as strong as the oaks;
I destroyed his fruit above,
and his roots beneath.
Also I brought you up out of the land of Egypt,
and led you forty years in the wilderness,
to possess the land of the Amorite.
And I raised up some of your sons for prophets,
and some of your young men for Nazirites.[24]
Is it not indeed so, O people of Israel?"
says the LORD.

"But you made the Nazirites drink wine,
and commanded the prophets,
saying, 'You shall not prophesy.'
Behold, I will press you down in your place,
as a cart full of sheaves presses down.
Flight shall perish from the swift,
and the strong shall not retain his strength,
nor shall the mighty save his life;
he who handles the bow shall not stand,
he who is swift of foot shall not save himself,
nor shall he who rides the horse save his life;
and he who is stout of heart among the mighty
shall flee away naked in that day,"
says the LORD.

Hear this word that the LORD has spoken against you, O people of Israel, against the whole family which I brought up out of the land of Egypt:

---

[23]Earlier inhabitants of the same land.

[24]A group of men who took ascetic religious vows. Among their prohibitions, they did not drink intoxicating beverages and did not cut their hair.

You only have I known
of all the families of the earth
therefore I will punish you
for all your iniquities.

Do two walk together,
unless they have made an appointment?
Does a lion roar in the forest,
when he has no prey?
Does a young lion cry out from his den,
if he has taken nothing?
Does a bird fall in a snare on the earth,
when there is no trap for it?
Does a snare spring up from the ground,
when it has taken nothing?
Is a trumpet blown in a city,
and the people are not afraid?
Does evil befall a city,
unless the LORD has done it?
Surely the Lord GOD does nothing,
without revealing his secret
to his servants the prophets.
The lion has roared;
who will not fear?
The Lord GOD has spoken;
who can but prophesy?"

• • •

Seek good, and not evil,
that you may live;
and so the LORD, the God of hosts, will be with you,
as you have said.
Hate evil, and love good,
and establish justice in the gate;
it may be that the LORD, the God of hosts,
will be gracious to the remnant of Joseph.[25]

Therefore thus says the LORD, the God of hosts, the Lord:

"In all the squares there shall be wailing;
and in all the streets they shall say, 'Alas! alas!'
They shall call the farmers to mourning
and to wailing those who are skilled in lamentation,
and in all vineyards there shall be wailing,
for I will pass through the midst of you,"
says the LORD.

Woe to you who desire the day of the LORD!
Why would you have the day of the LORD?
It is darkness, and not light;
as if a man fled from a lion,
and a bear met him;

---

[25]Jacob's son, who had begun the Hebrew sojourn in Egypt.

or went into the house and leaned with his hand against the wall,
and a serpent bit him.
Is not the day of the LORD darkness, and not light,
and gloom with no brightness in it?

"I hate, I despise your feasts,
and I take no delight in your solemn assemblies.
Even though you offer me your burnt offerings and cereal offerings
I will not accept them,
and the peace offerings of your fatted beasts
I will not look upon.
Take away from me the noise of your songs;
to the melody of your harps I will not listen.
But let justice roll down like waters,
and righteousness like an ever-flowing stream.

"Did you bring to me sacrifices and offerings the forty years in the wilderness, O house of Israel? You shall take up Sakkuth your king, and Kaiwan[26] your star-god, your images, which you made for yourselves; therefore I will take you into exile beyond Damascus," says the LORD, whose name is the God of hosts.

• • •

Then Amazi'ah the priest of Beth'el sent to Jerobo'am king of Israel, saying, "Amos has conspired against you in the midst of the house of Israel; the land is not able to bear all his words. For thus Amos has said.

'Jerobo'am shall die by the sword,
and Israel must go into exile
away from his land.'"

And Amazi'ah said to Amos, "O seer, go, flee away to the land of Judah and eat bread there, and prophesy there; but never again prophecy at Beth'el, for it is the king's sanctuary, and it is a temple of the kingdom."

Then Amos answered Amazi'ah, "I am no prophet, nor a prophet's son; but I am a herdsman, and a dresser of sycamore trees, and the LORD took me from following the flock, and the LORD said to me, Go; prophesy to my people Israel.'

Now therefore hear the word of
the LORD.
you say, 'Do not prophesy against
Israel,
and do not preach against the
house of Isaac'

Therefore thus says the LORD:

'Your wife shall be a harlot in the city,
and your sons and your daughters
shall fall by the sword,
and your land shall be parceled
out by line;
you yourself shall die in an unclean land,
and Israel shall surely go into
exile away from its land.'"

Thus the Lord GOD showed me: behold, a basket of summer fruit. And he said, "Amos, what do you see?" And I said, "A basket of summer fruit." Then the LORD said to me.

---

[26]Sakkuth and Kaiwan were Assyrian gods, worshipped in the form of carved images.

"The end has come upon my people Israel;
I will never again pass by them.
The songs of the temple shall become wailings in that day,"
says the Lord GOD

"the dead bodies shall be many;
in every place they shall be cast out in silence."

Hear this, you who trample upon the needy,
and bring the poor of the land to an end,
saying, "When will the new moon be over,
that we may sell grain?
And the sabbath,
that we may offer wheat for sale,
that we may make the ephah small and the shekel great,
and deal deceitfully with false balances,
that we may buy the poor for silver
and the needy for a pair of sandals,
and sell the refuse of the wheat?"

The Lord has sworn by the pride of Jacob:

"Surely I will never forget any of their deeds.
Shall not the land tremble on this account,
and every one mourn who dwells in it,
and all of it rise like the Nile,
and be tossed about and sink again, like the Nile of Egypt?
"And on that day," says the Lord GOD,
"I will make the sun go down at noon,
and darken the earth in broad daylight.
will turn your feasts into mourning,
and all your songs into lamentation;
will bring sackcloth upon all loins
and baldness on every head;
will make it like the mourning for an only son,
and the end of it like a bitter day."

• • •

I saw the LORD standing beside the altar, and he said:
Smite the capitals until the thresholds shake,
and shatter them on the heads of all the people;
and what are left of them I will slay with the sword;
not one of them shall flee away,
not one of them shall escape.

Though they dig into She'ol,[27]
from there shall my hand take them;
though they climb up to heaven,
from there I will bring them down.
Though they hide themselves on the top of Car'mel,
from there I will search out and take them;
and though they hide from my sight at the bottom of the sea,
there I will command the serpent, and it shall bite them.

[27]The underground place of the dead, similar to the Greek idea of Hades.

And though they go into captivity before their enemies,
there I will command the sword, and it shall slay them;
and I will set my eyes upon them for evil and not for good." . . .

Behold, the eyes of the Lord GOD are upon the sinful kingdom,
and I will destroy it from the surface of the ground;
except that I will not utterly destroy the house of Jacob,"
says the LORD.
For lo, I will command,
and shake the house of Israel among all the nations
as one shakes with a sieve,
but no pebble shall fall upon the earth.
All the sinners of my people shall die by the sword,
who say, 'Evil shall not overtake or meet us.'

"In that day I will raise up
the booth of [King] David that is fallen
and repair its breaches,
and raise up its ruins,
and rebuild it as in the days of old;
that they may possess the remnant of E'dom
and all the nations who are called by my name,"
says the LORD who does this.

"Behold, the days are coming," says the LORD,
"when the plowman shall overtake the reaper
and the treader of grapes him who sows the seed;
the mountains shall drip sweet wine,
and all the hills shall flow with it.
I will restore the fortunes of my people Israel,
and they shall rebuild the ruined cities and inhabit them;
they shall plant vineyards and drink their wine,
and they shall make gardens and eat their fruit.
I will plant them upon their land,
and they shall never again be plucked up
out of the land which I have given them,"
says the LORD your God.

Isaiah[28]

The Prophecy

45:8–25; 52:13–53:12

"Shower, O heavens, from above,
and let the skies rain down righteousness;
let the earth open, that salvation may sprout forth,
and let it cause righteousness to spring up also;
I the Lord have created it.

[28]The following passages from the latter part of the book of Isaiah were written by a famous prophet toward the end of the "Babylonian Exile." (After the fall of the southern kingdom of Judah, many Jews had been taken into captivity in Babylon, 586 B.C. With the approach of a mighty Persian army, which will defeat the force of Babylon (539 B.C.), the prophet joyfully anticipates the return to his homeland (Judah). The liberating Persians are viewed as a part of the universal God's historical plan.

Woe to him who strives with his Maker,
an earthen vessel with the potter!"
Does the clay say to him who fashions it, 'What are you making?'
or 'Your work has no handles'?
Woe to him who says to a father, 'What are you begetting?'
or to a woman, 'With what are you in travail?'"
Thus says the LORD,

the Holy One of Israel, and his Maker:
Will you question me about my children,
or command me concerning the work of my hands?
I made the earth,
and created man upon it;
it was my hands that stretched out the heavens,
and I commanded all their host.
I have aroused him in righteousness,
and I will make straight all his ways;
he shall build my city
and set my exiles free,
not for price or reward,"
says the LORD of hosts.

Thus says the LORD:

The wealth of Egypt and the merchandise of Ethiopia,
and the Sabe'ans, men of stature,
shall come over to you and be yours,
they shall follow you;
they shall come over in chains and bow down to you.
they will make supplication to you, saying:
God is with you only, and there is no other,
no god besides him.'"
Truly, thou art a God who hidest thyself,
O God of Israel; the Savior.
All of them are put to shame and confounded,
the makers of idols go in confusion together.
But Israel is saved by the LORD
with everlasting salvation;
you shall not be put to shame or confounded
to all eternity.

For thus says the LORD,
who created the heavens
(he is God!),
who formed the earth and made it
(he established it;
he did not create it a chaos,
he formed it to be inhabited!):
"I am the LORD, and there is no other.
I did not speak in secret,
in a land of darkness;
I did not say to the offspring of Jacob,
'Seek me in chaos.'
I the LORD speak the truth,

I declare what is right.

"Assemble yourselves and come,
draw near together,
you survivors of the nations!
They have no knowledge
who carry about their wooden idols,
and keep on praying to a god
that cannot save.
Declare and present your case;
let them take counsel together!
Who told this long ago?
Who declared it of old?
Was it not I, the LORD?
And there is no other god besides me,
a righteous God and a Savior;
there is none besides me.

"Turn to me and be saved,
all the ends of the earth!
For I am God, and there is no other.
By myself I have sworn,
from my mouth has gone forth in righteousness
a word that shall not return:
To me every knee shall bow,
every tongue shall swear.'
Only in the LORD, it shall be said of me,
are righteousness and strength;
to him shall come and be ashamed,
all who were incensed against him.
In the LORD all the offspring of Israel
shall triumph and glory."

• • •

Behold, my servant shall prosper,
he shall be exalted and lifted up,
and shall be very high.[29]
As many were astonished at him—
his appearance was so marred, beyond human semblance,
and his form beyond that of the sons of men—
so shall he startle many nations;
kings shall shut their mouths because of him;
for that which has not been told them they shall see,
and that which they have not heard they shall understand,

Who has believed what we have heard?
And to whom has the arm of the LORD been revealed?
For he grew up before him like a young plant,
and like a root out of dry ground;
he had no form or comeliness that we should look at him,

[29]This passage, often called the Song of the Suffering Servant, describes the Jewish people, collectively, as God's "servant"—a humiliated individual who endures his bruises without complaint. But now the Jews, who have suffered for all mankind, will be restored to their rightful place as God's chosen nation. (Christians would later interpret this passage as a prophecy of the coming and sacrifice of Jesus Christ.)

and no beauty that we should desire him.
He was despised and rejected by men;
a man of sorrows, and acquainted with grief;
and as one from whom men hide their faces
he was despised, and we esteemed him not.

Surely he has borne our griefs
and carried our sorrows;
yet we esteemed him stricken,
smitten by God, and afflicted.
But he was wounded for our transgressions,
he was bruised for our iniquities;
upon him was the chastisement that made us whole,
and with his stripes we are healed.
All we like sheep have gone astray;
we have turned every one to his own way;
and the Lord has laid on him
the iniquity of us all.

He was oppressed, and he was afflicted,
yet he opened not his mouth;
like a lamb that is led to the slaughter,
and like a sheep that before its shearers is dumb,
so he opened not his mouth.

By oppression and judgment he was taken away;
and as for his generation, who considered
that he was cut off out of the land of the living,
stricken for the transgression of my people?
And they made his grave with the wicked
and with a rich man in his death,
although he had done no violence,
and there was no deceit in his mouth.

Yet it was the will of the LORD to bruise him;
he has put him to grief;
when he makes himself an offering for sin,
he shall see his offspring, he shall prolong his days;
the will of the LORD shall prosper in his hand;
he shall see the fruit of the travail of his soul and be satisfied;
by his knowledge shall the righteous one, my servant,
make many to be accounted righteous;
and he shall bear their iniquities.
Therefore I will divide him a portion with the great,
and he shall divide the spoil with the strong;
because he poured out his soul to death,
and was numbered with the transgressors;
yet he bore the sin of many,
and made intercession for the transgressors.

THE ASSYRIAN ANNALS

The Assyrians were a Semitic people who had lived on the upper Tigris River in northern Mesopotamia since the Bronze Age. In the early Iron Age they embarked on an aggressive program of expansion, building an empire that ultimately included all of Mesopotamia, the entire Levant, and parts of neighboring lands such as Egypt. The Assyrian Empire reached its height in the mid-7th century B.C.

The Assyrian kings left detailed accounts of their exploits, including so-called "Annals" (i.e., a year by year narrative of events). These annals are the official accounts of the victories claimed by the Assyrian kings over various opponents. These documents are mostly inscriptions found by archaeologists when excavating the royal palaces. They follow a predictable pattern and usually include a series of battles (invariably described as victories) over named opponents at specific locations and specifics about such details as the number of captured soldiers (often afterwards forcibly incorporated into the Assyria army) and the kinds of booty.

The following excerpts from the Assyrian annals are typical examples of this kind of primary source. Although the evidence they provide is invaluable, one must remember that they are completely one-sided, representing only the Assyrian view and only presenting evidence favorable to the Assyrian side.

SARGON II (721-705 B.C.): CAMPAIGNS IN THE LEVANT

These texts were inscribed on the walls of the Assyrian palace at Khorsabad, which served as the Assyrian capital under Sargon and today lies in northern Iraq. Some of his campaigns were launched against former vassals who had allegedly proved disloyal. Of particular interest is the account of the siege and capture of Samaria, then the capital of the northern Kingdom of Israel. History is normally written by the victors but in this case we have an alternative account of this event in the Hebrew Bible/Old Testament (2 Kings 17:3-5; 18:9-11) which confirms the essential historicity of the Assyrian text.

(10—17)

At the begi[nning of my royal rule, I . . . the town of the Sama]rians [I besieged, conquered] (2 lines destroyed) [for the god . . . who le]t me achieve (this) my triumph. . . . I led away as prisoners [27,290 inhabitants of it (and) [equipped] from among [them (soldiers to man)] 50 chariots for my royal corps. . . . [The town I] re[built] better than (it was) before and [settled] therein people from countries which [I] myself [had con]quered. I placed an officer of mine as governor over them and imposed upon them tribute as (is customary) for Assyrian citizens.

---

[1]Republished with permission of Princeton University Press from *Ancient Near Eastern Texts: Relating to the Old Testament*, edited by James Pritchard, copyright © 1969. Permission conveyed through Copyright Clearance Center.

[2]For the textual and historical problems involved, cf. A. T. Olmstead, The Text of Sargon's Annals, in *AJSL*, XLVIII (1931), 259 ff.

[3]To this meaning of *enû*, cf. *ténû* discussed below, n.1, p. 289

[4]For this Egyptian name (mentioned also in II Kings 17:4) and the historical problems involved, cf. G. Steindorff, Die keilschriftliche Wiedergabe. aegyptischer Eigennamen (*BA*, 1, 339 ff.); also, Kees, *GGA*, 1926, p. 426; H. Ranke, *Keilschriftliches Material zur altaegyptischen Vokalisierung*, p. 38; and Helene von Zeissl, *Aethiopen und Assyrer in Aegypten, Beiträge zur Geschichie der ägyptischen "Spätzeit" Aegyptologische Forschungen*, Heft 14, 1944), p. 18 ff. Further, A. T. Olmstead, *History of Assyria* (New York, 1923), p. 204.

[5]The Assyrian word (attested since Shalmaneser III, but *tertennûtu* already in Boğozköi-Akkadian, *KBo*, 1, 3:29 and Ebeling, *KAJ*, 245:17 *amel tar-te-ni-šu-nu*) refers to a high military and administrative official, second in rank only to the king (cf. E. Unger's translation *Vizekönig* in *ZATW*, 1923, 204 ff.). Etymology uncertain; beside *turtanu*, also *tartanu* is attested.

[6]To the thorny problem of the identification of both, name of king and name of country, cf. E. F. Weidner, *AfO*, XIV (1941), 45 f. Also Helene von Zeissl, *op.cit.*, pp. 21 ff.

I besieged and conquered Samaria (*Sa-me-ri-na*), led away as booty 27,290 inhabitants of it. I formed from among them a contingent of 50 chariots and made remaining (inhabitants) assume their (social) positions.[3] I installed over them and officer of mine and imposed upon them the tribute of the former king. Hanno, king of Gaza and also *Sib'e,*[4] the *turtan*[5] of *Egypt (Mu-ṣu-ri),* set out from Rapihu against me to deliver a decisive battle. I defeated them; Sib'e ran away, afraid when he (only) heard the noise of my (approaching) army, and has not been seen again. Hanno, I captured personally. I received the tribute from Pir'u of Musuru,[6] from Samsi, queen of Arabia (and) It'*amar the Sabaean,* gold in dust-form, horses (and) camels.

(11—15)

Iamani from Ashdod, afraid of my armed force (lit.: weapons), left his wife and children and fled to the frontier of M{*usru*} which belongs to *Meluhha* (i.e., *Ethiopia*)) and hid (lit.: stayed) there like a thief. I installed an officer of mine as governor over his entire large country and its prosperous inhabitants, (thus) aggrandizing (again) the territory belonging to Ashur, the king of the gods. The terror (-inspiring) glamor of Ashur, my lord, overpowered (however) the king of *Meluhha* and he threw him (i.e. Iamani) in fetters on hands and feet, and sent him to me, to Assyria. I conquered and sacked the towns Shinuhtu (and) Samaria, and *all Israel* (lit.: "Omri-Land" *Bît Ḫu-um-ri-ia*). I caught, like a fish, the Greek (Ionians) who live (on islands) amidst the Western Sea.

(2) *Second Year.*

(23–57)

In the second year of my rule, Ilubi'[di, from Hamath] . . . a large [army] he brought together at the town Qarqar and, [forgetting] the oaths [which they had sworn . . .] the [cities of Arpad, Simirra], Damascus (*Di-maš-*[*qa*ᵏˡ]) and Samaria [revolted against me] (lacuna of uncertain length) he (i.e. Hanno of Gaza) made [an agreement with him (i.e. the Pharaoh)] and he (i.e. the Pharaoh) called up Sib'e his *turtan* to assist him (i.e. Hanno) and he (i.e. Sib'e) set out against me to deliver a decisive battle. I inflicted a defeat upon them (i.e. Hanno and Sib'e) upon an (oracle-) order[7] (given) by my lord Ashur, and Sib'e, like a s i p a (i.e. shepherd)[8] whose flock has been stolen, fled alone and disappeared. Hanno (however), I captured personally and brought him (with me) in fetters to my city Ashur. I destroyed Rapihu, tore down (its walls) and burned (it). I led away as prisoners 9,033 inhabitants with their numerous possessions.

(33–37)

Ia'ubidi from Hamath, a commoner[9] without claim to the throne, a cursed Hittite, schemed to become king of Hamath, induced the cities Arvad, Simirra, Damascus (*Di-maš-qa*ᵏˡ) and Samaria to desert me, made them collaborate and fitted out an army. I called up the masses of the soldiers of Ashur and besieged him and his warriors in Qarqar, his favorite city. I conquered (it) and burnt (it). Himself I flayed; the rebels I killed in their cities and established (again) peace and harmony. A contingent of 200 chariots and 600 men on horseback I formed from among the inhabitants of Hamath and added them to my royal corps.

(3) *Fifth Year.*

(72–76)

In the fifth year of my rule, Pisiri of Carchemish broke the oath sworn by the great gods and wrote messages to Midas (*Mi-ta-a*), king of Muski, (full) of hostile plans against Assyria. I lifted my hands (in prayer) made him, and

---

[7]The text has *siqru* "order," cf. von Soden, *ZA, XLI* (NF VII), 168.

[8]This is meant to be a pun.

[9]For the meaning of the term *ḫubšu* denoting in Akkadian (as well as Ugaritic) texts a special social class, cf. G. R. Driver and J. C. Miles, *The Assyrian Laws* (Oxford, 1935), p. 485 (with references); further, W. F. Albright, *BASOR,* 63 (1934), 29 f.; I. Mendelsohn, *BASOR,* 83 (1941), 36 ff.; and R. Lancheman, *BASOR,* 86 (1942), 36 f.

[10]Usually, the yoke of the king is mentioned in connection with the status of newly subjugated peoples. The present reference to the "Yoke of Ashur" could therefore indicate a special status of the Assyrians forcibly settled in Carchemish.

[11]These seeds are part of the Mesopotamian pharmacopoeia.

[12]For *talimu* "younger brother," cf. in extenso P. Koschaker, Fratriarchat, Hausgemeinschaft und Mutterrecht in Keilschriftrechten, in *ZA, XLI* (NF VII), 64 ff. In *RA, XVI* (1919), p. 193, and *JAOS, XLVIII* (1928), p. 182, W. F. Albright suggested the translation "uterine broher."

also his family, surrender (lit.: come out) (of Carchemish), (all) in fetters and with the gold, silver and his personal possessions. And the rebellious inhabitants of Carchemish who (had sided) with him, I led away as prisoners and brought (them) to Assyria. I formed from among them a contingent of 50 chariots, 200 men on horseback (and) 3,000 foot soldiers and added (it) to my royal corps. In the city of Carchemish I (then) settled inhabitants of Assyria and imposed upon their (neck) the yoke of Ashur, my lord.[10]

(4) *Seventh Year.*

Upon a trust (-inspiring oracle given by) my lord Ashur, I crushed the tribes of Tamud, Ibadidi, Marsimanu, and Haiapa, the Arabs who live, far away, in the desert (and) who know neither overseers nor official(s) and who had not (yet) brought their tribute to any king. I deported their survivors and settled (them) in Samaria.

From Pir'u, the king of Musru, Samsi, the queen of Arabia, It'amra, the Sabaean,—the(se) are the kings of the seashore and from the desert—I received as their presents, gold in the form of dust, precious stones, ivory, ebony-seeds,[11] all kinds of aromatic substances, horses (and) camels.

(5) *Eleventh Year.*

(249—262)

Azuri, king of Ashdod, had schemed not to deliver tribute (any more) and sent messages (full) of hostilities against Assyria to the kings (living) in his neighborhood. On account of the misdeed which he (thus) committed, I abolished his rule over the inhabitants of his country and made Ahimiti, his younger[12] brother, king over them. But the(se) Hittites, (always) planning treachery, hated his (i.e. Ahimiti's) reign and elevated to rule over them a Greek[13] who, without claim to the throne, knew, just as they (hemselves), no respect for authority. [In a sudden rage] I marched quickly—(even) in my state chariot[14] and (only) with my cavalry which never, even in friendly territory,[15] leaves my side—against Ashdod, his royal residence, and I besieged and conquered the cities Ashdod, Gath (*Gi-im-tu*) (and) Asdudimmu. I declared the gods residing therein, himself, as well as the inhabitants of his country, the gold, silver (and) his personal possessions as booty. I reorganized (the administration of) these cities[16] and placed an officer of mine as governor over them and declared them Assyrian citizens and they bore (as such) my yoke.[17]

(90—112)

Azuri, king of Ashdod, had schemed not to deliver tribute any more and sent messages (full) of hostilities against Assyria, to the kings (living) in his neighborhood. On account of the(se) act(s) which he committed, I abolished his rule over the people of his country and made Ahimiti, his younger brother, king over them. But the(se) Hittites, always planning evil deeds, hated his reign and elevated to rule over them a Greek (*Ia-ma-ni*) who, without any claim to the throne, had no respect for authority—just as they themselves. In a sudden rage, I did not (wait to) assemble the full might of my army (or to) prepare the camp(ing equipment), but started out towards Ashdod (only) with those of my warriors who, even in friendly areas, never leaves my side. But this Greek heard about the advance of my expedition, from afar, and he fled into the territory of *Egypt*—which *belongs (now) to Ethiopia*—and his (hiding) place could not be detected. I besieged (and) conquered the cities Ashdod, Gath, Asdudimmu; I declared his images, his wife, his children, all the possessions and treasures of his palace as well as the inhabitants of his country as booty. I reorganized, (the administration of) these cities (and) settled therein people from the [regions] of the East which I had conquered personally. I installed an officer of mine over them and declared them Assyrian citizens and they pulled (as such) the straps (of my yoke). *The king of Ethiopia who {lives} in {a distant country}*, in an inapproachable region, the road [to which is . . .], whose fathers never—from remote days until now[18]—had sent messengers to inquire after the health of my royal fore-fathers, he did hear, even (that) far away, of the might of Ashur, Nebo (and) Marduk. The awe-inspiring glamor of my kingship blinded him and terror over came him. He threw him (i.e. the Greek) in fetters, shackles and iron bands, and they brought him to Assyria, a long journey.

[13]The pertinent texts interchange the expressions *Iamani* (i.e. Ionian) and *Iadna*; cf. D. D. Luckenbill, *ZA,* XXVIII (1913), 92 ff.

[14]According to this passage, the vehicle termed *narkabat šêpē* was not destined for speedy transportation nor for warlike purposes.

[15]This translation is suggested by the context (differently Landsberger, *ZA,* XXXVII [NF III], 86 f. for *salimu*).

[16]For the meaning of the administrative terminus technicus *ana eššûti ṣabâtu*, cf. B. Meissner, *Babylonien und Assyrien* (Heidelberg, 1920), 1, p. 141.

[17]A very smilar version of this report is contained in the fragment BrM 81–7–23,3 published by E. F. Weidner, in *AfO,* XIV (1941), 40, with transliteration and translation on p. 50.

[18]*Sic,* against J. Lewy, in *HUCA,* XIX, 461.

SENNACHERIB (704–681)

The Siege of Jerusalem[1]

The prisms of the Assyrian King Sennacherib contain texts written in Akkadian cuneiform. They contain annals of this ruler. The excerpt below is a narrative of his third campaign, ca. 701 B.C. aimed at rebellious cities in the Levant. Of special interest is his campaign against Hezekiah, the King of Judah. Once again, as with the fall of Samaria, we have the exceptional survival of an alternative narrative of the same event from the Hebrew Bible/Old Testament (2 Kings 18:13-16), which confirms some of the details in this official Assyrian account.

(1) From the Oriental Institute Prism of Sennacherib, which contains—as does the so-called Taylor Prism.

(ii 37—iii 49)

In my third campaign I marched against Hatti. Luli, king of Sidon, whom the terror-inspiring glamor of my lordship had overwhelmed, fled far overseas and perished.[2] The awe-inspiring splendor of the "Weapon" of Ashur, my lord, overwhelmed his strong cities (such as) Great Sidon, Little Sidon, Bit-Zitti, Zaribtu, Mahalliba, Ushu (i.e. the mainland settlement of Tyre), Akzib (and) Akko, (all) his fortress cities, walled (and well) provided with feed and water for his garrisons, and they bowed in submission t my feet. I installed Ethba'al (*Tuba'lu*) upon the throne to be their king and imposed upon him tribute (due) to me (as his) overlord (to be paid) annually without interruption.

As to all the kings of Amurru—Menahem (*Mi-in-ḫi-im-mu*) from Samsimuruna, Tuba'lu from Sidon, Abdili'ti from Arvad, Urumilki from Byblos, Mitinti from Ashdod, Buduili from Beth-Ammon, Kammusunadbi from Moab (and) Aiarammu from Edom, they brought sumptuous gifts (*igisû*) and—fourfold—their heavy *tâmartu* -presents to me and kissed my feet. Sidqia, however, king of Ashkelon, who did not bow to my yoke, I deported and sent to Assyria, his family-gods, himself, his wife, his children, his brothers, all the male descendants of his family. I set Sharruludari, son of Rukibtu, their former king, over the inhabitants of Ashkelon and imposed upon him the payment of tribute (and of *katrû*) -presents (due) to me (as) overlord—and the (now) pulls the straps (of my yoke)!

In the continuation of my campaign I besieged Beth-Dagon, Joppa, Banai-Barqa, Azuru, cities belonging to Sidqia who did not bow to my feet quickly (enough); I conquered (them) and carried their spoils away. They officials, the patricians and the (common) people of Ekron[3]—who had thrown Padi, their king, into fetters (because he was) loyal to (his) solemn oath (sworn) by the god Ashur, and had handed him over to *Hezekiah, the Jew* (*Ha-za-qi-(i)a-ú* ^amel^*Ia-ú-da-ai*)—(and) he (Hezekiah) held him in prison, unlawfully, as if he (Padi) be an enemy—had become afraid and had *called (for help) upon the kings of Egypt* (*Muṣ(u)ri*) (and) the bowmen, the chariot (-corps) and the cavalry *of the king of Ethiopia* (*Meluḫḫa*), an army beyond counting—*and they (actually) had come to their assistance.* In the plain of Eltekeh (*Al-ta-qu-ú*), their battle lines were drawn up against me and they sharpened their weapons. Upon a trust (-inspiring) oracle (given) by Ashur, my lord, I fought with them and inflicted a defeat upon them. In the mêlée of the battle, I personally *captured alive the Egyptian* charioteers with the(ir) princes and (also) the charioteers of the king of *Ethiopia*. I besieged Eltekeh (and) Timnah (*Ta-am-na-a*), conquered (them) and carried

---

[1]Republished with permission of Princeton University Press from *Ancient Near Eastern Texts: Relating to the Old Testament*, edited by James Pritchard, copyright © 1969. Permission conveyed through Copyright Clearance Center.
[2]For the enigmatic idiom *Šadâ(šu) emêdu,* cf. E. F. Weidner, *AfO,* XIII (1940), 233 f. with the proposed translation "to die an infamous death."
[3]Note the social stratification indicated in this passage.

their spoils away. I assaulted Ekron and killed the officials and patricians who had committed the crime and hung their bodies on poles surrounding the city. The (common) citizens who were guilty of minor crimes, I considered prisoners of war. The rest of them, those who were not accused of crimes and misbehavior, I released. I made Padi, their king, come from Jerusalem (*Ur-sa-li-im-mu*) and set him as their lord on the throne, imposing upon him the tribute (due) to me (as) overlord.

As to Hezekiah, the Jew, he did not submit to my yoke, I laid siege to 46 of his strong cities, walled forts and to the countless small villages in their vicinity, and conquered (them) by means of well-stamped (earth-) ramps, and battering-rams brought (thus) near (to the walls) (combined with) the attack by foot soldiers, (using) mines, breeches as well as sapper work. I drove out (of them) 200,150 people, young and old, male and female, horses, mules, donkeys, camels, big and small cattle beyond counting, and considered (them) booty. *Himself I made a prisoner in Jerusalem,* his royal residence, like a bird in a cage. I surrounded him with earthwork in order to molest those who were leaving his city's gate. His towns which I had plundered, I took away from his country and gave them (over) to Mitinti, king of Ashdod, Padi, king of Ekron, and Sillibel, king of Gaza. Thus I reduced his country, but I still increased the tribute and the *katrû* -presents (due) to me (as his) overlord which I imposed (later) upon him beyond the former tribute, to be delivered annually. Hezekiah himself, whom the terror-inspiring splendor of my lordship had overwhelmed and whose irregular[4] and elite troops which he had brought into Jerusalem, his royal residence, in order to strengthen (it), had deserted him, *did send* me, later, to Nineveh, my lordly city, together *with 30 talents of gold, 800 talents of silver, Precious stones, antimony,*[5] large cuts of red stone, couches (inlaid) with ivory, *nîmedu* -chairs (inlaid) with ivory, elephant-hides, ebony-wood, boxwood (and) all kinds of valuable treasures, *his (own) daughters, concubines, male and female musicians.* In order to deliver the tribute and to do obeisance as a slave he sent his (personal) messenger.

[4]For ᵃᵐᵉˡ*urbu,* cf. H Winckler, in OLZ, IX (1906), 334, and, recently, Th. Bauer, *Assurbanipal,* II, I.

[5]This refers probably to stibnite, a vative sulphide of antimony (cf. J. R. Partington, *Origin and Development of Applied Chemistry* [London, 1935], p. 256; also R. C. Thompson, *A Dictionary of Assyrian Chemistry and Geology* [Oxford, 1936], p. 49), which might have been used as an eye paint (beside the cheaper and efficient substitute, burnt shells of almond and soot). Stibium is easily reduced and the metal is sporadically attested in Mesopotamia since the Neo-Sumerian period. For the provenience of the stibnite, of B. Meissner, *OLZ,* XVII (1915), 52 ff.

Part VI

PRIMARY SOURCES FROM ANCIENT GREECE

Homer

THE ILIAD

Literature probably began with oral poetry. The epic is among the earliest forms of such poetry—sung by bards who memorized and doubtless modified thousands of lines. It is, typically, a long narrative poem about some great struggle (for example, a war between great powers that ultimately destroys a civilization). The style is lofty and serious, and the central figure is a hero whose actions affect the fate of the whole group—his city, tribe, nation, or race. The "traditional" epic (also called "primary" or "folk" epic) was shaped by a poet or poets out of historical and legendary materials about their glorious past triumphs. Homer was such a shaper. According to ancient traditions he lived as a professional entertainer in the early Greek settlements on the eastern edge of the Aegean Sea around the eighth century B.C. In any case the oldest surviving epics of Western civilization, The Iliad *and* The Odyssey, *have been attributed to him. His poems certainly tell of a time long before his own, for the accepted date of the fall of Troy (Ilium), the event that occurs right after* The Iliad's *story and before* The Odyssey's, *is 1184 B.C. And whatever the facts of their creation, there is no doubt that across the centuries of Western literature these poems have been widely read and admired.*

The Iliad *is not only the tale of a war but more centrally the story of Achilles, its tragic hero, and the customs of his era and class; indeeed, the work might more properly have been called* The Achilleid. *As the poem begins, nine years of war between the Achaeans (Greeks) and the Trojans have passed, and Troy still stands. Helen, the Achaean woman whose desertion of her husband, King Menelaus, for the Trojan prince Paris is the cause of the war, still resides among the Trojans. So far, all the Achaeans have to show for their efforts to recapture her are the spoils of raids carried out in the region around the walled city. Nevertheless, as our selection of Book One shows, the events of these raids have brought matters to a crisis by inspiring the anger of Achilles toward his military chief, King Agamemnon. Achilles' withdrawal from the siege threatens the Achaean cause; for, by all opinion (including his own), he has excelled all others in battle and is indispensable to Achaean victory.*

As we read of the quarrel between the hero and Agamemnon, brother of Menelaus and commander of the combined Achaean armies, we see Achilles' tragic flaw—imperious, uncontrolled, unrelenting anger—which has led him to retire sullenly from battle. What follows, in the absence of his prowess, is a sharp reversal for his comrades—and for him, worse still, the death of Patroclus, his dearest friend.

The narrative of The Iliad *is filled largely with descriptions of ups and downs in the long combat and of the part played in it by the gods. More significantly, it also reveals the aristocratic interests and lifestyle of those Greeks who first heard the poem recited and of those who, later, were the first to read it. The climax of this epic work comes not with the predestined fall of Troy but with the struggle of Achilles to recover from his anger. It is this personal victory, this restoration of the "divine order," that satisfies the gods and the moral sense of the ancient Greeks.*

The Odyssey *continues Homer's narrative with the story of the aftermath of the war. It focuses upon the homecoming of another war hero, resourceful King Odysseus. Having offended Poseidon, god of the sea, he must spend ten years on the difficult journey. When he arrives at his own rocky island of Ithaca, alone and disguised, Odysseus takes bloody revenge on those who had abused his kingdom's hospitality during his absence. The Odyssey ends with restoration of the "proper" social order in Ithaca.*

Homer's original audience regarded the poems as part of their ancestral history. Thus, they already knew the main lines of the story. (Troy must fall, Achilles must eventually die before Troy's defeat, Odysseus must—after many adventures—make his way home, etc.) The audience's fascination with the epics, therefore, lay in the poet's skill—his development of character and beauty of language.

The epic poems of Homer have been translated many times from the original Greek and have been presented in several forms. One of the most charming and readable prose versions is that by the English scholar E. V. Rieu. The following excerpts from The Iliad *are taken from his translation.*

Book I: The Quarrel

The Wrath of Achilles is my theme, that fatal wrath which, in fulfilment of the will of Zeus,[1] brought the Achaeans[2] so much suffering and sent the gallant souls of many noblemen to Hades, leaving their bodies as carrion for the dogs and passing birds. Let us begin, goddess of song,[3] with the angry parting that took place between Agamemnon King of Men[4] and the great Achilles son of Peleus. Which of the gods was it that made them quarrel?

It was Apollo, Son of Zeus and Leto, who started the feud, when he punished the King for his discourtesy to Chryses, his priest, by inflicting a deadly plague on his army and destroying his men. Chryses had come to the Achaean ships to recover his captured daughter. He brought with him a generous ransom and carried the chaplet [wreath] of the Archer-god Apollo on a golden staff in his hand. He appealed to the whole Achaean army, and most of all to its two commanders, the sons of Atreus.[5]

'My lords, and you Achaean men-at-arms; you hope to sack King Priam's city and get home in safety. May the gods that live on Olympus grant your wish—on this condition, that you show your reverence for the Archer-god Apollo Son of Zeus by accepting this ransom and releasing my daughter.'

The troops applauded. They wished to see the priest respected and the tempting ransom taken. But this was not all to King Agamemnon's liking. He cautioned the man severely and rudely dismissed him.

'Old man,' he said, 'do not let me catch you loitering by the hollow ships to-day, nor coming back again, or you may find the god's staff and chaplet a very poor defence. Far from agreeing to set your daughter free, I intend her to grow old in Argos, in my house, a long way from her own country, working at the loom and sharing my bed. Off with you now, and do not provoke me if you want to save your skin.'

The old man trembled and obeyed him. He went off without a word along the shore of the sounding sea. But when he found himself alone he prayed fervently to King Apollo, Son of Leto of the Lovely Locks. 'Hear me, god of the Silver Bow, Protector of Chryse and holy Cilla, and Lord Supreme of Tenedos.[6] Smintheus,[7] if ever I built you a shrine that delighted you, if ever I burnt you the fat thighs of a bull or a goat, grant me this wish. Let the Danaans pay with your arrows for my tears.'

Phoebus Apollo heard his prayer and came down in fury from the heights of Olympus with his bow and covered quiver on his back. As he set out, the arrows clanged on the shoulder of the angry god; and his descent was like nightfall. He sat down opposite the ships and shot an arrow, with a dreadful twang from his silver bow. He attacked

---

[1]The chief of those twelve major gods who reside on Mount Olympus in northern Greece; he controls the heavens and exerts his considerable authority over the other gods.

[2]The ancient Greeks. Occasionally, Homer also refers to these warriors as Danaans (descendants of the legendary King Danaus), or as Argives.

[3]An invocation: for his great task Homer is requesting the aid of Calliope, Muse (patron goddess) of epic poetry.

[4]Agamemnon, king of Mycenae and the commander-in-chief of the expedition against Troy, was a kind of lord paramount or first among equals, for many other kings took part in the expedition.

[5]Agamemnon and his brother, Menelaus, king of Sparta. Homer's frequent reference to ancestry reflects a consciousness and pride of family among such warriors.

[6]Chryse (home of Chryses) and Cilla are towns near Troy; Tenedos is an island off the coast.

[7]Another name for Apollo, Olympian god of light, youth, medicine, music, archery, and prophecy. Smintheus literally means "mouse god." Since mice and rats are carriers of plague, Chryses' using the name of Smintheus as one of the titles by which he addresses Apollo is appropriate for the plague that will follow his prayer.

the mules first and the nimble dogs; then he aimed his sharp arrows at the men, and struck again and again. Day and night innumerable fires consumed the dead.

For nine days the god's arrows rained on the camp. On the tenth the troops were called to Assembly by order of Achilles—a measure that the white-armed goddess Here[8] prompted him to take, in her concern for the Danaans whose destruction she was witnessing. When all had assembled and the gathering was complete, the great runner Achilles rose to address them:

'Agamemnon my lord, what with the fighting and the plague, I fear that our strength will soon be so reduced that any of us who are not dead by then will be forced to give up the struggle and sail for home. But could we not consult a prophet or priest, or even some interpreter of dreams—for dreams too are sent by Zeus—and find out from him why Phoebus Apollo is so angry with us? He may be offended at some broken vow or some failure in our rites. If so, he might accept a savoury offering of sheep or of full-grown goats and save us from the plague.'

Achilles sat down, and Calchas son of Thestor rose to his feet. As an augur,[9] Calchas had no rival in the camp. Past, present and future held no secrets from him; and it was his second sight, a gift he owed to Apollo, that had guided the Achaean fleet to Ilium. He was a loyal Argive, and it was in this spirit that he took the floor.

'Achilles,' he said, 'my royal lord, you have asked me to account for the Archer-King Apollo's wrath; and I will do so. But listen to me first. Will you swear to come forward and use all your eloquence and strength to protect me? I ask this of you, being well aware that I shall make an enemy of one whose authority is absolute among us and whose word is law to all Achaeans. A commoner is no match for a king whom he offends. Even if the king swallows his anger for the moment, he will nurse his grievance till the day when he can settle the account. Consider, then, whether you can guarantee my safety.'

'Dismiss your fears,' said the swift Achilles, 'and tell us anything you may have learnt from Heaven. For by Apollo Son of Zeus, the very god, Calchas, in whose name you reveal your oracles, I swear that as long as I am alive and in possession of my senses not a Danaan of them all, here by the hollow ships, shall hurt you, not even if the man you mean is Agamemnon, who bears the title of our overlord.'

At last the worthy seer plucked up his courage and spoke out. 'There is no question,' he said, 'of a broken vow or any shortcoming in our rites. The god is angry because Agamemnon insulted his priest, refusing to take the ransom and free his daughter. That is the reason for our present sufferings and for those to come. The Archer-King will not release us from this loathsome scourge till we give the bright-eyed lady back to her father, without recompense or ransom, and send holy offerings to Chryse. When that is done we might induce him to relent.'

Calchas sat down, and the noble son of Atreus, imperial Agamemnon, leapt up in anger. His heart was seething with black passion and his eyes were like points of flame. He rounded first on Calchas, full of menace.

'Prophet of evil,' he cried, 'never yet have you said a word to my advantage. It is always trouble that you revel in foretelling. Not once have you fulfilled a prophecy of something good—you have never even made one! And now you hold forth as the army's seer, telling the men that the Archer-god is persecuting them because I refused the ransom for the girl Chryseis, princely though it was. And why did I refuse? Because I chose to keep the girl and take her home. Indeed, I like her better than my consort, Clytaemnestra. She is quite as beautiful, and no less clever or skilful with her hands. Still, I am willing to give her up, if that appears the wiser course. It is my desire to see my people safe and sound, not perishing like this. But you must let me have another prize at once, or I shall be the only one of us with empty hands, a most improper thing. You can see for yourselves that the prize I was given is on its way elsewhere.'

The swift and excellent Achilles leapt to his feet. 'And where,' he asked, 'does your majesty propose that our gallant troops should find a fresh prize to satisfy your unexampled greed? I have yet to hear of any public fund we have laid by. The plunder we took from captured towns has been distributed, and it is more than we can ask of the men to reassemble that. No; give the girl back now, as the god demands, and we will make you triple, fourfold, compensation, if Zeus ever allows us to bring down the battlements of Troy.'

King Agamemnon took him up at once. 'You are a great man, Prince Achilles, but do not imagine you can trick me into that. I am not going to be outwitted or cajoled by you. "Give up the girl," you say, hoping, I presume, to keep your own prize safe. Do you expect me tamely to sit by while I am robbed? No; if the army is prepared to give

---

[8]Here (more often spelled Hera) is Zeus's sister and queen. She favors the Greeks; many of the gods take sides in this earthly battle.
[9]An interpreter of omens, considered invaluable by ancient armies.

me a fresh prize, chosen to suit my taste and to make up for my loss, I have no more to say. If not, I shall come and help myself to your prize, or that of Aias; or I shall walk off with Odysseus'. And what an angry man I shall leave behind me! However, we can deal with all that later on. For the moment, let us run a black ship down into the friendly sea, give her a special crew, embark the animals for sacrifice, and put the girl herself, Chryseis of the lovely cheeks, on board. And let some Councillor of ours go as captain—Aias, Idomeneus, the excellent Odysseus, or yourself, my lord, the most redoubtable man we could choose—to offer the sacrifice and win us back Apollo's favour.'

Achilles the great runner gave him a black look. 'You shameless schemer,' he cried, 'always aiming at a profitable deal! How can you expect any of the men to give you loyal service when you send them on a raid or into battle? It was no quarrel with the Trojan spearmen that brought *me* here to fight. They have never done *me* any harm. They have never lifted cow or horse of mine, nor ravaged any crop that the deep soil of Phthia grows to feed her men; for the roaring seas and many a dark range of mountains lie between us. The truth is that we joined the expedition to please you; yes, you unconscionable cur, to get satisfaction from the Trojans for Menelaus and yourself—a fact which you utterly ignore.[10] And now comes this threat from you of all people to rob me of my prize, my hard-earned prize, which was a tribute from the ranks. It is not as though I am ever given as much as you when the Achaeans sack some thriving city of the Trojans. The heat and burden of the fighting fall on me, but when it comes to dealing out the loot, it is you that take the lion's share, leaving me to return exhausted from the field with something of my own, however small. So now I shall go back to Phthia. That is the best thing I can do—to sail home in my beaked ships. I see no point in staying here to be insulted while I pile up wealth and luxuries for you.'

'Take to your heels, by all means,' Agamemnon King of Men retorted, 'if you feel the urge to go. I am not begging you to stay on my account. There are others with me who will treat me with respect, and the Counsellor Zeus is first among them. Moreover, of all the princes here, you are the most disloyal to myself. To you, sedition, violence and fighting are the breath of life. What if you *are* a great soldier—who made you so but God? Go home now with your ships and your men-at-arms and rule the Myrmidons. I have no use for you; your anger leaves me cold. But mark my words. In the same way as Phoebus Apollo is robbing me of Chryseis, whom I propose to send off in my ship with my own crew, I am going to pay a visit to your hut and take away the beautiful Briseis, your prize, Achilles, to let you know that I am more powerful than you, and to teach others not to bandy words with me and openly defy their King.'

This cut Achilles to the quick. In his shaggy breast his heart was torn between two courses, whether to draw his sharp sword from his side, thrust his way through the crowd, and kill King Agamemnon, or to control himself and check the angry impulse. He was deep in this inward conflict, with his long sword half unsheathed, when Athene[11] came down to him from heaven at the instance of the white-armed goddess Here, who loved the two lords equally and was fretting for them both. Athene stood behind him and seized him by his golden locks. No one but Achilles was aware of her; the rest saw nothing. He swung round in amazement, recognized Pallas Athene at once—so terrible was the brilliance of her eyes—and spoke out to her boldly: 'And why have you come here, Daughter of aegis-bearing[12] Zeus? Is it to witness the arrogance of my lord Agamemnon? I tell you bluntly—and I make no idle threats—that he stands to pay for this outrage with his life.'

'I came from heaven,' replied Athene of the Flashing Eyes, 'in the hope of bringing you to your senses. It was Here, goddess of the White Arms, that sent me down, loving the two of you as she does and fretting for you both. Come now, give up this strife and take your hand from your sword. Sting him with words instead, and tell him what you mean to do. Here is a prophecy for you—the day shall come when gifts three times as valuable as what you now have lost will be laid at your feet in payment for this outrage. Hold your hand, then, and be advised by us.'

'Lady,' replied Achilles the great runner, 'when you two goddesses command, a man must obey, however angry he may be. Better for him if he does. The man who listens to the gods is listened to by them.'

With that he checked his great hand on the silver hilt and drove the long sword back into its scabbard, in obedience to Athene, who then set out for Olympus and the palace of aegis-bearing Zeus, where she rejoined the other gods.

[10]It was Agamemnon who personally persuaded the Greek princes to undertake a war to recover Helen, the wife of Menelaus.

[11]Daughter of Zeus, goddess of wisdom, who favors the Greek side. At this moment Athene brings some self-control to Achilles.

[12]In Homer the aegis is a thundercloud; in the works of later writers it is a garment of Athene.

Not that Achilles was appeased. He rounded on Atreides[13] once again with bitter taunts. 'You drunken sot,' he cried, 'with the eyes of a dog and the courage of a doe! You never have the pluck to arm yourself and go into battle with the men or to join the other captains in an ambush—you would sooner die. It pays you better to stay in camp, filching the prizes of anyone that contradicts you, and flourishing at your people's cost because they are too feeble to resist—feeble indeed; or else, my lord, this act of brigandage would prove your last.

'But mark my words, for I am going to take a solemn oath. Look at this staff.[14] Once cut from its stem in the hills, it can never put out leaves or twigs again. The billhook stripped it of its bark and foliage; it will sprout no more. Yet the men who in the name of Zeus safeguard our laws, the Judges of our nation, hold it in their hands. By this I swear (and I could not choose a better token) that the day is coming when the Achaeans one and all will miss me sorely, and you in your despair will be powerless to help them as they fall in their hundreds to Hector killer of men. Then, you will tear your heart out in remorse for having treated the best man in the expedition with contempt.'

The son of Peleus finished, flung down the staff with its golden studs, and resumed his seat, leaving Atreides to thunder at him from the other side. But Nestor now leapt up, Nestor, that master of the courteous word, the clear-voiced orator from Pylos, whose speech ran sweeter than honey off his tongue. He had already seen two generations come to life, grow up, and die in sacred Pylos, and now he ruled the third. Filled with benevolent concern, he took the floor. 'This is indeed enough to make Achaea weep!' he said. 'How happy Priam[15] and Priam's sons would be, how all the Trojans would rejoice, if they could hear of this rift between you two who are the leaders of the Danaans in policy and war. Listen to me. You are both my juniors. And what is more, I have mixed in the past with even better men than you and never failed to carry weight with them, the finest men I have ever seen or shall see, men like Peirithous and Dryas, Shepherd of the People, Caeneus, Exadius, the godlike Polyphemus and Aegeus' son, Theseus of heroic fame. They were the strongest men that Earth has bred, the strongest men pitted against the strongest enemies, a savage, mountain-dwelling tribe whom they utterly destroyed. Those were the men whom I left my home in Pylos to join. I travelled far to meet them, at their own request. I played my independent part in their campaign. And they were men whom not a soul on earth to-day could face in battle. Still, they listened to what I said and followed my advice. You two must do the same; you will not lose by it. Agamemnon, forget the privilege of your rank, and do not rob him of the girl. The army gave her to him: let him keep his prize. And you, my lord Achilles, drop your contentious bearing to the King. Through the authority he derives from Zeus, a sceptred king has more than ordinary claims on our respect. You, with a goddess for Mother, may be the stronger of the two; yet Agamemnon is the better man, since he rules more people. My lord Atreides, be appeased. I, Nestor, beg you to relent towards Achilles, our mighty bulwark in the stress of battle.'

'My venerable lord, no one could cavil at what you say,' replied King Agamemnon. 'But this man wants to get the whip-hand here; he wants to lord it over all of us, to play the king, and to give us each our orders, though I know one who is not going to stand for that. What if the everlasting gods did make a spearman of him? Does that entitle him to use insulting language?'

Here the noble Achilles broke in on the King: 'A pretty nincompoop and craven I shall be called if I yield to you at every point, no matter what you say. Command the rest, not me. I have done with obedience to you. And here is another thing for you to ponder. I am not going to fight you or anybody else with my hands for this girl's sake. You gave her to me, and now you take her back. But of all else I have beside my good black ship, you shall not rob me of a single thing. Come now and try, so that the rest may see what happens. Your blood will soon be flowing in a dark stream down my spear.'

The two stood up, when the war of words was over, and dismissed the Assembly by the Achaean fleet. Achilles, with Patroclus and his men, made off to his trim ships and huts; while Atreides launched a fast vessel on the sea, chose twenty oarsmen to man her, and after embarking the cattle to be offered to the god, fetched Chryseis of the lovely cheeks and put her on board. The resourceful Odysseus went as captain, and when everyone was in, they set out along the highways of the sea.

---

[13]Son of Atreus: Agamemnon. The Atreidae were of a family famous in Greek legend.
[14]A speaker in the Assembly claimed the group's attention so long as he held the staff which had been handed to him by a herald.
[15] King of Troy and father of Hector.

Meanwhile Agamemnon made his people purify themselves by bathing. When they had washed the filth from their bodies in the salt water, they offered a rich sacrifice of bulls and goats to Apollo on the shore of the unharvested sea; and savoury odours, mixed with the curling smoke, went up into the sky.

While his men were engaged on these duties in the camp, Agamemnon did not forget his quarrel with Achilles and the threat he had made to him at the meeting. He called Talthybius and Eurybates, his two heralds and obedient squires, and said to them: 'Go to the hut of Achilles son of Peleus, take the lady Briseis into your custody, and bring her here. If he refuses to let her go, I shall come in force to fetch her, which will be all the worse for him.'

He sent them off, and with his stern injunction in their ears, the two men made their unwilling way along the shore of the barren sea, till they reached the encampment and ships of the Myrmidons, where they found the prince himself sitting by his own black ship and hut. It gave Achilles no pleasure to see them. They came to a halt, too timid and abashed before the prince to address him and tell him what they wanted. But he knew without being told, and broke the silence. 'Heralds,' he said, 'ambassadors of Zeus and men, I welcome you. Come forward. My quarrel is not with you but with Agamemnon, who sent you here to fetch the girl Briseis. My lord Patroclus, will you bring the lady out and hand her over to these men? I shall count on them to be my witnesses before the happy gods, before mankind, before the brutal king himself, if the Achaeans ever need me again to save them from disaster. The man is raving mad. If he had ever learnt to look ahead, he would be wondering now how he is going to save his army when they are fighting by the ships.' Patroclus did as his friend had told him, brought out Briseis of the lovely cheeks from the hut, and gave her up to the two men, who made their way back along the line of ships with the unhappy girl.

Withdrawing from his men, Achilles wept. He sat down by himself on the shore of the grey sea, and looked across the watery wilderness. Then, stretching out his arms, he poured out prayers to his Mother.[16] 'Mother, since you, a goddess, gave me life, if only for a little while, surely Olympian Zeus the Thunderer owes me some measure of regard. But he pays me none. He has let me be flouted by imperial Agamemnon son of Atreus, who has robbed me of my prize and has her with him now.'

Achilles prayed and wept, and his Lady Mother heard him where she sat in the depths of the sea with her old Father. She rose swiftly from the grey water like a mist, came and sat by her weeping son, stroked him with her hand and spoke to him. 'My child,' she asked him, 'why these tears? What is it that has grieved you? Do not keep your sorrow to yourself, but tell me so that we may share it.'

Achilles of the swift feet sighed heavily. 'You know,' he said; 'and since you know, why should I tell you the whole story? We went to Thebe, Eëtion's sacred city; we sacked the place and brought back all our plunder, which the army shared out in the proper way, choosing Chryseis of the lovely cheeks as a special gift for Atreides. Presently Chryses, priest of the Archer-god Apollo, came to the ships of the bronze-clad Achaeans to set free his daughter, bringing a generous ransom and carrying the chaplet of the Archer Apollo on a golden staff in his hand. He importuned the whole Achaean army, but chiefly its two leaders, the Atreidae. The troops showed by their applause that they wished to see the priest respected and the tempting ransom taken. But this was not at all to Agamemnon's liking. He sent him packing, with a stern warning in his ears. So the old man went home in anger; but Apollo listened to his prayers, because he loved him dearly, and let his wicked arrows fly against the Argive army. The men fell thick and fast, for the god's shafts rained down on every part of our scattered camp. At last a seer who understood the Archer's will explained the matter to us. I rose at once and advised them to propitiate the god. This made Agamemnon furious. He leapt to his feet and threatened me. And now he has carried out his threats: the bright-eyed Achaeans are taking the girl to Chryse in a ship with offerings for the god, while the King's messengers have just gone from my hut with the other girl Briseis, whom the army gave to me.

'So now, if you have any power, protect your son. Go to Olympus, and if anything you have ever done or said has warmed the heart of Zeus, remind him of it as you pray to him. For instance, in my father's house I have often heard you proudly tell us how you alone among the gods saved Zeus the Darkener of the Skies from an inglorious fate, when some of the other Olympians—Here, Poseidon and Pallas Athene—had plotted to throw him into chains. You, goddess, went and saved him from that indignity. You quickly summoned to high Olympus the monster of the hundred arms whom the gods call Briareus, but mankind Aegaeon, a giant more powerful even than his father. He squatted by the Son of Cronos with such a show of force that the blessed gods slunk off in terror, leaving Zeus free.

---

[16]Achilles' mother, Thetis, was a divine sea-nymph, a daughter of Nereus, the Old Man of the Sea. This appeal to her includes the first reference to the hero's tragically short lease on life.

'Sit by him now, clasp his knees,[17] and remind him of that. Persuade him, if you can, to help the Trojans, to fling the Achaeans back on their ships, to pen them in against the sea and slaughter them. That would teach them to appreciate their King. That would make imperial Agamemnon son of Atreus realize what a fool he was to insult the noblest of them all.'

'My son, my son!" said Thetis, bursting into tears. 'Was it for this I nursed my ill-starred child? At least they might have left you carefree and at ease beside the ships, since Fate has given you so short a life, so little time. But it seems that you are not only doomed to an early death but to a miserable life. It was indeed an unlucky day when I brought you into the world. However, I will go to snowcapped Olympus to tell Zeus the Thunderer all this myself, and see whether I can move him. Meanwhile, stay by your gallant ships, keep up your feud with the Achaeans, and take no part in the fighting. Yesterday, I must tell you, Zeus left for Ocean Stream to join the worthy Ethiopians at a banquet, and all the gods went with him. But in twelve days' time he will be back on Olympus, and then you may rest assured that I shall go to his Bronze Palace, where I will throw myself at his feet. I am convinced that he will hear me.'

Thetis withdrew, leaving Achilles to his grief for the gentle lady whom they had forced him to give up. Meanwhile Odysseus and his men reached Chryse with the sacred offerings. When they had brought their craft into the deep waters of the port, they furled the sail and stowed it in the black ship's hold, dropped the mast neatly into its crutch by letting down the forestays, rowed her into her berth, cast anchor, made the hawsers [ropes] fast, and jumped out on the beach. The cattle for the Archer-god were disembarked, and Chryseis stepped ashore from the seagoing ship. Odysseus of the nimble wits led the girl to the altar and gave her back to her father. 'Chryses,' he said, 'Agamemnon King of Men has ordered me to bring you your daughter and to make ceremonial offerings to Phoebus on the Danaans' behalf, in the hope of pacifying the Archer-King, who has struck their army a grievous blow.' Then he handed the lady over to her father, who welcomed his daughter with joy.

The offerings destined to do honour to the god were quickly set in place round the well-built altar. The men rinsed their hands and took up the sacrificial grains.[18] Then Chryses lifted up his arms and prayed aloud for them: 'Hear me, God of the Silver Bow, Protector of Chryse and of holy Cilia, and Lord Supreme of Tenedos! My last petition found you kind indeed: you showed your regard for me and struck a mighty blow at the Achaean army. Now grant me a second wish and save the Danaans from their dreadful scourge.' Thus the old man prayed; and Phoebus Apollo heard him.

When they had made their petitions and scattered the grain, they first drew back the animals' heads, slit their throats and flayed them. Then they cut out slices from the thighs, wrapped them in folds of fat and laid raw meat above them. These pieces the old priest burnt on the faggots, while he sprinkled red wine over the flames and the young men gathered round him with five-pronged forks in their hands. When the thighs were burnt up and they had tasted the inner parts, they carved the rest into small pieces, pierced them with skewers, roasted them thoroughly, and drew them all off.

Their work done and the meal prepared, they fell to with a good will on the feast, in which all had equal shares. When their thirst and hunger were satisfied, the stewards filled the mixing-bowls to the brim with wine,[19] and after first pouring out a few drops in each man's cup,[20] served the whole company. And for the rest of the day these young Achaean warriors made music to appease the god, praising the Great Archer in a lovely song, to which Apollo listened with delight.

When the sun set and darkness fell, they lay down for sleep by the hawsers of their ship. But as soon as Dawn had lit the East with rosy hands, they set sail for the great Achaean camp, taking advantage of a breeze the Archer-god had sent them. They put up their mast and spread the white sail. The sail swelled out, struck full by the wind, and a dark wave hissed loudly round her stem as the vessel gathered way and sped through the choppy seas, forging ahead on her course. Thus they returned to the great Achaean camp, where they dragged their black ship high up on the mainland sands and underpinned her with long props. This done, they scattered to their several huts and ships.

---

[17]The sacred posture of the kneeling supplicant was to clasp the knees of the person appealed to with one hand and to reach for his chin with the other.

[18]Grains of barley were sprinkled between the horns of the sacrificial animal.

[19]In the ancient world wine was usually diluted with water; hence, the mixing-bowls.

[20]Before the whole company drank its wine, the steward put a few drops in each man's cup to be poured out on the ground as a liquid offering (libation) to the god.

Now all this time Achilles the great runner, the royal son of Peleus, had been sitting by his fast ships, nursing his anger. He not only kept away from the fighting but attended no meetings of the Assembly, where a man can win renown. He stayed where he was, eating his heart out and longing for the sound and fury of battle.

Eleven days went by, and at dawn on the twelfth the everlasting gods returned in full strength to Olympus, with Zeus at their head. Thetis, remembering her son's instructions, emerged in the morning from the depths of the sea, rose into the broad sky and reached Olympus. She found all-seeing Zeus sitting away from the rest on the topmost of Olympus' many peaks. She sank to the ground beside him, put her left arm round his knees, raised her right hand to touch his chin, and so made her petition to the Royal Son of Cronos. 'Father Zeus, if ever I have served you well among the gods, by word or deed, grant me a wish and show your favour to my son. He is already singled out for early death, and now Agamemnon King of Men has affronted him. He has stolen his prize and kept her for himself. Avenge my son, Olympian Judge, and let the Trojans have the upper hand till the Achaeans pay him due respect and make him full amends.'

The Marshaller of the Clouds made no reply to this. He sat in silence for a long time, with Thetis clinging to his knees as she had done throughout. At last she appealed to him once more: 'Promise me faithfully and bow your head, or else, since you have nothing to lose by doing so, refuse; and I shall know that there is no god who counts for less than I.'

Zeus the Cloud-gatherer was much perturbed. 'This is a sorry business!' he exclaimed. 'You will make me fall foul of Here, when she rails at me about it, as she will. Even as things are, she scolds me constantly before the other gods and accuses me of helping the Trojans in this war. However, leave me now, or she may notice us; and I will see the matter through. But first, to reassure you, I will bow my head—and the immortals recognize no surer pledge from me than that. When I promise with a nod, there can be no deceit, no turning back, no missing of the mark.'

Zeus, as he finished, bowed his sable brows. The ambrosial locks rolled forward from the immortal head of the King, and high Olympus shook.

The affair was settled, and the two now parted. Thetis swung down from glittering Olympus into the salt sea depths, while Zeus went to his own palace. There the whole company of gods rose from their chairs in deference to their Father. There was not one that dared to keep his seat as he approached; they all stood up to greet him. Zeus sat down on his throne; and Here, looking at him, knew at once that he and Thetis of the Silver Feet, the Daughter of the Old Man of the Sea, had hatched a plot between them. She rounded instantly on Zeus. 'What goddess,' she asked, 'has been scheming with you now, you arch-deceiver? How like you it is, when my back is turned, to settle things in your own furtive way. You never of your own accord confide in me.'

'Here,' the Father of men and gods replied, 'do not expect to learn all my decisions. You would find the knowledge hard to bear, although you are my Consort. What it is right for you to hear, no god or man shall know before you. But when I choose to take a step without referring to the gods, you are not to cross-examine me about it.'

'Dread Son of Cronos,' said the ox-eyed Queen, 'what are you suggesting now? Surely it never was my way to pester you with questions. I have always let you make your own decisions in perfect peace. But now I have a shrewd idea that you have been talked round by Thetis of the Silver Feet, the Daughter of the Old Man of the Sea. She sat with you this morning and clasped your knees. This makes me think that you have pledged your word to her to support Achilles and let the Achaeans be slaughtered at the ships.'

'Madam,' replied the Cloud-compeller, 'you think too much, and I can keep no secrets from you. But there is nothing you can *do*, except to turn my heart even more against you, which will be all the worse for yourself. If things are as you say, you may take it that my will is being done. Sit there in silence and be ruled by me, or all the gods in Olympus will not be strong enough to keep me off and save you from my unconquerable hands.'

This made the ox-eyed [large-eyed] Queen of Heaven tremble, and curbing herself with an effort she sat still. Zeus had daunted all the other Heavenly Ones as well, and there was silence in his palace, till at last Hephaestus the great Artificer[21] spoke up, in his anxiety to be of service to his Mother, white-armed Here. 'This is unbearable!' he exclaimed. 'A pretty pass we are coming to, with you two spoiling for a fight about mankind and setting the gods at loggerheads. How can a good dinner be enjoyed with so much trouble in the air? I do advise my Mother, who knows well enough what is best, to make her peace with my dear Father, Zeus, or she may draw another reprimand from him and our dinner be entirely spoilt. What if the Olympian, the Lord of the Lightning Flash, the strongest

---

[21]Hephaestus, son of Zeus and Here, is the god of fire and the metallic crafts. Being lame he is the only Olympian god not formed perfectly.

god in Heaven, should feel disposed to blast us from our seats? No, Mother, you must humbly ask his pardon, and the Olympian will be gracious to us again.'

As he said this, Hephaestus hurried forward with a two-handled cup and put it in his Mother's hand. 'Mother,' he said, 'be patient and swallow your resentment, or I that love you may see you beaten, here in front of me. A sorry sight for me—but what could I do to help you? The Olympian is a hard god to pit oneself against. Why, once before when I was trying hard to save you, he seized me by the foot and hurled me from the threshold of Heaven. I flew all day, and as the sun sank I fell half-dead in Lemnos, where I was picked up and looked after by the Sintians.'

The white-armed goddess Here smiled at this, and took the beaker from her Son, still smiling. Hephaestus then went on to serve the rest in turn, beginning from the left, with sweet nectar which he drew from the mixing-bowl; and a fit of helpless laughter seized the happy gods as they watched him bustling up and down the hall.[22]

So the feast went on, all day till sundown. Each of them had his equal share and they all ate with zest. There was music too, from a beautiful Harp played by Apollo, and from the Muses,[23] who sang in turn delightfully. But when the bright lamp of the Sun had set, they all went home to bed in the separate houses that the great lame god Hephaestus had built for them with skillful hands. Olympian Zeus, Lord of the Lightning, also retired to the upper room where he usually slept, and settled down for the night, with Here of the Golden Throne beside him.

---

[22]The sight of the lame god (instead of the usual attractive servers) hobbling around them with the nectar turned the carefree gods to laughter. Thus, the tension of the Zeus-Here argument was relieved, as Hephaestus had intended.

[23]Nine goddesses, daughters of Zeus and Mnemosyne (goddess of memory); each one of the Muses encouraged and protected a different art or science.

Xenophon

THE LAWS AND CUSTOMS OF THE SPARTANS

Xenophon (ca. 430- ca. 354 B.C.) was a citizen of Athens, born into an aristocratic family. At various times in his life he was also a mercenary soldier, historian, and philosopher. Little is known of his youth in Athens, other than for a time he was a student of the Athenian philosopher Socrates.

In 401 B.C. he joined a group of 10,000 Greek mercenary soldiers in an army supporting a Persian pretender attempting to seize the Persian throne. The defeat and death of this pretender in battle, along with most of the Greek mercenary officers, led to the elevation of Xenophon as one of the new leaders of the Greek mercenaries. Xenophon later recorded their successful retreat from northern Mesopotamia to the Black Sea as the Anabasis *(literally the "Going Up", as the army marched from the lowlands of Mesopotamia up through the mountains of eastern Anatolia to the Black Sea). Upon his return to Greece he served as a mercenary in the Spartan army, which led to his exile from his native Athens. He thus settled in Sparta where he lived for many years.*

In addition to the Anabasis, *his other works include accounts of his former teacher Socrates, the* Hellenica *(a continuation of Thucydides'* History of the Peloponnesian War, *taking it to its end in 404 B.C.), and* The Laws and Customs of the Spartans, *an excerpt of which is presented here. He thus offers the most detailed look still extant at Sparta, which so many ways was truly unique among the Greek city-states. Although Xenophon's eyewitness account of the Spartans is invaluable, several caveats must be kept in mind. First, Xenophon lived in Sparta in the early 4th century B.C. The Spartans themselves credited their entire unique system to a legendary lawgiver named Lycurgus, who likely lived centuries earlier, probably in the 7th century B.C. Many modern scholars believe that the Spartan system was probably not the work of a single individual but rather evolved over time, perhaps not coming into full form until the early 5th century B.C. Second, it must be remembered that Xenophon was an unabashed admirer of the Spartans and so his account must be considered in that light.*

Nevertheless, Xenophon offers many intriguing observations of this unique society, one that has fascinated both scholars and the general public ever since. The result was the most proficient army in the Greek world although at a considerable cost to both citizens and non-citizens within the Spartan city-state.

The Regulations of Lycurgus Respecting Marriage and the Treatment of Children

But reflecting once how Sparta, one of the least populous of states, had proved the most powerful and celebrated city in Greece, I wondered by what means this result had been produced. When I proceeded, however, to contemplate the institutions of the Spartans, I wondered no longer.

Lycurgus, who made the laws[1] for them, by obedience to which they have flourished, I not only admire, but consider to have been in the fullest sense a wise man; for he rendered his country preëminent in prosperity, not by imitating other states, but by making ordinances contrary to those of most governments.

With regard, for example, to the procreation of children, that I may begin from the beginning, other people feed their young women, who are about to produce offspring, and who are of the class regarded as well brought up, on the most moderate quantity of vegetable food possible, and on the least possible quantity of meat, while they either keep them from wine altogether, or allow them to use it only when mixed with water; and as the greater number of the men engaged in trades are sedentary, so the rest of the Greeks think it proper that their young women should sit quiet and spin wool. But how can we expect that women thus treated should produce a vigorous progeny? Lycurgus, on the contrary, thought that female slaves were competent to furnish clothes; and, considering that the production of children was the noblest duty of the free, he enacted, in the first place, that the female should practice bodily exercises no less than the male sex; and he then appointed for the women contests with one another, just as for the men, expecting that when both parents were rendered strong, a stronger offspring would be born from them.

Observing, too, that the men of other nations, when women were united to husbands, associated with their wives during the early part of their intercourse without restraint, he made enactments quite at variance with this practice; for he ordained that a man should think it shameful to be seen going in to his wife, or coming out from her. When married people meet in this way, they must feel stronger desire for the company of one another, and whatever offspring is produced must thus be rendered far more robust than if the parents were satiated with each other's society.

In addition to these regulations, he also took from the men the liberty of marrying when each of them pleased, and appointed that they should contract marriages only when they were in full bodily vigour, deeming this injunction also conducive to the production of an excellent offspring. Seeing also that if old men chanced to have young wives, they watched their wives with the utmost strictness, he made a law quite opposed to this feeling; for he appointed that an old man should introduce to his wife whatever man in the prime of life he admired for his corporeal and mental qualities, in order that she might have children by him. If, again, a man was unwilling to associate with his wife, and yet was desirous of having proper children, he made a provision also with respect to him, that whatever women he saw likely to have offspring, and of good disposition, he might, on obtaining the consent of her husband, have children by her. Many similar permissions he gave; for the women are willing to have two families, and the men to receive brothers to their children, who are equal to them in birth and standing, but have no claim to share in their property.

Let him who wishes, then, consider whether Lycurgus, in thus making enactments different from those of other legislators, in regard to the procreation of children, secured for Sparta a race of men eminent for size and strength.

On the Training and Education of Children

Having given this account of the procreation of children, I wish also to detail the education of those of both sexes. Of the other Greeks, those who say that they bring up their sons best set slaves over them to take charge of them, as soon as the children can understand what is said to them, and send them, at the same time, to schoolmasters, to learn letters, and music, and the exercises of the palaestra.[2] They also render their children's feet delicate by the use of sandals, and weaken their bodies by changes of clothes; and as to food, they regard their appetite as the measure of what they are to take. But Lycurgus, instead of allowing each citizen to set slaves as guardians over his children, appointed a man to have the care of them all, one of those from whom the chief magistrates are chosen; and he is called the paedonomus. He invested this man with full authority to assemble the boys, and, if he found that any one was negligent of his duties, to punish him severely. He assigned him also some of the grown-up boys as whip-carriers, that they might inflict whatever chastisement was necessary; so that great dread of disgrace, and great willingness to obey, prevailed among them.

Instead, also, of making their feet soft with sandals, he enacted that they should harden them by going without sandals; thinking that, if they exercised themselves in this state, they would go up steep places with far greater ease, and descend declivities with greater safety; and that they would also leap, and skip, and run faster unshod, if they had their feet inured to doing so, than shod. Instead of being rendered effeminate, too, by a variety of dresses, he made it a practice that they should accustom themselves to one dress throughout the year; thinking that they would thus be better prepared to endure cold and heat.

---

[1] These laws of Sparta had not been written down, but were learned and practiced from generation to generation.
[2] A public area used for athletic training.

As to food, he ordained that they should exhort the boys to take only such a quantity as never to be oppressed with overeating, and not to be strangers to living somewhat frugally; supposing that, being thus brought up, they would be the better able, if they should be required, to support toil under a scarcity of supplies, would be the more likely to persevere in exertion, should it be imposed on them, on the same quantity of provisions, and would be less desirous of sauces, more easily satisfied with any kind of food, and pass their lives in greater health. He also considered that the fare which rendered the body slender would be more conducive to increasing its stature than that which expanded it with nutriment. Yet that the boys might not suffer too much from hunger, Lycurgus, though he did not allow them to take what they wanted without trouble, gave them liberty to steal certain things to relieve the cravings of nature; and he made it honourable to steal as many cheeses as possible. That he did not give them leave to form schemes for getting food because he was at a loss what to allot them, I suppose no one is ignorant; as it is evident that he who designs to steal must be wakeful during the night, and use deceit, and lay plots; and, if he would gain anything of consequence, must employ spies. All these things, therefore, it is plain that he taught the children from a desire to render them more dexterous in securing provisions, and better qualified for warfare.

Some one may say, "Why, then, if he thought it honourable to steal, did he inflict a great number of whiplashes on him who was caught in the act?" I answer, that in other things which men teach, they punish him who does not follow his instructions properly; and that the Spartans accordingly punished those who were detected as having attempted to steal in an improper manner. These boys he gave in charge to others to whip them at the altar of Diana Orthia; designing to show by this enactment that it is possible for a person, after enduring pain for a short time, to enjoy pleasure with credit for a long time. It is also shown by this punishment that, where there is need of activity, the inert person benefits himself the least, and occasions himself most trouble.

In order, too, that the boys, in case of the paedonomus being absent, may never be in want of a president, he appointed that whoever of the citizens may happen at any time to be present is to assume the direction of them, and to enjoin whatever he may think advantageous for them, and punish them if they do anything wrong. By doing this, Lycurgus has also succeeded in rendering the boys much more modest; for neither boys nor men respect any one so much as their rulers. And that if, on any occasion, no full-grown man happen to be present, the boys may not even in that case be without a leader, he ordained that the most active of the grown-up youths take the command of each band; so that the boys there are never without a superintendent.

It appears to me that I must say something also of the boys as objects of affection; for this has likewise some reference to education. Among the other Greeks, a man and boy either form a union, as among the Boeotians, and associate together, or, as among the Eleians, the men gain the favour of the youths by means of attentions bestowed upon them; but there are some of the Greeks who prohibit the suitors for the boys' favours from having the least conversation with them. But Lycurgus, acting contrary to all these people also, thought proper, if any man, being himself such as he ought to be, admired the disposition of a youth, and made it his object to render him a faultless friend, and to enjoy his society, to bestow praise upon him, and regarded this as the most excellent kind of education; but if any man showed that his affections were fixed only on the bodily attractions of a youth, Lycurgus, considering this as most unbecoming, appointed that at Lacedaemon suitors for the favours of boys should abstain from intimate connexion with them, not less strictly than parents abstain from such intercourse with their children, or children of the same family from that with one another. That such a state of things is disbelieved by some, I am not surprised; for in most states the laws are not at all adverse to the love of youths; but Lycurgus, for his part, took such precautions with reference to it.

• • •

Meals Taken in Public. On Temperance

The employments which Lycurgus appointed for each period of life have now been almost all specified. What mode of living he instituted for all the citizens, I will next endeavour to explain.

Lycurgus, then, having found the Spartans, like the other Greeks, taking their meals at home, and knowing that most were guilty of excess at them, caused their meals to be taken in public, thinking that his regulations would thus be less likely to be transgressed. He appointed them such a quantity of food, that they should neither be overfed nor feel stinted. Many extraordinary supplies are also furnished from what is caught in hunting, and for these the rich sometimes contribute bread; so that the table is never without provisions, as long as they design the meal to last, and yet is never expensive.

Having put a stop likewise to all unnecessary drinking, which weakens alike the body and the mind, he gave permission that every one should drink when he was thirsty, thinking that the drink would thus be most innoxious and most pleasant. When they take their meals together in this manner, how can any one ruin either himself or his family by gluttony or drunkenness? In other states, equals in age generally associate together, and with them modesty has but very little influence; but Lycurgus, at Sparta, mixed citizens of different ages, so that the younger are for the most part instructed by the experience of the older. It is a custom at these public meals, that whatever any one has done to his honour in the community is related; so that insolence or disorder from intoxication, or any indecency in conduct or language, has there no opportunity of showing itself. The practice of taking meals away from home is also attended with these advantages, that the people are obliged to walk in taking their departure homewards, and to be careful that they may not stagger from the effects of wine, knowing that they will not remain where they dined, and that they must conduct themselves in the night just as in the day; for it is not allowable for any one who is still liable to military duty to walk with a torch.

As Lycurgus observed, too, that those who, after taking food, exercise themselves, become well-complexioned, plump, and robust, while those who are inactive are puffy, unhealthy-looking, and feeble, he did not neglect to give attention to that point; and as he perceived that when any one engages in labour from his own inclination, he proves himself to have his body in efficient condition, he ordered that the oldest in each place of exercise should take care that those belonging to it should never be overcome by taking too much food. With regard to this matter, he appears to me to have been by no means mistaken, for no one would easily find men more healthy, or more able-bodied, than the Spartans; for they exercise themselves alike in their legs, in their hands, and in their shoulders.

Rules Regarding Children, Slaves, and Property

In the following particulars, also, he made enactments contrary to the usage of most states; for in other communities each individual has the control over his own children, and servants, and property; but Lycurgus, wishing to order things so that the citizens might enjoy some advantage from one another, unattended with any reciprocal injury, ordained that each should have authority not only over his own children, but over those of others. But when a person is conscious that his fellow-citizens are fathers of the children over whom he exercises authority, he must exercise it in such a way as he would wish it to be exercised over his own. If a boy, on any occasion, receive blows from another boy, and complain of that boy to his father, it is considered dishonourable in the father not to inflict additional blows on his son. Thus they trust to one another to impose nothing disgraceful on the children.

He enacted also that a person might use his neighbour's servants, if he had need of them. He introduced, too, a community of property in hunting-dogs; so that those who require them call on their owner to hunt, who, if he is not at leisure to hunt himself, cheerfully sends them out. They use horses also in like manner; for whoever is sick, or wants a vehicle, or desires to go to some place speedily, takes possession of a horse, if he sees one anywhere, and, after making proper use of it, restores it.

Nor, in regard to the following point, did he allow that which is customary among other people should be practised among his countrymen. For when men, from being overtaken by night in hunting, are in want of provisions, unless they have previously furnished themselves with them, he directed that, in such a case, those who have partaken of what they need, leave the rest ready for use, and that those who require a supply, having opened the seals, and taken as much as they want, seal the remainder up again and leave it. As they share thus, then, with one another, those who possess but little participate, whenever they are in need, in all the produce of the country.

Restrictions on the Employments of the Spartans

The following practices, too, Lycurgus established in Sparta, at variance with those of the rest of Greece. In other communities all gain as much by traffic[3] as they can; one cultivates land, another trades by sea, another engages in general commerce, another maintains himself by art. But at Sparta, Lycurgus prohibited free men from having any connexion with traffic, and enjoined them to consider as their only occupation whatever secures freedom to states. How, indeed, could wealth be eagerly sought in a community where he had appointed that

---

[3]That is, by commerce.

the citizens should contribute equally to their necessary maintenance, and should take their meals in common, and had thus provided that they should not desire wealth with a view to sensual gratifications? Nor had they, moreover, to get money for the sake of clothing; for they think themselves adorned, not by expensive raiment, but by a healthy personal appearance. Nor have they to gather money for the purpose of spending it on those who eat with them, since he has made it more honourable for a person to serve his neighbours by bodily exertion, than by putting himself to pecuniary expense; making it apparent that the one proceeds from the mind, and the other from fortune.

From acquiring money by unjust means, he prohibited them by such methods as the following. He instituted, in the first place, such a kind of money, that, even if but ten minae[4] came into a house, it could never escape the notice either of masters or of servants; for it would require much room, and a carriage to convey it. In the next place, gold and silver are searched after, and, if they are discovered anywhere, the possessor of them is punished. How, then, could gain by traffic be an object of pursuit, in a state where the possession of money occasions more pain than the use of it affords pleasure?

Obedience to the Magistrates and Laws

That at Sparta the citizens pay the strictest obedience to the magistrates [officials] and laws, we all know. I suppose, however, that Lycurgus did not attempt to establish such an excellent order of things, until he had brought the most powerful men in the state to be of the same mind with regard to it. I form my opinion on this consideration, that, in other states, the more influential men are not willing even to appear to fear the magistrates, but think that such fear is unbecoming free men; but in Sparta, the most powerful men not only put themselves under the magistrates, but even count it an honour to humble themselves before them, and to obey, when they are called upon, not walking, but running; supposing that if they themselves are the first to pay exact obedience, others will follow their example; and such has been the case. It is probable, also, that the chief men established the offices of the Ephors[5] in conjunction with Lycurgus, as they must have been certain that obedience is of the greatest benefit, alike in a state, and in an army, and in a family; and they doubtless considered that the greater power magistrates have, the greater effect will they produce on the citizens in enforcing obedience. The Ephors, accordingly, have full power to impose a fine on whomsoever they please, and to exact the fine without delay; they have power also to degrade magistrates even while they are in office, and to put them in prison, and to bring them to trial for their life. Being possessed of such authority, they do not, like the magistrates in other states, always permit those who are elected to offices to rule during the whole year as they choose, but, like despots and presidents in gymnastic contests, punish on the instant whomsoever they find acting at all contrary to the laws.

Though there were many other excellent contrivances adopted by Lycurgus, to induce the citizens to obey the laws, the most excellent of all appears to me to be, that he did not deliver his laws to the people until he had gone, in company with the most eminent of his fellow-citizens, to Delphi, and consulted the god whether it would be more beneficial and advantageous for Sparta to obey the laws which he had made. As the god replied that it would be more beneficial in every way, he at once delivered them, deciding that it would be not only illegal, but impious, to disobey laws sanctioned by the oracle.

Infamy and Penalties of Cowardice

It is deserving of admiration, too, in Lycurgus, that he made it a settled principle in the community, that an honourable death is preferable to a dishonourable life; for whoever pays attention to the subject will find that fewer of those who hold this opinion die than of those who attempt to escape danger by flight. Hence we may say with truth, that safety attends for a much longer period on valour than on cowardice; for valour is not only attended with less anxiety and greater pleasure, but is also more capable of assisting and supporting us. It is evident, too, that good report [reputation] accompanies valour; for almost everybody is willing to be in alliance with the brave.

---

[4]Large iron coins (really weights) of the Spartans.
[5]A five-man board, elected annually, that had nearly unlimited executive powers, except command in war.

How he contrived that such sentiments should be entertained, it is proper not to omit to mention. He evidently, then, intended a happy life for the brave, and a miserable one for the cowardly. In other communities, when a man acts as a coward, he merely brings on himself the name of coward, but the coward goes to the same market, and sits or takes exercise, if he pleases, in the same place with the brave men; at Sparta, however, every one would be ashamed to admit a coward into the same tent with him, or to allow him to be his opponent in a match at wrestling. Frequently, too, a person of such character, when they choose opposite parties to play at ball, is left without any place; and in forming a chorus he is thrust into the least honourable position. On the road he must yield the way to others, and at public meetings he must rise up, even before his juniors. His female relatives he must maintain at home, and they too must pay the penalty of his cowardice, since no man will marry them. He is also not allowed to take a wife, and must at the same time pay the customary fine for being a bachelor. He must not walk about with a cheerful expression, or imitate the manners of persons of blameless character; else he will have to receive whipping from his betters. Since, then, such disgrace is inflicted on cowards, I do not at all wonder that death is preferred at Sparta to a life so dishonourable and infamous.

Honors Paid to Old Age. Encouragement of Virtue

Lycurgus seems to me to have provided also, with great judgment, how virtue might be practised even to old age; for by adding to his other enactments the choice of senators at an advanced stage of life,[6] he caused honour and virtue not to be disregarded even in old age.

It is worthy of admiration in him, too, that he attached consideration to the old age of the well-deserving; for by making the old men arbiters in the contest for superiority in mental qualifications, he rendered their old age more honourable than the vigour of those in the meridian of life. This contest is deservedly held in the greatest esteem among the people, for gymnastic contests are attended with honour, but they concern only bodily accomplishments; the contest for distinction in old age involves a decision respecting merits of the mind. In proportion, therefore, as the mind is superior to the body, so much are contests for mental eminence more worthy of regard than those concerning bodily superiority.

Is it not highly worthy of admiration, also, in Lycurgus, that when he saw that those who are disinclined to practice virtue are not qualified to increase the power of their country, he obliged all the citizens of Sparta to cultivate every kind of virtue publicly. As private individuals, accordingly, who practise virtue, are superior in it to those who neglect it, so Sparta is naturally superior in virtue to all other states, as it is the only one that engages in a public cultivation of honour and virtue. Is it not also deserving of commendation, that, when other states punish any person that injures another, Lycurgus inflicted no less punishment on any one that openly showed himself unconcerned with becoming as good a man as possible? He thought, as it appears, that by those who make others slaves, or rob them, or steal anything, the individual sufferers only are injured, but that by the unprincipled and cowardly whole communities are betrayed; so that he appears to me to have justly imposed the heaviest penalties on such characters.

He also imposed on his countrymen an obligation, from which there is no exception, of practising every kind of political virtue; for he made the privileges of citizenship equally available to all those who observed what was enjoined by the laws, without taking any account either of weakness of body or scantiness of means; but if any one was too indolent to perform what the laws prescribed, Lycurgus appointed that he should be no longer counted in the number of equally privileged citizens.

That these laws are extremely ancient is certain; for Lycurgus is said to have lived in the time of the Heracleidae;[7] but, ancient as they are, they are still very new to other communities; for, what is the most wonderful of all things, all men extol such institutions, but no state thinks proper to imitate them.

---

[6]The twenty-eight senators, along with the two hereditary kings, formed the principal law-making body of Sparta (the Council of Elders); the senators were elected for life and had to be over sixty years of age.
[7]Children of the legendary Greek hero Heracles.

Of the Spartan Army

The regulations which I have mentioned are beneficial alike in peace and in war; but if any one wishes to learn what he contrived better than other legislators with reference to military proceedings, he may attend to the following particulars.

In the first place, then, the Ephors proclaim the age limits for the citizen draft to the army; artisans (non-citizens) are also called by the same order to serve supplying the troops. For the Spartans provide themselves in the field with an abundance of all those things which people use in a city; and of whatever instruments an army may require in common, orders are given to bring some on waggons, and others on beasts of burden, as by this arrangement anything left behind is least likely to escape notice.

For engagements in the field he made the following arrangements. He ordered that each soldier should have a purple robe and a brazen shield; for he thought that such a dress had least resemblance to that of women, and was excellently adapted for the field of battle, as it is soonest made splendid, and is longest in growing soiled. He permitted also those above the age of puberty to let their hair grow, as he thought that they thus appeared taller, more manly, and more terrifying in the eyes of the enemy. . . .

Herodotus

HISTORY

Herodotus (ca. 484- ca.425 B.C.) is often called the "Father of History" and for good reason. His history of the Persian War is not only the earliest surviving such work but also one of the best, serving as a model for all subsequent historians down to our own day.

Little is actually known about his personal life. A native of the Greek city-state of Halicarnassus on the eastern coast of the Aegean Sea, he was forced into exile from his homeland and traveled extensively throughout the eastern Mediterranean, including Egypt, and even reaching Mesopotamia. He eventually settled for some time in Athens and later migrated to an Athenian colony at Thurii in southern Italy.

His extensive travels allowed him to conduct "researches" (the Greek word "historie") into the greatest event of his immediate past, the war between the Persians and the Greeks in the early 5th century B.C. Of special importance is his use of the **historical method,** *now routinely used by all historians. Since Herodotus was not an eyewitness to this war, he had to conduct his research by other means, including interviews with actual participants who were still living and visiting the locations where key events took place. He thus often identifies the accounts of his varied sources (e.g., "It is said that . . ."), subjects these sources to critical analysis, and then offers his own interpretation, explaining his reasoning for doing so. Some elements of his account, such as the size of the Persian army which invaded Greece in 480 B.C., have rightly been questioned. Nevertheless, most scholars accept the bulk of his history as essentially reliable.*

It is important to note that Herodotus intended his history to be recited orally before a public audience (as he apparently did in Athens) rather than simply to be read by individuals. Thus his history was intended at least in part as entertainment and is full of fascinating stories, often with clear moral lessons, to engage an audience. Of particular interest is his sympathetic attitude towards non-Greeks, even the Persians, at a time when many Greeks regarded all non-Greeks as "barbarians".

The excerpt presented here covers the invasion of European Greece by the Persian King Xerxes in 480 B.C., leading up to the famous Battle of Thermopylae, where 300 Spartans plus several thousand other Greeks attempted to stop the advance of Xerxes' invading army."

Account of the Persian Invasion

After the conquest of Egypt, when he was on the point of taking in hand the expedition against Athens, Xerxes[1] called a conference of the leading men in the country, to find out their attitude towards the war and explain to them his own wishes. When they met, he addressed them as follows: 'Do not suppose, gentlemen, that I am departing from precedent in the course of action I intend to undertake. We Persians have a way of living, which I have

[1]King of Persia from 485 to 465 B.C., invaded Greece in 480 B.C.

inherited from my predecessors and propose to follow. I have learned from my elders that ever since Cyrus[2] deposed Astyages and we took over from the Medes the sovereign power we now possess, we have never yet remained inactive. This is God's guidance, and it is by following it that we have gained our great prosperity. Of our past history you need no reminder; for you know well enough the famous deeds of Cyrus, Cambyses, and my father .Darius, and their additions to our empire. Now I myself, ever since my accession, have been thinking how not to fall short of the kings who have sat upon this throne before me, and how to add as much power as they did to the Persian empire. And now at last I have found a way to win for Persia not glory only but a country as large and as rich as our own—indeed richer than our own[3]—and at the same time to get satisfaction and revenge. That, then, is the object of this meeting—that I may disclose to you what it is that I intend to do. I will bridge the Hellespont[4] and march an army through Europe into Greece, and punish the Athenians for the outrage they committed upon my father and upon us.[5] As you saw, Darius himself was making his preparations for war against these men; but death prevented him from carrying out his purpose. I therefore on his behalf, and for the benefit of all my subjects, will not rest until I have taken Athens and burnt it to the ground, in revenge for the injury which the Athenians without provocation once did to me and my father. These men, you remember, came to Sardis with Aristagoras the Milesian, a subject of ours, and burnt the temples and sacred groves; and you know all too well how they served our troops under Datis and Artaphernes,[6] when they landed upon Greek soil. For these reasons I have now prepared to make war upon them, and, when I consider the matter, I find several advantages in the venture; if we crush the Athenians and their neighbours in the Peloponnese,[7] we shall so extend the empire of Persia that its boundaries will be God's own sky, so that the sun will not look down upon any land beyond the boundaries of what is ours. With your help I shall pass through Europe from end to end and make it all one country. For if what I am told is true, there is not a city or nation in the world which will be able to withstand us, once these are out of the way. Thus the guilty and the innocent alike shall bear the yoke of servitude.

'If, then, you wish to gain my favour, each one of you must present himself willingly and in good heart on the day which I shall name whoever brings with him the best equipped body of troops I will reward with those marks of distinction held in greatest value by our countrymen. That is what you must do; but so that I shall not appear to consult only my own whim, I will throw the whole matter into open debate, and ask any of you who may wish to do so, to express his views.'

The first to speak after the king was Mardonius. 'Of all Persians who have ever lived,' he began, 'and of all who are yet to be born, you my lord, are the greatest. Every word you have spoken is true and excellent, and you will not allow the wretched Ionians[8] in Europe to make fools of us. It would indeed be an odd thing if we who have defeated and enslaved the Sacae, Indians, Ethiopians, Assyrians, an many other great nations for no fault of their own, but merely to extend the boundaries of our empire, should fail now to punish the Greeks who have been guilty of injuring us without provocation. Have we anything to fear from them? The size of their army? Their wealth? The question is absurd; we know how they fight; we know how slender their resources are. People of their race we have already reduced to subjection—I mean the Greeks of Asia, Ionians, Aeolians, and Dorians.[9] I myself before now have had some experience of these men, when under orders from your father I invaded their country; and I got as far as Macedonia—indeed almost to Athens itself—without a single soldier daring to oppose me. Yet, from what I hear, the Greeks are pugnacious enough, and start fights on the spur of the moment without sense or judgement to justify them. When they declare war on each other, they go off together to the smoothest and levellest bit of ground they can find, and have their battle on it—with the result that even the victors never get off without heavy losses, and

---

[2]Founder of the Persian Empire (559–529 B.C.), father of Cambyses.
[3]Xerxes greatly-overstates the size and wealth of the Greek city-states.
[4]The strait separating Europe from Asia, near the site of ancient Troy.
[5]In 499 B.C. some ethnic Greeks on the coast of Asia Minor had revolted against Darius, their Persian king. With the aid of Athenian infantry, the rebels had burned the city of Sardis. Focussing his revenge on Athens, Darius invaded Greece in 490 B.C. but was defeated at Marathon near Athens. He died while preparing a new invasion which his son, Xerxes, would now push forward.
[6]Persian commanders in the failed campaign of 490 B.C.
[7]The southern portion of Greece.
[8]Greek "tribal" group that included both those in Asia Minor who had revolted against their Persian lords in 499 B.C. and their kinsmen in Athens, the source of Ionian power.
[9]All three Greek tribal groups—Ionian, Aeolian, and Dorian—had some of their population migrate to Asia Minor where they had become subjects of the Persian Empire.

as for the losers—well, they're wiped out. Now surely, as they all talk the same language, they ought to be able to find a better way of settling their differences: by negotiation, for instance, or an interchange of views—indeed by anything rather than fighting. Or if it is really impossible to avoid coming to blows, they might at least employ the elements of strategy and look for a strong position to fight from. In any case, the Greeks, with their absurd notions of warfare, never even thought of opposing me when I led my army to Macedonia.

'Well then, my lord, who is likely to resist you when you march against them with the millions of Asia at your back, and the whole Persian fleet? Believe me, it is not in the Greek character to take so desperate a risk. But should I be wrong and they be so foolish as to do battle with us, then they will learn that we are the best soldiers in the world. Nevertheless, let us take this business seriously and spare no pains; success is never automatic in this world—nothing is achieved without trying.'

Xerxes' proposals were made to sound plausible enough by these words of Mardonius, and when he stopped speaking there was a silence. For a while nobody dared to put forward the opposite view, until Artabanus, taking courage from the fact of his relationship to the king—he was a son of Hystaspes and therefore Xerxes' uncle—rose to speak. 'My lord,' he said, 'without a debate in which both sides of a question are expressed, it is not possible to choose the better course. All one can do is to accept whatever it is that has been proposed. But grant a debate, and there is a fair choice to be made. We cannot assess the purity of gold merely by looking at it: we test it by rubbing it on other gold—then we can tell which is the purer. I warned your father—Darius my own brother—not to attack the Scythians, those wanderers who live in a cityless land. But he would not listen to me. Confident in his power to subdue them he invaded their country, and before he came home again many fine soldiers who marched with him were dead. But you, my lord, mean to attack a nation greatly superior to the Scythians: a nation with the highest reputation for valour both on land and at sea. It is my duty to tell you what you have to fear from them: you have said you mean to bridge the Hellespont and march through Europe to Greece. Now suppose—and it is not impossible—that you were to suffer a reverse by sea or land, or even both. These Greeks are said to be great fighters—and indeed one might well guess as much from the fact that the Athenians alone destroyed the great army we sent to attack them under Datis and Artaphernes. Or, if you will, suppose they were to succeed upon one element only—suppose they fell upon our fleet and defeated it, and then sailed to the Hellespont and destroyed the bridge: then, my lord, you would indeed be in peril. It is no special wisdom of my own that makes me argue as I do; but just such a disaster as I have suggested did, in fact, very nearly overtake us when your father bridged the Thracian Bosphorus and the Danube to take his army into Scythia. You will remember how on that occasion the Scythians went to all lengths in their efforts to induce the Ionian guard to break the Danube bridge, and how Histiaeus, the lord of Miletus, merely by following the advice of the other Ionian despots instead of rejecting it, as he did, had it in his power to ruin Persia Surely it is a dreadful thing even to hear said, that the fortunes of the king once wholly depended upon a single man.

'I urge you, therefore, to abandon this plan; take my advice and do not run any such terrible risk when there is no necessity to do so. Break up this conference; turn the matter over quietly by yourself, and then, when you think fit, announce your decision. Nothing is more valuable to a man than to lay his plans carefully and well; even if things go against him, and forces he cannot control bring his enterprise to nothing, he still has the satisfaction of knowing that is was not his fault—the plans were all laid; if, on the other hand, he leaps headlong into danger and succeeds by luck—well, that's a bit of luck indeed, but he still has the shame of knowing that he was ill prepared.

'You know, my lord, that amongst living creatures it is the great ones that God [Zeus] smites with his thunder, out of envy of their pride. The little ones do not vex him. It is always the great buildings and the tall trees which are struck by lightning. It is God's way to bring the lofty low. Often a great army is destroyed by a little one, when God in his envy puts fear into the men's hearts, or sends a thunderstorm, and they are cut to pieces in a way they do not deserve. For God tolerates pride in none but Himself. Haste is the mother of failure—and for failure we always pay a heavy price; it is in delay our profit lies—perhaps it may not immediately be apparent, but we shall find it, sure enough, as times goes on. . . .

'This, my lord, is the advice I offer you. . . .'

All the Persian nobles who had attended the conference hurried home to their respective provinces; and as every one of them hoped to win the reward which Xerxes had offered, no pains were spared in the subsequent preparations, and Xerxes, in the process of assembling his, armies, had every corner of the continent ransacked. For the four years following the conquest of Egypt the mustering of troops and the provision of stores and equipment continued, and towards the close of the fifth Xerxes, at the head of his enormous force, began his march.

The army was indeed far greater than any other in recorded history. . . .

There was not a nation in Asia that he did not take with him against Greece; save for the great rivers there was not a stream his army drank from that was not drunk dry. Some nations provided ships, others formed infantry units; from some cavalry was requisitioned, from others horse-transports and crews; from others, again, warships for floating bridges, or provisions and naval craft of various kinds. . . .

In Sardis Xerxes' first act was to send representatives to every place in Greece except Athens and Sparta with a demand for earth and water and a further order to prepare entertainment for him against his coming. This renewed demand for submission was due to his confident belief that the Greeks who had previously refused to comply with the demand of Darius would now be frightened into complying with his own. It was to prove whether or not he was right that he took this step.

He then prepared to move forward to Abydos, where a bridge had already been constructed across the Hellespont from Asia to Europe. Between Sestos and Madytus in the Chersonese there is a rocky headland running out into the water opposite Abydos. It was here not long afterwards that the Greeks under Xanthippus the son of Ariphron took Artaÿctes the Persian governor of Sestos, and nailed him alive to a plank—he was the man who collected women in the temple of Protesilaus at Elaeus and committed various acts of sacrilege. This headland was the point to which Xerxes' engineers carried their two bridges from Abydos—a distance of seven furlongs.[10] One was constructed by the Phoenicians using flax cables, the other by the Egyptians with papyrus cables. The work was successfully completed, but a subsequent storm of great violence smashed it up and carried everything away. Xerxes was very angry when he learned of the disaster, and gave orders that the Hellespont should receive three hundred lashes and have a pair of fetters [leg shackles] thrown into it. I have heard before now that he also sent people to brand it with hot irons. He certainly instructed the men with the whips to utter, as they wielded them, the barbarous and presumptuous words: 'You salt and bitter stream, your master lays this punishment upon you for injuring him, who never injured you. But Xerxes the King will cross you, with or without your permission. No man sacrifices to you, and you deserve the neglect by your acid and muddy waters.' In addition to punishing the Hellespont Xerxes gave orders that the men responsible for building the bridges should have their heads cut off. The men who received these invidious orders duly carried them out, and other engineers completed the work. . . .

No sooner had the troops begun to move than the sun vanished from his place in the sky and it grew dark as night, though the weather was perfectly clear and cloudless. Xerxes, deeply troubled, asked the Magi[11] to interpret the significance of this strange phenomenon, and was given to understand that God meant to foretell to the Greeks the eclipse of their cities—for it was the sun which gave warning of the future to Greece, just as the moon did to Persia. Having heard this Xerxes continued the march in high spirits.

The army, however, had not gone far when Pythius the Lydian, in alarm at the sign from heaven, was emboldened by the presents he had received to come to Xerxes with a request. 'Master,' he said, 'there is a favour I should like you to grant me—a small thing, indeed, for you to perform, but to me of great importance, should you consent to do so Xerxes, who thought the request would be almost anything but what it actually turned out to be, agreed to grant it and told Pythius to say what it was he wanted. This generous answer raised Pythius' hopes, and he said, 'My lord, I have five sons, and it happens that every one of them is serving in your army in the campaign against Greece. I am an old man, Sire, and I beg you in pity to release from service one of my sons—the eldest—to take care of me and my property. Take the other four—and may you return with your purpose accomplished.'

Xerxes was furiously angry. 'You miserable fellow,' he cried, 'have you the face to mention your son, when I, in person, am marching to the war against Greece with my sons and brothers and kinsmen and friends—*you*, my slave, whose duty it was to come with me with every member of your house, including your wife? Mark my words: it is through the ears you can touch a man to pleasure or rage—let the spirit which dwells there hear good things, and it will fill the body with delight; let it hear bad, and it will swell with fury. When you did me good service, and offered more, you cannot boast that you were more generous than I; and now your punishment will be less than your impudence deserves. Yourself and four of your sons are saved by the entertainment you gave me; but you shall pay with the life of the fifth, whom you cling to most.'

---

[10]A furlong is a unit of distance equal to 220 yards, an eighth of a mile. (The translator has here converted Greek into English measurements.)
[11]Persian priest-oracles.

Having answered Pythius in these words Xerxes at once gave orders that the men to whom such duties fell should find Pythius' eldest son and cut him in half and put the two halves one on each side of the road, for the army to march out between them. The order was performed.

From the European shore Xerxes watched his troops coming over under the whips. The crossing occupied seven days and nights without a break. There is a story that some time after Xerxes had passed the bridge, a native of the country thereabouts exclaimed: 'Why, O God, have you assumed the shape of a man of Persia, and changed your name to Xerxes, in order to lead everyone in the world to the conquest and devastation of Greece? You could have destroyed Greece without going to that trouble.' . . .

As nobody has left a record, I cannot state the precise number of men provided by each separate nation, but the grand total, excluding the naval contingent, turned out to be 1,700,000.[12] The counting was done by first packing ten thousand men as close together as they could stand and drawing a circle round them on the ground; they were then dismissed, and a fence, about navel-high, was constructed round the circle; finally other troops were marched into the area thus enclosed and dismissed in their turn, until the whole army had been counted. After the counting, the army was reorganized in divisions according to nationality. . . .

Having sailed from one end to the other of the line of anchored ships, Xerxes went ashore again and sent for Demaratus,[13] the son of Ariston, who was accompanying him in the march to Greece. 'Demaratus,' he said, 'it would give me pleasure at this point to put to you a few questions. You are a Greek, and a native, moreover, of by no means the meanest or weakest city in that country—as I learn not only from yourself but from the other Greeks I have spoken with. Tell me, then—will the Greeks dare to lift a hand against me? My own belief is that all the Greeks and all the other western peoples gathered together would be insufficient to withstand the attack of my army—and still more so if they are not united. But it is your opinion upon this subject that I should like to hear.'

'My lord,' Demaratus replied, 'is it a true answer you would like, or merely an agreeable one?'

'Tell me the truth,' said the king: 'and I promise that you will not suffer by it.' Encouraged by this Demaratus continued: 'My lord, you bid me speak nothing but the truth, to say nothing which might later be proved a lie. Very well then; this is my answer: poverty is my country's inheritance from of old, but valour she won for herself by wisdom and the strength of law. By her valour Greece now keeps both poverty and bondage at bay.

'I think highly of all Greeks of the Dorian lands, but what I am about to say will apply not to all Dorians, but to the Spartans only. First then, they will not under any circumstances accept terms from you which would mean slavery for Greece; secondly, they will fight you even if the rest of Greece submits. Moreover, there is no use in asking if their numbers are adequate to enable them to do this; suppose a thousand of them take the field—then that thousand will fight you; and so will any number, greater than this or less.'

Xerxes laughed. 'My dear Demaratus,' he exclaimed, 'what an extraordinary thing to say! Do you really suppose a thousand men would fight an army like mine? Now tell me, would *you*, who were once, as you say, king of these people, be willing at this moment to fight ten men single-handed? I hardly think so; yet, if things in Sparta are really as you have described them, then, according to your laws, you as king ought to take on a double share—so that if every Spartan is a match for ten men of mine, I should expect you to be a match for twenty. Only in that way can you prove the truth of your claim. But if you Greeks, who think so much of yourselves, are all of the size and quality of those I have spoken with when they have visited my court—and of yourself, Demaratus—there is some danger of your words being nothing but an empty boast. But let me put my point as reasonably as I can—how is it possible that a thousand men, or ten thousand, or fifty thousand, should stand up to an army as big as mine, especially if they were not under a single master, but all perfectly free to do as they pleased? Suppose them to have five thousand men: in that case we should be more than a thousand to one! If, like ours, their troops were subject to the control of a single man, then possibly for fear of him, in spite of the disparity in numbers, they might show some sort of factitious courage, or let themselves be whipped into battle; but, as every man is free to follow his fancy, it is not conceivable that they should do either. Indeed, my own opinion is that even on equal terms the Greeks could hardly face the Persians alone. We, too, have this thing that you were speaking of—I do not say it is common, but it does exist; for instance, amongst the Persians in my bodyguard there are men who would willingly fight with three Greeks together. But you know nothing of such things, or you could not talk such nonsense.'

[12]Herodotus' figure is impossibly huge. The estimates of modern scholars are, nevertheless, still impressive. They range from 100,000 to 400,000 combatants in the Persian army, and from 700 to 1000 ships in the navy.

[13]A former king of Sparta who had been dethroned by his own countrymen on a false charge of illegitimacy.

My lord,' Demaratus answered, 'I knew before I began that if I spoke the truth you would not like it. But, as you demanded the plain truth and nothing less, I told you how things are with the Spartans. Yet you are well aware that I now feel but little affection for my countrymen, who robbed me of my hereditary power and privileges and made me a fugitive without a home—whereas your father welcomed me at his court and gave me the means of livelihood and somewhere to live. Surely it is unreasonable to reject kindness; any sensible man will cherish it. Personally I do not claim to be able to fight ten men—or two; indeed I should prefer not even to fight with one. But should it be necessary—should there be some great cause to urge me on—then nothing would give me more pleasure than to stand up to one of those men of yours who claim to be a match for three Greeks. So it is with the Spartans; fighting singly, they are as good as any, but fighting together they are the best soldiers in the world. They are free—yes—but not entirely free; for they have a master, and that master is Law, which they fear much more than your subjects fear you. Whatever this master commands, they do; and his command never varies: it is never to retreat in battle, however great the odds, but always to stand firm, and to conquer or die. If, my lord, you think that what I have said is nonsense—very well; I am willing henceforward to hold my tongue. This time I spoke because you forced me to speak. In any case, I pray that all may turn out as you desire.'

Xerxes burst out laughing at Demaratus' answer, and good-humouredly let him go.

After the conversation I have recorded above, Xerxes . . . continued his march through Thrace towards Greece.

• • •

The position, then, was that Xerxes was lying with his force at Trachis in Malian territory, while the Greeks occupied the pass[14] known locally as Pylae—though Thermopylae is the common Greek name. Such were the respective positions of the two armies, one being in control of all the country from Trachis northward, the other of the whole mainland to the south. The Greek force which here awaited the coming of Xerxes was made up of the following contingents: 300 heavy-armed infantry from Sparta, 500 from Tegea, 500 from Mantinea, 120 from Orchomenus in Arcadia, 1000 from the rest of Arcadia; from Corinth there were 400, from Phlius 200, and from Mycenae 80. In addition to these troops from the Peloponnese, there were the Boeotian contingents of 700 from Thespiae and 400 from Thebes. The Locrians of Opus and the Phocians had also obeyed the call to arms, the former sending all the men they had, the latter one thousand. The other Greeks had induced these two towns to send troops by a message to the effect that they themselves were merely an advance force, and that the main body of the confederate [allied] army was daily expected; the sea, moreover, was strongly held by the fleet of Athens and Aegina and the other naval forces. Thus there was no cause for alarm—for, after all, it was not a god who threatened Greece, but a man, and there neither was nor ever would be a man who was not born with a good chance of misfortune—and the greater the man, the greater the misfortune. The present enemy was no exception; he too was human, and was sure to be disappointed of his great expectations.

The appeal succeeded, and Opus and Phocis sent their troops to Trachis. The contingents of the various states were under their own officers, but the most respected was Leonidas the Spartan, who was in command of the whole army. Leonidas traced his descent directly back to Heracles,[15] through Anaxandrides and Leon (his father and grandfather), Anaxander, Eurycrates, Polydorus, Alcamenes, Teleches, Archelaus, Agesilaus, Doryssus, Labotas, Echestratus, Agis, Eurysthenes, Aristodemus, Aristomachus, Cleodaeus—and so to Hyllus, who was Heracles' son. He had come to be king of Sparta quite unexpectedly, for as he had two elder brothers, Cleomenes and Dorieus, he had no thought of himself succeeding to the throne. Dorieus, however, was killed in Sicily, and when Cleomenes also died without an heir, Leonidas found himself next in the succession. He was older than Cleombrotus, Anaxandrides' youngest son, and was, moreover, married to Cleomenes' daughter. The three hundred men whom he brought on this occasion to Thermopylae were chosen by himself, all fathers of living sons. He also took with him the Thebans I mentioned, under the command of Leontiades, the son of Eurymachus. The reason why he made a special point of taking troops from Thebes, and from Thebes only, was that the Thebans were strongly suspected of Persian sympathies, so he called upon them to play their part in the war in order to see if they would answer the call, or openly refuse to join the confederacy. They did send troops, but their secret sympathy was nevertheless with the enemy. Leonidas and his three hundred were sent by Sparta in advance of the main army, in order that the sight of them might encourage the

---

[14]The width of the pass, the distance between a high cliff and the sea, was only about fourteen yards.

[15]It was common for aristocrats to trace their lineage back to some famous hero. For a Spartan warrior, Heracles (Roman Hercules) would have been an especially appropriate ancestor as he was noted for his strength, courage, and endurance.

other confederates to fight and prevent them from going over to the enemy, as they were quite capable of doing if they knew that Sparta was hanging back; the intention was, when the Carneia was over (for it was that festival which prevented the Spartans from taking the field in the ordinary way), to leave a garrison in the city and march with all the troops at their disposal. The other allied states proposed to act similarly; for the Olympic festival happened to fall just at this same period. None of them ever expected the battle at Thermopylae to be decided so soon—which was the reason why they sent only advance parties there.

The Persian army was now close to the pass, and the Greeks, suddenly doubting their power to resist, held a conference to consider the advisability of retreat. It was proposed by the Peloponnesians generally that the army should fall back upon the Peloponnese and hold the Isthmus; but when the Phocians and Locrians expressed their indignation at this suggestion, Leonidas gave his voice for staying where they were and sending, at the same time, an appeal for reinforcements to the various states of the confederacy, as their numbers were inadequate to cope with the Persians.

During the conference Xerxes sent a man on horseback to ascertain the strength of the Greek force and to observe what the troops were doing. He had heard before he left Thessaly that a small force was concentrated here, led by the Lacedaemonians [Spartans] under Leonidas of the house of Heracles. The Persian rider approached the camp and took a thorough survey of all he could see—which was not, however, the whole Greek army; for the men on the further side of the wall which, after its reconstruction, was now guarded, were out of sight. He did, none the less, carefully observe the troops who were stationed on the outside of the wall. At that moment these happened to be Spartans, and some of them were stripped for exercise, while others were combing their hair. The Persian spy watched them in astonishment; nevertheless he made sure of their numbers, and of everything else he needed to know, as accurately as he could, and then rode quietly off. No one attempted to catch him, or took the least notice of him.

Back in his own camp he told Xerxes what he had seen. Xerxes was bewildered; the truth, namely that the Spartans were preparing themselves to die and deal death with all their strength, was beyond his comprehension, and what they were doing seemed to him merely absurd. Accordingly he sent for Demaratus, the son of Ariston, who had come with the army, and questioned him about the spy's report, in the hope of finding out what the behaviour of the Spartans might mean. 'Once before,' Demaratus said, 'when we began our march against Greece, you heard me speak of these men. I told you then how I saw this enterprise would turn out, and you laughed at me. I strive for nothing, my lord, more earnestly than to observe the truth in your presence; so hear me once more. These men have come to fight us for possession of the pass, and for that struggle they are preparing. It is the common practice of the Spartans to pay careful attention to their hair when they are about to risk their lives. But I assure you that if you can defeat these men and the rest of the Spartans who are still at home, there is no other people in the world who will dare to stand firm or lift a hand against you. You have now to deal with the finest kingdom in Greece, and with the bravest men.'

Xerxes, unable to believe what Demaratus said, asked further how it was possible that so small a force could fight with his army. 'My lord,' Demaratus replied, 'treat me as a liar, if what I have foretold does not take place.' But still Xerxes was unconvinced.

For four days Xerxes waited, in constant expectation that the Greeks would make good their escape; then, on the fifth, when still they had made no move and their continued presence seemed mere impudent and reckless folly, he was seized with rage and sent forward the Medes and Cissians[16] with orders to take them alive and bring them into his presence. The Medes charged, and in the struggle which ensued many fell; but others took their places, and in spite of terrible losses refused to be beaten off. They made it plain enough to anyone, and not least to the king himself, that he had in his army many men, indeed, but few soldiers. All day the battle continued; the Medes, after their rough handling, were at length withdrawn and their place was taken by Hydarnes and his picked Persian troops—the King's Immortals—who advanced to the attack in full confidence of bringing the business to a quick and easy end. But, once engaged, they were no more successful than the Medes had been; all went as before, the two armies fighting in a confined space, the Persians using shorter spears than the Greeks and having no advantage from their numbers.

On the Spartan side it was a memorable fight; they were men who understood war pitted against an inexperienced enemy, and amongst the feints they employed was to turn their backs on a body and pretend to be retreating

---

[16]Allies of the Persians.

in confusion, whereupon the enemy would pursue them with a great clatter and roar; but the Spartans, just as the Persians were on them, would wheel and face them and inflict in the new struggle innumerable casualties. The Spartans had their losses too, but not many. At last the Persians, finding that their assaults upon the pass, whether by divisions or by any other way they could think of, were all useless, broke off the engagement and withdrew. Xerxes was watching the battle from where he sat; and it is said that in the course of the attacks three times, in terror for his army, he leapt to his feet.

Next day the fighting began again, but with no better success for the Persians, who renewed their onslaught in the hope that the Greeks, being so few in number, might be badly enough disabled by wounds to prevent further resistance. But the Greeks never slackened; their troops were ordered in divisions corresponding to the states from which they came, and each division took its turn in the line except the Phocian, which had been posted to guard the track over the mountains. So when the Persians found that things were no better for them than on the previous day, they once more withdrew.

How to deal with the situation Xerxes had no idea; but just then, a man from Malis, Ephialtes, the son of Eurydemus, came, in hope of a rich reward, to tell the king about the track which led over the hills to Thermopylae—and thus he was to prove the death of the Greeks who held the pass.[17] . . .

The Greeks at Thermopylae had their first warning of the death that was coming with the dawn from the seer Megistias, who read their doom in the victims of sacrifice;[18] deserters, too, came in during the night with news of the Persian flank movement, and lastly, just as day was breaking, the look-out men came running from the hills. In council of war their opinions were divided, some urging that they must not abandon their post, others the opposite. The result was that the army split: some dispersed, contingents returning to their various cities, while others made ready to stand by Leonidas. It is said that Leonidas himself dismissed them, to spare their lives, but thought it unbecoming for the Spartans under his command to desert the post which they had originally come to guard. I myself am inclined to think that he dismissed them when he realized that they had no heart for the fight and were unwilling to take their share of the danger; at the same time honour forbade that he himself should go. And indeed by remaining at his post he left a great name behind him, and Sparta did not lose her prosperity, as might otherwise have happened; for right at the outset of the war the Spartans had been told by the Delphic oracle[19] that either their city must be laid waste by the foreigner or a Spartan king be killed. . . .

I believe it was the thought of this oracle, combined with his wish to lay up for the Spartans a treasure of fame in which no other city should share, that made Leonidas dismiss those troops; I do not think that they deserted, or went off without orders, because of a difference of opinion. Moreover, I am strongly supported in this view by the case of the seer Megistias, who was with the army—an Acarnanian, said to be of the clan of Melampus—who foretold the coming doom from his inspection of the sacrificial victims. He quite plainly received orders from Leonidas to quit Thermopylae, to save him from sharing the army's fate. He refused to go, but he sent his only son, who was serving with the forces.

Thus it was that the confederate troops, by Leonidas' orders, abandoned their posts and left the pass, all except the Thespians and the Thebans who remained with the Spartans.[20] The Thebans were detained by Leonidas as hostages very much against their will; but the Thespians of their own accord refused to desert Leonidas and his men, and stayed, and died with them. They were under the command of Demophilus the son of Diadromes.

In the morning Xerxes poured a libation to the rising sun, and then waited till it was well up before he began to move forward. This was according to Ephialtes' instructions, for the way down from the ridge is much shorter and more direct than the long and circuitous ascent.[21] As the Persian army advanced to the assault, the Greeks under Leonidas, knowing that they were going to their deaths, went out into the wider part of the pass much further

[17]The track led *around* the pass, to the rear of the Greek forces. (Ephialtes came from the local region. Some ten years later, when he had returned from his place of refuge, Ephialtes was assassinated.)

[18]Cattle and sheep were the most usual victims of the ritual sacrifice to the gods of the Greeks. (Note Odysseus' offering in Book One of *The Iliad*—selection 1, pp. 13–14.) Seers told the future by examining the animals' entrails.

[19]Delphi, on the Greek mainland, was the site of the ancient world's most famous oracle. Questioners would come there seeking advice on matters concerning religious ritual, morality, and the course of the future. (Note Oedipus' journey to Delphi.)

[20]Some modern estimates number the total Greek forces under Leonidas, including his 300 Spartans, at about 7,000 men. Before the final stand, when most of the units were allowed to march away, 1,100 stayed with the Spartans.

[21]The instructions allowed time for the troops led by Ephialtes to reach the rear of the Greek force at about the same time as the main Persian frontal attack.

than they had done before; in the previous days' fighting they had been holding the wall and making sorties from behind it into the narrow neck, but now they fought outside the narrows. Many of the invaders fell; behind them the company commanders plied their whips indiscriminately, driving the men on. Many fell into the sea and were drowned, and still more were .trampled to death by their friends. No one could count the number of the dead. The Greeks, who knew that the enemy were on their way round by the mountain track and that death was inevitable, put forth all their strength and fought with fury and desperation. By this time most of their spears were broken, and they were killing Persians with their swords.

In the course of that fight Leonidas fell, having fought most gallantly, and many distinguished Spartans with him—their names I have learned, as those of men who deserve to be remembered; indeed, I have learned the names of all the three hundred. Amongst the Persian dead, too, were many men of high distinction, including two brothers of Xerxes. . . .

There was a bitter struggle over the body of Leonidas; four times the Greeks drove the enemy off, and at last by their valour rescued it. So it went on, until the troops with Ephialtes were close at hand; and then, when the Greeks knew that they had come, the character of the fighting changed. They withdrew again into the narrow neck of the pass, behind the wall, and took up a position in a single compact body—all except the Thebans—on the little hill at the entrance to the pass, where the stone lion in memory of Leonidas stands to-day. Here they resisted to the last, with their swords, if they had them, and, if not, with their hands and teeth, until the Persians, coming on from the front over the ruins of the wall and closing in from behind, finally overwhelmed them with missile weapons.

Of all the Spartans and Thespians who fought so valiantly the most signal proof of courage was given by the Spartan Dieneces. It is said that before the battle he was told by a native of Trachis that, when the Persians shot their arrows, there were so many of them that they hid the sun. Dieneces, however, quite unmoved by the thought of the strength of the Persian army, merely remarked: 'This is pleasant news that the stranger from Trachis brings us: if the Persians hide the sun, we shall have our battle in the shade.' . . .

The dead were buried where they fell, and with them the men who had been killed before those dismissed by Leonidas left the pass. Over them is this inscription, in honour of the whole force:

> *Four thousand here from Pelops' land*
> *Against three million once did stand.*

The Spartans have a special epitaph; it runs:

> *Go tell the Spartans, you who read:*
> *We took their orders, and are dead.*

[Editor's note: After the battle at Thermopylae the Persians continued their advance. The Athenians evacuated their city which was captured by the Persians who burned down the temples on the Acropolis (the high citadel which dominated the city). In the following months, however, there was a great naval battle in the narrow waters between the island of Salamis and the mainland; there was also a major land battle near Plataea. On both occasions the Persians were totally routed. After those battles never again did a Persian military force threaten the European mainland.]

• • •

Thucydides

HISTORY OF THE PELOPONNESIAN WAR

The Persian Wars, described in Herodotus' account of the heroic Greek stand at Thermopylae, were the prelude to Greek glory. The Peloponnesian War (431–404 B.C.), fought mainly between Athens and Sparta, brought suffering and disaster to Greece. In the years following the victory over the Persians, the democratic city-state of Athens expanded into imperial power by using the financial contributions from other city-states, intended for the common defense of Greece, to build up the powerful Athenian navy and its own economic prosperity. Thus, the conflict with Sparta, which had the stronger army, was "inevitable" (the historian Thucydides tells us) because of "the growth of Athenian power and the fear which this caused in Sparta."

The task of recording and analyzing that bitter struggle of Greek against Greek fell to Thucydides (ca. 460–ca. 400 B.C.). Born in Athens to an aristocratic and wealthy family, Thucydides was chosen in 424 B.C. to command a fleet against the Spartans in the northern Aegean Sea. For allowing himself to be outmaneuvered and defeated by the enemy, he was exiled and did not return to Athens until 404. Thucydides thus had ample opportunity to observe the Peloponnesian War from both sides; he spent his twenty years of exile in various parts of Greece, recording the tragedy of his own times. Behind his narrative lay the deeper purpose of searching for an answer to the following question: "Why had Athens, with the fairest prospects of victory, been beaten?" Thucydides' History is, in essence, an analysis of the causes of the Athenian defeat; hence, it has been well described as a study in the pathology of imperialism and war.

Thucydides' own reflections on issues and motives are found in the forty or more "set speeches" for which the History is famous. These speeches—which appear as direct quotations from the individual participants, but were actually written by Thucydides—represent a common device in ancient Greek literature. Like the oration and the dialogue they must be accounted for by the importance of the spoken word in Greek culture. Thucydides, describing his method, stated that "while keeping as closely as possible to the general sense of the words that were actually used, [I] . . . make the speakers say what, in my opinion, was called for by each situation."

The first speech in the following group of selections gives a foreigner's view of the Athenian character. It shows clearly a sharp contrast to the Spartan traits described by Xenophon. This contrast is further developed in the second selection, the most famous speech of the History—the "Funeral Oration" by Pericles, the leading Athenian statesman, in honor of those who had died in the war's first campaign. Like Abraham Lincoln's "Gettysburg Address," which bears many similarities to Pericles' speech, it is both an appeal to patriotism and a reasoned explanation of a free and open democracy's superiority to rival forms of government.

In the summer following the public funeral a dreadful plague broke out among the people crowded inside the walls of Athens. The city lost more than a quarter of its inhabitants, a blow from which it never fully recovered. (Pericles died in the following year from the lingering effects of the plague.) Thucydides, too, was a victim, but

From *The History of the Peloponnesian War* by Thucydides, translated by Rex Warner, with an introduction and notes by M.I. Finley (Penguin Classics 1954, Revised edition 1972). Translation copyright © Rex Warner, 1954. Introduction and Appendices copyright © M.I. Finley, 1972. Reproduced by permission of Penguin Books Ltd.

he recovered. His medical and sociological description of the plague's symptoms and results, included here, is remarkable for its scientific objectivity.

The last excerpt is "The Melian Dialogue," in which the monstrous realities of the conflict are stripped bare. To the question, "Why was Athens beaten?" Thucydides implies the answer that Athens, deprived of Pericles' strong but humanely moderate leadership, pursued a policy of barbarous extremism. At Melos, after some fifteen years of brutalizing war, the Athenians justified their empire solely on the grounds of self-serving power.

Thucydides says he composed his History *(which breaks off, unfinished among the events of 411 B.C.) so that its readers could "understand clearly the events which happened in the past and which (human nature being what it is) will, at some time or other and in much the same ways, be repeated in the future." It was written "to last forever." The* History *is impartial and reflective, conveying both the Periclean ideals favored by Thucydides and the later moral degeneration and disillusionment that result when the life of reason is sacrificed for wealth and power. There is in his writing none of the sentiment or supernaturalism that make the recitations of Herodotus so entertaining, but lovers of Thucydides' objectivity and human insight have hailed him as the supreme historian of all time.*

The Debate at Sparta and Declaration of War [432 B.C.][1]

You have never yet tried to imagine what sort of people these Athenians are against whom you will have to fight—how much, indeed how completely different from you. An Athenian is always an innovator, quick to form a resolution and quick at carrying it out. You, on the other hand, are good at keeping things as they are; you never originate an idea, and your action tends to stop short of its aim. Then again, Athenian daring will outrun its own resources; they will take risks against their better judgement, and still, in the midst of danger, remain confident. But your nature is always to do less than you could have done, to mistrust your own judgement, however sound it may be, and to assume that dangers will last forever. Think of this, too: while you are hanging back, they never hesitate; while you stay at home, they are always abroad; for they think that the farther they go the more they will get, while you think that any movement may endanger what you have already. If they win a victory, they follow it up at once, and if they suffer a defeat, they scarcely fall back at all. As for their bodies, they regard them as expendable for their city's sake, as though they were not their own; but each man cultivates his own intelligence, again with a view to doing something notable for his city. If they aim at something and do not get it, they think that they have been deprived of what belonged to them already; whereas, if their enterprise is successful, they regard that success as nothing compared to what they will do next. Suppose they fail in some undertaking; they make good the loss immediately by setting their hopes in some other direction. Of them alone it may be said that they possess a thing almost as soon as they have begun to desire it, so quickly with them does action follow upon decision. And so they go on working away in hardship and danger all the days of their lives, seldom enjoying their possessions because they are always adding to them. Their view of a holiday is to do what needs doing; they prefer hardship and activity to peace and quiet. In a word, they are by nature incapable of either living a quiet life themselves or of allowing anyone else to do so.

• • •

Pericles' Funeral Oration [430 B.C.]

In the same winter[2] the Athenians, following their annual custom, gave a public funeral for those who had been the first to die in the war. These funerals are held in the following way: two days before the ceremony the bones of the fallen are brought and put in a tent which has been erected, and people make whatever offerings they wish to their own dead. Then there is a funeral procession in which coffins of cypress wood are carried on wagons. There is one coffin for each tribe, which contains the bones of members of that tribe. One empty bier is decorated and carried in the procession: this is for the missing, whose bodies could not be recovered. Everyone who wishes to, both citizens and

---

[1]Representatives from Corinth, a city-state bitterly hostile to Athens, have called together at Sparta an assembly of delegates from other Greek cities. After giving the others a chance to air their grievances against Athenian aggression, the Corinthians speak, pointing out Athenian encroachments upon the territories of others and urging immediate invasion of Attica, the home region of Athens. (Sparta had the only army could effectively oppose Athens.) In this excerpt the Corinthians address the Spartans and urge them to action, contrasting Spartan caution to Athenian quickness and versatility. At the conclusion of the speeches, Sparta and her allies would declare war against Athens.
[2]431–430 B.C.

foreigners, can join in the procession and the women who are related to the dead are there to make their laments at the tomb. The bones are laid in the public burial-place, which is in the most beautiful quarter outside the city walls. Here the Athenians always bury those who have fallen in war. The only exception is those who died at Marathon,[3] who, because their achievement was considered absolutely outstanding, were buried on the battlefield itself.

When the bones have been laid in the earth, a man chosen by the city for his intellectual gifts and for his general reputation makes an appropriate speech in praise of the dead, and after the speech all depart. This is the procedure at these burials, and all through the war, when the time came to do so, the Athenians followed this ancient custom. Now, at the burial of those who were the first to fall in the war Pericles, the son of Xanthippus, was chosen to make the speech. When the moment arrived, he came forward from the tomb and, standing on a high platform, so that he might be heard by as many people as possible in the crowd, he spoke as follows:

'Many of those who have spoken here in the past have praised the institution of this speech at the close of our ceremony. It seemed to them a mark of honour to our soldiers who have fallen in war that a speech should be made over them. I do not agree. These men have shown themselves valiant in action, and it would be enough, I think, for their glories to be proclaimed in action, as you have just seen it done at this funeral organized by the state. Our belief in the courage and manliness of so many should not be hazarded on the goodness or badness of one man's speech. Then it is not easy to speak with a proper sense of balance, when a man's listeners find it difficult to believe in the truth of what one is saying. The man who knows the facts and loves the dead may well think that an oration tells less than what he knows and what he would like to hear: others who do not know so much may feel envy for the dead, and think the orator over-praises them, when he speaks of exploits that are beyond their own capacities. Praise of other people is tolerable only up to a certain point, the point where one still believes that one could do oneself some of the things one is hearing about. Once you get beyond this point, you will find people becoming jealous and incredulous. However, the fact is that this institution was set up and approved by our forefathers, and it is my duty to follow the tradition and do my best to meet the wishes and the expectations of every one of you.

'I shall begin by speaking about our ancestors, since it is only right and proper on such an occasion to pay them the honour of recalling what they did. In this land of ours there have always been the same people living from generation to generation up till now, and they, by their courage and their virtues, have handed it on to us, a free country. They certainly deserve our praise. Even more so do our fathers deserve it. For to the inheritance they had received they added all the empire we have now, and it was not without blood and toil that they handed it down to us of the present generation. And then we ourselves, assembled here today, who are mostly in the prime of life, have, in most directions, added to the power of our empire and have organized our State in such a way that it is perfectly well able to look after itself both in peace and in war.

'I have no wish to make a long speech on subjects familiar to you all: so I shall say nothing about the warlike deeds by which we acquired our power or the battles in which we or our fathers gallantly resisted our enemies, Greek or foreign. What I want to do is, in the first place, to discuss the spirit in which we faced our trials and also our constitution and the way of life which has made us great. After that I shall speak in praise of the dead, believing that this kind of speech is not inappropriate to the present occasion, and that this whole assembly, of citizens and foreigners, may listen to it with advantage.

'Let me say that our system of government does not copy the institutions of our neighbours. It is more the case of our being a model to others, than of our imitating anyone else. Our constitution is called a democracy because power is in the hands not of a minority but of the whole people. When it is a question of settling private disputes, everyone is equal before the law; when it is a question of putting one person before another in positions of public responsibility, what counts is not membership of a particular class, but the actual ability which the man possesses. No one, so long as he has it in him to be of service to the state, is kept in political obscurity because of poverty. And, just as our political life is free and open, so is our day-to-day life in our relations with each other. We do not get into a state with our next-door neighbour if he enjoys himself in his own way, nor do we give him the kind of black looks which, though they do no real harm, still do hurt people's feelings. We are free and tolerant in our private lives; but in public affairs we keep to the law. This is because it commands our deep respect.

'We give our obedience to those whom we put in positions of authority, and we obey the laws themselves, especially those which are for the protection of the oppressed, and those unwritten laws which it is an acknowledged shame to break.

---

[3]The site, twenty-six miles from Athens, where the Athenians defeated the first Persian invasion (490 B.C.).

'And here is another point. When our work is over, we are in a position to enjoy all kinds of recreation for our spirits. There are various kinds of contests and sacrifices regularly throughout the year; in our own homes we find a beauty and a good taste which delight us every day and which drive away our cares. Then the greatness of our city brings it about that all the good things from all over the world flow in to us, so that to us it seems just as natural to enjoy foreign goods as our own local products.

'Then there is a great difference between us and our opponents, in our attitude towards military security. Here are some examples: Our city is open to the world, and we have no periodical deportations in order to prevent people observing or finding out secrets which might be of military advantage to the enemy. This is because we rely, not on secret weapons, but on our own real courage and loyalty. There is a difference, too, in our educational systems. The Spartans, from their earliest boyhood, are submitted to the most laborious training in courage; we pass our lives without all these restrictions, and yet are just as ready to face the same dangers as they are. Here is a proof of this: When the Spartans invade our land, they do not come by themselves, but bring all their allies with them; whereas we, when we launch an attack abroad, do the job by ourselves, and, though fighting on foreign soil, do not often fail to defeat opponents who are fighting for their own hearths and homes. As a matter of fact none of our enemies has ever yet been confronted with our total strength, because we have to divide our attention between our navy and the many missions on which our troops are sent on land. Yet, if our enemies engage a detachment of our forces and defeat it, they give themselves credit for having thrown back our entire army; or, if they lose, they claim that they were beaten by us in full strength. There are certain advantages, I think, in our way of meeting danger voluntarily, with an easy mind, instead of with a laborious training, with natural rather than with state-induced courage. We do not have to spend our time practising to meet sufferings which are still in the future; and when they are actually upon us we show ourselves just as brave as these others who are always in strict training. This is one point in which, I think, our city deserves to be admired. There are also others:

'Our love of what is beautiful does not lead to extravagance; our love of the things of the mind does not make us soft. We regard wealth as something to be properly used, rather than as something to boast about. As for poverty, no one need be ashamed to admit it: the real shame is in not taking practical measures to escape from it. Here each individual is interested not only in his own affairs but in the affairs of the state as well: even those who are mostly occupied with their own business are extremely well-informed on general politics—this is a peculiarity of ours: we do not say that a man who takes no interest in politics is a man who minds his own business; we say that he has no business here at all. We Athenians, in our own persons, take our decisions on policy or submit them to proper discussions: for we do not think that there is an incompatibility between words and deeds; the worst thing is to rush into action before the consequences have been properly debated. And this is another point where we differ from other people. We are capable at the same time of taking risks and of estimating them beforehand. Others are brave out of ignorance; and, when they stop to think, they begin to fear. But the man who can most truly be accounted brave is he who best knows the meaning of what is sweet in life and of what is terrible, and then goes out undeterred to meet what is to come.

'Again, in questions of general good feeling there is a great contrast between us and most other people. We make friends by doing good to others, not by receiving good from them. This makes our friendship all the more reliable, since we want to keep alive the gratitude of those who are in our debt by showing continued goodwill to them: whereas the feelings of one who owes us something lack the same enthusiasm, since he knows that, when he repays our kindness, it will be more like paying back a debt than giving something spontaneously. We are unique in this. When we do kindnesses to others, we do not do them out of any calculations of profit or loss: we do them without afterthought, relying on our free liberality. Taking everything together then, I declare that our city is an education to Greece, and I declare that in my opinion each single one of our citizens, in all the manifold aspects of life, is able to show himself the rightful lord and owner of his own person, and do this, moreover, with exceptional grace and exceptional versatility. And to show that this is no empty boasting for the present occasion, but real tangible fact, you have only to consider the power which our city possesses and which has been won by those very qualities which I have mentioned. Athens, alone of the states we know, comes to her testing time in a greatness that surpasses what was imagined of her. In her case, and in her case alone, no invading enemy is ashamed at being defeated, and no subject can complain of being governed by people unfit for their responsibilities. Mighty indeed are the marks and monuments of our empire which we have left. Future ages will wonder at us, as the present age wonders at us now. We do not need the praises of a Homer, or of anyone else whose words may delight us for the moment, but whose estimation of facts will fall short of what is really true. For our adventurous spirit has forced an entry into every sea and into every land; and everywhere we have left behind us everlasting memorials of good done to our friends or suffering inflicted on our enemies.

'This, then, is the kind of city for which these men, who could not bear the thought of losing her, nobly fought and nobly died. It is only natural that every one of us who survive them should be willing to undergo hardships in her service. And it was for this reason that I have spoken at such length about our city, because I wanted to make it clear that for us there is more at stake than there is for others who lack our advantages; also I wanted my words of praise for the dead to be set in the bright light of evidence. And now the most important of these words has been spoken. I have sung the praises of our city; but it was the courage and gallantry of these men, and of people like them, which made her splendid. Nor would you find it true in the case of many of the Greeks, as it is true of them, that no words can do more than justice to their deeds.

'To me it seems that the consummation which has overtaken these men shows us the meanings of manliness in its first revelation and in its final proof. Some of them, no doubt, had their faults; but what we ought to remember first is their gallant conduct against the enemy in defence of their native land. They have blotted out evil with good, and done more service to the commonwealth than they ever did harm in their private lives. No one of these men weakened because he wanted to go on enjoying his wealth: no one put off the awful day in the hope that he might live to escape his poverty and grow rich. More to be desired than such things, they chose to check the enemy's pride. This, to them, was a risk most glorious, and they accepted it, willing to, strike down the enemy and relinquish everything else. As for success or failure, they left that in the doubtful hands of Hope, and when the reality of battle was before their faces, they put their trust in their own selves. In the fighting, they thought it more honourable to stand their ground and suffer death than to give in and save their lives. So they fled from the reproaches of men, abiding with life and limb the brunt of battle; and, in a small moment of time, the climax of their lives, a culmination of glory, not of fear, were swept away from us.

'So and such they were, these men—worthy of their city. We who remain behind may hope to be spared their fate, but must resolve to keep the same daring spirit against the foe. It is not simply a question of estimating the advantages in theory. I could tell you a long story (and you know it as well as I do) about what is to be gained by beating the enemy back. What I would prefer is that you should fix your eyes every day on the greatness of Athens as she really is, and should fall in love with her. When you realize her greatness, then reflect that what made her great was men with a spirit of adventure, men who knew their duty, men who were ashamed to fall below a certain standard. If they ever failed in an enterprise, they made up their minds that at any rate the city should not find their courage lacking to her, and they gave to her the best contribution that they could. They gave her their lives, to her and to all of us, and for their own selves they won praises that never grow old, the most splendid of sepulchres—not the sepulchre in which their bodies are laid, but where their glory remains eternal in men's minds, always there on the right occasion to stir others to speech or to action. For famous men have the whole earth as their memorial: it is not only the inscriptions on their graves in their own country that mark them out; no, in foreign lands also, not in any visible form but in people's hearts, their memory abides and grows. It is for you to try to be like them. Make up your minds that happiness depends on being free, and freedom depends on being courageous. Let there be no relaxation in face of the perils of the war. The people who have most excuse for despising death are not the wretched and unfortunate, who have no hope of doing well for themselves, but those who run the risk of a complete reversal in their lives, and who would feel the difference most intensely, if things went wrong for them. Any intelligent man would find a humiliation caused by his own slackness more painful to bear than death, when death comes to him unperceived, in battle, and in the confidence of his patriotism.

'For these reasons I shall not commiserate with those parents of the dead, who are present here. Instead I shall try to comfort them. They are well aware that they have grown up in a world where there are many changes and chances. But this is good fortune—for men to end their lives with honour, as these have done, and for you honourably to lament them: their life was set to a measure where death and happiness went hand in hand. I know that it is difficult to convince you of this. When you see other people happy you will often be reminded of what used to make you happy too. One does not feel sad at not having some good thing which is outside one's experience: real grief is felt at the loss of something which one is used to. All the same, those of you who are of the right age must bear up and take comfort in the thought of having more children. In your own homes these new children will prevent you from brooding over those who are no more, and they will be a help to the city, too, both in filling the empty places, and in assuring her security. For it is impossible for a man to put forward fair and honest views about our affairs if he has not, like everyone else, children whose lives may be at stake. As for those of you who are now too old to have children, I would ask you to count as gain the greater part of your life, in which you have been happy, and remember that what remains is not long, and let your hearts be lifted up at the thought of the fair fame of the dead. One's sense of honour is the only thing that does not grow old, and the last pleasure, when one is worn out with age, is not, as the poet said, making money,[4] but having the respect of one's fellow men.

'As for those of you here who are sons or brothers of the dead, I can see a hard struggle in front of you. Everyone always speaks well of the dead, and, even if you rise to the greatest heights of heroism, it will be a hard thing for you to get the reputation of having come near, let alone equalled, their standard. When one is alive, one is always liable to the jealousy of one's competitors, but when one is out of the way, the honour one receives is sincere and unchallenged.

'Perhaps I should say a word or two on the duties of women to those among you who are now widowed. I can say all I have to say in a short word of advice. Your great glory is not to be inferior to what God has made you, and the greatest glory of a woman is to be least talked about by men, whether they are praising you or criticizing you. I have now, as the law demanded, said what I had to say. For the time being our offerings to the dead have been made, and for the future their children will be supported at the public expense by the city, until they come of age. This is the crown and prize which she offers, both to the dead and to their children, for the ordeals which they have faced. Where the rewards of valour are the greatest, there you will find also the best and bravest spirits among the people. And now, when you have mourned for your dear ones, you must depart.'

The Plague [430 B.C.]

In this way the public funeral was conducted in the winter that came at the end of the first year of the war. At the beginning of the following summer the Peloponnesians[5] and their allies, with two-thirds of their total forces as before, invaded Attica, again under the command of the Spartan King Archidamus, the son of Zeuxidamus. Taking up their positions, they set about the devastation of the country.

They had not been many days in Attica before the plague first broke out among the Athenians. Previously attacks of the plague had been reported from many other places in the neighbourhood of Lemnos[6] and elsewhere, but there was no record of the disease being so virulent anywhere else or causing so many deaths as it did in Athens. At the beginning the doctors were quite incapable of treating the disease because of their ignorance of the right methods. In fact mortality among the doctors was the highest of all, since they came more frequently in contact with the sick. Nor was any other human art or science of any help at all. Equally useless were prayers made in the temples, consultation of oracles, and so forth; indeed, in the end people were so overcome by their sufferings that they paid no further attention to such things.

The plague originated, so they say, in Ethiopia in upper Egypt, and spread from there into Egypt itself and Libya and much of the territory of the King of Persia. In the city of Athens it appeared suddenly, and the first cases were among the population of Piraeus,[7] where there were no wells at that time, so that it was supposed by them that the Peloponnesians had poisoned the reservoirs. Later, however, it appeared also in the upper [central] city, and by this time the deaths were greatly increasing in number. As to the question of how it could first have come about or what causes can be found adequate to explain its powerful effect on nature, I must leave that to be considered by other writers, with or without medical experience. I myself shall merely describe what it was like, and set down the symptoms, knowledge of which will enable it to be recognized, if it should ever break out again. I had the disease myself and saw others suffering from it.

That year, as is generally admitted, was particularly free from all other kinds of illness, though those who did have any illness previously all caught the plague in the end. In other cases, however, there seemed to be no reason for the attacks. People in perfect health suddenly began to have burning feelings in the head; their eyes became red and inflamed; inside their mouths there was bleeding from the throat and tongue, and the breath became unnatural

---

[4]A reference to that worldly view exemplified by a well-known remark of Simonides (ca. 556–ca. 468 B.C.), a famous poet and businessman. When criticized for his love of money, he replied that since he had been deprived by old age of all other pleasures, he could still be comforted by profit.

[5]The Peloponnesian peninsula forms the south of Greece; its dominant city-state was Sparta.

[6]An island in the Aegean Sea colonized by kinsmen of the Athenians.

[7]The chief port of Athens, five miles from the central city.

and unpleasant. The next symptoms were sneezing and hoarseness of voice, and before long the pain settled on the chest and was accompanied by coughing. Next the stomach was affected with stomach-aches and with vomitings of every kind of bile that has been given a name by the medical profession, all this being accompanied by great pain and difficulty. In most cases there were attacks of ineffectual retching, producing violent spasms; this sometimes ended with this stage of the disease, but sometimes continued long afterwards. Externally the body was not very hot to the touch, nor was there any pallor: the skin was rather reddish and livid, breaking out into small pustules and ulcers. But inside there was a feeling of burning, so that people could not bear the touch even of the lightest linen clothing, but wanted to be completely naked, and indeed most of all would have liked to plunge into cold water. Many of the sick who were uncared for actually did so, plunging into the water-tanks in an effort to relieve a thirst which was unquenchable; for it was just the same with them whether they drank much or little. Then all the time they were afflicted with insomnia and the desperate feeling of not being able to keep still.

In the period when the disease was at its height, the body, so far from wasting away, showed surprising powers of resistance to all the agony, so that there was still some strength left on the seventh or eighth day, which was the time when, in most cases, death came from the internal fever. But if people survived this critical period, then the disease descended to the bowels, producing violent ulceration and uncontrollable diarrhea, so that most of them died later as a result of the weakness caused by this. For the disease, first settling in the head, went on to affect every part of the body in turn, and even when people escaped its worst effects, it still left its traces on them by fastening upon the extremities of the body. It affected the genitals, the fingers, and the toes, and many of those who recovered lost the use of these members; some, too, went blind. There were some also who, when they first began to get better, suffered from a total loss of memory, not knowing who they were themselves and being unable to recognize their friends.

Words indeed fail one when one tries to give a general picture of this disease; and as for the sufferings of individuals, they seemed almost beyond the capacity of human nature to endure. Here in particular is a point where this plague showed itself to be something quite different from ordinary diseases: though there were many dead bodies lying about unburied, the birds and animals that eat human flesh either did not come near them or, if they did taste the flesh, died of it afterwards. Evidence for this may be found in the fact that there was a complete disappearance of all birds of prey: they were not to be seen either round the bodies or anywhere else. But dogs, being domestic animals, provided the best opportunity of observing this effect of the plague.

These, then, were the general features of the disease, though I have omitted all kinds of peculiarities which occurred in various individual cases. Meanwhile, during all this time there was no serious outbreak of any of the usual kinds of illness; if any such cases did occur, they ended in the plague. Some died in neglect, some in spite of every possible care being taken of them. As for a recognized method of treatment, it would be true to say that no such thing existed: what did good in some cases did harm in others. Those with naturally strong constitutions were no better able than the weak to resist the disease, which carried away all alike, even those who were treated and dieted with the greatest care. The most terrible thing of all was the despair into which people fell when they realized that they had caught the plague; for they would immediately adopt an attitude of utter hopelessness, and, by giving in in this way, would lose their powers of resistance. Terrible, too, was the sight of people dying like sheep through having caught the disease as a result of nursing others. This indeed caused more deaths than anything else. For when people were afraid to visit the sick, then they died with no one to look after them; indeed, there were many houses in which all the inhabitants perished through lack of any attention. When, on the other hand, they did visit the sick, they lost their own lives, and this was particularly true of those who made it a point of honour to act properly. Such people felt ashamed to think of their own safety and went into their friends' houses at times when even the members of the household were so overwhelmed by the weight of their calamities that they had actually given up the usual practice of making laments for the dead. Yet still the ones who felt most pity for the sick and the dying were those who had had the plague themselves and had recovered from it. They knew what it was like and at the same time felt themselves to be safe, for no one caught the disease twice, or, if he did, the second attack was never fatal. Such people were congratulated on all sides, and they themselves were so elated at the time of their recovery that they fondly imagined that they could never die of any other disease in the future.

A factor which made matters much worse than they were already was the removal of people from the country into the city,[8] and this particularly affected the incomers. There were no houses for them, and, living as they did during the

---

[8]This was done because of the war raging outside the city's walls.

hot season in badly ventilated huts, they died like flies. The bodies of the dying were heaped one on top of the other, and half-dead creatures could be seen staggering about in the streets or flocking around the fountains in their desire for water. The temples in which they took up their quarters were full of the dead bodies of people who had died inside them. For the catastrophe was so overwhelming that men, not knowing what would happen next to them, became indifferent to every rule of religion or of law. All the funeral ceremonies which used to be observed were now disorganized, and they buried the dead as best they could. Many people, lacking the necessary means of burial because so many deaths had already occurred in their households, adopted the most shameless methods. They would arrive first at a funeral pyre that had been made by others, put their own dead upon it and set it alight; or, finding another pyre burning, they would throw the corpse that they were carrying on top of the other one and go away.

In other respects also Athens owed to the plague the beginnings of a state of unprecedented lawlessness. Seeing how quick and abrupt were the changes of fortune which came to the rich who suddenly died and to those who had previously been penniless but now inherited their wealth, people now began openly to venture on acts of self-indulgence which before then they used to keep dark. Thus they resolved to spend their money quickly and to spend it on pleasure, since money and life alike seemed equally ephemeral. As for what is called honour, no one showed himself willing to abide by its laws, so doubtful was it whether one would survive to enjoy the name for it. It was generally agreed that what was both honourable and valuable was the pleasure of the moment and everything that might conceivably contribute to that pleasure. No fear of god or law of man had a restraining influence. As for the gods, it seemed to be the same thing whether one worshipped them or not, when one saw the good and the bad dying indiscriminately. As for offences against human law, no one expected to live long enough to be brought to trial and punished: instead everyone felt that already a far heavier sentence had been passed on him and was hanging over him, and that before the time for its execution arrived it was only natural to get some pleasure out of life.

This, then, was the calamity which fell upon Athens, and the times were hard indeed, with men dying inside the city and the land outside being laid waste.

• • •

The Melian Dialogue [416 B.C.]

The Athenians also made an expedition against the island of Melos. . . .

The Melians are a colony from Sparta. They had refused to join the Athenian empire like the other islanders, and at first had remained neutral without helping either side; but afterwards, when the Athenians had brought force to bear on them by laying waste their land, they had become open enemies of Athens.

Now the generals Cleomedes, the son of Lycomedes, and Tisias, the son of Tisimachus, encamped with the above force in Melian territory and, before doing any harm to the land, first of all sent representatives to negotiate. The Melians did not invite these representatives to speak before the people, but asked them to make the statement for which they had come in front of the governing body and the few. The Athenian representatives then spoke as follows:

'So we are not to speak before the people, no doubt in case the mass of the people should hear once and for all and without interruption an argument from us which is both persuasive and incontrovertible, and should so be led astray. This, we realize, is your motive in bringing us here to speak before the few. Now suppose that you who sit here should make assurance doubly sure. Suppose that you, too, should refrain from dealing with every point in detail in a set speech, and should instead interrupt us whenever we say something controversial and deal with that before going on to the next point? Tell us first whether you approve of this suggestion of ours.'

The Council of the Melians replied as follows:

'No one can object to each of us putting forward our own views in a calm atmosphere. That is perfectly reasonable. What is scarcely consistent with such a proposal is the present threat, indeed the certainty, of your making war on us. We see that you have come prepared to judge the argument yourselves, and that the likely end of it all will be either war, if we prove that we are in the right, and so refuse to surrender, or else slavery.'

ATHENIANS. If you are going to spend the time in enumerating your suspicions about the future, or if you have met here for any other reason except to look the facts in the face and on the basis of these facts to consider how you can save your city from destruction, there is no point in our going on with this discussion. If, however, you will do as we suggest, then we will speak on.

MELIANS. It is natural and understandable that people who are placed as we are should have recourse to all kinds of arguments and different points of view. However, you are right in saying that we are met together here to discuss the safety of our country and, if you will have it so, the discussion shall proceed on the lines that you have laid down.

ATHENIANS. Then we on our side will use no fine phrases saying, for example, that we have a right to our empire because we defeated the Persians, or that we have come against you now because of the injuries you have done us—a great mass of words that nobody would believe. And we ask you on your side not to imagine that you will influence us by saying that you, though a colony of Sparta, have not joined Sparta in the war, or that you have never done us any harm. Instead we recommend that you should try to get what it is possible for you to get, taking into consideration what we both really do think; since you know as well as we do that, when these matters are discussed by practical people, the standard of justice depends on the equality of power to compel and that in fact the strong do what they have the power to do and the weak accept what they have to accept.

MELIANS. Then in our view (since you force us to leave justice out of account and to confine ourselves to self-interest)—in our view it is at any rate useful that you should not destroy a principle that is to the general good of all men—namely, that in the case of all who fall into danger there should be such a thing as fair play and just dealing, and that such people should be allowed to use and to profit by arguments that fall short of a mathematical accuracy. And this is a principle which affects you as much as anybody, since your own fall would be visited by the most terrible vengeance and would be an example to the world.

ATHENIANS. As for us, even assuming that our empire does come to an end, we are not despondent about what would happen next. One is not so much frightened of being conquered by a power which rules over others, as Sparta does (not that we are concerned with Sparta now), as of what would happen if a ruling power is attacked and defeated by its own subjects. So far as this point is concerned, you can leave it to us to face the risks involved. What we shall do now is to show you that it is for the good of our own empire that we are here and that it is for the preservation of your city that we shall say what we are going to say. We do not want any trouble in bringing you into our empire, and we want you to be spared for the good both of yourselves and of ourselves.

MELIANS. And how could it be just as good for us to be the slaves as for you to be the masters?

ATHENIANS. You, by giving in, would save yourselves from disaster; we, by not destroying you, would be able to profit from you.

MELIANS. So you would not agree to our being neutral, friends instead of enemies, but allies of neither side?

ATHENIANS. No, because it is not so much your hostility that injures us; it is rather the case that, if we were on friendly terms with you, our subjects would regard that as a sign of weakness in us, whereas your hatred is evidence of our power.

MELIANS. Is that your subjects' idea of fair play—that no distinction should be made between people who are quite unconnected with you and people who are mostly your own colonists or else rebels whom you have conquered?

ATHENIANS. So far as right and wrong are concerned they think that there is no difference between the two, that those who still preserve their independence do so because they are strong, and that if we fail to attack them it is because we are afraid. So that by conquering you we shall increase not only the size but the security of our empire. We rule the sea and you are islanders, and weaker islanders too than the others; it is therefore particularly important that you should not escape.

MELIANS. But do you think there is no security for you in what we suggest? For here again, since you will not let us mention justice, but tell us to give in to your interests, we, too, must tell you what our interests are and, if yours and ours happen to coincide, we must try to persuade you of the fact. Is it not certain that you will make enemies of all states who are at present neutral, when they see what is happening here and naturally conclude that in course of time you will attack them too? Does not this mean that you are strengthening the enemies you have already and are forcing others to become your enemies even against their intentions and their inclinations?

ATHENIANS. As a matter of fact we are not so much frightened of states on the continent. They have their liberty, and this means that it will be a long time before they begin to take precautions against us. We are more concerned about islanders like yourselves, who are still unsubdued, or subjects who have already become embittered by the constraint which our empire imposes on them. These are the people who are most likely to act in a reckless manner and to bring themselves and us, too, into the most obvious danger.

MELIANS. Then surely, if such hazards are taken by you to keep your empire and by your subjects to escape from it, we who are still free would show ourselves great cowards and weaklings if we failed to face everything that comes rather than submit to slavery.

ATHENIANS. No, not if you are sensible. This is no fair fight, with honour on one side and shame on the other. It is rather a question of saving your lives and not resisting those who are far too strong for you.

MELIANS. Yet we know that in war fortune sometimes makes the odds more level than could be expected from the difference in numbers of the two sides. And if we surrender, then all our hope is lost at once, whereas, so long as we remain in action, there is still a hope that we may yet stand upright.

ATHENIANS. Hope, that comforter in danger! If one already has solid advantages to fall back upon, one can indulge in hope. It may do harm, but will not destroy one. But hope is by nature an expensive commodity, and those who are risking their all on one cast[9] find out what it means only when they are already ruined; it never fails them in the period when such a knowledge would enable them to take precautions. Do not let this happen to you, you who are weak and whose fate depends on a single movement of the scale. And do not be like those people who, as so commonly happens, miss the chance of saving themselves in a human and practical way, and, when every clear and distinct hope has left them in their adversity, turn to what is blind and vague, to prophecies and oracles and such things which by encouraging hope lead men to ruin.

MELIANS. It is difficult, and you may be sure that we know it, for us to oppose your power and fortune, unless the terms be equal. Nevertheless we trust that the gods will give us fortune as good as yours, because we are standing for what is right against what is wrong; and as for what we lack in power, we trust that it will be made up for by our alliance with the Spartans, who are bound, if for no other reason, than for honour's sake, and because we are their kinsmen, to come to our help. Our confidence, therefore, is not so entirely irrational as you think.

ATHENIANS. So far as the favour of the gods is concerned, we think we have as much right to that as you have. Our aims and our actions are perfectly consistent with the beliefs men hold about the gods and with the principles which govern their own conduct. Our opinion of the gods and our knowledge of men lead us to conclude that it is a general and necessary law of nature to rule whatever one can. This is not a law that we made ourselves, nor were we the first to act upon it when it was made. We found it already in existence, and we shall leave it to exist for ever among those who come after us. We are merely acting in accordance with it, and we know that you or anybody else with the same power as ours would be acting in precisely the same way. And therefore, so far as the gods are concerned, we see no good reason why we should fear to be at a disadvantage. But with regard to your views about Sparta and your confidence that she, out of a sense of honour, will come to your aid, we must say that we congratulate you on your simplicity but do not envy you your folly. In matters that concern themselves or their own constitution the Spartans are quite remarkably good; as for their relations with others, that is a long story, but it can be expressed shortly and clearly by saying that of all people we know the Spartans are most conspicuous for believing that what they like doing is honourable and what suits their interests is just. And this kind of attitude is not going to be of much help to you in your absurd quest for safety at the moment.

MELIANS. But this is the very point where we can feel most sure. Their own self-interest will make them refuse to betray their own colonists, the Melians, for that would mean losing the confidence of their friends among the Hellenes [Greeks] and doing good to their enemies.

ATHENIANS. You seem to forget that if one follows one's self-interest one wants to be safe, whereas the path of justice and honour involves one in danger. And, where danger is concerned, the Spartans are not, as a rule, very venturesome.

MELIANS. But we think that they would even endanger themselves for our sake and count the risk more worth taking than in the case of others, becuase we are so close to the Peloponnese that they could operate more easily, and because they can depend on us more than on others, since we are of the same race and share the same feelings.

ATHENIANS. Goodwill shown by the party that is asking for help does not mean security for the prospective ally. What is looked for is a positive preponderance of power in action. And the Spartans pay attention to this point even more than others do. Certainly they distrust their own native resources so much that when they attack a neighbour they bring a great army of allies with them. It is hardly likely therefore that, while we are in control of the sea, they will cross over to an island.

MELIANS. But they still might send others. The Cretan sea is a wide one, and it is harder for those who control it to intercept others than for those who want to slip through to do so safely. And even if they were to fail in this,

---

[9]That is, one throw of the dice.
[10]A successful Spartan general.

they would turn against your own land and against those of your allies left unvisited by Brasidas.[10] So, instead of troubling about a country which has nothing to do with you, you will find trouble nearer home, among your allies, and in your own country.

ATHENIANS. It is a possibility, something that has in fact happened before. It may happen in your case, but you are well aware that the Athenians have never yet relinquished a single siege operation through fear of others. But we are somewhat shocked to find that, though you announced your intention of discussing how you could preserve yourselves, in all this talk you have said absolutely nothing which could justify a man in thinking that he could be preserved. Your chief points are concerned with what you hope may happen in the future, while your actual resources are too scanty to give you a chance of survival against the forces that are opposed to you at this moment. You will therefore be showing an extraordinary lack of common sense if, after you have asked us to retire from this meeting, you still fail to reach a conclusion wiser than anything you have mentioned so far. Do not be led astray by a false sense of honour—a thing which often brings men to ruin when they are faced with an obvious danger that somehow affects their pride. For in many cases men have still been able to see the dangers ahead of them, but this thing called dishonour, this word, by its own force of seduction, has drawn them into a state where they have surrendered to an idea, while in fact they have fallen voluntarily into irrevocable disaster, in dishonour that is all the more dishonourable because it has come to them from their own folly rather than their misfortune. You, if you take the right view, will be careful to avoid this. You will see that there is nothing disgraceful in giving way to the greatest city in Hellas [Greece] when she is offering you such reasonable terms—alliance on a tribute-paying basis and liberty to enjoy your own property. And, when you are allowed to choose between war and safety, you will not be so insensitively arrogant as to make the wrong choice. This is the safe rule—to stand up to one's equals, to behave with deference toward one's superiors, and to treat one's inferiors with moderation. Think it over again, then, when we have withdrawn from the meeting, and let this be a point that constantly recurs to your minds—that you are discussing the fate of your country, that you have only one country, and that its future for good or ill depends on this one single decision which you are going to make.

The Athenians then withdrew from the discussion. The Melians, left to themselves, reached a conclusion which was much the same as they had indicated in their previous replies. Their answer was as follows:

'Our decision, Athenians, is just the same as it was at first. We are not prepared to give up in a short moment the liberty which our city has enjoyed from its foundation for 700 years. We put our trust in the fortune that the gods will send and which has saved us up to now, and in the help of men—that is, of the Spartans; and so we shall try to save ourselves. But we invite you to allow us to be friends of yours and enemies to neither side, to make a treaty which shall be agreeable to both you and us, and so to leave our country.'

The Melians made this reply, and the Athenians, just as they were breaking off the discussion, said:

'Well, at any rate, judging from this decision of yours, you seem to us quite unique in your ability to consider the future as something more certain than what is before your eyes, and to see uncertainties as realities, simply because you would like them to be so. As you have staked most on and trusted most in Spartans, luck, and hopes, so in all these you will find yourselves most completely deluded.'

The Athenian representatives then went back to the army, and the Athenian generals, finding that the Melians would not submit, immediately commenced hostilities and built a wall completely round the city of Melos, dividing the work out among the various states. Later they left behind a garrison of some of their own and some allied troops to blockade the place by land and sea, and with the greater part of their army returned home. The force left behind stayed on and continued with the siege. . . .

Meanwhile the Melians made a night attack and captured the part of the Athenian lines opposite the market-place. They killed some of the troops, and then, after bringing in corn [grain] and everything else useful that they could lay their hands on, retired again and made no further move, while the Athenians took measures to make their blockade more efficient in future. So the summer came to an end.

In the following winter . . . the Melians again captured another part of the Athenian lines where there were only a few of the garrison on guard. As a result of this, another force came out afterwards from Athens under the command of Philocrates, the son of Demeas. Siege operations were now carried on vigorously and, as there was also some treachery from inside, the Melians surrendered unconditionally to the Athenians, who put to death all the men of military age whom they took, and sold the women and children as slaves. Melos itself they took over for themselves, sending out later a colony of 500 men.

Plato

APOLOGY

Socrates of Athens (469-399 B.C.) was the first of the great Athenian philosophers. Socrates himself wrote nothing which has survived, and thus we are entirely dependent upon what others wrote about him. The most important of these writers was one of his students, Plato (429-347 B.C.), also of Athens. Socrates was an Athenian citizen and loyally served his polis *on several campaigns as a hoplite in the Peloponnesian War. Although a stonemason by trade, Socrates seems to have been much more interested in intellectual pursuits, especially challenging conventional views in a search for true wisdom. He attracted a number of young Athenian aristocrats as informal students, including Xenophon, Alcibiades, and Plato, using the "Socratic Method" (teaching by asking students a series of leading questions).*

In 399 B.C. Socrates was formally charged by the Athenian government with 1) denying belief in the traditional gods while inventing new false gods and 2) with corrupting the youth of Athens by instilling such beliefs. He was tried before a jury of 501 Athenians chosen by lot. The Apology is an account of this trial written by Plato. It is important to note that the word "apologia" in Greek (from which we derive the English word "apology", which now means an expression of regret) originally meant "defense" or "justification". Thus Plato's Apology is actually the "defense" of Socrates. Therefore, remember that we only have one side of this trial. Although much of the prosecution's case can be reconstructed by Socrates' own responses to the charges, we nevertheless lack the full case presented by the prosecution. Further, one must also recognize that Plato greatly admired Socrates and likely presents a somewhat idealized portrait of his beloved teacher.

{*To the jury:*}

How you, O Athenians, have been affected by my accusers, I cannot tell; but I know that they almost made me forget who I was—so persuasively did they speak; and yet they have hardly uttered a word of truth. But of the many falsehoods told by them, there was one which quite amazed me;—I mean when they said that you should be upon your guard and not allow yourselves to be deceived by the force of my eloquence. To say this, when they were certain to be detected as soon as I opened my lips and proved myself to be anything but a great speaker, did indeed appear to me most shameless—unless by the force of eloquence they mean the force of truth; for if such is their meaning, I admit that I am eloquent. But in how different a way from theirs! Well, as I was saying, they have scarcely spoken the truth at all; from me you shall hear the whole truth, but not delivered after their manner in a set oration duly ornamented with fine words and phrases. No, by heaven! I shall use the words and arguments which occur to me at the moment, for I am confident in the justice of my cause: at my time of life I ought not to be appearing before you, O men of Athens, in the character of a boy inventing falsehoods—let no one expect it of me. And I must particularly beg of you to grant me this favour:—If I defend myself in my accustomed manner, and you hear me using the words which many of you have heard me using habitually in the agora,[1] at the tables of the money-changers, and elsewhere, I would ask you not to be surprised, and not to interrupt me on this account. For I am more than seventy years of age, and appearing now for the first time before a court of law, I am quite a stranger to the language of the place; and therefore I would have you regard me as if I were really a stranger, whom you would excuse if he spoke

---

[1]The market place, a favorite social center of the citizens.

in his native tongue, and after the fashion of his country:—Am I making an unfair request of you? Never mind the manner, which may or may not be good; but think only of the truth of my words, and give heed to that: let the speaker speak truly and the judge decide justly.

And first, I have to reply to the older charges and to my first accusers,[2] and then I will go on to the later ones. For of old I have had many accusers, who have accused me falsely to you during many years; and I am more afraid of them than of Anytus[3] and his associates, who are dangerous, too, in their own way. But far more dangerous are the others, who began when most of you were children, and took possession of your minds with their falsehoods, telling of one Socrates, a wise man, who speculated about the heaven above, and searched into the earth beneath, and made the worse appear the better cause.[4] The men who have besmeared me with this tale are the accusers whom I dread; for their hearers are apt to fancy that such inquirers do not believe in the existence of the gods. And they are many, and their charges against me are of ancient date, and they were made by them in the days when some of you were more impressible than you are now—in childhood, or it may have been in youth—and the cause went by default, for there was none to answer. And hardest of all, I do not know and cannot tell the names of my accusers; unless in the chance case of a comic poet.[5] All who from envy and malice have persuaded you—some of them having first convinced themselves—all this class of men are most difficult to deal with; for I cannot have them up here, and cross-examine them, and therefore I must simply fight with shadows in my own defence, and argue when there is no one who answers. I will ask you then to take it from me that my opponents are of two kinds; one recent, the other ancient: and I hope that you will see the "propriety of my answering the latter first, for these accusations you heard long before the others, and much oftener.

Well, then, I must make my defence, and endeavour to remove from your minds in a short time, a slander which you have had a long time to take in. May I succeed, if to succeed be for my good and yours, or likely to avail me in my cause! The task is not an easy one; I quite understand the nature of it. And so leaving the event with God, in obedience to the law I will now make my defence.

I will begin at the beginning, and ask what is the accusation which has given rise to the slander of me, and in fact has encouraged Meletus to prefer this charge against me. Well, what do the slanderers say? They shall be my prosecutors, and this is the information they swear against me: 'Socrates is an evil-doer; a meddler who searches into things under the earth and in heaven, and makes the worse appear the better cause, and teaches the aforesaid practices to others.' Such is the nature of the accusation: it is just what you have yourselves seen in the comedy of Aristophanes, who has introduced a man whom he calls Socrates, swinging about and saying that he walks on air, and talking a deal of nonsense concerning matters of which I do not pretend to know either much or little—not that I mean to speak disparagingly of anyone who is a student of natural philosophy. May Meletus never bring so many charges against me as to make me do that! But the simple truth is, O Athenians, that I have nothing to do with physical speculations. Most of those here present are witnesses to the truth of this, and to them I appeal. Speak then, you who have heard me, and tell your neighbours whether any of you have ever known me hold forth in few words or in many upon such matters. . . . You hear their answer. And from what they say of this part of the charge you will be able to judge of the truth of the rest.

As little foundation is there for the report that I am a teacher, and take money;[6] this accusation has no more truth in it than the other. Although, if a man were really able to instruct mankind, this too would, in my opinion, be an honour to him. . . .

I dare say, Athenians, that someone among you will reply, 'Yes, Socrates, but what *is* your occupation? What is the origin of these accusations which are brought against you; there must have been something strange which

[2]Socrates had been much criticized for many years before his trial; here, he states that he will deal first with the old falsehoods that created the prejudices that are the real cause of the current charges against him.
[3]Anytus, Meletus, and Lycon were the three men pressing charges against Socrates. (Anytus was a wealthy merchant whose son was intellectually gifted and wished to be a follower of Socrates; Anytus had angrily refused and insisted his son go into the family's business; the young man—according to tradition—became an alcoholic.)
[4]Socrates was accused by some of being a natural philosopher (physical scientist) who speculated, or theorized, about the material nature of the universe—and was thought, therefore, to be an atheist. He was also accused of being a Sophist, a teacher of public speaking who taught people to argue their law cases without regard for truth. Actually, he had lost interest in natural philosophy decades earlier and had never been a Sophist.
[5]Aristophanes (see selection 7), whose satirical comedy, *The Clouds* (423 B.C.), portrayed Socrates as a ridiculous fake who had contempt for religion and tradition.
[6]The Sophists often charged high fees. Socrates, on the other hand, charged no fees at all for his philosophical questioning.

you have been doing? All these rumours and this talk about you would never have arisen if you had been like other men: tell us, then, what is the cause of them, for we should be sorry to judge hastily of you.' Now I regard this as a fair challenge, and I will endeavour to explain to you the reason why I am called wise and have such an evil fame. Please to attend then. And although some of you may think that I am joking, I declare that I will tell you the entire truth. Men of Athens, this reputation of mine has come of a certain sort of wisdom which I possess. If you ask me what kind of wisdom, I reply, wisdom such as may perhaps be attained by man, for to that extent I am inclined to believe that I am wise; whereas the persons of whom I was speaking have a kind of superhuman wisdom,[7] which I know not how to describe, because I have it not myself; and he who says that I have, speaks falsely, and is taking away my character. And here, O men of Athens, I must beg you not to interrupt me, even if I seem to say something extravagant. For the word which I will speak is not mine. I will refer you to a witness who is worthy of credit; that witness shall be the god of Delphi[8]—he will tell you about my wisdom, if I have any, and of what sort it is. You must have known Chaerephon; he was early a friend of mine, and also a friend of yours, for he shared in the recent exile of the people, and returned with you.[9] Well, Chaerephon, as you know, was very impetuous in all his doings, and he went to Delphi and boldly asked the oracle to tell him whether—as I was saying, I must beg you not to interrupt—he actually asked the oracle to tell him whether anyone was wiser than I was, and the Pythian prophetess answered that there was no man wiser. Chaerephon is dead himself; but his brother, who is in court, will confirm the truth of what I am saying.

Why do I mention this? Because I am going to explain to you why I have such an evil name. When I heard the answer, I said to myself, What can the god mean? and what is the interpretation of his riddle? for I know that I have no wisdom, small or great. What then can he mean when he says that I am the wisest of men? And yet he is a god, and cannot lie; that would be against his nature. After long perplexity, I thought of a method of trying the question. I reflected that if I could only find a man wiser than myself, then I might go to the god with a refutation in my hand. I should say to him, 'Here is a man who is wiser than I am; but you said that I was the wisest.' Accordingly I went to one who had the reputation of wisdom, and observed him—his name I need not mention, he was a politician; and in the process of examining him and talking with him, this, men of Athens, was what I found. I could not help thinking that he was not really wise, although he was thought wise by many, and still wiser by himself; and thereupon I tried to explain to him that he thought himself wise, but was not really wise; and the consequence was that he hated me, and his enmity was shared by several who were present and heard me. So I left him, saying to myself as I went away: Well, although I do not suppose that either of us knows anything really worth knowing, I am at least wiser than this fellow—for he knows nothing, and thinks that he knows; I neither (know nor think that I know. In this one little point, then, I seem to have the advantage of him. Then I went to another who had still higher pretensions to wisdom, and my conclusion was exactly the same. Whereupon I made another enemy of him, and of many others besides him.

Then I went to one man after another, being not unconscious of the enmity which I provoked, and I lamented and feared this: but necessity was laid upon me,—the word of God [Apollo], I thought, ought to be considered first. And I said to myself, Go I must to all who appear to know, and find out the meaning of the oracle. And I swear to you, Athenians,—for I must tell you the truth—the result of my mission was just this: I found that the men most in repute were nearly the most foolish; and that others less esteemed were really closer to wisdom. I will tell you the tale of my wanderings and of the 'Herculean' labours, as I may call them, which I endured only to find at last the oracle irrefutable. After the politicians, I went to the poets; tragic, dithyrambic, and all sorts. And there, I said to myself, you will be instantly detected; now you will find out that you are more ignorant than they are. Accordingly, I took them some of the most elaborate passages in their own writings, and asked what was the meaning of them—thinking that they would teach me something. Will you believe me? I am ashamed to confess the truth, but I must say that there is hardly a person present who would not have talked better about their poetry than they did themselves. So I learnt that not by wisdom do poets write poetry, but by a sort of

---

[7]Socrates, with his customary ironic (sarcastic) humor, is speaking here of the Sophists.

[8]Apollo's most famous temple was at Delphi, about seventy-five miles northwest of Athens; the Pythia, Apollo's priestess, there uttered the god's oracles (divine statements).

[9]Five years before Socrates' trial, after the defeat of Athens ended the Peloponnesian War in 404 B.C., the "Thirty Tyrants" drove the democratic leadership of Athens (including Socrates' friend Chaerephon) into exile. The democracy was restored in 403.

genius and inspiration; they are like diviners or soothsayers who also say many fine things, but do not understand the meaning of them. The poets appeared to me to be much in the same case; and I further observed that upon the strength of their poetry they believed themselves to be the wisest of men in other things; in which they were not wise. So I departed, conceiving myself to be superior to them for the same reason that I was superior to the politicians.

At last I went to the skilled craftsmen for I was conscious that I knew nothing at all, as I may say, and I was sure that they knew many fine things; and here I was not mistaken, for they did know many things of which I was ignorant, and in this they certainly were wiser than I was. But I observed that even the good craftsmen fell into the same error as the poets;—because they were good workmen they thought that they also knew all sorts of high matters, and this defect in them overshadowed their wisdom; and therefore I asked myself on behalf of the oracle, whether I would like to be as I was, neither having their knowledge nor their ignorance, or like them in both; and I made answer to myself and to the oracle that I was better off as I was.

This inquiry has led to my having many enemies of the worst and most dangerous kind, and has given rise also to many imputations, including the name of 'wise'; for my hearers always imagine that I myself possess the wisdom which I find wanting in others. But the truth is, O men of Athens, that God only is wise; and by his answer he intends to show that the wisdom of men is worth little or nothing; although speaking of Socrates, he is only using my name by way of illustration, as if he said, He, O men, is the wisest, who, like Socrates, knows that his wisdom is in truth worth nothing. And so I go about the world, obedient to the god, and search and make inquiry into the wisdom of anyone, whether citizen or stranger, who appears to be wise; and if he is not wise, then in vindication of the oracle I show him that he is not wise; and my occupation quite absorbs me, and I have had no time to do anything useful either in public affairs or in any concern of my own, but I am in utter poverty by reason of my devotion to the god.

There is another thing:—young men of the richer classes, who have not much to do, come about me of their own accord; they like to hear people examined, and they often imitate me, and proceed to do some examining themselves; there are plenty of persons, as they quickly discover, who think that they know something, but really know little or nothing; and then those who are examined by them instead of being angry with themselves are angry with me: This confounded Socrates, they say; this villainous misleader of youth!—and then if somebody asks them, Why, what evil does he practise or teach? they do not know, and cannot tell; but in order that they may not appear to be at a loss, they repeat the ready-made charges which are used against all philosophers about teaching things up in the clouds and under the earth, and having no gods, and making the worse appear the better cause; for they do not like to confess that their pretence of knowledge has been detected—which is the truth; and as they are numerous and ambitious and energetic, and speak vehemently with persuasive tongues, they have filled your ears with their loud and inveterate slanders. And this is the reason why my three accusers, Meletus and Anytus and Lycon, have set upon me. . . .

I have said enough in my defence against the first class of my accusers; I turn to the second class. They are headed by Meletus, that good man and true lover of his country, as he calls himself. Against these, too, I must try to make a defence:—Let their affidavit be read: it contains something of this kind: It says that Socrates is a doer of evil, inasmuch as he corrupts the youth, and does not receive the gods whom the state receives, but has a new religion of his own. Such is the charge; and now let us examine the particular counts. He says that I am a doer of evil, and corrupt the youth; but I say, O men of Athens, that Meletus is a doer of evil, in that he is playing a solemn farce, recklessly bringing men to trial from a pretended zeal and interest about matters in which he really never had the smallest interest. And the truth of this I will endeavor to prove to you.

Come hither, Meletus, and let me ask a question of you. You attach great importance to the improvement of youth?

Yes, I do.

Tell the judges, then, who is their improver; for you must know, as you take such interest in the subject, and have discovered their corrupter, and are citing and accusing me in this court. Speak, then, and tell the judges who is the improver of youth:—Observe, Meletus, that you are silent, and have nothing to say. But is this not rather disgraceful, and a very considerable proof of what I was saying, that you have no interest in the matter? Speak up, friend, and tell us who their improver is.

The laws.

But that, my good sir, is not my question: Can you not name some person—whose first qualification will be that he knows the laws?[10]

The judges, Socrates, who are present in court.

What, do you mean to say, Meletus, that they are able to instruct and improve youth?

Certainly they are.

What, all of them, or some only and not others?

All of them.

Truly, that is good news! There are plenty of improvers, then. And what do you say of the audience,—do they improve them?

Yes, they do.

And the senators?

Yes, the senators improve them.

But perhaps the members of the assembly corrupt them?—or do, they too improve them?

They improve them.

Then every Athenian improves and elevates them; all with the exception of myself; and I alone am their corrupter? Is that what you affirm?

That is what I stoutly affirm.

I am very unfortunate if you are right. But suppose I ask you a question: Is it the same with horses? Does one man do them harm and all the world good? Is not the exact opposite the truth? One man is able to do them good, or at least very few;—the trainer of horses, that is to say, does them good, but the ordinary man does them harm if he has to do with them? Is not that true, Meletus, of horses, or of any other animals? Most assuredly it is; whether you and Anytus say yes or no. Happy indeed would be the condition of youth if they had one corrupter only, and all the rest of the world were their benefactors. But you, Meletus, have sufficiently shown that you never had a thought about the young: your carelessness is plainly seen in your not caring about the very things which you bring against me. . . .

It will be very clear to you, Athenians, as I was saying, that Meletus has never had any care, great or small, about the matter. But still I should like to know, Meletus, in what I am affirmed to corrupt the young I suppose you mean, as I infer from your indictment, that I teach them not to acknowledge the gods which the state acknowledges, but some other new divinities or spiritual agencies in their stead. These are the lessons by which I corrupt the youth, as you say.

Yes, that I say emphatically.

Then, by the gods, Meletus, of whom we are speaking, tell me and the court, in somewhat plainer terms, what you mean! for I do not as yet understand whether you affirm that I teach other men to acknowledge some gods, and therefore that I do believe in gods, and am not an entire atheist—this you do not lay to my charge,—but only you say that they are not the same gods which the city recognizes—the charge is that they are different gods. Or, do you mean that I am an atheist simply, and a teacher of atheism?

I mean the latter—that you are a complete atheist.

What an extraordinary statement! Why do you think so, Meletus? Do you mean that I do not believe in the god-head of the sun or moon, like the rest of mankind?[11]

I assure you, judges, that he does not: for he says that the sun is stone, and the moon earth.

Friend Meletus, do you think that you are accusing Anaxagoras?[12] Have you such a low opinion of the judges, that you fancy them so illiterate as not to know that these doctrines are found in the books of Anaxagoras the

---

[10]In the following series of questions Socrates, as part of his right to cross-examine his accuser, playfully uses his logical method (*dialectic*) to make the angrily squirming Meletus look foolish. Meletus is first forced, by Socrates' questions, to define the "improver of youth" as all the "judges" (the entire jury of 501); then as the non-voting "audience"; then as the "senators" (the Council of 500 which drafted the laws and supervised their carrying out); and finally, as the "assembly" (all the adult male citizens, who voted approval of the laws of Athens).

[11]Apollo was the sun god, Artemis the moon goddess. Whether or not those two divine personalities were meant in Socrates' question, reverence for the sun and moon themselves was expected of all Greeks.

[12]A natural philosopher from Clazomenae, a town in Asia Minor. Condemned for impiety, he was forced to leave Athens partly because of his materialist, anti-supernatural views of the sun and moon.

Clazomenian, which are full of them? And so, forsooth, the youth are said to be taught them by Socrates, when they can be bought in the book-market for one drachma[13] at the most; and they might pay their money, and laugh at Socrates if he pretends to father these extraordinary views. And so, Meletus, you really think that I do not believe in any god?

I swear by Zeus that you verily believe in none at all.

Nobody will believe you, Meletus, and I am pretty sure that you do not believe yourself I cannot help thinking, men of Athens, that Meletus is reckless and impudent, and that he has brought this indictment in a spirit of mere wantonness and youthful bravado. Has he not compounded a riddle, thinking to try me? He said to himself:— I shall see whether the wise Socrates will discover my facetious self-contradiction, or whether I shall be able to deceive him and the rest of them. For he certainly does appear to me to contradict himself in the indictment as much as if he said that Socrates is guilty of not believing in the gods, and yet of believing in them—but this is not like a person who is in earnest.

I should like you, O men of Athens, to join me in examining what I conceive to be his inconsistency; and do you, Meletus, answer. And I must remind the audience of my request that they would not make a disturbance if I speak in my accustomed manner:

Did ever man, Meletus, believe in the existence of human things, and not of human beings? . . . I wish, men of Athens, that he would answer, and not be always trying to get up an interruption. Did ever any man believe in horsemanship, and not in horses? or in flute-playing, and not in flute-players? My friend, no man ever did; I answer to you and to the court, as you refuse to answer for yourself. But now please to answer the next question: Can a man believe in the existence of things spiritual and divine, and not in spirits or demigods?

He cannot.

How lucky I am to have extracted that answer, by the assistance of the court! But then you swear in the indictment that I teach and believe in divine or spiritual things (new or old, no matter for that); at any rate, I believe in spiritual things,—so you say and swear in the affidavit; and yet if I believe in them, how can I help believing in spirits or demigods;—must I not? To be sure I must; your silence gives consent. Now what are spirits or demigods? are they not either gods or the sons of gods?

Certainly they are.

But this is what I call the facetious riddle invented by you: the demigods or spirits are gods, and you say first that I do not believe in gods, and then again that I do believe in gods; that is, if I believe in demigods. For if the demigods are the illegitimate sons of gods, whether by nymphs, or by other mothers, as some are said to be—what human being will ever believe that there are no gods when there are sons of gods? You might as well affirm the existence of mules, and deny that of horses and asses.[14] Such nonsense, Meletus, could only have been intended by you to make trial of me. You have put this into the indictment because you could think of nothing real of which to accuse me. But no one who has a particle of understanding will ever be convinced by you that a man can believe in the existence of things divine and superhuman, and the same man refuse to believe in gods and demigods and heroes.

I have said enough in answer to the charge of Meletus: any elaborate defence is unnecessary. You know well the truth of my statement that I have incurred many violent enmities; and this is what will be my destruction if I am destroyed;—not Meletus, nor yet Anytus, but the envy and detraction of the world, which has been the death of many good men, and will probably be the death of many more; there is no danger of my being the last of them.

Someone will say: And are you not ashamed, Socrates, of a course of life which is likely to bring you to an untimely end? To him I may fairly answer: There you are mistaken: a man who is good for anything ought not to calculate the chance of living or dying; he ought only to consider whether in doing anything he is doing right or wrong—acting the part of a good man or of a bad. . . .

Strange, indeed, would be my conduct, O men of Athens, if I who, when I was ordered by the generals whom you chose to command me at Potidaea and Amphipolis and Delium,[15] remained where they placed me, like any other man, facing death—if now, when, as I conceive and imagine, God orders me to fulfil the philosopher's

[13]A Greek coin of small value.
[14]A mule is a sterile work animal produced by the mating of a mare with a male donkey (jackass).

[15]Sites of battles during the Peloponnesian War where Socrates had fought as an Athenian infantryman.

mission of searching into myself and other men, I were to desert my post through fear of death, or any other fear; that would indeed be strange, and I might justly be arraigned in court for denying the existence of the gods, if I disobeyed the oracle because I was afraid of death, fancying that I was wise when I was not wise. For the fear of death is indeed the pretence of wisdom, and not real wisdom, being a pretence of knowing the unknown; and no one knows whether death, of which men are afraid because they apprehend it to be the greatest evil, may not be the greatest good. Is not this ignorance of a disgraceful sort, the ignorance which is the conceit that a man knows what he does not know? And in this respect only I believe myself to differ from men in general, and may perhaps claim to be wiser than they are:—that whereas I know but little of the world below,[16] I do not suppose that I know: but I do know that injustice and disobedience to a better, whether God or man, is evil and dishonourable, and I will never fear or avoid a possible good rather than a certain evil. And therefore if you let me go now, and . . . if you say to me, Socrates, this time we will not mind Anytus, and you shall be let off, but upon one condition: that you are not to inquire and speculate in this way any more, and that if you are caught doing so again you shall die. If this was the condition on which you let me go, I should reply: Men of Athens, I honour and love you; but I shall obey God rather than you, and while I have life and strength I shall never cease from the practice and teaching of philosophy, exhorting any one of you whom I meet and saying to him after my manner: You, my friend,—a citizen of the great and mighty and wise city of Athens,—are you not ashamed of heaping up the largest amount of money and honour and reputation, and caring so little about wisdom and truth and the greatest improvement of the soul, which you never regard nor heed at all? And if the person with whom I am arguing, says; Yes, but I do care; then I shall not leave him nor let him go at once, but proceed to interrogate and examine and cross-examine him, and if I think that he has no virtue in him but only says that he has, I shall reproach him with undervaluing the most precious, and overvaluing the less. And I shall repeat the same words to everyone whom I meet, young and old, citizen and alien, but especially to you citizens, inasmuch as you are my brethren. . . . This is my teaching, and if it corrupts the young, it is mischievous; but if anyone says that this is not my teaching, he is speaking an untruth. Wherefore, O men of Athens, I say to you, do as Anytus bids or not as Anytus bids, and either acquit me or not; but whichever you do, understand that I shall never alter my ways, not even if I have to die many times.

Men of Athens, do not interrupt,[17] but hear me; I begged you before to listen to me without interruption, and I beg you now to hear me to the end. I have something more to say, at which you may be inclined to cry out; but I believe that to hear me will be good for you, and therefore I beseech you to restrain yourselves. I would have you know, that if you kill such an one as I am, you will injure yourselves more than you will injure me. Nothing will injure me, not Meletus nor yet Anytus—they cannot, for a bad man is not permitted to injure a better than himself. I do not deny that Anytus may, perhaps, kill him, or drive him into exile, or deprive him of civil rights; and he may imagine, and others may imagine, that he is inflicting a great injury upon him: but there I do not agree. For the evil of doing as he is doing—the evil of seeking unjustly to take the life of another—is far greater.

And now, Athenians, I am not going to argue for my own sake, as you may think, but for yours, that you may not sin against God by condemning me, who am his gift to you. For if you kill me you will not easily find a successor to me, who, if I may use such a ludicrous figure of speech, am a sort of gadfly,[18] given to the state by God; and the state is a great and noble horse who is tardy in his motions owing to his very size, and requires to be stirred into life. I am that gadfly which God has attached to the state, and all day long and in all places am always fastening upon you, arousing and persuading and reproaching you. You will not easily find another like me, and therefore I would advise you to spare me. I dare say that you may feel out of temper (like a person who is suddenly awakened from sleep), and you think that you might easily strike me dead as Anytus advises, and then you would sleep on for the remainder of your lives, unless God in his care of you sent you another gadfly. When I say that I am given to you by God, the proof of my mission is this:—if I had been like other men, I should not have neglected all my own concerns or patiently seen the neglect of them during all these years, and have been doing yours, coming to you

---

[16]The afterlife, thought by the Greeks to be in an underground place called Hades.

[17]Apparently, Socrates is now speaking over noises from the crowd, as he directly defies the city's power in stating that he will never alter his ways.

[18]A fly that bites and annoys horses and livestock.

individually like a father or elder brother, exhorting you to regard virtue; such conduct, I say, would be unlike human nature. . . .

Someone may wonder why I go about in private giving advice and busying myself with the concerns of others, but do not venture to come forward in public and advise the state. I will tell you why. You have heard me speak at different times and places of a superhuman oracle or sign which comes to me, and is the divinity which Meletus ridicules in the indictment. This sign, which is a kind of voice, first began to come to me when I was a child; from time to time it forbids me to do something which I am going to do, but never commands anything. This is what deters me from being a politician. And rightly, as I think. For I am certain, O men of Athens, that if I had engaged in politics, I should have perished long ago, and done no good either to you or to myself. And do not be offended at my telling you the truth: for the truth is, that no man who sets himself firmly against you or any other multitude, honestly striving to keep the state from many lawless and unrighteous deeds, will save his life; he who will fight for the right, if he would live even for a brief space, must have a private station and not a public one. . . .

[Editor's note: At the end of his defense, in which—contrary to accepted custom—Socrates refused to appeal to the sympathetic emotions of the jury, he was found guilty. The vote was 280 to 221. In the next phase of the trial, the prosecution and the convicted person each propose a *penalty*. The jury must then vote for one or the other penalty.]

There are many reasons why I am not grieved, O men of Athens, at the vote of condemnation. I expected it, and am only surprised that the votes are so nearly equal; for I had thought that the majority against me would have been far larger; but now, had thirty votes gone over to the other side, I should have been acquitted. . . .

And so he [Meletus] proposes death as the penalty. And what shall I propose on my part, O men of Athens? Clearly that which is my due. And what is my due? What ought I to have done to me, or to pay—a man who has never had the wit to keep quiet during his whole life; but has been careless of what the many care for—wealth, and family interests, and military offices, and speaking in the assembly, and magistracies, and plots, and parties. Reflecting that I was really too honest a man to be a politician and live, I did not go where I could do no good to you or to myself; but where I could do privately the greatest good (as I affirm it to be) to everyone of you, thither I went, and sought to persuade every man among you that he must look to himself, and seek virtue and wisdom before he looks to his private interests, and look to the state before he looks to the interests of the state; and that this should be the order which he observes in all his actions. What shall be done to such an one? Doubtless some good thing, O men of Athens, if he has his reward; and the good should be of a kind suitable to him. What would be a reward suitable to a poor man who is your benefactor, and who desires leisure that he may instruct you? There can be no reward so fitting as a full pension in the Prytaneum,[19] O men of Athens, a reward which he deserves far more than the citizen who has won the prize at Olympia in the horse or chariot race, whether the chariots were drawn by two horses or by many. For I am in want, and he has enough; and he only gives you the appearance of happiness, and I give you the reality. And if I am to estimate the penalty fairly, I should say that maintenance in the Prytaneum is the just return.

Perhaps you think that I am braving you in what I am saying now, as in what I said before about the tears and prayers. But this is not so. I speak rather because I am convinced that I never intentionally wronged anyone, although I cannot convince you—the time has been too short; if there were a law at Athens, as there is in other cities, that a capital cause should not be decided in one day, then I believe that I should have convinced you. But I cannot in a moment refute great slanders; and, as I am convinced that I never wronged another, I will assuredly not wrong myself. I will not say of myself that I deserve any evil, nor propose any penalty. Why should I? Because I am afraid of the penalty of death which Meletus proposes? When I do not know whether death is a good or an evil, why should I propose a penalty which would certainly be an evil? Shall I say imprisonment? And why should I live in prison, and be the slave of the magistrates of the year? . . . Or shall the penalty be a fine, and imprisonment until the fine is paid? There is the same objection. I should have to lie in prison, for money I have none, and cannot pay. And if I say exile (and this may possibly be the penalty which you will affix), I must indeed be blinded by the

---

[19]The place where benefactors of Athens and winners of the athletic contests at Olympia were entertained as guests.

love of life, if I am so irrational as to expect that when you, who are my own citizens, cannot endure my discourses and arguments, and have found them so grievous and odious that you will have no more of them, others are likely to endure them. No indeed, men of Athens, that is not very likely. And what a life should I lead, at my age, wandering from city to city, ever changing my place of exile, and always being driven out! For I am quite sure that wherever I go, there, as here, the young men will flock to listen to me; and if I drive them away, their elders will drive me out at their request; and if I let them come, their fathers and friends will drive me out for their sakes.

Someone will say: Yes, Socrates, but cannot you hold your tongue, and then you may go into a foreign city, and no one will interfere with you? Now I have great difficulty in making you understand my answer to this. For if I tell you that to do as you say would be a disobedience to God, and therefore that I cannot hold my tongue, you will not believe that I am serious; and if I say again that daily to discourse about virtue, and of those other things about which you hear me examining myself and others, is the greatest good of man, and that the unexamined life is no life for a human being, you are still less likely to believe me. Yet I say what is true, although a thing of which it is hard for me to persuade you. Also, I have never been accustomed to think that I deserve to suffer any harm. Had I money I might have estimated the offence at what I was able to pay, and not have been much the worse. But I have none, and therefore I must ask you to proportion the fine to my means. Well, perhaps I could afford a mina,[20] and therefore I propose that penalty: Plato, Crito, Critobulus, and Apollodorus, my friends here, bid me say thirty minas, and they will be the sureties. Let thirty minas be the penalty; for which sum they will be ample security to you.

[Editor's note: The jury, insulted by Socrates' suggestion that he be rewarded for his service to Athens, voted for the death penalty, 360 to 141.]

Not much time will be gained, O Athenians, in return for the evil name which you will get from the detractors of the city, who will say that you killed Socrates, a wise man; for they will call me wise, even though I am not wise, when they want to reproach you. If you had waited a little while, your desire would have been fulfilled in the course of nature. For I am far advanced in years, as you may perceive, and not far from death. I am speaking now not to all of you, but only to those who have condemned me to death. And I have another thing to say to them: You think that I was convicted because I had no words of the sort which would have procured my acquittal—I mean, if I had thought fit to leave nothing undone or unsaid. Not so; the deficiency which led to my conviction was not of words—certainly not. But I had not the boldness nor impudence nor inclination to address you as you would have liked me to do, weeping and wailing and lamenting, and saying and doing many things, such indeed as you have been accustomed to hear from others, but I maintain to be unworthy of myself. I thought at the time that I ought not to do anything common or mean when in danger: nor do I now repent the style of my defence; I would rather die having spoken after my manner, than speak in your manner and live. For neither in war nor yet at law ought I or any man to use every way of escaping death. Often in battle there can be no doubt that if a man will throw away his arms, and fall on his knees before his pursuers, he may escape death; and in other dangers there are other ways of escaping death, if a man has the hardihood to say and do anything. The difficulty, my friends, is not to avoid death, but to avoid unrighteousness; for that runs faster than death. I am old and move slowly, and the slower runner has overtaken me; my accusers are keen and quick, and the faster runner, who is wickedness, has overtaken them. And now I depart hence condemned by you to suffer the penalty of death,—they too go their ways condemned by the truth to suffer the penalty of villainy and wrong; and I must abide by my award—let them abide by theirs. I suppose that these things may be regarded as fated,—and I think that they are well.

And now, O men who have condemned me, I would fain prophesy to you; for I am about to die, and in the hour of death men are gifted with prophetic power. And I prophesy to you who are my murderers, that immediately after my departure punishment far heavier than you have inflicted on me surely awaits you. Me you have killed because you wanted to escape the accuser, and not to give an account of your lives. But that will not be as you suppose: far otherwise. For I say that there will be more accusers of you than there are now; accusers whom hitherto I have restrained: and as they are younger they will be more severe with you, and you will be more offended at them.

[20]A valuable coin, probably equal to 100 drachmas.

If you think that by killing men you will stop all censure of your evil lives, you are mistaken; that is not a way of escape which is either very possible, or honourable; the easiest and the noblest way is not to be disabling others, but to be improving yourselves. This is the prophecy which I utter before my departure to the judges who have condemned me.

Friends, who would have acquitted me, I would like also to talk with you about the thing which has come to pass, while the magistrates are busy, and before I go to the place at which I must die. Stay then a little, for we may as well talk with one another while there is time. You are my friends, and I should like to show you the meaning of this event which has happened to me. O my judges—for you I may truly call judges—I should like to tell you of a wonderful circumstance. Hitherto the divine faculty of which my inner voice is the source has constantly been in the habit of opposing me even about trifles, if I was going to make a slip or error in any matter; and now as you see there has come upon me that which may be thought, and is generally believed to be, the last and worst evil. But the oracle made no sign of opposition, either when I was leaving my house in the morning, or when I was on my way to the court, or while I was speaking, at anything which I was going to say; and yet I have often been stopped in the middle of a speech, but now in nothing I either said or did touching the matter in hand has the oracle opposed me. What do I take to be the explanation of this silence? I will tell you. It is an intimation that what has happened to me is a good, and therefore those of us who think that death is an evil must be in error. I have this conclusive proof; the customary sign would surely have opposed me had I been going to evil and not to good.

Let us reflect in another way, and we shall see that there is great reason to hope that death is a good; for one of two things—either death is a state of nothingness and utter unconsciousness, or, as men say, there is a change and migration of the soul from this world to another. Now if you suppose that there is no consciousness, but a sleep like the sleep of him who is undisturbed even by dreams, death will be an unspeakable gain. For if a person were to select the night in which his sleep was undisturbed even by dreams, and were to compare with this the other days and nights of his life, and then were to tell us how many days and nights he had passed in the course of his life better and more pleasantly than this one, I think that any man, I will not say a private man, but even the great king will not find many such days or nights, when compared with the others. Now if death be of such a nature, I say that to die is gain; for eternity is then only a single night. But if death is the journey to another place, and there, as men say, all the dead abide, what good, O my friends and judges, can be greater than this? If indeed when the pilgrim arrives in the world below, he is delivered from our earthly professors of justice, and finds the true judges who are said to give judgement there . . . and other sons of God who were righteous in their own life, that pilgrimage will be worth making. What would not a man give if he might converse with Orpheus and Musaeus and Hesiod and Homer?[21] Nay, if this be true, let me die again and again. . . . Above all, I shall then be able to continue my search into true and false knowledge, as in this world, so also in the next; and I shall find out who is wise, and who pretends to be wise, and is not. . . . In another world they do not put a man to death for asking questions: assuredly not. For besides being happier than we are, they will be immortal, if what is said is true.

Wherefore, O judges, be of good cheer about death, and know of a certainty that no evil can happen to a good man, either in life or after death, and that he and his are not neglected by the gods. Nor has my own approaching end happened by mere chance; I see clearly that the time had arrived when it was better for me to die and be released from trouble; therefore the oracle gave no sign, and therefore also I am not at all angry with my condemners, or with my accusers. But although they have done me no harm, they intended it; and for this I may properly blame them.

Still I have a favour to ask of them. When my sons are grown up, I would ask you, O my friends, to punish them; I would have you trouble them, as I have troubled you, if they seem to care about riches, or anything, more than about virtue; or if they pretend to be something when they are really nothing,—then reprove them, as I have reproved you, for not caring about that for which they ought to care, and thinking that they are something when they are really nothing. And if you do this, I shall have received justice at your hands, and so will my sons.

The hour of departure has arrived, and we go our ways—I to die, and you to live. Which is better God only knows.

---

[21]Orpheus and Musaeus were poets in ancient mythological accounts; Hesiod and Homer were historical figures—Greek poets of the eighth century B.C.

Plato

REPUBLIC

Plato (429-347 B.C.) was the most famous student of Socrates and the second of the great Athenian philosophers. Unlike his teacher, Plato was by birth a member of the Athenian aristocracy. But his entire childhood, adolescence, and youth were spent observing the decline, defeat, and humiliation of his democratic city-state, Athens, throughout the long and disastrous Peloponnesian War (41-404 B.C.). Five years later Plato witnessed the arrest, trial and execution of his beloved teacher Socrates, again at the hands of the democratic Athenian government.

Thoroughly disillusioned with democracy, Plato left Athens for about twelve years, returning only in 387 B.C. He soon founded a philosophical school, the Academy, just outside the city of Athens, which would remain a major center of learning in the Mediterranean World for the next nine hundred years. Plato's most famous student at the Academy was Aristotle (384-322 B.C.), the third of the great Athenian philosophers of this era.

Plato wrote a number of philosophical works, presented as dialogues, and most with Socrates as the principal speaker. However it is clear that, although Socrates is serving as a convenient mouthpiece in these dialogues, the ideas are clearly those of Plato. This was a common literary device in classical antiquity.

Plato's Republic is the most famous of these works. It attempts to outline a blueprint for a just society that can best assure happiness for all its people. Since Plato is a Greek of the classical age, his ideal state must be a polis (city-state). But this will be a polis of a special type and will bear little resemblance to Athens or any other Greek city-state. His ideal state will be ruled by a small group of self-selected "philosopher-kings" who will have absolute power. The decisions of these rulers will be enforced by a larger group of "Guardians", selected on the basis of merit from among the best of all the other citizens, who will have no political rights and will serve as workers in this ideal state.

The following excerpt focuses on the selection and training of these so-called "Guardians", presented as a dialogue with Socrates as the main speaker and employing the "Socratic Method". But remember that the ideas expressed here are those of Plato, not Socrates. Especially note Plato's attitude towards the role of women in this ideal state, which is truly revolutionary.

[Editor's note: Earlier in the dialogue, the discussion has turned about the preliminary education of the Guardians,[1] ending at the age of twenty, intended to develop a harmony of mental, physical, and "philosophic" elements in their character. As we begin the selected passage, Socrates moves on to a higher level of training: to the "kingly science" that prepares the best individuals for rule.]

Good, said Socrates; and what is the next point to be settled? Is it not the question, which of these Guardians are to be rulers and which are to obey?

No doubt, said Glaucon.

Well, it is obvious that the elder must have authority over the young, and that the rulers must be the best.

Yes.

---

[1] The Guardians were authoritarian, but their function was custodianship, not leadership. Unlike some twentieth-century dictators, they would work to preserve values, not to bring about change.

And as among farmers the best are those with a natural turn for farming, so, if we want the best among our Guardians, we must take those naturally fitted to watch over a commonwealth. They must have the right sort of intelligence and ability; and also they must look upon the commonwealth as their special concern—the sort of concern that is felt for something so closely bound up with oneself that its interests and fortunes, for good or ill, are held to be identical with one's own.

Exactly.

So the kind of men we must choose from among the Guardians will be those who, when we look at the whole course of their lives, are found to be full of zeal to do whatever they believe is for the good of the commonwealth and never willing to act against its interest.

Yes, they will be the men we want.

We must watch them, I think, at every age and see whether they are capable of preserving this conviction that they must do what is best for the community, never forgetting it or allowing themselves to be either forced or bewitched into throwing it over.

How does this throwing over come about?

I will explain. When a belief passes out of the mind, a man may be willing to part with it, if it is false and he has learnt better, or unwilling, if it is true.

I see how he might be willing to let it go; but you must explain how he can be unwilling.

Where is your difficulty? Don't you agree that men are unwilling to be deprived of good, though ready enough to part with evil? Or that to be deceived about the truth is evil, to possess it good? Or don't you think that possessing truth means thinking of things as they really are?

You are right. I do agree that men are unwilling to be robbed of a true belief.

When that happens to them, then, it must be by theft, or violence, or bewitchment.

Again I do not understand.

Perhaps my metaphors are too high-flown. I call it theft when one is persuaded out of one's belief or forgets it. Argument in the one case, and time in the other, steal it away without one's knowing what is happening. You understand now?

Yes.

And by violence I mean being driven to change one's mind by pain or suffering.

That too I understand, and you are right.

And bewitchment, as I think you would agree, occurs when a man is beguiled out of his opinion by the allurements of pleasure or scared out of it under the spell of panic.

Yes, all delusions are like a sort of bewitchment.

As I said just now, then, we must find out who are the best guardians of this inward conviction that they must always do what they believe to be best for the commonwealth. We shall have to watch them from earliest childhood and set them tasks in which they would be most likely to forget or to be beguiled out of this duty. We shall then choose only those whose memory holds firm and who are proof against delusion.

Yes.

We must also subject them to ordeals of toil and pain and watch for the same qualities there. And we must observe them when exposed to the test of yet a third kind of bewitchment. As people lead colts up to alarming noises to see whether they are timid, so these young men must be brought into terrifying situations and then into scenes of pleasure, which will put them to severer proof than gold tried in the furnace. If we find one bearing himself well in all these trials and resisting every enchantment, a true guardian of himself, preserving always that perfect rhythm and harmony of being which he has acquired from his training in music and poetry, such a one will be of the greatest service to the commonwealth as well as to himself. Whenever we find one who has come unscathed through every test in childhood, youth, and manhood, we shall set him as a Ruler to watch over the commonwealth; he will be honoured in life, and after death receive the highest tribute of funeral rites and other memorials. All who do not reach this standard we must reject. And that, I think, my dear Glaucon, may be taken as an outline of the way in which we shall select Guardians to be set in authority as Rulers.

I am very much of your mind.

These, then, may properly be called Guardians in the fullest sense, who will ensure that neither foes without shall have the power, nor friends within the wish, to do harm. Those young men whom up to now we have been speaking of as Guardians, will be better described as Auxiliaries, who will enforce the decisions of the Rulers.

I agree.

Now, said I, can we devise something in the way of those convenient fictions we spoke of earlier, a single bold flight of invention,[2] which we may induce the community in general, and if possible the Rulers themselves, to accept?

What kind of fiction?

Nothing new; something like an Eastern tale of what, according to the poets, has happened before now in more than one part of the world. The poets have been believed; but the thing has not happened in our day, and it would be hard to persuade anyone that it could ever happen again.

You seem rather shy of telling this story of yours.

With good reason, as you will see when I have told it.

Out with it; don't be afraid.

Well, here it is; though I hardly know how to find the courage or the words to express it. I shall try to convince, first the Rulers and the soldiers, and then the whole community, that all that nurture and education which we gave them was only something they seemed to experience as it were in a dream. In reality they were the whole time down inside the earth, being moulded and fostered while their arms and all their equipment were being fashioned also; and at last, when they were complete, the earth sent them up from her womb into the light of day. So now they must think of the land they dwell in as a mother and nurse, whom they must take thought for and defend against any attack, and of their fellow citizens as brothers born of the same soil.

You might well be bashful about coming out with your fiction.

No doubt; but still you must hear the rest of the story. It is true, we shall tell our people in this fable, that all of you in this land are brothers; but the god who fashioned you mixed gold in the composition of those among you who are fit to rule, so that they are of the most precious quality; and he put silver in the Auxiliaries, and iron and brass in the farmers and craftsmen. Now, since you are all of one stock, although your children will generally be like their parents, sometimes a golden parent may have a silver child or a silver parent a golden one, and so on with all the other combinations. So the first and chief injunction laid by heaven upon the Rulers is that, among all the things of which they must show themselves good guardians, there is none that needs to be so carefully watched as the mixture of metals in the souls of the children. If a child of their own is born with an alloy of iron or brass, they must, without the smallest pity, assign him the station proper to his nature and thrust him out among the craftsmen or the farmers. If, on the contrary, these classes produce a child with gold or silver in his composition, they will promote him, according to his value, to be a Guardian or an Auxiliary. They will appeal to a prophecy that ruin will come upon the state when it passes into the keeping of a man of iron or brass. Such is the story; can you think of any device to make them believe it?

Not in the first generation; but their sons and descendants might believe it, and finally the rest of mankind.

Well, said I, even so it might have a good effect in making them care more for the commonwealth and for one another; for I think I see what you mean.

So, I continued, we will leave the success of our story to the care of popular tradition; and now let us arm these sons of Earth and lead them, under the command of their Rulers, to the site of our city. There let them look round for the best place to fix their camp, from which they will be able to control any rebellion against the laws from within and to beat off enemies who may come from without like wolves to attack the fold. When they have pitched their camp and offered sacrifice to the proper divinities, they must arrange their sleeping quarters; and these must be sufficient to shelter them from winter cold and summer heat.

Naturally. You mean they are going to live there?

Yes, said I; but live like soldiers, not like men of business.

What is the difference?

I will try to explain. It would be very strange if a shepherd were to disgrace himself by keeping, for the protection of his flock, dogs who were so ill-bred and badly trained that hunger or unruliness or some bad habit or other would set them worrying the sheep and behaving no better than wolves. We must take every precaution against our Auxiliaries treating the citizens in any such way and, because they are stronger, turning into savage tyrants instead of friendly allies; and they will have been furnished with the best of safeguards, if they have really been educated in the right way.

---

[2]Sometimes translated as "the noble lie"; but, although a fiction, it was "true in spirit" and intended for the good of all. The Guardians themselves were to accept it.

But surely there is nothing wrong with their education.

We must not be too positive about that, my dear Glaucon; but we can be sure of what we said not long ago, that if they are to have the best chance of being gentle and humane to one another and to their charges, they must have the right education, whatever that may be.

We were certainly right there.

Then besides that education, it is only common sense to say that the dwellings and other belongings provided for them must be such as will neither make them less perfect Guardians nor encourage them to maltreat their fellow citizens.

True.

With that end in view, let us consider how they should live and be housed. First, none of them must possess any private property beyond the barest necessaries. Next, no one is to have any dwelling or storehouse that is not open for all to enter at will. Their food, in the quantities required by men of temperance and courage who are in training for war, they will receive from the other citizens as the wages of their guardianship, fixed so that there shall be just enough for the year with nothing over; and they will have meals in common and all live together like soldiers in a camp. Gold and silver, we shall tell them, they will not need, having the divine counterparts of those metals always in their souls as a god-given possession, whose purity it is not lawful to sully by the acquisition of that mortal dross, current among mankind, which has been the occasion of so many unholy deeds. They alone of all the citizens are forbidden to touch and handle silver or gold, or to come under the same roof with them, or wear them as ornaments, or drink from vessels made of them. This manner of life will be their salvation and make them the saviours of the commonwealth. If ever they should come to possess land of their own and houses and money, they will give up their guardianship for the management of their farms and households and become tyrants at enmity with their fellow citizens instead of allies. And so they will pass all their lives in hating and being hated, plotting and being plotted against, in much greater fear of their enemies at home than of any foreign foe, and fast heading for the destruction that will soon overwhelm their country with themselves. For all these reasons let us say that this is how our Guardians are to be housed and otherwise provided for, and let us make laws accordingly.

By all means, said Glaucon.

Here Adeimantus interposed. Socrates, he said, how would you meet the objection that you are not making these people particularly happy? It is their own fault too, if they are not; for they are really masters of the state, and yet they get no good out of it as other rulers do, who own lands, build themselves fine houses with handsome furniture, offer private sacrifices to the gods, and entertain visitors from abroad; who possess, in fact, that gold and silver you spoke of, with everything else that is usually thought necessary for happiness. These people seem like nothing so much as a garrison of mercenaries posted in the city and perpetually mounting guard.

Yes, I said, and what is more they will serve for their food only without getting a mercenary's pay, so that they will not be able to travel on their own account or to make presents to a mistress or to spend as they please in other ways, like the people who are commonly thought happy. You have forgotten to include these counts in your indictment, and many more to the same effect.

Well, take them as included now.

And you want to hear the answer?

Yes.

We shall find one, I think, by keeping to the line we have followed so far. We shall say that, though it would not be surprising if even these people were perfectly happy under such conditions, our aim in founding the commonwealth was not to make any one class specially happy, but to secure the greatest possible happiness for the community as a whole. We thought we should have the best chance of finding justice in a state so constituted, just as we should find injustice where the constitution was of the worst possible type; we could then decide the question which has been before us all this time. For the moment, we are constructing, as we believe, the state which will be happy as a whole, not trying to secure the well-being of a select few; we shall study a state of the opposite kind presently. It is as if we were colouring a statue[3] and someone came up and blamed us for not putting the most beautiful colours on the noblest parts of the figure; the eyes, for instance, should be painted crimson, but we had made them black. We should think it a fair answer to say: Really, you must not expect us to paint eyes so handsome as not to look like eyes at all. This applies to all the parts: the question is whether,

---

[3]Greek sculpture was usually painted.

by giving each its proper colour, we make the whole beautiful. So too, in the present case, you must not press us to endow our Guardians with a happiness that will make them anything rather than guardians. We could quite easily clothe our farmers in gorgeous robes, crown them with gold, and invite them to till the soil at their pleasure; or we might set our potters to lie on couches by their fire, passing round the wine and making merry, with their wheel at hand to work at whenever they felt so inclined. We could make all the rest happy in the same sort of way, and so spread this well-being through the whole community. But you must not put that idea into our heads; if we take your advice, the farmer will be no farmer, the potter no longer a potter; none of the elements that make up the community will keep its character. In many cases this does not matter so much: if a cobbler goes to the bad and pretends to be what he is not, he is not a danger to the state; but, as you must surely see, men who make only a vain show of being guardians of the laws and of the commonwealth bring the whole state to utter ruin, just as, on the other hand, its good government and well-being depend entirely on them. We, in fact, are making genuine Guardians who will be the last to bring harm upon the commonwealth; if our critic aims rather at producing a happiness like that of a party of peasants feasting at a fair, what he has in mind is something other than a civic community. So we must consider whether our aim in establishing Guardians is to secure the greatest possible happiness for them, or happiness is something of which we should watch the development in the whole commonwealth. If so, we must compel these Guardians and Auxiliaries of ours to second our efforts; and they, and all the rest with them, must be induced to make themselves perfect masters each of his own craft. In that way, as the community grows into a well-ordered whole, the several classes may be allowed such measure of happiness as their nature will compass.

I think that is an admirable reply.

• • •

We must go back, then, said Socrates, to a subject which ought, perhaps, to have been treated earlier in its proper place; though, after all, it may be suitable that the women should have their turn on the stage when the men have quite finished their performance, especially since you are so insistent. In my judgement, then, the question under what conditions people born and educated as we have described should possess wives and children, and how they should treat them, can be rightly settled only by keeping to the course on which we started them at the outset. We undertook to put these men in the position of watch-dogs guarding a flock. Suppose we follow up the analogy and imagine them bred and reared in the same sort of way. We can then see if that plan will suit our purpose.

How will that be?

In this way. Which do we think right for watch-dogs: should the females guard the flock and hunt with the males and take a share in all they do, or should they be kept within doors as fit for no more than bearing and feeding their puppies, while all the hard work of looking after the flock is left to the males?

They are expected to take their full share, except that we treat them as not quite so strong.

Can you employ any creature for the same work as another, if you do not give them both the same upbringing and education?

No.

Then, if we are to set women to the same tasks as men, we must teach them the same things. They must have the same two branches of training for mind and body and also be taught the art of war, and they must receive the same treatment.

That seems to follow.

Possibly, if these proposals were carried out, they might be ridiculed as involving a good many breaches of custom.

They might indeed.

The most ridiculous—don't you think?—being the notion of women exercising naked along with the men in the wrestling-schools; some of them elderly women too, like the old men who still have a passion for exercise when they are wrinkled and not very agreeable to look at.

Yes that would be thought laughable, according to our present notions.

Now we have started on this subject, we must not be frightened of the many witticisms that might be aimed at such a revolution, not only in the matter of bodily exercise but in the training of women's minds, and not least when it comes to their bearing arms and riding on horse-back. Having begun upon these rules, we must not draw back from the harsher provisions. The wits may be asked to stop being witty and try to be serious; and we may remind them that it is not so long since the Greeks, like most foreign nations of the present day, thought it ridiculous and shameful for men to be seen naked. When gymnastic exercises were first introduced in Crete and later at Sparta, the humorists had their chance to make fun of them; but when experience had shown that nakedness is better uncovered than muffled up, the laughter died down and a practice which the reason approved ceased to look ridiculous to the eye. This shows how idle it is to think anything ludicrous but what is base. One who tries to raise a laugh at any spectacle save that of baseness and folly will also, in his serious moments, set before himself some other standard than goodness of what deserves to be held in honour.

Most assuredly.

The first thing to be settled, then, is whether these proposals are feasible; and it must be open to anyone, whether a humorist or serious-minded, to raise the question whether, in the case of mankind, the feminine nature is capable of taking part with the other sex in all occupations, or in none at all, or in some only; and in particular under which of these heads this business of military service falls. Well begun is half done, and would not this be the best way to begin?

Yes.

Shall we take the other side in this debate and argue against ourselves? We do not want the adversary's position to be taken by storm for lack of defenders.

I have no objection.

Let us state his case for him. "Socrates and Glaucon," he will say, "there is no need for others to dispute your position; you yourselves, at the very outset of founding your commonwealth, agreed that everyone should do the one work for which nature fits him." Yes, of course; I suppose we did. "And isn't there a very great difference in nature between man and woman?" Yes, surely. "Does not that natural difference imply a corresponding difference in the work to be given to each?" Yes. . . .

If, then, we find that either the male sex or the female is specially qualified for any particular form of occupation, then that occupation, we shall say, ought to be assigned to one sex or the other. But if the only difference appears to be that the male begets and the female brings forth, we shall conclude that no difference between man and woman has yet been produced that is relevant to our purpose. We shall continue to think it proper for our Guardians and their wives to share in the same pursuits.

And quite rightly.

The next thing will be to ask our opponent to name any profession or occupation in civic life for the purposes of which woman's nature is different from man's.

That is a fair question.

He might reply, as you did just now, that it is not easy to find a satisfactory answer on the spur of the moment, but that there would be no difficulty after a little reflection.

Perhaps.

Suppose, then, we invite him to follow us and see if we can convince him that there is no occupation concerned with the management of social affairs that is peculiar to women. We will confront him with a question: When you speak of a man having a natural talent for something, do you mean that he finds it easy to learn, and after a little instruction can find out much more for himself; whereas a man who is not so gifted learns with difficulty and no amount of instruction and practice will make him even remember what he has been taught? Is the talented man one whose bodily powers are readily at the service of his mind, instead of being a hindrance? Are not these the marks by which you distinguish the presence of a natural gift for any pursuit?

Yes, precisely.

Now do you know of any human occupation in which the male sex is not superior to the female in all these respects? Need I waste time over exceptions like weaving and watching over saucepans and batches of cakes, though women are supposed to be good at such things and get laughed at when a man does them better?

It is true, he replied, in almost everything one sex is easily beaten by the other. No doubt many women are better at many things than many men; but taking the sexes as a whole, it is as you say.

To conclude, then, there is no occupation concerned with the management of social affairs which belongs either to woman or to man, as such. Natural gifts are to be found here and there in both creatures alike; and every occupation is open to both, so far as their natures are concerned, though woman is for all purposes the weaker.

Certainly. . . .

It follows that one woman will be fitted by nature to be a Guardian, another will not; because these were the qualities for which we selected our men Guardians. So for the purpose of keeping watch over the commonwealth, woman has the same nature as man, save in so far as she is weaker.

So it appears.

It follows that women of this type must be selected to share the life and duties of Guardians with men of the same type, since they are competent and of a like nature, and the same natures must be allowed the same pursuits.

Yes.

We come round, then, to our former position, that there is nothing contrary to nature in giving our Guardians' wives the same training for mind and body. The practice we proposed to establish was not impossible or visionary, since it was in accordance with nature. Rather, the contrary practice which now prevails turns out to be unnatural.

So it appears.

Well, we set out to inquire whether the plan we proposed was feasible and also the best. That it is feasible is now agreed; we must next settle whether it is the best.

Obviously.

Now, for the purpose of producing a woman fit to be a Guardian, we shall not have one education for men and another for women, precisely because the nature to be taken in hand is the same.

True.

What is your opinion on the question of one man being better than another? Do you think there is no such difference?

Certainly I do not.

And in this commonwealth of ours which will prove the better men—the Guardians who have received the education we described, or the shoemakers who have been trained to make shoes?

It is absurd to ask such a question.

Very well. So these Guardians will be the best of all the citizens?

By far.

And these women the best of all the women?

Yes.

Can anything be better for a commonwealth than to produce in it men and women of the best possible type?

No.

And that result will be brought about by such a system of mental and bodily training as we have described?

Surely.

We may conclude that the institution we proposed was not only practicable, but also the best for the commonwealth.

Yes.

The wives of our Guardians, then, must strip for exercise, since they will be clothed with virtue, and they must take their share in war and in the other social duties of guardianship. They are to have no other occupation; and in these duties the lighter part must fall to the women, because of the weakness of their sex. The man who laughs at naked women, exercising their bodies for the best of reasons, is like one that "gathers fruit unripe," for he does not know what it is that he is laughing at or what he is doing. There will never be a finer saying than the one which declares that whatever does good should be held in honour, and the only shame is in doing harm.

That is perfectly true. . . . So far, then, in regulating the position of women, we may claim to have come safely through with one hazardous proposal, that male and female Guardians shall have all occupations in common. The consistency of the argument is an assurance that the plan is a good one and also feasible. We are like swimmers who have breasted the first wave without being swallowed up.

Not such a small wave either.

You will not call it large when you see the next.

Let me have a look at the next one, then.

Here it is: a law which follows from that principle and all that has gone before, namely that, of these Guardians, no one man and one woman are to set up house together privately: wives are to be held in common by all; so too are the children, and no parent is to know his own child, nor any child his parent.

It will be much harder to convince people that that is either a feasible plan or a good one.

As to its being a good plan, I imagine no one would deny the immense advantage of wives and children being held in common, provided it can be done. I should expect dispute to arise chiefly over the question whether it is possible.

There may well be a good deal of dispute over both points.

You mean, I must meet attacks on two fronts. I was hoping to escape one by running away: if you agreed it was a good plan, then I should only have had to inquire whether it was feasible.

No, we have seen through that maneuver. You will have to defend both positions.

Well, I must pay the penalty for my cowardice. But grant me one favour. Let me indulge my fancy, like one who entertains himself with idle day-dreams on a solitary walk. Before he has any notion how his desires can be realized, he will set aside that question, to save himself the trouble of reckoning what may or may not be possible. He will assume that his wish has come true, and amuse himself with settling all the details of what he means to do then. So a lazy mind encourages itself to be lazier than ever; and I am giving way to the same weakness myself. I want to put off till later that question, how the thing can be done. For the moment, with your leave, I shall assume it to be possible, and ask how the Rulers will work out the details in practice; and I shall argue that the plan, once carried into effect, would be the best thing in the world for our commonwealth and for its Guardians. That is what I shall now try to make out with your help, if you will allow me to postpone the other question.

Very good; I have no objection.

Well, if our Rulers are worthy of the name, and their Auxiliaries likewise, these latter will be ready to do what they are told, and the Rulers, in giving their commands, will themselves obey our laws and will be faithful to their spirit in any details we leave to their discretion.

No doubt.

It is for you, then, as their lawgiver, who have already selected the men, to select for association with them women who are so far as possible of the same natural capacity. Now since none of them will have any private home of his own, but they will share the same dwelling and eat at common tables, the two sexes will be together; and meeting without restriction for exercise and all through their upbringing, they will surely be drawn towards union with one another by a necessity of their nature—necessity is not too strong a word, I think?

Not too strong for the constraint of love, which for the mass of mankind is more persuasive and compelling than even the necessity of mathematical proof.

Exactly. But in the next place, Glaucon, anything like unregulated unions would be a profanation in a state whose citizens lead the good life. The Rulers will not allow such a thing.

No, it would not be right.

Clearly, then, we must have marriages, as sacred as we can make them; and this sanctity will attach to those which yield the best results.

Certainly. . . .

This, then, Glaucon, is the manner in which the Guardians of your commonwealth are to hold their wives and children in common. Must we not next find arguments to establish that it is consistent with our other institutions and also by far the best plan?

Yes, surely.

We had better begin by asking what is the greatest good at which the lawgiver should aim in laying down the constitution of a state, and what is the worst evil. We can then consider whether our proposals are in keeping with that good and irreconcilable with the evil.

By all means.

Does not the worst evil for a state arise from anything that tends to rend it asunder and destroy its unity, while nothing does it more good than whatever tends to bind it together and make it one?

That is true.

And are not citizens bound together by sharing in the same pleasures and pains, all feeling glad or grieved on the same occasions of gain or loss; whereas the bond is broken when such feelings are no longer universal, but any event of public or personal concern fills some with joy and others with distress?

Certainly.

And this disunion comes about when the words "mine" and "not mine," "another's" and "not another's" are not applied to the same things throughout the community. The best ordered state will be the one in which the largest number of persons use these terms in the same sense, and which accordingly most nearly resembles a single person. When one of us hurts his finger, the whole extent of those bodily connexions which are gathered up in the soul and unified by its ruling element is made aware and it all shares as a whole in the pain of the suffering part; hence we say that the man has a pain in his finger. The same thing is true of the pain or pleasure felt when any other part of the person suffers or is relieved.

Yes; I agree that the best organized community comes nearest to that condition.

And so it will recognize as a part of itself the individual citizen to whom good or evil happens, and will share as a whole in his joy or sorrow.

• • •

But really, Socrates, Glaucon continued, if you are allowed to go on like this, I am afraid you will forget all about the question you thrust aside some time ago: whether a society so constituted can ever come into existence, and if so, how. No doubt, if it did exist, all manner of good things would come about. I can even add some that you have passed over. Men who acknowledged one another as fathers, sons, or brothers and always used those names among themselves would never desert one another; so they would fight with unequalled bravery: And if their womenfolk went out with them to war, either in the ranks or drawn up in the rear to intimidate the enemy and act as a reserve in case of need, I am sure all this would make them invincible. At home, too, I can see many advantages you have not mentioned. But, since I admit that our commonwealth would have all these merits and any number more, if once it came into existence, you need not describe it in further detail. All we have now to do is to convince ourselves that it can be brought into being and how.

This is a very sudden onslaught, said I; you have no mercy on my shilly-shallying. Perhaps you do not realize that, after I have barely escaped the first two waves,[4] the third, which you are now bringing down upon me, is the most formidable of all. When you have seen what it is like and heard my reply, you will be ready to excuse the very natural fears which made me shrink from putting forward such a paradox for discussion.

The more you talk like that, he said, the less we shall be willing to let you off from telling us how this constitution can come into existence; so you had better waste no more time.

Well, said I, let me begin by reminding you that what brought us to this point was our inquiry into the nature of justice and injustice.

True; but what of that?

Merely this: suppose we do find out what justice is, are we going to demand that a man who is just shall have a character which exactly corresponds in every respect to the ideal of justice? Or shall we be satisfied if he comes as near to the ideal as possible and has in him a larger measure of that quality than the rest of the world?

That will satisfy me.

If so, when we set out to discover the essential nature of justice and injustice and what a perfectly just and a perfectly unjust man would be like, supposing them to exist, our purpose was to use them as ideal patterns: we were to observe the degree of happiness or unhappiness that each exhibited, and to draw the necessary inference that our own destiny would be like that of the one we most resembled. We did not set out to show that these ideals could exist in fact.

That is true.

Then suppose a painter had drawn an ideally beautiful figure complete to the last touch, would you think any the worse of him, if he could not show that a person as beautiful as that could exist?

No, I should not.

Well, we have been constructing in discourse the pattern of an ideal state. Is our theory any the worse, if we cannot prove it possible that a state so organized could be actually founded?

Surely not.

That, then, is the truth of the matter. But if, for your satisfaction, I am to do my best to show under what conditions our ideal would have the best chance of being realized, I must ask you once more to admit that the same principle applies here. Can theory ever be fully realized in practice? Is it not in the nature of things that action should come less close to truth than thought? People may not think so; but do you agree or not?

I do.

Then you must not insist upon my showing that this construction we have traced in thought could be reproduced in fact down to the last detail. You must admit that we shall have found a way to meet your demand for realization, if we can discover how a state might be constituted in the closest accordance with our description. Will not that content you? It would be enough for me.

And for me too.

---

[4]Socrates is referring to the difficulties ("waves" of public opinion) he has overcome in proposing equality for women and an end to the traditional family unit.

Then our next attempt, it seems, must be to point out what defect in the working of existing states prevents them from being so organized, and what is the least change that would effect a transformation into this type of government—a single change if possible, or perhaps two; at any rate let us make the changes as few and insignificant as may be.

By all means.

Well, there is one change which, as I believe we can show, would bring about this revolution—not a small change, certainly, nor an easy one, but possible.

What is it?

I have now to confront what we called the third and greatest wave. But I must state my paradox, even though the wave should break in laughter over my head and drown me in ignominy. Now mark what I am going to say.

Go on.

Unless either philosophers become kings in their countries or those who are now called kings and rulers come to be sufficiently inspired with a genuine desire for wisdom; unless, that is to say, political power and philosophy meet together, while the many natures who now go their several ways in the one or the other direction are forcibly debarred from doing so, there can be no rest from troubles, my dear Glaucon, for states, nor yet, as I believe, for all mankind; nor can this commonwealth which we have imagined ever till then see the light of day and grow to its full stature. This it was that I have so long hung back from saying; I knew what a paradox it would be, because it is hard to see that there is no other way of happiness either for the state or for the individual.

• • •

Next, said I, here is a parable[5] to illustrate the degrees in which our nature may be enlightened or unenlightened. Imagine the condition of men living in a sort of cavernous chamber underground, with an entrance open to the light and a long passage all down the cave. Here they have been from childhood, chained by the leg and also by the neck, so that they cannot move and can see only what is in front of them, because the chains will not let them turn their heads. At some distance higher up is the light of a fire burning behind them; and between the prisoners and the fire is a track with a parapet built along it, like the screen at a puppetshow, which hides the performers while they show their puppets over the top.

I see, said he.

Now behind this parapet imagine persons carrying along various artificial objects, including figures of men and animals in wood or stone or other materials, which project above the parapet. Naturally, some of these persons will be talking, others silent.

It is a strange picture, he said, and a strange sort of prisoners.

Like ourselves, I replied; for in the first place prisoners so confined would have seen nothing of themselves or of one another, except the shadows thrown by the fire-light on the wall of the Cave facing them, would they?

Not if all their lives they had been prevented from moving their heads.

And they would have seen as little of the objects carried past.

Of course.

Now, if they could talk to one another, would they not suppose that their words referred only to those passing shadows which they saw?

Necessarily.

And suppose their prison had an echo from the wall facing them? When one of the people crossing behind them spoke, they could only suppose that the sound came from the shadow passing before their eyes.

No doubt.

In every way, then, such prisoners would recognize as reality nothing but the shadows of those artificial objects.

Inevitably.

Now consider what would happen if their release from the chains and the healing of their unwisdom should come about in this way. Suppose one of them set free and forced suddenly to stand up, turn his head, and walk with eyes lifted to the light; all these movements would be painful, and he would be too dazzled to make out the objects whose shadows he had been used to see. What do you think he would say, if someone told him that what he had formerly seen was meaningless illusion, but now, being somewhat nearer to reality and turned towards more real

[5]What follows is Plato's view of human alienation—not from a personal God or from society, but from Plato's concept of Reality. This parable, or fable, is often referred to as the "Allegory of the Cave."

objects, he was getting a truer view? Suppose further that he were shown the various objects being carried by and were made to say, in reply to questions, what each of them was. Would he not be perplexed and believe the objects now shown him to be not so real as what he formerly saw?

Yes, not nearly so real.

And if he were forced to look at the fire-light itself, would not his eyes ache, so that he would try to escape and turn back to the things which he could see distinctly, convinced that they really were clearer than these other objects now being shown to him?

Yes.

And suppose someone were to drag him away forcibly up the steep and rugged ascent and not let him go until he had hauled him out into the sunlight, would he not suffer pain and vexation at such treatment, and, when he had come out into the light, find his eyes so full of its radiance that he could not see a single one of the things that he was now told were real?

Certainly he would not see them all at once.

He would need, then, to grow accustomed before he could see things in that upper world. At first it would be easiest to make out shadows, and then the images of men and things reflected in water, and later on the things themselves. After that, it would be easier to watch the heavenly bodies and the sky itself by night, looking at the light of the moon and stars rather than the Sun and the Sun's light in the day-time.

Yes, surely.

Last of all, he would be able to look at the Sun and contemplate its nature, not as it appears when reflected in water or any alien medium, but as it is in itself in its own domain.

No doubt.

And now he would begin to draw the conclusion that it is the Sun that produces the seasons and the course of the year and controls everything in the visible world, and moreover is in a way the cause of all that he and his companions used to see.

Clearly he would come at last to that conclusion.

Then if he called to mind his fellow prisoners and what passed for wisdom in his former dwelling-place, he would surely think himself happy in the change and be sorry for them. They may have had a practice of honouring and commending one another, with prizes for the man who had the keenest eye for the passing shadows and the best (memory for the order in which they followed or accompanied one another, so that he could make a good guess as to which was going to come next. Would our released prisoner be likely to covet those prizes or to envy the men exalted to honour and power in the Cave? Would he not feel like Homer's Achilles, that he would far sooner "be on earth as a hired servant in the house of a landless man"[6] or endure anything rather than go back to his old beliefs and live in the old way?

Yes, he would prefer any fate to such a life.

Now imagine what would happen if he went down again to take his former seat in the Cave. Coming suddenly out of the sunlight, his eyes would be filled with darkness. He might be required once more to deliver his opinion on those shadows, in competition with the prisoners who had never been released, while his eyesight was still dim and unsteady; and it might take some time to become used to the darkness. They would laugh at him and sây that he had gone up only to come back with his sight ruined; it was worth no one's while even to attempt the ascent. If they could lay hands on the man who was trying to set them free and lead them up, they would kill him.[7]

Yes, they would.

Every feature in this parable, my dear Glaucon, is meant to fit our earlier analysis. The prison dwelling corresponds to the region revealed to us through the sense of sight, and the fire-light within it to the power of the Sun. The ascent to see the things in the upper world you may take as standing for the upward journey of the soul into the region of the intelligible; then you will be in possession of what I surmise, since that is what you wish to be told. Heaven knows whether it is true; but this, at any rate, is how it appears to me. In the world of knowledge, the last thing to be perceived and only with great difficulty is the essential Form of Goodness. Once it is perceived, the conclusion must follow that, for all things, this is the cause of whatever is right and good; in the visible world

---

[6] Achilles was the mightiest of the warriors who had died at Troy. In Homer's epic poem *The Odyssey,* the soul of the dead Achilles states that he would rather be the lowliest slave up on earth than the king of the departed souls in the underworld of Hades.
[7] As happened to Socrates.

it gives birth to light and to the lord of light, while it is itself sovereign in the intelligible world and the parent of intelligence and truth. Without having had a vision of this Form no one can act with wisdom, either in his own life or in matters of state.

So far as I can understand, I share your belief. . . .

You will see, then, Glaucon, that there will be no real injustice in compelling our philosophers to watch over and care for the other citizens. We can fairly tell them that their peers in other states may quite reasonably refuse to collaborate: there they have sprung up, like a self-sown plant, in despite of their country's institutions; no one has fostered their growth, and they cannot be expected to show gratitude for a care they have never received. "But," we shall say, "it is not so with you. We have brought you into existence for your country's sake as well as for your own, to be like leaders and king-bees in a hive; you have been better and more thoroughly educated than those others and hence you are more capable of playing your part both as men of thought and as men of action. You must go down, then, each in his turn, to live with the rest and let your eyes grow accustomed to the darkness. You will then see a thousand times better than those who live there always; you will recognize every image for what it is and know what it represents, because you have seen justice, beauty, and goodness in their reality; and so you and we shall find life in our commonwealth no mere dream, as it is in most existing states, where men live fighting one another about shadows and quarrelling for power, as if that were a great prize; whereas in truth government can be at its best and free from dissension only where the destined rulers are least desirous of holding office."

Aristophanes

LYSISTRATA

Little is known about the life of Aristophanes (ca. 446- ca. 386 B.C.) of Athens, the only author of the "Old Comedy" whose work survives. Aristophanes was clearly from the Athenian aristocracy and seems to have cared little for the democracy of his own city-state. His plays are thus often anti-democratic in tone. He wrote more than forty plays but only eleven have survived, mostly written during the Peloponnesian War (431-404 B.C.).

Unlike Greek tragedy, which was strongly based on mythological themes from the past, Greek comedy was highly topical, focusing and often satirizing contemporary times. His plays satirized prominent figures of Athens, including for example Pericles and Socrates, as well "stock types" of characters. Although the plays are filled with humor, including much sexual innuendo and imagery, they also are intended to convey messages to the Athenian audience.

An excellent example is the Lysistrata, *first performed in 411 B.C. The date is important because the Peloponnesian Ware was now twenty years old and there was still no end in sight. Just two years earlier Athens had endured its worst defeat of the entire war, the disastrous expedition to Syracuse in Sicily. Aristophanes uses a completely fictional "sex strike" organized women led by by the title character to ridicule the stupidity of Greek versus Greek warfare. One may note the significance of the fact that this strongly anti-war play which was harshly critical of the Athenian government was produced in war time and paid for in part by the very same government! Although the play underscores the power of women, one may seriously question to what degree it reflects the actual reality of gender relations in 5th century B.C. Athens.*

Characters of the Play

LYSISTRATA }

KLEONIKE } *Athenian women*[1]

MYRRHINE }

LAMPITO, *a Spartan woman*

ISMENIA, *a Boiotian girl*

KORINTHIAN GIRL

POLICEWOMAN

---

[1]As often happens in ancient Greek comedy, some of the characters' names match their roles; for example, *Lysistrata* means, in Greek, "dismisser of armies"; *Kleonike* means "dried weed"; *Myrrhine* suggests a slang word for the female sexual organ; *Kinesias,* the name of Myrrhine's husband, is derived from the Greek verb *kinein* ("to move") and is used here as a punning reference to the movements of intercourse. (The letter "K," as shown here in the English equivalent of the Greek letter, is often shown in other translations as "C.")

KORYPHAIOS [Chorus Leader] OF THE MEN

CHORUS OF OLD MEN *of Athens*

KORYPHAIOS [Chorus Leader] OF THE WOMEN

CHORUS OF OLD WOMEN *of Athens*

COMMISSIONER *of Public Safety*

FOUR POLICEMEN

KINESIAS, *Myrrhine's husband*

CHILD *of Kinesias and Myrrhine*

SLAVE

SPARTAN HERALD

SPARTAN AMBASSADOR

FLUTE-PLAYER

ATHENIAN WOMEN

PELOPONNESIAN WOMEN

PELOPONNESIAN MEN

ATHENIAN MEN

SCENE: *A street in Athens. In the background, the Akropolis;[2] center, its gateway, the Propylaia. The time is early morning. Lysistrata is discovered alone, pacing back and forth injurious impatience.*

LYSISTRATA
Women!
Announce a debauch in honor of Bacchos,[3] a spree for Pan,[4] some footling fertility fieldday, and traffic stops—the streets are absolutely clogged with frantic females banging on tambourines. No urging for an orgy!

But *today*—there's not one woman here.

Enter Kleonike.

Correction: one. Here comes my next door neighbor.—Hello, Kleonike.

KLEONIKE
Hello to *you*, Lysistrata.—But what's the fuss? Don't look so barbarous, baby; knitted brows just aren't your style.

LYSISTRATA
It doesn't matter, Kleonike—I'm on fire right down to the bone. I'm positively ashamed to be a woman—a member of a sex which can't even live up to male slanders! To hear our husbands talk, we're *sly:* deceitful, always plotting, monsters of intrigue. . . .

KLEONIKE

Proudly.

[2]The steep plateau dominating the city; upon its crest were built the major temples. The greatest of these, the Parthenon, contained a gold and ivory statue of Athene—and the city's treasury.
[3]Bacchos (Dionysos) was the god of wine, revelry, and fertility; he was also the patron god of the drama.
[4]A woodland god of flocks and shepherds.

That's us!

LYSISTRATA
And so we agreed to meet today and plot an intrigue that really deserves the name of monstrous
. . . and WHERE are the women?
    Slyly asleep at home—they won't get up for anything!

KLEONIKE
Relax, honey. They'll be here. You know a woman's way is hard—mainly the way out of the
house: fuss over hubby, wake the maid up, put the baby down, bathe him, feed him . . .

LYSISTRATA
Trivia. They have more fundamental business to engage in.

KLEONIKE
Incidentally, Lysistrata, just why are you calling this meeting? Nothing teeny, I trust?

LYSISTRATA
Immense.

KLEONIKE
Hmmm. And pressing?

LYSISTRATA
Unthinkably tense.

KLEONIKE
Then where IS everybody?

LYSISTRATA
Nothing like that. If it were, we'd already be in session. Seconding motions.—No, *this* came to
hand some time ago. I've spent my nights kneading it, mulling it, filing it down. . . .

KLEONIKE
Too bad. There can't be very much left.

LYSISTRATA
Only this: the hope and salvation of Hellas lies with the WOMEN!

KLEONIKE
Lies with the women? Now *there's* a last resort.

LYSISTRATA
It lies with us to decide affairs of state and foreign policy.
    The Spartan Question: Peace or Extirpation?

KLEONIKE
How *fun!*
    I cast an Aye for Extirpation!

LYSISTRATA
The Utter Annihilation of every last Boiotian?[5]

KLEONIKE
AYE!—I mean Nay. Clemency, please, for those scrumptious eels.[6]

---

[5]Boiotia is a region near Athens; its cities were allied with Sparta.

LYSISTRATA

And as for Athens . . . I'd rather not put the thought into words. Just fill in the blanks, if you will. —To the point: If we can meet and reach agreement here and now with the girls from Thebes and the Peloponnese,[7] we'll form an alliance and save the States of Greece!

KLEONIKE

Us? Be practical. Wisdom from women? There's nothing cosmic about cosmetics—and Glamor is our only talent. All we can do is *sit,* primped and painted, made up and dressed up,

Getting carried away in spite of her argument.

ravishing in saffron wrappers, peekaboo peignoirs, exquisite negligees, those chic, expensive little slippers that come from the East. . .

LYSISTRATA

Exactly. You've hit it. I see our way to salvation in just such ornamentation—in slippers and slips, rouge and perfumes, negligees and decolletage. . . .

KLEONIKE

How so?

LYSISTRATA

So effectively that not one husband will take up his spear against another. . . .

KLEONIKE

Peachy!

I'll have that kimono dyed . . .

LYSISTRATA

. . . or shoulder his shield . . .

KLEONIKE

. . . squeeze into that daring negligee . . .

LYSISTRATA

. . . or unsheathe his sword!

KLEONIKE

. . . and buy those slippers!

LYSISTRATA

Well, now. Don't you think the girls should be here?

KLEONIKE

Be here? Ages ago—they should have flown!

She stops.

But no. You'll find out. These are authentic Athenians: no matter what they do, they do it late.

LYSISTRATA

But what about the out-of-town delegations? There isn't a woman here from the Shore; none from Salamis . . .[8]

---

[6]Eels from Boiotia, in short supply because of the war, were considered a great delicacy in Athens.

[7]Thebes is in Boiotia; the Peloponnese is a peninsula, forming the southern part of Greece, and includes Sparta.

[8]An island just across the bay from the port of Athens and under its control. (Lysistrata's plan is to gather women from cities both allied with and opposed to Athens.)

KLEONIKE

That's quite a trip. They usually get on board at sunup. Probably riding at anchor now.

LYSISTRATA

I thought the girls from Acharnai would be here first. I'm especially counting on them. And they're not here.

KLEONIKE

I think Theogenes' wife[9] is under way. When I went by, she was hoisting her sandals . . .

Looking off right.

But look! Some of the girls are coming!

Women enter from the right. Lysistrata looks off to the left where more—a ragged lot—are straggling in.

LYSISTRATA

And more over here!

KLEONIKE

Where did you find *that* group?

LYSISTRATA

They're from the outskirts.

KLEONIKE

Well, that's something. If you haven't done anything else, you've really ruffled up the outskirts.

Myrrhine enters guiltily from the right,

MYRRHINE

Oh, Lysistrata, we aren't late, are we?
Well, *are* we?
      Speak to me!

LYSISTRATA

What is it, Myrrhine? Do you want a medal for tardiness? Honestly, such behavior, with so much at stake . . .

MYRRHINE

I'm sorry. I couldn't find my girdle in the dark. And anyway, we're here now. So tell us all about it, whatever it is.

KLEONIKE

No, wait a minute. Don't begin just yet. Let's wait for those girls from Thebes and the Peloponnese.

LYSISTRATA

Now *there* speaks the proper attitude.

Lampito, a strapping Spartan woman, enters left, leading a pretty Boiotian girl (Ismenia) and a huge, steatopygous {fat-buttocked}Korinthian.

And here's our lovely Spartan.
      He*llo*, Lampito dear. Why, darling, you're simply ravishing! Such a blemishless complexion—so clean, so out-of-doors! And will you look at that figure—the pink of perfection!

---

[9]Theogenes was a member of the political group in Athens that was urging agressive continuation of the war.

KLEONIKE
I'll bet you could strangle a bull.

LAMPITO
I calklate so.[10] Hit's fitness whut done it, fitness and dancin'. You know the step?

Demonstrating.

Foot it out back'ards an' toe yore twitchet.

The women crowd around Lampito.

KLEONIKE
What unbelievably beautiful bosoms!

LAMPITO
Shuckins, whut fer you tweedlin' me up so? I feel like a heifer come fair-time.

LYSISTRATA

Turning to Ismenia.

And who is this young lady here?

LAMPITO
Her kin's purt-near the bluebloodiest folk in Thebes—the First Fam'lies of Boiotia.

LYSISTRATA

As they inspect Ismenia.

Ah, picturesque Boiotia: her verdant meadows, her fruited plain . . .

KLEONIKE

Peering more closely.

Her sunken garden where no grass grows. A cultivated country.

LYSISTRATA

Gaping at the gawking Korinthian.

And who is *this*—er—little thing?

LAMPITO
She hails from over by Korinth, but her kinfolk's quality—mighty big back there.

KLEONIKE

On her tour of inspection.

She's mighty big back *here*.

LAMPITO
The womenfolk's all assemblied. Who-all's notion was this-hyer confabulation?

LYSISTRATA
Mine.

LAMPITO
Git on with the give-out. I'm hankerin' to hear.

---

[10]To Aristophanes' Athenian audience, the Spartans were not only their military enemies but also their cultural inferiors. Thus, the American translator has given a hillbilly dialect to Lampito and to other Spartans.

MYRRHINE

Me, too! I can't imagine what could be so important. Tell us about it!

LYSISTRATA

Right away.—But first, a question. It's not an involved one. Answer yes or no.

A pause.

MYRRHINE

Well, ASK it!

LYSISTRATA

It concerns the fathers of your children—your husbands, absent on active service. I know you all have men abroad.

—Wouldn't you like to have them home?

KLEONIKE

My husband's been gone for the last five months! Way up to Thrace, watchdogging military waste. It's horrible!

MYRRHINE

Mine's been posted to Pylos for seven whole months!

LAMPITO

My man's no sooner rotated out of the line than he's plugged back in. Hain't no discharge in this war!

KLEONIKE

And lovers can't be had for love or money, not even synthetics. Why, since those beastly Milesians revolted and cut off the leather trade, that handy do-it-yourself kit's *vanished* from the open market![11]

LYSISTRATA

If I can devise a scheme for ending the war, I gather I have your support?

KLEONIKE

You can count on me! If you need money, I'll pawn the shift off my back—

Aside.

and drink up the cash before the sun goes down.

MYRRHINE

Me, too! I'm ready to split myself right up the middle like a mackerel, and give you half!

LAMPITO

Me, too! I'd climb Taygetos Mountain plumb to the top to git the leastes' peek at Peace!

LYSISTRATA

Very well, I'll tell you. No reason to keep a secret.

Importantly, as the women cluster around her.

We can force our husbands to negotiate Peace, Ladies, by exercising steadfast Self-Control—By Total Abstinence . . .

A pause.

KLEONIKE
From WHAT?

---

[11]Miletus, apparently the source of artificial phalluses made from leather, had left its Athenian alliance and joined the Spartan alliance in the preceding year.

MYRRHINE

Yes, what?

LYSISTRATA

You'll do it?

KLEONIKE

Of course we'll do it! We'd even *die!*

LYSISTRATA

Very well, then here's the program:
Total Abstinence from SEX!

The cluster of women dissolves.

—Why are you turning away? Where are you going?

Moving among the women.

—What's this? Such stricken expressions! Such gloomy gestures!—Why so pale?
—Whence these tears?
—What IS this?
Will you do it or won't you? Cat got your tongue?

KLEONIKE

Afraid I can't make it. Sorry.
On with the War!

MYRRHINE

Me neither. Sorry.
On with the War!

LYSISTRATA

This from my little mackerel? The girl who was ready, a minute ago, to split herself right up the middle?

KLEONIKE

Breaking in between Lysistrata and Myrrhine.

Try something else. Try anything. If you say so, I'm willing to walk through fire barefoot. But not to give up SEX—there's nothing like it, Lysistrata!

LYSISTRATA

To Myrrhine.

And you?

MYRRHINE

Me, too! I'll walk through fire.

LYSISTRATA

Women!
Utter sluts, the entire sex! Will-power, nil. We're perfect raw material for Tragedy, the stuff of heroic lays. "Go to bed with a god and then get rid of the baby"—that sums us up!

Turning to Lampito.

—Oh, Spartan, be a dear. If *you* stick by me, just you, we still may have a chance to win. Give me your vote.

LAMPITO

Hit's right onsettlin' fer gals to sleep all lonely-like, withouten no humpin'. But I'm on yore side. We shore need Peace, too.

LYSISTRATA

You're a darling—the only woman here worthy of the name!

KLEONIKE

Well, just suppose we *did,* as much as possible, abstain from . . . what you said, you know—not that we *would*—could something like that bring Peace any sooner?

LYSISTRATA

Certainly. Here's how it works: We'll paint, powder, and pluck ourselves to the last detail, and stay inside, wearing those filmy tunics that set off everything we *have*—
and then slink up to the men. They'll snap to attention, go absolutely *mad* to love us—
   but we won't let them. We'll Abstain.—I imagine they'll conclude a treaty rather quickly.

LAMPITO

Nodding.

Menelaos he tuck one squint at Helen's bubbies all nekkid, and plumb throwed up.

Pause for thought.

Throwed up his sword.[12]

KLEONIKE

Suppose the men just leave us flat?

LYSISTRATA

In that case, we'll have to take things into our own hands.

KLEONIKE

There simply isn't any reasonable facsimile!—Suppose they take up by force and drag us off to the bedroom against our wills?

LYSISTRATA

Hang on to the door.

KLEONIKE

Suppose they beat us?

LYSISTRATA

Give in—but be bad sports. Be nasty about it—they don't enjoy these forced affairs. So make them suffer. Don't worry; they'll stop soon enough. A married man wants harmony—cooperation, not rape.

KLEONIKE

Well, I suppose so . . .

Looking from Lysistrata to Lampito

If *both* of you approve this, then so do we.

---

[12]Menelaos [Menelaus] was a mythical king of Sparta. His wife, Helen, ran away with Paris, a prince of Troy, thus causing the famous Trojan War. (See selection 1, *The Iliad*, p. 1.) As the Greek forces were destroying Troy, Menelaos changed his mind about his personal revenge against Helen when, once again, he saw her beauty.

LAMPITO

Hain't worried over our menfolk none. We'll bring 'em round to makin' a fair, straightfor'ard Peace withouten no nonsense about it. But take this rackety passel in Athens; I misdoubt no one could make 'em give over thet blabber of theirn.

LYSISTRATA

They're our concern. Don't worry. We'll bring them around.

LAMPITO

Not likely. Not long as they got ships kin still sail straight, an' thet fountain of money up thar in Athene's temple.[13]

LYSISTRATA

That point is quite well covered:

We're taking over the Akropolis, including Athene's temple, today. It's set: Our oldest women have their orders. They're up there now, pretending to sacrifice, waiting for us to reach an agreement. As soon as we do, they seize the Akropolis.

LAMPITO

They way you put them thengs, I swear I can't see how we kin possibly lose!

LYSISTRATA

Well, now that it's settled, Lampito, let's not lose any time. Let's take the Oath to make this binding.[14]

LAMPITO

Just trot out thet-thar Oath. We'll swear it.

LYSISTRATA

Excellent.

—Where's a policewoman?

A huge girl, dressed as a Skythian archer (the Athenian police) with bow and circular shield, lumbers up and gawks.

—What are *you* looking for?

Pointing to a spot in front of the women.

Put your shield down here.

The girl obeys.

No, hollow *up!*

The girl reverses the shield. Lysistrata looks about brightly.

—Someone give me the entrails.

A dubious silence.

KLEONIKE

Lysistrata, what kind of an Oath are we supposed to swear?

LYSISTRATA

The Standard. Aischylos used it in a play, they say—the one where you slaughter a sheep and swear on a shield.

[13]The Parthenon, the temple of Athene Parthenos ("the Maiden").
[14]The oath that follows is a parody (takeoff) of a standard ritual animal sacrifice and an oath of loyalty.

KLEONIKE
Lysistrata, you *do not* swear an Oath for *Peace* on a *shield!*

LYSISTRATA
What Oath do you want?

Exasperated.

Something bizzare and expensive? A fancier victim—"Take one white horse and disembowel"?

KLEONIKE

White horse? The symbolism's too obscure.

LYSISTRATA

Then how do we swear this oath?

KLEONIKE
Oh, *I* can tell you *that*, if you'll let me.
First, we put an enormous black cup right here—hollow up, of course. Next, into the cup we slaughter a jar of Thasian wine, and swear a mighty Oath that we won't . . . dilute it with water.

LAMPITO

To Kleonike.

Let me corngratulate you—that were the beatenes' Oath I ever heerd on!

LYSISTRATA

Calling inside.

Bring out a cup and a jug of wine!

Two women emerge, the first staggering under the weight of a huge black cup, the second even more burdened with a tremendous wine jar. Kleonike addresses them.

KLEONIKE
You darlings! What a tremendous display of pottery!

Fingering the cup.

A girl could get a glow just *holding* a cup like this!

She grabs it away from the first woman, who exits.

LYSISTRATA

Taking the wine jar from the second serving woman (who exits), she barks at Kleonike.

Put that down and help me butcher this boar!

Kleonike puts down the cup, over which she and Lysistrata together hold the jar of wine (the "boar"). Lysistrata prays.

O Mistress Persuasion,
O Cup of Devotion,
Attend our invocation:
Accept this oblation,
Grant our petition,
Favor our mission.

Lysistrata and Kleonike tip up the jar and pour the gurgling wine into the cup. Myrrhine, Lampito, and the others watch closely.

MYRRHINE
Such an attractive shade of blood. And the spurt—pure Art!

LAMPITO
>Hit shore do smell mighty purty!

Lysistrata and Kleonike put down the empty wine jar.

KLEONIKE
>Girls, let me be the first

Launching herself at the cup.

>to take the Oath!

LYSISTRATA

Hauling Kleonike back.

>You'll have to wait your turn like everyone else.—Lampito, how do we manage with this mob?
>Cumbersome.—Everyone place her right hand on the cup.

The women surround the cup and obey.

>I need a spokeswoman. One of you to take the Oath in behalf of the rest.

The women edge away from Kleonike, who reluctantly finds herself elected.

>The rite will conclude with a General Pledge of Assent by all of you, thus confirming the Oath.
>Understood?

Nods from the women. Lysistrata addresses Kleonike.

>Repeat after me:

LYSISTRATA
>**I will withhold all rights of access or entrance**

KLEONIKE
>*I will withhold all rights of access or entrance*

LYSISTRATA
>**From every husband, lover, or casual acquaintance**

KLEONIKE
>*from every husband, lover, or casual acquaintance*

LYSISTRATA
>**Who moves in my direction in erection.**
>   —Go on.

KLEONIKE

>*who m-moves in my direction in erection.*

>Ohhhhh!
>   —Lysistrata, my knees are shaky. Maybe I'd better . . .

LYSISTRATA
>**I will create, imperforate in cloistered chastity,**

KLEONIKE
>*I will create, imperforate in cloistered chastity,*

LYSISTRATA
>**A newer, more glamorous, supremely seductive me**

KLEONIKE
a newer, more glamorous, supremely seductive me

LYSISTRATA
And fire my husband's desire with my molten allure—

KLEONIKE
and fire my husband's desire with my molten allure—

LYSISTRATA
But remain, to his panting advances, icily pure.

KLEONIKE
but remain, to his panting advances, icily pure.

LYSISTRATA
If he should force me to share the connubial couch,

KLEONIKE
If he should force me to share the connubial couch,

LYSISTRATA
I refuse to return his stroke with the teeniest twitch.

KLEONIKE
I refuse to return his stroke with the teeniest twitch.

LYSISTRATA
I will not lift my slippers to touch the thatch

KLEONIKE
I will not lift my slippers to touch the thatch

LYSISTRATA
Or submit sloping prone in a hangdog crouch.

KLEONIKE
or submit sloping prone in a hangdog crouch.

LYSISTRATA
If I this oath maintain, may I drink this glorious wine.

KLEONIKE
If I this oath maintain, may I drink this glorious wine.

LYSISTRATA
But if I slip or falter, let me drink water.

KLEONIKE
But if I slip or falter, let me drink water.

LYSISTRATA
—And now the General Pledge of Assent:

WOMEN
A-MEN!

LYSISTRATA
Good. I'll dedicate the oblation.

She drinks deeply.

KLEONIKE

Not too much, darling. You know how anxious we are to become allies and friends.
Not to mention *staying* friends.

She pushes Lysistrata away and drinks. As the women take their turns at the cup, loud cries and alarums are heard offstage.

LAMPITO

What-all's that bodacious ruckus?

LYSISTRATA

Just what I told you: It means the women have taken the Akropolis. Athene's Citadel is ours!
It's time for you to go, Lampito, and set your affairs in order in Sparta.

Indicating the other women in Lampito's group.

Leave these girls here as hostages.

Lampito exits left. Lysistrata turns to the others.

Let's hurry inside the Akropolis and help the others shoot the bolts.

KLEONIKE

Don't you think the men will send reinforcements against us as soon as they can?

LYSISTRATA

So where's the worry? The men can't burn their way in or frighten us out. The Gates are ours—
they're proof against fire and fear—and they open only on our conditions.

KLEONIKE

Yes!
That's the spirit—let's deserve our reputations:

As the women hurry off into the Akropolis.

UP THE SLUTS!
WAY FOR THE OLD IMPREGNABLES!

The door shuts behind the women, and the stage is empty.

A pause, and the Chorus of Men shuffles on from the left in two groups, led by their Koryphaios [Chorus Leader]. They are incredibly aged Athenians; though they may acquire spryness later in the play, at this point they are sheer decrepitude. Their normally shaky progress is impeded by their burdens; each man not only staggers under a load of wood across his shoulders, but has his hands full as well—in one, an earthen pot containing fire (which is in constant danger of going out); in the other, a dried vinewood torch, not yet lit. Their progress toward the Akropolis is very slow.

KORYPHAIOS OF MEN

To the right guide of the First Semichorus, who is stumbling along in mild agony.

Forward, Swifty, keep 'em in step! Forget your shoulder. I know these logs are green and
heavy—but duty, boy, duty!

SWIFTY

Somewhat inspired, he quavers into slow song to set a pace for his group.

I'm never surprised. At my age, life
is just one damned thing after another.
And yet, I never thought my wife
was anything more than a home-grown bother.
But now, dadblast her,
she's a National Disaster!

FIRST SEMICHORUS OF MEN

What a catastrophe—
MATRIARCHY!
They've brought Athene's statue to heel,
they've put the Akropolis under a seal,
they've copped the whole damned commonweal . . .
What is there left for them to steal?

KORYPHAIOS OF MEN

To the right guide of the Second Semichorus—a slower soul, if possible, than Swifty.

Now, Chipper, speed's the word. The Akropolis, on the double! Once we're there, we'll pile these logs around them, and convene a circuit court for a truncated trial. Strictly impartial: With a show of hands, we'll light a spark of justice under every woman who brewed this scheme. We'll burn them all on the first ballot—and the first to go is Ly . . .

Pause for thought.

is Ly . . .

Remembering and pointing at a spot in the audience.

is *Lykon's* wife—and there she is, right over there![15]

CHIPPER

Taking up the song again.

I won't be twitted, I won't be guyed,
I'll teach these women not to trouble us!
Kleomenes the Spartan tried
expropriating our Akropolis[16]
some time ago—
ninety-five years or so—
SECOND SEMICHORUS OF MEN
but he suffered damaging losses
when he ran across US!
He breathed defiance—and more as well:
No bath for six years—you could tell.
We fished him out of the Citadel
and quelled his spirit—but not his smell.

KORYPHAIOS OF MEN
That's how I took him. A savage siege:
Seventeen ranks of shields were massed at that gate, with blanket infantry cover. I slept like a baby.
So when mere women (who gall the gods and make Euripides sick)[17] try the same trick, should I sit idly by?
Then demolish the monument I won at Marathon![18]

---

[15]At this moment the Koryphaios breaks the dramatic illusion in order to ridicule someone in the audience—Rhodia, wife of the politician Lykon, a woman often criticized for her loose morals.
[16]Kleomenes, a king of Sparta, had occupied the Akropolis in 508 B.C. for a couple of days—not the six years the senile men's chorus "remembers."
[17]Euripides, the tragic dramatist, is always presented in Aristophanes' comedies as a woman-hater.
[18]In 490 B.C. on the plain of Marathon, the Athenians defeated the first Persian invasion of Greece. The "monument" is a mound of earth, still to be seen, erected over the Athenian dead. Obviously, Aristophanes is joking about the decrepitude of the old men's chorus, since they would have had to be over a century old to actually remember Kleomenes and Marathon.

FIRST SEMICHORUS OF MEN

Singly.

—The last lap of our journey!
—I greet it with some dismay.
—The danger doesn't deter me,
—but it's uphill
—all the way.
—Please, somebody,
—find a jackass to drag these logs
—to the top.
—I ache to join the fracas
—but my shoulder's aching
—to stop.

SWIFTY

Backward there's no turning.
Upward and onward, men!
And keep those firepots burning, or
we make this trip again.

CHORUS OF MEN

Blowing into their firepots, which promptly send forth clouds of smoke.

With a puff (pfffff) . . . .
and a cough (hhhhhh) . . . .
The smoke! I'll choke! Turn it off!

SECOND SEMICHORUS OF MEN

Singly.

—Damned embers.
—Should be muzzled.
—There oughta be a law.
—They jumped me
—when I whistled
—and then they gnawed my eyeballs
—raw.
—There's lava in my lashes.
—My lids are oxidized.
—My brows are braised.
—These ashes are volcanoes
—in disguise.

CHIPPER

This way, men. And remember,
the Goddess needs our aid.
So don't be stopped by cinders. Let's
press on to the stockade!

CHORUS OF MEN

Blowing again into their firepots, which erupt as before.

With a huff (hfffff) . . . .
and a chuff (chffff) . . . .
Drat that smoke. Enough is enough!

KORYPHAIOS OF MEN

Signalling the Chorus, which has now tottered into position before the Akropolis gate, to stop, and peering into his firepot.

Praise be to the gods, it's awake. There's fire in the old fire yet.—Now the directions. See how they strike you:
First, we deposit these logs at the entrance and light our torches. Next, we crash the gate. When that doesn't work, we request admission. Politely. When *that* doesn't work, we burn the damned door down, and smoke these women into submission.
That seem acceptable? Good.

Down with the load . . . ouch, that smoke! Sonofabitch!

A horrible tangle results as the Chorus attempts to deposit the logs. The Koryphaios turns to the audience.

Is there a general in the house? We have a logistical problem . . . .

No answer. He shrugs.

Same old story. Still at loggerheads over in Samos.[19]

With great confusion, the logs are placed somehow.

That's better. The pressure's off. I've got my backbone back.

To his firepot.

What, pot? You forgot your part in the plot?
Urge that smudge to be hot on the dot and scorch my torch.
Got it, pot?

Praying.

Queen Athene, let these strumpets
crumple before our attack.
Grant us victory, male supremacy . . .
and a testimonial plaque.

The men plunge their torches into firepots and arrange themselves purposefully before the gate. Engaged in their preparations, they do not see the sudden entrance, from the right, of the Chorus of Women, led by their Koryphaios. These wear long cloaks and carry pitchers of water. They are very old—though not so old as the men—but quite spry. In their turn, they do not perceive the Chorus of Men.

KORYPHAIOS OF WOMEN

Stopping suddenly.

What's this—soot? And smoke as well? I may be all wet, but this might mean fire. Things look dark, girls; we'll have to dash.

They move ahead, at a considerably faster pace than the men.

FIRST SEMICHORUS OF WOMEN

Singly.

Speed! Celerity!   Save our sorority
from arson. Combustion.   And heat exhaustion.
Don't let our sisterhood   shrivel to blisterhood.
Fanned into slag by hoary typhoons.
By flatulent, nasty, gusty baboons.
We're late! Run!
The girls might be done!

---

[19]At the time of the play's production, the headquarters of the Athenian military forces was on the distant island of Samos.

Tutte. {All together}

Filling my pitcher   was absolute torture;
The fountains in town   are so *crowded* at dawn,
glutted with masses   of the lower classes
blatting and battering,   shoving, and shattering
jugs. But I juggled   my burden, and wriggled
away to extinguish   the igneous anguish
    of neighbor, and sister, and daughter—
        Here's Water!

SECOND SEMICHORUS OF WOMEN

Singly.

Get wind of the news?   The gaffers are loose.
The blowhards are off   with fuel enough
to furnish a bathhouse.   But the finish is pathos:
They're scaling the heights with a horrid proposal.
They're threatening women with rubbish disposal!
        How ghastly—how gauche!
        burned up with the trash!

Tutte.

Preserve me, Athene,   from gazing on any
matron or maid   auto-da-fé'd.[20]
Cover with grace   these redeemers of Greece
from battles, insanity,   Man's inhumanity.
Gold-browed goddess,   hither to aid us!
Fight as our ally,   join in our sally
    against pyromaniac slaughter—
        Haul Water!

KORYPHAIOS OF WOMEN

Noticing for the first time the Chorus of Men, still busy at their firepots, she cuts off a member of her Chorus who seems about to continue the song.

Hold it. What have we here? You don't catch true-blue patriots red-handed. These are authentic degenerates, male, taken *in flagrante.*[21]

KORYPHAIOS OF MEN
Oops. Female troops. This could be upsetting. I didn't expect such a flood of reserves.

KORYPHAIOS OF WOMEN
Merely a spearhead. If our numbers stun you, watch that yellow streak spread.
    We represent just one percent of one percent of This Woman's Army.

KORYPHAIOS OF MEN
Never been confronted with such backtalk. Can't allow it. Somebody pick up a log and pulverize that brass.
    Any volunteers?

There are none among the male chorus

---

[20]That is, burned to death.
[21]Part of a Latin legal term indicating that the person has been caught in the act of committing the offense.

KORYPHAIOS OF WOMEN
Put down the pitchers, girls. If they start waving that lumber, we don't want to be encumbered.

KORYPHAIOS OF MEN
Look, men, a few sharp jabs will stop that jawing. It never fails.
   The poet Hipponax swears by it.[22]

Still no volunteers. The Koryphaios of Women advances.

KORYPHAIOS OF WOMEN
Then step right up. Have a jab at me. Free shot.

KORYPHAIOS OF MEN

Advancing reluctantly to meet her.

Shut up! I'll peel your pelt. I'll pit your pod.

KORYPHAIOS OF WOMEN
The name is Stratyllis. I dare you to lay one finger on me.

KORYPHAIOS OF MEN
I'll lay on you with a fistful. Er—any specific threats?

KORYPHAIOS OF WOMEN

Earnestly.

I'll crop your lungs and reap your bowels, bite by bite, and leave no balls on the body for other bitches to gnaw.

KORYPHAIOS OF MEN

Retreating hurriedly.

Can't beat Euripides for insight. And I quote:
No creature's found so lost to shame as Woman.
   Talk about realist playwrights!

KORYPHAIOS OF WOMEN
Up with the water, ladies. Pitchers at the ready, place!

KORYPHAIOS OF MEN
Why the water, you sink of iniquity?
   More sedition?

KORYPHAIOS OF WOMEN
Why the fire, you walking boneyard? Self-cremation?

KORYPHAIOS OF MEN
I brought this fire to ignite a pyre and fricassee your friends.

KORYPHAIOS OF WOMEN
I brought this water to douse your pyre. Tit for tat.

KORYPHAIOS OF MEN

You'll douse my fire?

   Nonsense!

---

[22]Hipponax was a satirical poet who threatened, in one of his verses, to "sock [the sculptor] Boupalos in the jaw" for having made an ugly statue of him.

KORYPHAIOS OF WOMEN
You'll see, when the facts soak in.

KORYPHAIOS OF MEN
I have the torch right here. Perhaps I should barbecue *you.*

KORYPHAIOS OF WOMEN
If you have any soap, I could give you a bath.

KORYPHAIOS OF MEN
A bath from those polluted hands?

KORYPHAIOS OF WOMEN
Pure enough for a blushing young bridegroom.

KORYPHAIOS OF MEN
Enough of that insolent lip.

KORYPHAIOS OF WOMEN
It's merely freedom of speech.

KORYPHAIOS OF MEN
I'll stop that screeching!

KORYPHAIOS OF WOMEN
You're helpless outside of the jury-box.[23]

KORYPHAIOS OF MEN
Urging his men, torches at the ready, into a charge.

Burn, fire, burn!

KORYPHAIOS OF WOMEN
As the women empty their pitchers over the men.

And cauldron bubble.

KORYPHAIOS OF MEN
Like his troops, soaked and routed.

Arrgh!

KORYPHAIOS OF WOMEN
Goodness. What seems to be the trouble? Too hot?

KORYPHAIOS OF MEN
Hot, hell!
    Stop it! What do you think you're doing?

KORYPHAIOS OF WOMEN
If you must know, I'm gardening. Perhaps you'll bloom.

KORYPHAIOS OF MEN
Perhaps I'll fall right off the vine! I'm withered, frozen, shaking . . .

KORYPHAIOS OF WOMEN
Of course. But, providentially, you brought along your smudgepot.
    The sap should rise eventually.

---

[23]Jury duty was a frequent—sometimes the only—source of income for older male Athenians.

Shivering, the Chorus of Men retreats in utter defeat.

A Commissioner of Public Safety enters from the left, followed quite reluctantly by a squad of police—four Skythian archers {from a region north of Greece}. He surveys the situation with disapproval.

COMMISSIONER

Fire, eh? Females again—spontaneous combustion of lust. Suspected as much.

Rubadubdubbing, incessant incontinent keening for wine, damnable funeral foofaraw for Adonis resounding from roof to roof—heard it all before . . .[24]

Savagely, as the Koryphaios of Men tries to interpose a remark.

and WHERE?

The ASSEMBLY!

Recall, if you can, the debate on the Sicilian Question: That bullbrained demagogue Demostratos[25] (who will rot, I trust) rose to propose a naval task force.

His wife, writhing with religion on a handy roof, bleated a dirge:

"BEREFT! OH WOE OH WOE FOR ADONIS!"

And so of course Demostratos, taking his cue, outblatted her:

"A DRAFT! ENROLL THE WHOLE OF ZAKYNTHOS!"

His wife, a smidgin stewed, renewed her yowling:

"OH GNASH YOUR TEETH AND BEAT YOUR BREASTS FOR ADONIS!"

And so of course Demostratos (that god-detested blot, that foul-lunged son of an ulcer) gnashed tooth and nail and voice, and bashed and rammed his program through. And THERE is the Gift of Women:

MORAL CHAOS!

KORYPHAIOS OF MEN

Save your breath for actual felonies, Commissioner; see what's happened to us! Insolence, insults, these we pass over, but not lese-majesty:[26]

We're flooded with indignity from those bitches' pitchers—like a bunch of weak-bladdered brats. Our cloaks are sopped. We'll sue!

COMMISSIONER

Useless. Your suit won't hold water. Right's on their side. For female depravity, gentlemen, WE stand guilty—we, their teachers, preceptors of prurience, accomplices before the fact of fornication. We sowed them in sexual license, and now we reap rebellion.

The proof?

Consider. Off we trip to the goldsmith's to leave an order:

"That bangle you fashioned last spring for my wife is sprung. She was thrashing around last night, and the prong popped out of the bracket. I'll be tied up all day—I'm boarding the ferry right now—but my wife'll be home. If you get the time, please stop by the house in a bit and see if you can't do something—anything—to fit a new prong into the bracket of her bangle." And bang.

Another one ups to a cobbler—young, but no apprentice, full kit of tools, ready to give his awl—and delivers this gem:

"My wife's new sandals are tight. The cinch pinches her pinkie right where she's sensitive. Drop in at noon with something to stretch her cinch and give it a little play."

---

[24]At the time when the disastrous Athenian expedition to Sicily was setting forth, the female followers of the cult of Adonis were ritually—publicly—lamenting their hero's death. The expedition to Sicily was aimed against the city of Syracuse, an ally of Sparta. Later, the women's wailing was seen as having put ill-luck upon the expedition.

[25]One of the most enthusiastic initiators of the Sicilian expedition. Demostratos had also proposed drafting soldiers into the Athenian forces from the island of Zakynthos (an allied state) on their way to Sicily.

[26]An attack against the dignity of a ruler or a revered group (like the senior male citizens of Athens).

And a cinch it is. Such hanky-panky we have to thank for today's Utter Anarchy: I, a Commissioner of Public Safety, duly invested with extraordinary powers to protect the State in the Present Emergency, have secured a source of timber to outfit our fleet and solve the shortage of oarage. I need the money immediately . . . and WOMEN, no less, have locked me out of the Treasury!

Pulling himself together.

—Well, no profit in standing around.

To one of the archers.

Bring the crowbars. I'll jack these women back on their pedestals!—WELL, you slack-jawed jackass? What's the attraction? Wipe that thirst off your face. I said *crow*bar, not saloon!—All right, men, all together. Shove those bars underneath the gate and HEAVE!

Grabbing up a crowbar.

I'll take this side. And now let's root them out, men, ROOT them out. One, Two . . .

The gates to the Akropolis burst open suddenly, disclosing Lysistrata. She is perfectly composed and bears a large spindle. The Commissioner and the Police fall back in consternation.

LYSISTRATA
Why the moving equipment? I'm quite well motivated, thank you, and here I am. Frankly, you don't need crowbars nearly so much as brains.

COMMISSIONER
Brains? O name of infamy! Where's a policeman?
He grabs wildly for the First Archer and shoves him toward Lysistrata.

Arrest that woman!
     Better tie her hands behind her.

LYSISTRATA
By Artemis,[27] goddess of the hunt, if he lays a finger on me, he'll rue the day he joined the force!

She jabs the spindle viciously at the First Archer, who leaps, terrified, back to his comrades.

COMMISSIONER
What's this—retreat? Never! Take her on the flank.

The First Archer hangs back. The Commissioner grabs the Second Archer.

—Help him.
—Will the two of you kindly
     TIE HER UP?

He shoves them toward Lysistrata. Kleonike, carrying a large chamber pot, springs out of the entrance and advances on the Second Archer.

KLEONIKE
By Artemis, goddess of the dew, if you so much as touch her, I'll stomp the shit right out of you!

The two Archers run back to their group.

COMMISSIONER
Shit? Shameless! Where's another policeman?

---

[27]Virgin goddess of the hunt, the moon, and childbirth; twin sister of Apollo.

He grabs the Third Archer and propels him toward Kleonike.

> Handcuff *her* first. Can't stand a foul-mouthed female.

Myrrhine, carrying a large, blazing lamp, appears at the entrance and advances on the Third Archer.

MYRRHINE
By Artemis, bringer of light, if you lay a finger on her, you won't be able to stop the swelling!

The Third Archer dodges her swing and runs back to the group.

COMMISSIONER
Now what? Where's an officer?

Pushing the Fourth Archer toward Myrrhine.

> Apprehend that woman! I'll see that *somebody* stays to take the blame!

Ismenia the Boiotian, carrying a huge pair of pincers, appears at the entrance and advances on the Fourth Archer.

ISMENIA
By Artemis, goddess of [Skythian] Tauris, if you go near that girl, I'll rip the hair right out of your head!

The Fourth Archer retreats hurriedly.

COMMISSIONER
What a colossal mess: Athens' Finest—finished!

Arranging the Archers.

> —Now, men, a little *esprit de corps.*
> Worsted by women? Drubbed by drabs?
> *Never!*
> Regroup, reform that thin red line.
> Ready?
> CHARGE!

He pushes them ahead of him.

LYSISTRATA
I warn you. We have four battalions behind us—full-armed combat infantrywomen, trained from the cradle . . .

COMMISSIONER
Disarm them, Officers!
> Go for the hands!

LYSISTRATA

Calling inside the Akropolis.

MOBILIZE THE RESERVES!

A horde of women, armed with household articles, begins to pour from the Akropolis.

> Onword you ladies from hell!
> Forward, you market militia, you battle-hardened bargain hunters, old sales campaigners, grocery grenadiers, veterans never bested by an overcharge!
> You troops of the breadline, doughgirls—
> INTO THE FRAY!
> Show them no mercy!
> Push!

Jostle!
Shove!
Call them nasty names!
    Don't be ladylike.

The women charge and rout the Archers in short order.

Fall back—don't strip the enemy!
    The day is ours!

The women obey, and the Archers run off left. The Commissioner, dazed, is left muttering to himself.

COMMISSIONER
Gross ineptitude. A sorry day for the Force.

LYSISTRATA
Of course. What did you expect? We're not slaves; we're freeborn Women, and when we're scorned, we're full of fury. Never Underestimate the Power of a Woman.

COMMISSIONER
Power? You mean Capacity. I should have remembered the proverb: *The lower the tavern, the higher the dudgeon.*[28]

KORYPHAIOS OF MEN
Why cast your pearls before swine, Commissioner? I know you're a civil servant, but don't overdo it. Have you forgotten the bath they gave us—in public, fully dressed, totally soapless? Keep rational discourse for *people!*

He aims a blow at the Koryphaios of Women, who dodges and raises her pitcher.

KORYPHAIOS OF WOMEN
I might point out that lifting one's hand against a neighbor is scarcely civilized behavior—and entails, for the lifter, a black eye.
    I'm really peaceful by nature, compulsively inoffensive—a perfect doll. My ideal is a well-bred repose that doesn't even stir up dust . . .

Swinging at the Koryphaios of Men with the pitcher.

unless some no-good lowlife tries to rifle my hive and gets my dander up!

The Koryphaios of Men backs hurriedly away, and the Chorus of Men goes into a worried dance.

CHORUS OF MEN
Singly.

O Zeus, what's the use of this constant abuse?
How do we deal with this female zoo?
Is there no solution to Total Immersion?
    What can a poor man DO?

Tutti. {All together}

Query the Adversary!
Ferret out their story!
What end did they have in view,
to seize the city's sanctuary,
snatch its legendary eyrie,[29]
snare an area so very
    terribly taboo?

---

[28]That is, the lower the social class, the greater the resentment.
[29]Lofty nest (Athene's chamber in the Parthenon).

KORYPHAIOS OF MEN

To the Commissioner.

> Scrutinize those women! Scour their depositions—assess their rebuttals!
> Masculine honor demands this affair be probed to the bottom!

COMMISSIONER

Turning to the women from the Akropolis.

> All right, you. Kindly inform me, dammit, in your own words: What possible object could you
> have had in blockading the Treasury?

LYSISTRATA

We thought we'd deposit the money in escrow and withdraw you men from the war.

COMMISSIONER

The money's the cause of the war?

LYSISTRATA

And all our internal disorders—the Body Politic's chronic bellyaches: What causes Peisandros'
frantic rantings, or the raucous caucuses of the Friends of Oligarchy?[30] The chance for graft.

> But now, with the money up there, they can't upset the City's equilibrium—or lower its
> balance.

COMMISSIONER

And what's your next step?

LYSISTRATA

Stupid question. We'll budget the money.

COMMISSIONER

You'll budget the money?

LYSISTRATA

Why should you find that so shocking? We budget the household accounts, and you don't
object at all.

COMMISSIONER

That's different.

LYSISTRATA

Different? How?

COMMISSIONER

The War Effort needs this money!

LYSISTRATA

Who needs the War Effort?

COMMISSIONER

Every patriot who pulses to save all that Athens holds near and dear . . .

LYSISTRATA

Oh, *that*. Don't worry. We'll save you.

COMMISSIONER

_____

[30]A corrupt politician and his party, which would shortly overthrow the democratic constitution of Athens (in May, 411 B.C.).

You will save us?

LYSISTRATA
Who else?

COMMISSIONER
But this is unscrupulous!

LYSISTRATA
We'll save you. You can't deter us.

COMMISSIONER
Scurrilous!

LYSISTRATA
You seem disturbed. This makes it difficult. But, still—we'll save you.

COMMISSIONER
Doubtless illegal!

LYSISTRATA
We deem it a duty. For friendship's sake.

COMMISSIONER
Well, forsake this, friend: I DO NOT WANT TO BE SAVED, DAMMIT!

LYSISTRATA
All the more reason. It's not only Sparta; now we'll have to save you from *you.*

COMMISSIONER
Might I ask where you women conceived this concern about War and Peace?

LYSISTRATA

Loftily.

We shall explain.

COMMISSIONER

Making a fist.

Hurry up, and you won't get hurt.

LYSISTRATA
Then *listen.* And do try to keep your hands to yourself.

COMMISSIONER

Moving threateningly toward her.

I can't. Righteous anger forbids restraint, and decrees . . .

KLEONIKE

Brandishing her chamber pot.

Multiple fractures?

COMMISSIONER

Retreating.

Keep those croaks for yourself, you old crow!

To Lysistrata.

All right, lady, I'm ready. Speak.

LYSISTRATA
I shall proceed:
When the War began, like the prudent, dutiful wives that we are, we tolerated you men, and endured your actions in silence. (Small wonder—you wouldn't let us say boo.)
You were not precisely the answer to a matron's prayer—we knew you too well, and found out more. Too many times, as we sat in the house, we'd hear that you'd done it again—manhandled another affair of state with your usual staggering incompetence.
Then, masking our worry with a nervous laugh, we'd ask you, brightly, "How was the Assembly today, dear?
Anything in the minutes about Peace?" And my husband would give his stock reply.
    "What's that to you? Shut up!" And I did.

KLEONIKE

Proudly.

I never shut up!

COMMISSIONER
I trust you were shut up. Soundly.

LYSISTRATA
Regardless, *I* shut up.
    And then we'd learn that you'd passed another decree, fouler than the first, and we'd ask again: "Darling, how *did* you manage anything so idiotic?" And my husband, with his customary glare, would tell me to spin my thread, or else get a clout on the head. And of course he'd quote from Homer:

The menne must husband the warred.[31]

COMMISSIONER
Apt and irrefutably right.

LYSISTRATA

Right, you miserable misfit?

To keep us from giving advice while you fumbled the City away in the Senate? Right, indeed!
But this time was really too much: Wherever we went, we'd hear you engaged in the same conversation:
"What Athens needs is a Man." "But there isn't a Man in the country."
"You can say that again."
    There was obviously no time to lose. We women met in immediate convention and passed a unanimous resolution: To work in concert for safety and Peace in Greece. We have valuable advice to impart, and if you can possibly deign to emulate our silence, and take your turn as audience, we'll rectify you—we'll straighten you out and set you right.

COMMISSIONER

You'll set *us* right? You go too far. I cannot permit such a statement to . . .

LYSISTRATA
Shush.

[31]That is, the men must manage the war.

COMMISSIONER

I categorically decline to shush for some confounded woman, who wears—as a constant reminder of congenital inferiority, an injunction to public silence—a veil! Death before such dishonor!

LYSISTRATA

Removing her veil.

If that's the only obstacle . . .
I feel you need a new panache,
so take the veil, my dear Commissioner,
and drape it thus—
                    and SHUSH!

As she winds the veil around the startled Commissioner's head, Kleonike and Myrrhine, with carding-comb and wool-basket, rush forward and assist in transforming him into a woman.

KLEONIKE

Accept, I pray, this humble comb.

MYRRHINE

Receive this basket of fleece as well.

LYSISTRATA

Hike up your skirts, and card your wool, and gnaw your beans—and stay at home!
While we rewrite Homer:
       The WOMEN must WIVE the wane!

To the chorus of Women, as the Commissioner struggles to remove his new outfit.

Women, weaker vessels, arise!
       Put down your pitchers. It's our turn, now. Let's supply our friends with some moral support.

The Chorus of Women dances to the same tune as the Men, but with much more confidence.

CHORUS OF WOMEN

Singly.

Oh, yes! I'll dance to bless their success.
Fatigue won't weaken my will. Or my knees.
I'm ready to join in any jeopardy, with girls as good as *these!*

Tutte.

       A tally of their talents
       convinces me they're giants
       of excellence. To commence:
       there's Beauty, Duty, Prudence,
       Science, Self-Reliance, Compliance, Defiance,
       and Love of Athens in balanced alliance with Common Sense!

KORYPHAIOS OF WOMEN

To the women from the Akropolis.

Autochthonous[32] daughters of Attika,[33] sprung from the soil that bore your mothers, the spiniest, spikiest nettles known to man, prove your mettle and attack! Now is no time to dilute your anger. You're running ahead of the wind!

---

[32]Native.
[33]The region of which Athens was the dominant city.

LYSISTRATA

We'll wait for the wind from heaven. The gentle breath of Love and his Kyprian mother[34] will imbue our bodies with desire, and raise a storm to tense and tauten these blasted men until they crack. And soon we'll be on every tongue in Greece—the *Pacifiers*.[35]

COMMISSIONER

That's quite a mouthful.
    How will you win it?

LYSISTRATA

First, we intend to withdraw that crazy Army of Occupation from the downtown shopping section.

KLEONIKE

Aphrodite be praised!

LYSISTRATA

The pottery shop and the grocery stall are overstocked with soldiers, clanking around like those maniac Korybants,[36] armed to the teeth for a battle.

COMMISSIONER

A Hero is Always Prepared!

LYSISTRATA

I suppose he is. But it does look silly to shop for sardines from behind a shield.

KLEONIKE

I'll second that. I saw a cavalry captain buy vegetable soup on horseback. He carried the whole mess home in his helmet.

    And then that fellow from Thrace, shaking his buckler and spear—a menace straight from the stage. The saleslady was stiff with fright. He was hogging her ripe figs—free.

COMMISSIONER

I admit, for the moment, that Hellas'[37] affairs are in one hell of a snarl. But how can you set them straight?

LYSISTRATA

Simplicity itself.

COMMISSIONER

Pray demonstrate.

LYSISTRATA

It's rather like yarn. When a hank's in a tangle, we lift it—*so*—and work out the snarls by winding it up on spindles, now this way, now that way.

    That's how we'll wind up the War, if allowed; We'll work out the snarls by sending Special Commissions—back and forth, now this way, now that way—to ravel these tense international kinks.

COMMISSIONER

I lost your thread, but I know there's a hitch. Spruce up the world's disasters with spindles— typically wooly female logic.

---

[34]Aphrodite, goddess of feminine beauty and love, was associated with the island of Kypros (Cyprus); her son was "Love" (Eros, Cupid).
[35]A play upon the meaning of Lysistrata's name.
[36]The armed priests of the goddess Cybele, whose rites included frenzied dances and music.
[37]Hellas was the name the Greeks gave to their own civilization. The name, Greece, was applied to Hellas later by the Romans.

LYSISTRATA

If *you* had a scrap of logic, you'd adopt our wool as a master plan for Athens.

COMMISSIONER

What course of action does the wool advise?

LYSISTRATA

Consider the City as fleece, recently shorn.[38] The first step is Cleansing: Scrub it in a public bath, and remove all corruption, offal, and sheepdip.

Next, to the couch for Scutching and Plucking: Cudgel the leeches and similar vermin loose with a club, then pick the prickles and cockleburs out. As for the clots—those lumps that clump and cluster in knots and snarls to snag important posts—you comb these out, twist off their heads, and discard.

Next, to raise the City's nap, you card the citizens together in a single basket of common weal and general welfare. Fold in our loyal Resident Aliens, all Foreigners of proven and tested friendship, and any Disenfranchised Debtors. Combine these closely with the rest.

Lastly, cull the colonies settled by our own people: these are nothing but flocks of wool from the City's fleece, scattered throughout the world. So gather home these far-flung flocks, amalgamate them with the others.

Then, drawing this blend of stable fibers into one fine staple, you spin a mighty bobbin of yarn—and weave, without bias or seam, a cloak to clothe the City of Athens!

COMMISSIONER

This is too much! The City's died in the wool, worsted by the distaff side—by women who bore no share in the War. . . .

LYSISTRATA

None, you hopeless hypocrite? The quota we bear is double. First, we delivered our sons to fill out the front lines in Sicily . . .

COMMISSIONER

Don't tax me with that memory.

LYSISTRATA

Next, the best years of our lives were levied. Top-level strategy attached our joy, and we sleep alone.

But it's not the matrons like us who matter. I mourn for the virgins, bedded in single blessedness, with nothing to do but grow old.

COMMISSIONER

Men *have* been known to age, as well as women.

LYSISTRATA

No, not as well as—better.

A man, an absolute antique, comes back from the war, and he's barely doddered into town before he's married the veriest nymphet. But a woman's season is brief; it slips, and she'll have no husband, but sit out her life groping at omens—and finding no men.

COMMISSIONER

Lamentable state of affairs. Perhaps we can rectify matters:

To the audience.

TO EVERY MAN JACK, A CHALLENGE: ARISE!
    Provided you can . . .

---

[38]Lysistrata's response is actually a conservative political allegory.

LYSISTRATA

Instead, Commissioner, why not simply curl up and *die?*
    Just buy a coffin; here's the place.

Banging him on the head with her spindle.

    I'll knead you a cake for the wake—and *these*

Winding the threads from the spindle around him.

    make excellent wreaths. So Rest In Peace.

KLEONIKE

Emptying the chamber pot over him.

    Accept these tokens of deepest grief.

MYRRHINE

Breaking her lamp over his head.

    A final garland for the dear deceased.

LYSISTRATA

May I supply any last request?
    Then run along. You're due at the wharf: Charon's anxious to sail—you're holding up the
boat for Hell![39]

COMMISSIONER

This is monstrous—maltreatment of a public official—maltreatment of ME!
    I must repair directly to the Board of Commissioners, and present my colleagues concrete
evidence of the sorry specifics of this shocking attack!

He staggers off left. Lysistrata calls after him.

LYSISTRATA

You won't haul us into court on a charge of neglecting the dead, will you? (How like a man to
insist on his rights—even his last ones.) Two days between death and funeral, that's the rule.
    Come back here early day after tomorrow, Commissioner: We'll lay you out.

Lysistrata and her women re-enter the Akropolis. The Koryphaios of Men advances to address the audience.

KORYPHAIOS OF MEN

Wake up, Athenians! Preserve your freedom—the time is Now!

To the Chorus of Men.

    Strip for action, men. Let's cope with the current mess.

The men put off their long mantles, disclosing short tunics underneath, and advance toward the audience.

CHORUS OF MEN

This trouble may be terminal; it has a loaded odor, an ominous aroma of constitutional rot.
My nose gives a prognosis of radical disorder—it's just the first installment of an absolutist plot!
The Spartans are behind it: they must have masterminded some morbid local contacts
(engineered by Kleisthenes).[40]

---

[39]In Greek mythology, Charon was the god whose boat ferried the dead souls across the River Styx to Hades (the underworld). Lysistrata's earlier "cake for the wake" is a reference to the honey cake needed by the dead souls to please Cerberus, the three-headed dog who guarded the entrance to Hades.
[40]A notoriously effeminate bisexual—and one of Aristophanes' favorite targets of ridicule.

Predictably infected, these women straightway acted to commandeer the City's cash. They're feverish to freeze

my be-all,

my end-all . . .

my *payroll!*

KORYPHAIOS OF MEN

The symptoms are clear. Our birthright's already nibbled. And oh, so daintily: WOMEN ticking off troops for improper etiquette.

WOMEN propounding their featherweight views on the fashionable use and abuse of the shield. And (if any more proof were needed) WOMEN nagging us to trust the Nice Spartan, and put our heads in his toothy maw—to make a dessert and call it Peace.

They've woven the City a seamless shroud, bedecked with the legend DICTATORSHIP. But I won't be hemmed in. I'll use their weapon against them, and uphold the right by sneakiness.

With knyf under cloke, gauntlet in glove, sword in olivebranch,

Slipping slowly toward the Koryphaios of Women.

I'll take up my post in Statuary Row, beside our honored National Heroes, the natural foes of tyranny: Harmodios, Aristogeiton,[41] and Me.

Next to her.

Striking an epic pose, so, with the full approval of the immortal gods,
I'll bash this loathesome hag in the jaw!

He does, and runs cackling back to the Men. She shakes a fist after him.

KORYPHAIOS OF WOMEN

Mama won't know her little boy when he gets home!

To the Women, who are eager to launch a full-scale attack.

Let's not be hasty, fellow. . . hags. Cloaks off first.

The Women remove their mantles, disclosing tunics very like those of the Men, and advance toward the audience.

CHORUS OF WOMEN

We'll address you, citizens, in beneficial, candid, patriotic accents, as our breeding says we must, since, from the age of seven, Athens graced me with a splendid string of civic triumphs to signalize her trust:
I was a Relic-Girl quite early,
then advanced to Maid of Barley;
in Artemis' "Pageant of the Bear" I played the lead.
To cap this proud progression,[42]
I led the whole procession
at Athene's Celebration, certified and pedigreed
—that cachet
so distingué—

a *Lady!*

KORYPHAIOS OF WOMEN

To the audience.

I trust this establishes my qualifications. I may, I take it, address the City to its profit? Thank you.

---

[41]A reference to a famous statuary group in the Athenian marketplace representing two young men who, in 514 B.C., had killed a tyrant.
[42]The chorus mentions four past public festivals in which, as upper class Athenian girls, they had each played a part.

I admit to being a woman—but don't sell my contribution short on that account. It's better than the present panic. And my word is as good as my bond, because I hold stock in Athens— stock I paid for in sons.

To the Chorus of Men.

—But you, you doddering bankrupts, where are your shares in the State?

Slipping slowly toward the Koryphaios of Men

Your grandfathers willed you the Mutual Funds from the Persian War—
and where are they?[43]

Nearer.

You dipped into capital, then lost interest . . . and now a pool of your assets won't fill a hole in the ground. All that remains is one last potential killing—Athens. Is there any rebuttal?

The Koryphaios of Men gestures menacingly. She ducks down, as if toward off a blow, and removes a slipper.

Force is a footling resort. I'll take my very sensible shoe, and paste you in the jaw!

She does so, and runs back to the women.

CHORUS OF MEN
Their native respect for our manhood is small, and keeps getting smaller. Let's bottle their gall.
    The man who won't battle has no balls at all!

KORYPHAIOS OF MEN
All right, men, skin out of the skivvies. Let's give them a whiff of Man, full strength. No point in muffling the essential Us.

The men remove their tunics.

CHORUS OF MEN
A century back, we soared to the Heights and beat down Tyranny there.
    Now's the time to shed our moults and fledge our wings once more, to rise to the skies in our reborn force, and beat back Tyranny here!

KORYPHAIOS OF MEN
No fancy grappling with these grannies; straightforward strength.
The tiniest toehold, and those nimble, fiddling fingers will have their foot in the door, and we're done for.
No amount of know-how can lick a woman's knack.
They'll want to build ships . . . next thing we know, we're all at sea, fending off female boarding parties. (Artemisia fought us at Salamis.[44] Tell me, has anyone caught her yet?)
But we're *really* sunk if they take up horses. Scratch the Cavalry:
A woman is an easy rider with a natural seat.
Take her over the jumps bareback, and she'll never slip her mount. (That's how the Amazons nearly took Athens. On horseback.
Check on Mikon's mural down in the Stoa.)[45]
Anyway, the solution is obvious. Put every woman in her place—stick her in the stocks.
    To do this, first snare your woman around the neck.

[43]The original treasury of the Delian League had been on the island of Delos. The League was an alliance of most Greek states, organized in 477 B.C. for the purpose of maintaining the common defense against any Persian attack. The treasury was transferred by the Athenians to their Akropolis in 454 and, thereafter, was turned mainly to Athenian purposes. Obviously, this misuse of the common treasury was a contributing cause of the Peloponnesian War. After the heavy expenses of the Sicilian expedition, the women's question is very embarrassing to the men.
[44]Artemisia was a queen of Halikarnassos in Asia Minor. She was allied with the Persian King Xerxes in his invasion of Greece in 480 B.C. and fought bravely at the naval battle of Salamis.
[45]A Stoa was a roofed colonnade, with a wall on one side, often serving the same purpose as a modern shopping mall. The wall was usually decorated with paintings; the subject of the painting referred to here was a common one: an attack by Amazons, a mythical race of warrior-women.

He attempts to demonstrate on the Koryphaios of Women. After a brief tussle, she works loose and chases him back to the Men.

CHORUS OF WOMEN

The beast in me's eager and fit for a brawl.
Just rile me a bit and she'll kick down the wall.
    You'll bawl to your friends that you've no balls at all.

KORYPHAIOS OF WOMEN

All right, ladies, strip for action. Let's give them a whiff of *Femme Enragée*—piercing and pungent, but not at all tart.

The women remove their tunics.

CHORUS OF WOMEN

We're angry. The brainless bird who tangles with *us* has gummed his last mush.
In fact, the coot who even heckles is being daringly rash.
    So look to your nests, you reclaimed eagles—whatever you lay, we'll squash!

KORYPHAIOS OF WOMEN

Frankly, you don't faze me. *With* me, I have my friends—Lampito from Sparta; that genteel girl from Thebes, Ismenia—committed to me forever. *Against* me, you—permanently out of commission. So do your damnedest.
Pass a law.
Pass seven. Continue the winning ways that have made your name a short and ugly household word.
Like yesterday:
I was giving a little party, nothing fussy, to honor the goddess Hekate. Simply to please my daughters, I'd invited a sweet little thing from the neighborhood—flawless pedigree, perfect taste, a credit to any gathering—a Boiotian eel.
But she had to decline. Couldn't pass the border.
You'd passed a law.
    Not that you care for my party. You'll overwork your right of passage till your august body is overturned, and you break your silly neck!

She deftly grabs the Koryphaios of Men by the ankle and upsets him. He scuttles back to the Men, who retire in confusion.

Lysistrata emerges from the citadel, obviously distraught.

KORYPHAIOS OF WOMEN

Mock-tragic.

Mistress, queen of this our subtle scheme, why burst you from the hall with brangled brow?

LYSISTRATA

Oh, wickedness of woman! The female mind does sap my soul and set my wits a-totter.

KORYPHAIOS OF WOMEN

What drear accents are these?

LYSISTRATA

The merest truth.

KORYPHAIOS OF WOMEN

Be nothing loath to tell the tale to friends.

LYSISTRATA

'Twere shame to utter, pain to hold unsaid.

KORYPHAIOS OF WOMEN

Hide not from me affliction which we share.

LYSISTRATA

In briefest compass,

Dropping the paratragedy.

we want to get laid.

KORYPHAIOS OF WOMEN
By Zeus!

LYSISTRATA
No, no, not HIM!
Well, that's the way things are. I've lost my grip on the girls—they're mad for men! But sly—
they slip out in droves.
A minute ago, I caught one scooping out the little hole that breaks through just below
Pan's grotto.[46]
One had jerry-rigged some block-and-tackle business and was wriggling away on a rope.
Another just flat deserted. Last night I spied one mounting a sparrow, all set to take off for the
nearest bawdyhouse. I hauled her back by the hair.
And excuses, pretexts for overnight passes? I've heard them all.
    Here comes one. Watch.

To the First Woman, as she runs out of the Akropolis.

    —You, there! What's your hurry?

FIRST WOMAN
I have to get home. I've got all this lovely Milesian wool in the house, and the moths will
simply batter it to bits!

LYSISTRATA
I'll bet. Get back inside.

FIRST WOMAN
I swear I'll hurry right back!—Just time enough to spread it out on the couch?

LYSISTRATA
Your wool will stay unspread. And you'll stay here.

FIRST WOMAN
Do I have to let my piecework *rot?*

LYSISTRATA
Possibly.

The Second Woman runs on.

SECOND WOMAN
Oh dear, oh goodness, what shall I do—my flax!
    I left and forgot to peel it!

LYSISTRATA
Another one. She suffers from unpeeled flax.
    —Get back inside!

SECOND WOMAN
I'll be right back. I just have to pluck the fibers.

---

[46]A cave just outside the defensive wall that surrounded the top (the Citadel) of the Akropolis.

LYSISTRATA

No. No plucking. You start it, and everyone else will want to go and do their plucking, too.

The Third Woman, swelling conspicuously, hurries on, praying loudly.

THIRD WOMAN

O Goddess of Childbirth, grant that I not deliver until I get me from out this sacred precinct!

LYSISTRATA

What sort of nonsense is *this?*

THIRD WOMAN

I'm due—any second!

LYSISTRATA

You weren't pregnant yesterday.

THIRD WOMAN

Today I am—a miracle!
    Let me go home for a midwife, *please!* I may not make it!

LYSISTRATA

Restraining her.

You can do better than that.

Tapping the woman's stomach and receiving a metallic clang.

What's this? It's hard.

THIRD WOMAN

I'm going to have a boy.

LYSISTRATA

Not unless he's made of bronze. Let's see.

She throws open the Third Woman's cloak, exposing a huge bronze helmet.

Of all the brazen . . . You've stolen the helmet from Athene's statue! Pregnant, indeed!

THIRD WOMAN

I am *so* pregnant!

LYSISTRATA

Then why the helmet?

THIRD WOMAN

I thought my time might come while I was still on forbidden ground.[47] If it did, I could climb inside Athene's helmet and have my baby there.
    The pigeons do it all the time.

LYSISTRATA

Nothing but excuses!

Taking the helmet.

This is your baby. I'm afraid you'll have to stay until we give it a name.

THIRD WOMAN

But the Akropolis is *awful.* I can't even sleep! I saw the snake that guards the temple.

---

[47]Childbirth was taboo on the holy ground of the Akropolis.

LYSISTRATA

That snake's a fabrication.[48]

THIRD WOMAN

I don't care *what* kind it is—I'm *scared!*

The other women, who have emerged from the citadel, crowd around.

KLEONIKE

And those goddamned holy owls![49] All night long, *tu-wit, tu-wu*—they're hooting me into my grave!

LYSISTRATA

Darlings, let's call a halt to this hocus-pocus. You miss your men—now isn't that the trouble?

Shamefaced nods from the group.

Don't you think they miss you just as much?
I can assure you, their nights are every bit as hard as yours. So be good girls; endure!
Persist a few days more, and Victory is ours.

It's fated: a current prophecy declares that the men will go down to defeat before us, provided that *we* maintain a United Front.

Producing a scroll.

I happen to have a copy of the prophecy.

KLEONIKE

Read it!

LYSISTRATA

Silence, *please:*

Reading from the scroll.

> But when the swallows, in flight from the
>   hoopoes,[50] have flocked to a hole
> on high, and stoutly eschew their
>   accustomed perch on the pole,
> yea, then shall Thunderer Zeus to
>   their suff'ring establish a stop,
> by making the lower the upper . . .

KLEONIKE

Then *we'll* be lying on top?

LYSISTRATA

> But should these swallows, indulging their
>   lust for the perch, lose heart,
> dissolve their flocks in winged dissension,
>   and singly depart
> the sacred stronghold, breaking the
>   bands that bind them together—
> then know them as lewd, the pervertedest
>   birds that ever wore feather.

[48]A snake, never actually seen, was mythically associated with the cult of Athene as I guardian of the Akropolis.
[49]Birds sacred to Athene.
[50]A family of birds, here identified with the male sex.

KLEONIKE
There's nothing obscure about *that* oracle. Ye gods!

LYSISTRATA
Sorely beset as we are, we must not flag or falter. So back to the citadel!

As the women troop inside.

And if we fail that oracle, darlings, our image is absolutely *mud!*

She follows them in. A pause, and the Choruses assemble.

CHORUS OF MEN
I have a simple
tale to relate you
a sterling example
of masculine virtue:

The huntsman bold Melanion
was once a harried quarry.
The women in town tracked him down
and badgered him to marry.

Melanion knew the cornered male
eventually cohabits.
Assessing the odds, he took to the woods
and lived by trapping rabbits.

He stuck to the virgin stand, sustained
by rabbit meat and hate,
and never returned, but ever remained
an alfresco celibate.

Melanion is our ideal;
his loathing makes us free.
Our dearest aim is the gemlike flame
of his misogyny.[51]

OLD MAN
Let me kiss that wizened cheek. . . .

OLD WOMAN

Threatening with a fist.

A wish too rash for that withered flesh,

OLD MAN
and lay you low with a highflying kick.

He tries one and misses.

OLD WOMAN
Exposing an overgrown underbrush.

OLD MAN
A hairy behind, historically, means masculine force: Myronides harassed the foe with his mighty mane, and furry Phormion swept the seas of enemy ships, never meeting his match—such was the nature of his thatch.

---

[51]Hatred for women.

CHORUS OF WOMEN
I offer an anecdote for your opinion, an adequate antidote for your Melanion:
Timon, the noted local grouch, put rusticating hermits out of style by building his wilds inside the city limits.
He shooed away society with natural battlements: his tongue was edgèd; his shoulder, frigid; his beard, a picket fence.
When random contacts overtaxed him, he didn't stop to pack, but loaded curses on the male of the species, left town, and never came back.
Timon, you see, was a misanthrope[52] in a properly narrow sense: his spleen was vented only on men . . . *we* were his dearest friends.

OLD WOMAN

Making a fist.

Enjoy a chop to that juiceless chin?

OLDMAN

Backing away.

I'm jolted already. Thank you, no.

OLD WOMAN
Perhaps a trip from a well-turned shin?

She tries a kick and misses.

OLD MAN
Brazenly baring the mantrap below.

OLD WOMAN
At least it's *neat*. I'm not too sorry to have you see my daintiness.
My habits are still depilatory; age hasn't made me a bristly mess.
Secure in my smoothness, I'm never in doubt—though even down is out.

Lysistrata mounts the platform and scans the horizon. When her gaze reaches the left, she stops suddenly.

LYSISTRATA
Ladies, attention! Battle stations, please!
And quickly!

A general rush of women to the battlements.

KLEONIKE
What is it?

MYRRHINE
What's all the shouting for?

LYSISTRATA
A MAN!

Consternation.

Yes, it's a man. And he's coming this way! Hmm. Seems to have suffered a seizure. Broken out with a nasty attack of love.

[52]Hater of men.

Prayer, aside

O Aphrodite, Mistress all-victorious, mysterious, voluptuous, you who make the crooked straight . . .

don't let this happen to US!

KLEONIKE
I don't care who he is—*where is he?*

LYSISTRATA

Pointing.

Down there—just flanking that temple—Demeter the Fruitful.

KLEONIKE
My. Definitely a man.

MYRRHINE

Craning for a look.

I wonder who it can be?

LYSISTRATA
See for yourselves.—Can anyone identify him?

MYRRHINE
Oh lord, I can.

That is my husband—Kinesias.

LYSISTRATA

To Myrrhine.

Your duty is clear.

Pop him on the griddle, twist the spit, braize him, baste him, stew him in his own juice, do him to a turn. Sear him with kisses, coyness, caresses, *everything*—but stop where Our Oath begins.

MYRRHINE
Relax. I can take care of this.

LYSISTRATA
Of course you can, dear. Still, a little help can't hurt, now can it? I'll just stay around for a bit and—er—poke up the fire.

—Everyone else inside!

Exit all the women but Lysistrata, on the platform, and Myrrhine, who stands near the Akropolis entrance, hidden from her husband's view. Kinesias staggers on, in erection and considerable pain, followed by a male slave who carries a baby boy.

KINESIAS
OUCH!
Omigod.
Hypertension, twinges. . . . I can't hold out much more. I'd rather be dismembered.
How long, ye gods, how long?

LYSISTRATA

Officially.

WHO GOES THERE?
WHO PENETRATES OUR POSITIONS?

KINESIAS
Me.

LYSISTRATA
A Man?

KINESEAS
Every inch.

LYSISTRATA
Then inch yourself out of here. Off Limits to Men.

KINESIAS
This *is* the limit. Just who are *you* to throw me out?

LYSISTRATA
The Lookout.

KINESIAS
Well, look here, Lookout. I'd like to see Myrrhine. How's the outlook?

LYSISTRATA
Unlikely. Bring Myrrhine to you? The idea!
    Just by the by, who are you?

KINESIAS
A private citizen. Her husband, Kinesias.

LYSISTRATA
No!
        Meeting you—I'm overcome!

        Your name, you know, is not without its fame among us girls.

Aside.

—Matter of fact, we have a name for *it.*—I swear, you're never out of Myrrhine's mouth. She won't even nibble a quince, or swallow an egg, without reciting, "Here's to Kinesias!"

KINESIAS
For god's sake, will you . . .

LYSISTRATA

Sweeping on over his agony.

Word of honor, it's true. Why, when we discuss our husbands (you know how women are), Myrrhine refuses to argue. She simply insists: "Compared with Kinesias, the rest have *nothing!*" Imagine!

KINESIAS

Bring her out here!

LYSISTRATA
Really? And what would I get out of this?

KINESIAS
You see my situation. I'll raise whatever I can. This can all be yours.

LYSISTRATA
Goodness. It's really her place. I'll go and get her.

She descends from the platform and moves to Myrrhine, out of Kinesias' sight.

KINESIAS
Speed!
—Life is a husk. She left our home, and happiness went with her. Now pain is the tenant. Oh, to enter that wifeless house, to sense that awful emptiness, to eat that tasteless, joyless food—it makes it hard, I tell you.
        Harder all the time.

MYRRHINE

Still out of his sight, in a voice to be overheard.

Oh, I *do* love him! I'm mad about him! But he doesn't want my love. Please don't make me see him.

KINESIAS
Myrrhine darling, why do you *act* this ways? Come down here!

MYRRHINE

Appearing at the wall.

Down there? Certainly not!

KINESIAS
It's me, Myrrhine. I'm begging you. Please come down.

MYRRHINE
I don't see why you're begging me. You don't need me.

KINESIAS
I don't need you? I'm at the end of my rope!

MYRRHINE
I'm leaving.

She turns. Kinesias grabs the boy from the slave.

KINESIAS
No! Wait! At least you'll have to listen to the voice of your child.

To the boy, in a fierce undertone.

—(Call your mother!)

Silence.

. . . to the voice of your very own child . . .
        —(Call your mother, brat!)

CHILD
MOMMYMOMMYMOMMY!

KINESIAS
Where's your maternal instinct? He hasn't been washed or fed for a week. How can you be so pitiless?

MYRRHINE
Him I pity. Of all the pitiful excuses for a father. . . .

KINESIAS
Come down here, dear. For the baby's sake.

MYRRHINE

Motherhood! I'll have to come. I've got no choice.

KINESIAS

Soliloquizing as she descends.

It may be me, but I'll swear she looks years younger—and gentler—her eyes caress me. And then they flash: that anger, that verve, that high-and-mighty air! She's fire, she's ice—and I'm stuck right in the middle.

MYRRHINE

Taking the baby.

Sweet babykins with such a nasty daddy!
    Here, let Mummy kissums. Mummy's little darling.

KINESIAS

The injured husband.

You should be ashamed of yourself, letting those women lead you around. Why do you DO these things? You only make me suffer and hurt your poor, sweet self.

MYRRHINE

Keep your hands away from me!

KINESIAS

But the house, the furniture, everything we own—you're letting it go to hell!

MYRRHINE

Frankly, I couldn't care less.

KINESIAS

But your weaving's unraveled—the loom is full of chickens! You couldn't care less about *that?*

MYRRHINE

I certainly couldn't.

KINESIAS

And the holy rites of Aphrodite?[53] Think how long that's been.
    Come on, darling, let's go home.

MYRRHINE

I absolutely refuse!
    Unless you agree to a truce to stop the war.

KINESIAS

Well, then, if that's your decision, we'll STOP the war.

MYRRHINE

Well, then, if that's your decision, I'll come back—*after* it's done.
    But, for the present, I've sworn off.

KINESIAS

At least lie down for a minute. We'll talk.

MYRRHINE

I know what you're up to—NO!
    —And yet . . . I really can't say I don't love you . . .

[53]That is, the act of lovemaking.

KINESIAS
You love me?
So what's the trouble? *Lie down.*

MYRRHINE
Don't be disgusting. In front of the baby?

KINESIAS
Er . . . no. Heaven Forfend.

Taking the baby and pushing it at the slave.

—Take this home.

The slave obeys.

—Well, darling, we're rid of the kid . . . let's go to bed!

MYRRHINE
Poor dear.
But where does one do this sort of thing?

KINESIAS
Where? All we need is a little nook. . . . We'll try Pan's grotto. Excellent spot.

MYRRHINE

With a nod at the Akropolis.

I'll have to be pure to get back in *there.* How can I expunge my pollution?

KINESIAS
Sponge off in the pool next door.

MYRRHINE
I did swear an Oath. I'm supposed to perjure myself?

KINESIAS
Bother the Oath. Forget it—I'll take the blame.
A pause.

MYRRHINE
Now I'll go get us a cot.

KINESIAS
No! Not a cot! The ground's enough for us.

MYRRHINE
I'll get the cot. For all your faults, I refuse to put you to bed in the dirt.

She exits to the Akropolis.

KINESIAS
She certainly loves me. That's nice to know.

MYRRHINE

Returning with a rope-tied cot.

Here. You hurry to bed while I undress.
Kinesias lies down.

Gracious me—I forgot. We need a mattress.

KINESIAS
Who wants a mattress? Not me!

MYRRHINE
Oh, yes, you do. It's perfectly squalid on the ropes.

KINESIAS
Well, give me a kiss to tide me over.

MYRRHINE
Voilà.

She pecks at him and leaves.

KINESIAS
OoolaLAlala!
      —Make it a quick trip, dear.

MYRRHINE

Entering with the mattress, she waves Kinesias off the cot and lays the mattress on it.

      Here we are. Our mattress. Now hurry to bed while I undress.

Kinesias lies down again.

      Gracious me—I forgot. You don't have a pillow.

KINESIAS
I do *not* need a pillow.

MYRRHINE
I know, but *I* do.

She leaves.

KINESIAS
What a lovefeast! Only the table gets laid.

MYRRHINE

Returning with a pillow.

      Rise and shine!

Kinesias jumps up. She places the pillow.

      And now I have everything I need.

KINESIAS

Lying down again.

      You certainly do.
            Come here, my little jewelbox!

MYRRHINE
Just taking off my bra.
      Don't break your promise: no cheating about the Peace.

KINESIAS
I swear to god, I'll die first!

MYRRHINE

Coming to him.

> Just look. You don't have a blanket.

KINESIAS
I didn't plan to go camping—I want to make love!

MYRRHINE
Relax. You'll get your love. I'll be right back.

She leaves.

KINESIAS
Relax? I'm dying a slow death by dry goods!

MYRRHINE

Returning with the blanket.

> Get up!

KINESIAS

Getting out of bed.

> I've been up for hours. I was up before I was up.

Myrrhine spreads the blanket on the mattress, and he lies down again.

MYRRHINE
I presume you want perfume?

KINESIAS
Positively NO!

MYRRHINE
Absolutely yes—whether you want it or not.

She leaves.

KINESIAS
Dear Zeus, I don't ask for much—but please let her spill it.

MYRRHINE

Returning with a bottle.

> Hold out your hand like a good boy.
> Now rub it in.

KINESIAS

Obeying and sniffing.

This is to quicken desire? Too strong. It grabs your nose and bawls out: *Try again tomorrow.*

MYRRHINE
I'm *awful!* I brought you that rancid Rhodian brand.

She starts off with the bottle.

KINESIAS
This is just *lovely*. Leave it, woman!

MYRRHINE
Silly!

She leaves.

KINESIAS
God damn the clod who first concocted perfume!

MYRRHINE

Returning with another bottle.

Here, try this flask.

KINESIAS
Thanks—but you try mine. Come to bed, you witch—
and please stop bringing things!

MYRRHINE
That is exactly what I'll do. There go my shoes.

Incidentally, darling, you *will* remember to vote for the truce?

KINESIAS
I'LL THINK IT OVER!

Myrrhine runs off for good.

That woman's laid me waste—destroyed me, root and branch!
I'm scuttled, gutted, up the spout!

And Myrrhine's gone!

In a parody of tragic style

Out upon't! But how? But where?
Now I have lost the fairest fair,
how screw my courage to yet another
sticking-place? Aye, there's the rub—
And yet, this wagging, wanton babe
must soon be laid to rest, or else . . .
Ho Pandar!⁵⁴

                    Pandar!
I'd hire a nurse.

KORYPHAIOS OF MEN
Grievous your bereavement, cruel
the slow tabescence⁵⁵ of your soul.
I bid my liquid pity mingle.

Oh, where the soul, and where, alack!
the cod to stand the taut attack
of swollen prides, the scorching tensions
that ravine up the lumbar regions?
        His morning lay
        has gone astray.

KINESIAS

---

⁵⁴The translator has here adapted the common Greek name Pandaros whose English form ("pander") means "pimp."
⁵⁵Wasting away.

It agony.

>O Zeus, reduce the throbs, the throes!

KORYPHAIOS OF MEN
I turn my tongue to curse the cause
of your affliction—that jade, that slut,
that hag, that ogress . . .

KINESIAS
No! Slight not
my light-o'-love, my dove, my sweet!

KORYPHAIOS OF MEN
Sweet!
O Zeus who rul'st the sky,
snatch that slattern up on high,
crack thy winds, unleash thy thunder,
tumble her over, trundle her under,
juggle her from hand to hand;
twirl her ever near the ground—
drop her in a well-aimed fall
on our comrade's tool!

>That's all.

Kinesias exits left.

A Spartan herald enters from the right, holding his cloak together in a futile attempt to conceal his condition.

HERALD
This Athens? Where-all kin I find the Council of Elders or else the Executive Board? I brung some news.

The Commissioner, swathed in his cloak, enters from the left.

COMMISSIONER
And what are you—a man? a signpost? a joint-stock company?

HERALD
A herald, sonny, a honest-to-Kastor[56] herald. I come to chat 'bout thet-there truce.

COMMISSIONER
. . . carrying a concealed weapon? Pretty underhanded.

HERALD

Twisting to avoid the Commissioner's direct gaze.

>Hain't done no sech a thang!

COMMISSIONER
Very well, stand still. Your cloak's out of crease—hernia? Are the roads that bad?

SPARTAN
I swear this feller's plumb fetched in the haid!

COMMISSIONER

---

[56]A son of Zeus.

Throwing open the Spartan's cloak, exposing the phallus.

> You clown, you've got an erection!

SPARTAN

Wildly embarrassed.

> Hain't got no sech a thang!
> You stop this-hyer foolishment!

COMMISSIONER
> What *have* you got there, then?

SPARTAN
> Thet-thur's a Spartan epistle. In code.[57]

COMMISSIONER
> I have the key.

Throwing open his cloak.

> Behold another Spartan epistle. In code.

Tiring of teasing.

> Let's get down to cases. I know the score, so tell me the truth.
>   How are things with you in Sparta?

HERALD
> Thangs is up in the air. The whole Alliance is purt-near 'bout to explode. We-uns'll need barrels, 'stead of women.

COMMISSIONER
> What was the cause of this outburst? The great god Pan?[58]

HERALD
> Nope. I'll lay 'twere Lampito, most likely. She begun, and then they was off and runnin' at the post in a bunch, every last little gal in Sparta, drivin' their menfolk away from the winner's circle.

COMMISSIONER
> How are you taking this?

HERALD
> Painful-like. Everyone's doubled up worse as a midget nursin' a wick in a midnight wind come moon-dark time. Cain't even tetch them little old gals on the moosey without we all agree to a Greece-wide Peace.

COMMISSIONER
> Of course!
> A universal female plot—all Hellas risen in rebellion—I should have known!
> Return to Sparta with this request:
>   Have them despatch us a Plenipotentiary Commission, fully empowered to conclude an armistice. I have full confidence that I can persuade our Senate to do the same, without extending myself. The evidence is at hand.

---

[57]For their coded communications the Spartans inscribed their messages on a leather strip wound around a slender rod. When the strip was delivered, it had to be wound around a rod identical in size and shape—or else the message would appear to be a meaningless collection of letters.

[58]The woodland god, Pan, sometimes caused fits of madness or "panic"—which might also be expressed as fits of sexual excess.

HERALD
I'm a-flyin', Sir! I hev never heered your equal!

Exeunt hurriedly, the Commissioner to the left, the Herald to the right.

KORYPHAIOS OF MEN
The most unnerving work of nature,
the pride of applied immorality,
is the common female human.
No fire can match, no beast can best her.
O Unsurmountability, the name—worse luck—is Woman.

KORYPHAIOS OF WOMEN
After such knowledge, why persist
in wearing out this feckless
war between the sexes?
When can I apply for the post
of ally, partner, and general friend?

KORYPHAIOS OF MEN
I won't be ployed to revise, re-do,
amend, extend, or bring to an end
my irreversible credo:
Misogyny Forever!
    —The answer's never.

KORYPHAIOS OF WOMEN
All right. Whenever you choose.
But, for the present, I refuse
to let you look your absolute worst,
parading around like an unfrocked freak:
I'm coming over and get you dressed.

She dresses him in his tunic, an action (like others in this scene) imitated by the members of the Chorus of Women toward their opposite members in the Chorus of Men.

KORYPHAIOS OF MEN
This seems sincere. It's not a trick.
Recalling the rancor with which I stripped,
I'm overlaid with chagrin.

KORYPHAIOS OF MEN
Now you resemble a man,
not some ghastly practical joke.
And if you show me a little respect
(and promise not to kick), I'll extract
the beast in you.

KORYPHAIOS OF MEN

Searching himself.

What beast in me?

KORYPHAIOS OF MEN
That insect. There. The bug that's stuck in your eye.

KORYPHAIOS OF MEN

Playing along dubiously.

This gnat?

KORYPHAIOS OF WOMEN
Yes, nitwit!

KORYPHAIOS OF MEN
Of course.
That steady, festering agony. . . .
You've put your finger on the source
of all my lousy troubles. Please
roll back the lid and scoop it out.
I'd like to see it.

KORYPHAIOS OF WOMEN
All right, I'll do it.

Removing the imaginary insect.

Although, of all the impossible cranks. . . .
Do you sleep in a swamp? Just look at this.
I've never seen a bigger chigger.

KORYPHAIOS OF MEN
Thanks. Your kindness touches me deeply. For years, that thing's been sinking wells in my eye.
Now you've unplugged me. Here come the tears.

KORYPHAIOS OF WOMEN
I'll dry your tears, though I can't say why.

Wiping away the tears.

Of all the irresponsible boys. . . .
And I'll kiss you.

KORYPHAIOS OF WOMEN
Don't you kiss me!

KORYPHAIOS OF WOMEN
What made you think you had a choice?

She kisses him.

KORYPHAIOS OF MEN
All right, damn you, that's enough of that ingrained palaver.
I can't dispute the truth or logic of the pithy old proverb:
> *Life with women is hell.*
> *Life without women is hell, too.*
And so we conclude a truce with you, on the following terms: in future, a mutual moratorium
on mischief in all its forms. Agreed?—Let's make a single chorus and start our song.

The two Choruses unite and face the audience.

CHORUS OF MEN
We're not about to introduce
the standard personal abuse—the Choral Smear
Of Present Persons (usually, in every well-made comedy, inserted here).
Instead, in deed and utterance, we shall now indulge in philanthropy because we feel
that members of the audience
endure, in the course of current events, sufficient hell.
Therefore, friends, be rich! Be flush!

Apply to us, and borrow cash in large amounts.
The Treasury stands behind us—there—
and we can personally take care of small accounts.
Drop up today. Your credit's good.
Your loan won't have to be repaid in full until
the war is over. And then, your debt is only the money you actually get—nothing at all.

CHORUS OF WOMEN
Just when we meant to entertain
some madcap gourmets from out of town
—such flawless taste!—
the present unpleasantness intervened,
and now we fear the feast we planned will go to waste.
The soup is waiting, rich and thick;
I've sacrificed a suckling pig
—the pièce de résistance—
whose toothsome cracklings should amaze
the most fastidious gourmets—
you, for instance.
To everybody here, I say
take potluck at my house today
with me and mine.
Bathe and change as fast as you can,
bring the children, hurry down,
and walk right in.
Don't bother to knock. No need at all.
My house is yours. Liberty Hall.
What are friends for?
Act self-possessed when you come over;
it may help out when you discover
I've locked the door.

A delegation of Spartans enters from the right, with difficulty. They have removed their cloaks, but hold them before themselves in an effort to conceal their condition.

KORYPHAIOS OF MEN
What's this? Behold the Spartan ambassadors, dragging their beards, pussy-footing along. It appears they've developed a hitch in the crotch.

Advancing to greet them.

Men of Sparta, I bid you welcome!
And now to the point: What predicament brings you among us?

SPARTAN
We-uns is up a stump. Hain't fit fer chatter.

Flipping aside his cloak.

Here's our predicament. Take a look for yourselfs.

KORYPHAIOS OF MEN
Well, I'll be damned—a regular disaster area.
    Inflamed. I imagine the temperature's rather intense?

SPARTAN
Hit ain't the heat, hit's the tumidity.

But words won't help what ails us. We-uns come after Peace.
Peace from any person, at any price.

Enter the Athenian delegation from the left, led by Kinesias. They are wearing cloaks, but are obviously in as much travail as the Spartans.

KORYPHAIOS OF MEN
Behold our local Sons of the Soil, stretching their garments away from their groins, like wrestlers. Grappling with their plight. Some sort of athlete's disease, no doubt. An outbreak of epic proportions.
Athlete's foot?
No. Could it be athlete's . . . ?

KINESIAS

Breaking in.

Who can tell us how to get hold of Lysistrata? We've come as delegates to the Sexual Congress.

Opening his cloak.

Here are our credentials.

KORYPHAIOS OF MEN

Ever the scientist, looking from the Athenians to the Spartans and back again.

The words are different, but the malady seems the same.

To Kinesias.

Dreadful disease. When the crisis reaches its height, what do you take for it?

KINESIAS
Whatever comes to hand. But now we've reached the bitter end. It's Peace or we fall back on Kleisthenes.
And he's got a waiting list.

KORYPHAIOS OF MEN

To the Spartans.

Take my advice and put your clothes on. If someone from that self-appointed Purity League comes by, you may be docked. They do it to the statues of Hermes, they'll do it to you.[59]

KINESIAS

Since he has not yet noticed the Spartans, he interprets the warning as meant for him, and hurriedly pulls his cloak together, as do the other Athenians.

Excellent advice.

SPARTAN
Hit shorely is. Hain't nothing to argue after. Let's git dressed.

As they put on their cloaks, the Spartans are finally noticed by Kinesias.

KINESIAS
Welcome, men of Sparta! This is a shameful disgrace to masculine honor.

---

[59]Squared stone posts with the head and phallus of Hermes, messenger of the gods, were set up at Athenian street intersections and in front of houses. The sacrilegious mutilation of these statues by unknown persons, just before the sailing of the Sicilian expedition, had caused great consternation among the citizens and disruption among the leadership.

SPARTAN

Hit could be worser.

Ef them Herm-choppers seed us all fired up, they'd *really* take us down a peg or two.

KINESIAS

Gentlemen, let's descend to details. Specifically, why are you here?

SPARTAN

Ambassadors. We come to dicker 'bout thet-thur Peace.

KINESIAS

Perfect! Precisely our purpose. Let's send for Lysistrata. Only she can reconcile our differences. There'll be no Peace for us without her.

SPARTAN

We-uns ain't fussy. Call Lysistratos, too, if you want.

The gates to the Akropolis open, and Lysistrata emerges, accompanied by her handmaid, Peace—a beautiful girl without a stitch on. Peace remains out of sight by the gates until summoned.

KORYPHAIOS OF MEN

Hail, most virile of women! Summon up all your experience:

Be terrible and tender, lofty and lowbrow, severe and demure.

Here stand the Leaders of Greece, enthralled by your charm.

They yield the floor to you and submit their claims for your arbitration.

LYSISTRATA

Really, it shouldn't be difficult, if I can catch them all bothered, before they start to solicit each other. I'll find out soon enough. Where's Peace?

    —Come here.

Peace moves from her place by the gates to Lysistrata. The delegations goggle at her.

Now, dear, first get those Spartans and bring them to me. Take them by the hand, but don't be pushy about it, not like our husbands (no savoir-faire[60] at all!).

Be a lady, be proper, do just what you'd do at home: if hands are refused, conduct them by the handle.

Peace leads the Spartans to a position near Lysistrata.

And now a hand to the Athenians—it doesn't matter where; accept any offer—and bring *them* over.

Peace conducts the Athenians to a position near Lysistrata, opposite the Spartans.

You Spartans move up closer—right *here*—

To the Athenians.

and *you* stand over *here*.

    —And now attend my speech.

This the delegations do with some difficulty, because of the conflicting attractions of Peace, who is standing beside her mistress.

I am a woman—but not without some wisdom:

my native wit is not completely negligible,

and I've listened long and hard to the discourse of

my elders—my education is not entirely despicable.

Well, now that I've got you, I intend to give you hell,

and I'm perfectly right. Consider your actions:

[60]Sophistication (literally, in French, "knowing how to do").

At festivals, in Pan-Hellenic harmony, like true blood-brothers, you share the selfsame basin of holy water, and sprinkle altars all over Greece—Olympia, Delphoi, Thermopylai . . . (I could go on and on, if length were my only object.)

But now, when the Persians sit by and wait, in the very presence of your enemies, you fight each other, destroy *Greek* men, destroy *Greek* cities!

—Point One of my address is now concluded.

KINESIAS

Gazing at Peace.

I'm destroyed, if this is drawn out much longer!

LYSISTRATA

Serenely unconscious of the interruption.

>—Men of Sparta, I direct these remarks to you. Have you forgotten that a Spartan suppliant once came to beg assistance from Athens? Recall Perikleidas: Fifty years ago, he clung to our altar, his face dead-white above his crimson robe, and pleaded for an army. Messene was pressing you hard in revolt, and to this upheaval, Poseidon, the Earthshaker, added another.

>But Kimon took four thousand troops from Athens—an army which saved the state of Sparta. Such treatment have you received at the hands of Athens, you who devastate the country that came to your aid!

KINESIAS

Stoutly; the condemnation of his enemy has made him forget the girl momentarily.

>You're right, Lysistrata. The Spartans are clearly in the wrong!

SPARTAN

Guiltily backing away from Peace whom he has attempted to pat.

>Hit's wrong, I reckon, but that's the purtiest behind. .

LYSISTRATA

Turning to the Athenians.

>—Men of Athens, do you think I'll let *you* off?
>Have you forgotten the Tyrant's days,[61] when you wore the smock of slavery, when the Spartans turned to the spear, cut down the pride of Thessaly, despatched the friends of tyranny, and dispossessed your oppressors?
>Recall:

>On that great day, your only allies were Spartans; your liberty came at their hands, which stripped away your servile garb and clothed you again in Freedom!

SPARTAN

Indicating Lysistrata.

>Hain't never seed no higher type of woman.

KINESIAS

Indicating Peace.

>Never saw one I wanted so much to top.

LYSISTRATA

---

[61]The reign of the tyrant Hippias; he was expelled by the Athenians in 510 B.C. with the help of the Spartans who defeated Hippias' Thessalian allies.

Oblivious to the byplay, addressing both groups.

With such a history of mutual benefits conferred and received, why are you fighting? Stop this wickedness! Come to terms with each other! What prevents you?

SPARTAN
We'd a heap sight druther make Peace, if we was indemnified with a plumb strategic location.

Pointing at Peace's rear.

We'll take thet butte.

LYSISTRATA
Butte?

SPARTAN
The Promontory of Pylos[62]—Sparta's Back Door. We've missed it fer a turrible spell.

Reaching.

Hev to keep our hand in.

KINESIAS

Pushing him away.

The price is too high—you'll never take that!

LYSISTRATA
Oh, let them have it.

KINESIAS
What room will we have left for maneuvers?

LYSISTRATA
Demand another spot in exchange.

KINESIAS

Surveying Peace like a map as he addresses the Spartan.

Then you hand over to us—uh, let me see—let's try Thessaly—

Indicating the relevant portions of Peace.

First of all, Easy Mountain . . . then the Maniac Gulf behind it . . .
    and down to Megara for the legs . . .

SPARTAN
You cain't take all of thet! Yore plumb out of yore mind!

LYSISTRATA

To Kinesias.

Don't argue. Let the legs go.

Kinesias nods. A pause. General smiles of agreement.

KINESIAS

Doffing his cloak.

I feel an urgent desire to plow a few furrows.

SPARTAN

---

[62]Pylos was once Spartan territory, held during the war by the Athenians. (The geographical references in this exchange correspond to portions of the anatomy of the young lady, Peace.)

Doffing his cloak.

Hit's time to work a few loads of fertilizer in.

LYSISTRATA

Conclude the treaty and the simple life is yours. If such is your decision, convene your councils, and then deliberate the matter with your allies.

KINESIAS

Deliberate? Allies?

We're over-extended already!
    Wouldn't every ally approve of our position—*Union Now?*

SPARTAN

I know I kin speak for ourn.

KINESIAS

And I for ours.
    They're just a bunch of gigolos.

LYSISTRATA

I heartily approve.
    Now first attend to your purification, then we, the women, will welcome you to the Citadel and treat you to all the delights of a home-cooked banquet. Then you'll exchange your oaths and pledge your faith, and every man of you will take his wife and depart for home.

Lysistrata and Peace enter the Akropolis.

KINESIAS

Let's hurry!

SPARTAN

Lead on, everwhich way's yore pleasure.

KINESIAS

This way, then—and HURRY!

The delegations exeunt at a run.

CHORUS OF WOMEN

I'd never stint on anybody.
And now I include, in my boundless bounty, the younger set.
Attention, you parents of teenage girls about to debut in the social whirl.
Here's what you get: Embroidered linens, lush brocades, a huge assortment of ready-mades, from mantles to shifts; *plus* bracelets and bangles of solid gold—every item my wardrobe holds—absolute gifts!
Don't miss this offer. Come to my place, barge right in, and make your choice.
You can't refuse.
Everything there must go today.
Finders keepers—cart it away!
How can you lose?
Don't spare me. Open all the locks.
Break every seal. Empty every box.
Keep ferreting—
    And your sight's considerably better than mine if you should possibly chance to find a single thing.

CHORUS OF MEN

Troubles, friend? Too many mouths to feed, and not a scrap in the house to see you through?
Faced with starvation? Don't give it a thought
Pay attention; I'll tell you what I'm gonna do.
I overbought. I'm overstocked.
Every room in my house is clogged with flour (best ever), glutted with luscious loaves whose
size you wouldn't believe. I need the space; do me a favor:
Bring gripsacks, knapsacks, duffle bags, pitchers, cisterns, buckets, and kegs around to me.
A courteous servant will see to your needs; he'll fill them up with A-1 wheat—and all for free!
—Oh. Just one final word before you turn your steps to my front door:
I happen to own a dog. Tremendous animal.
        Can't stand a leash. And bites like hell—better stay home.

The united Chorus flocks to the door of the Akropolis.

KORYPHAIOS OF MEN

Banging at the door.

        Hey, open up in there!

The door opens, and the Commissioner appears. He wears a wreath, carries a torch, and is slightly drunk. He addresses the Koryphaios.

COMMISSIONER

You know the Regulations. Move along!

He sees the entire Chorus.

        —And why are YOU lounging around? I'll wield my trusty torch and scorch the lot!

The Chorus backs away in mock horror. He stops and looks at his torch.

        —*This* is the bottom of the barrel. A cheap burlesque bit. I refuse to do it. I have my pride.

With a start, he looks at the audience, as though hearing a protest. He shrugs and addresses the audience.

        —No choice, eh?
        Well, if that's the way it is, we'll take the trouble.
            Anything to keep you happy.

The Chorus advances eagerly

KORYPHAIOS OF MEN

Don't forget us! We're in this, too. Your trouble is ours!

COMMISSIONER

Resuming his character and jabbing with his torch at the Chorus.

        Keep moving!
        Last man out of the way goes home without hair!
        Don't block the exit. Give the Spartans some room.
        They've dined in comfort; let them go home in peace.

The Chorus shrinks back from the door. Kinesias, wreathed and quite drunk, appears at the door. He speaks his first speech in Spartan.

KINESIAS

Hain't never seed sech a spread! Hit were splendiferous!

COMMISSIONER
I gather the Spartans won friends and influenced people?

KINESIAS
And *we've* never been so brilliant. It was the wine.

COMMISSIONER
Precisely.

The reason? A sober Athenian is just *non compos*.[63] If I can carry a little proposal I have in mind, our Foreign Service will flourish, guided by this rational rule:

No Ambassador Without a Skinful [of wine].

Reflect on our past performance: Down to a Spartan parley we troop, in a state of disgusting sobriety, looking for trouble. It muddles our senses: we read between the lines; we hear, not what the Spartans say, but what we suspect they might have been about to be going to say. We bring back paranoid reports—cheap fiction, the fruit of temperance. Cold-water diplomacy, pah!

Contrast this evening's total pleasure, the free-and-easy give-and-take of friendship: If we were singing,

> *Just Kleitagora and me,*
> *Alone in Thessaly,*

and someone missed his cue and cut in loudly,

> *Ajax, son of Telamon,*
> *He was one hell of a man—*

no one took it amiss, or started a war;
we clapped him on the back and gave three cheers.

During this recital, the Chorus has sidled up to the door.

—Dammit, are you back here again?

Waving his torch

Scatter! Get out of the road! Gangway, you gallowsbait!

KINESIAS
Yes, everyone out of the way. They're coming out.

Through the door emerge the Spartan delegation, a flutist, the Athenian delegation, Lysistrata, Kleonike, Myrrhine, and the rest of the women from the citadel, both Athenian and Peloponnesian. The Chorus splits into its male and female components and draws to the sides to give the procession room.

To the flutist.

Friend and kinsman, take up them pipes a yourn. I'd like fer to shuffle a bit and sing a right sweet song in honor of Athens and us'uns, too.

COMMISSIONER

To the flutist.

Marvelous, marvelous—come, take up your pipes!

To the Spartan.

I certainly love to see you Spartans dance.

The flutist plays, and the Spartan begins a slow dance.

---

[63]Latin: *non compos mentis*: "not of sound mind."

SPARTAN

Memory send me your Muse, who knows our glory, knows Athens'—
Tell the story:
At Artemision[64] like gods, they stampeded the hulks of the Medes, and beat them.
And Leonidas[65] leading us—the wild boars whetting their tusks.
And the foam flowered, flowered and flowed, down our cheeks to our knees below.
The Persians there like the sands of the sea—
Hither, huntress, virgin, goddess,[66] tracker, slayer, to our truce!
Hold us ever fast together; bring our pledges love and increase; wean us from the fox's wiles—
Hither, huntress!
Virgin, hither!

LYSISTRATA

Surveying the assemblage with a proprietary air.

Well, the preliminaries are over—very nicely, too. So, Spartans,
Indicating the Peloponnesian women who have been hostages. take these girls back home. And *you*

To the Athenian delegation, indicating the women from the Akropolis.

take *these* girls. Each man stand by his wife, each wife by her husband. Dance to the gods' glory, and thank them for the happy ending. And, from now on, please be careful. Let's not make the same mistakes again.
The delegations obey; the men and women of the chorus join again for a rapid ode.

CHORUS

Start the chorus dancing,
Summon all the Graces,
Send a shout to Artemis in invocation.
Call upon her brother,
healer, chorus master,
Call the blazing Bacchos, with his maddened muster.

Call the flashing, fiery Zeus, and
call his mighty, blessed spouse, and
call the gods, call all the gods,
to witness now and not forget
our gentle, blissful Peace—the gift,
the deed of Aphrodite,
Ai!
Alalai!   Paion!
Leap you!   Paion!
Victory!   Alalai!
Hail!   Hail!   Hail!

LYSISTRATA

Spartan, let's have another song from you, a new one.

---

[64]Site of a sea battle in 480 B.C. in which the Athenians defeated the invading Persians.
[65]Spartan king and general who, with 300 of his infantry, fought to the death to hold the pass at Thermopylae (in central Greece) against a vast Persian army.
[66]Artemis.

SPARTAN

Leave darlin' Taygetos,[67]
Spartan Muse! Come to us once more, flyin' and glorifyin'

Spartan themes: the god at Amyklai, bronze-house Athene,[68]

Tyndaros' twins,[69] the valiant ones, playin' still by Eurotas' streams.
Up! Advance!
Leap to the dance!
Help us hymn Sparta,
lover of dancin',
lover of foot-pats,
where girls go prancin'
like fillies along Eurotas' banks,
whirlin' the dust, twinklin' their shanks,
shakin' their hair
like Maenads[70]playin'
and jugglinl' the thyrsis,
in frenzy obeyin'
Leda's daughter, the fair, the pure
Helen, the mistress of the choir.
Here, Muse, here!
Bind up your hair!
Stamp like a deer! Pound your feet!
Clap your hands! Give us a beat!
Sing the greatest,
sing the mightiest,
sing the conqueror,
sing to honor her—
Athene of the Bronze House!
Sing Athene!

Exeunt omnes[71] *dancing and singing.*

---

[67]A high mountain near Sparta. (All of the references in the following passage are to personages and places sacred to the Spartans.)
[68]The bronze-plated temple of Athene in Sparta.
[69]Leda, wife of Tyndaros the Spartan, was raped by Zeus, chief of the gods, in the form of a swan. Born from that union were the heroic twins, Kastor and Polydeukes, as well as Helen (whose abduction caused the Trojan War).
[70]Literally "mad women": intoxicated, dancing followers of the god Bacchos. They sometimes carried a thyrsis, a staff topped with a pine cone and twined with vines.
[71]Latin: *All leave.*

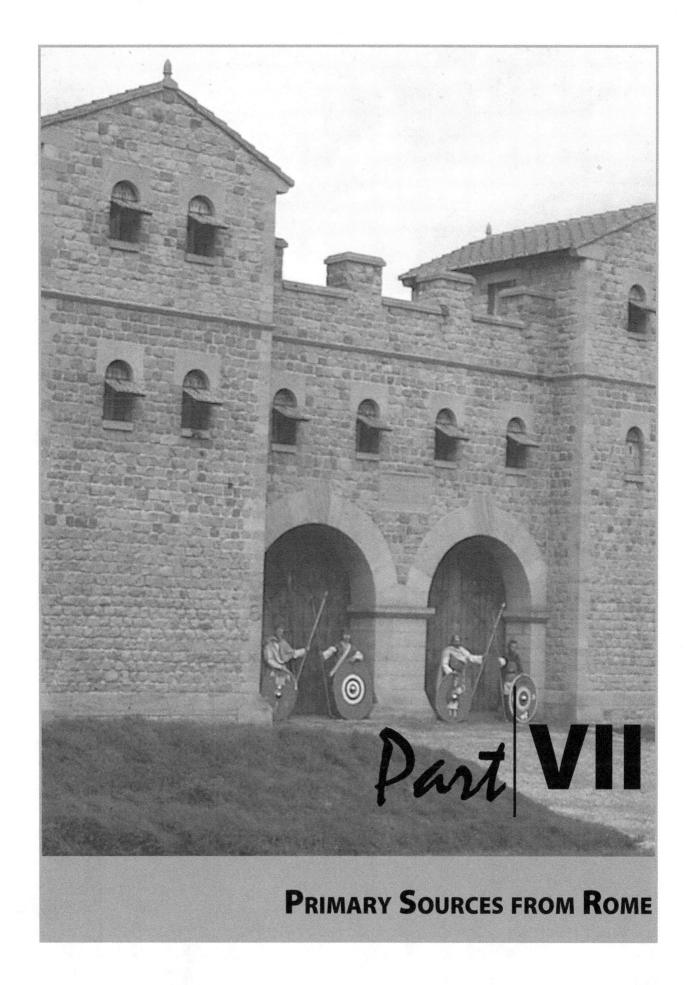

Part VII

PRIMARY SOURCES FROM ROME

Livy

THE HISTORY OF ROME FROM ITS FOUNDATION

All historians see the past through the prism of their present. A member of the Roman aristocracy, Titus Livy (ca. 59- B.C.-A.D. 17) lived in tumultuous times that witnessed the collapse of the Roman Republic and the foundation of the Roman Empire. His massive history originally consisted of 142 books that narrated Rome's history from its foundation down to 9 B.C., although only 35 books survive today.

In some ways Roman historians were strongly influenced by their Greek predecessors, from whom they modeled their own historical writing. Yet, in a significant departure from earlier Greek historians, such as Herodotus and Thucydides, Livy used history in a didactic way to teach moral lessons. Livy tries to explain how a small insignificant village on the banks of the Tiber in central Italy could rise to dominate the entire Mediterranean world. He believes that Rome rose to unparalleled greatness and power through the moral virtue of its citizens: patriotism, honor, courage, frugality, and disdain for material wealth. Yet, for Livy, the very success of the Roman Republic brought about the seeds of its own decline as the Romans were eventually corrupted by the extraordinary wealth and power they amassed, ultimately leading to the fall of the Republic itself.

The surviving books, including the excerpts included here, deal with Rome's early rise and thus display for all to see the outstanding virtues which made Rome great. The historicity of such anecdotes has long been questioned and certainly the many speeches are likely the invention of Livy himself. He himself had few documentary sources for the early period of Roman history and even these may have been of questionable reliability. But he nevertheless provides our only surviving connected narrative of the early history of Rome.

The task of writing a history of our nation from Rome's earliest days fills me, I confess, with some misgiving, and even were I confident in the value of my work, I should hesitate to say so. I am aware that for historians to make extravagant claims is, and always has been, all too common: every writer on history tends to look down his nose at his less cultivated predecessors, happily persuaded that he will better them in point of style, or bring new facts to light. But however that may be, I shall find satisfaction in contributing—not, I hope, ignobly—to the labour of putting on record the story of the greatest nation in the world. Countless others have written on this theme and it may be that I shall pass unnoticed amongst them; if so, I must comfort myself with the greatness and splendour of my rivals, whose work will rob my own of recognition.

My task, moreover, is an immensely laborious one. I shall have to go back more than seven hundred years, and trace my story from its small beginning up to these recent times when its ramifications are so vast that any adequate treatment is hardly possible. I am aware, too, that most readers will take less pleasure in my account of how

Rome began and in her early history; they will wish to hurry on to more modern times and to read of the period, already a long one, in which the might of an imperial people is beginning to work its own ruin. My own feeling is different; I shall find antiquity a rewarding study, if only because, while I am absorbed in it, I shall be able to turn my eyes from the troubles which for so long have tormented the modern world, and to write without any of that over-anxious consideration which may well plague a writer on contemporary life, even if it does not lead him to conceal the truth.

Events before Rome was born or thought of have come to us in old tales with more of the charm of poetry than of a sound historical record, and such traditions I propose neither to affirm nor refute. There is no reason, I feel, to object when antiquity draws no hard line between the human and the supernatural; it adds dignity to the past, and, if any nation deserves the privilege of claiming a divine ancestry, that nation is our own. And so great is the glory won by the Roman people in their wars that, when they declare that Mars himself was their first parent and father of the man who founded their city,[1] all the nations of the world might well allow the claim as readily as they accept Rome's imperial dominion.

These, however, are comparatively trivial matters and I set little store by them. I invite the reader's attention to the much more serious consideration of the kind of lives our ancestors lived, of who were the men, and what the means both in politics and war by which Rome's power was first acquired and subsequently expanded; I would then have him trace the process of our moral decline, to watch, first, the sinking of the foundations of morality as the old teaching was allowed to lapse, then the rapidly increasing disintegration, then the final collapse of the whole edifice, and the dark dawning of our modern day when we can neither endure our vices nor face the remedies needed to cure them. The study of history is the best medicine for a sick mind; for in history you have a record of the infinite variety of human experience plainly set out for all to see; and in that record you can find for yourself and your country both examples and warnings: fine things to take as models, base things, rotten through and through, to avoid.

I hope my passion for Rome's past has not impaired my judgement; for I do honestly believe that no country has ever been greater or purer than ours or richer in good citizens and noble deeds; none has been free for so many generations from the vices of avarice and luxury; nowhere have thrift and plain living been for so long held in such esteem, Indeed, poverty, with us, went hand in hand with contentment. Of late years wealth has made us greedy, and self-indulgence has brought us, through every form of sensual excess, to be, if I may so put it, in love with death both individual and collective.

But bitter comments of this sort are not likely to find favour, even when they have to be made. Let us have no more of them, at least at the beginning of our great story. On the contrary, I should prefer to borrow from the poets and begin with good omens and with prayers to all the host of heaven to grant a successful issue to the work which lies before me.

● ● ●

But (I must believe) it was already written in the book of fate that this great city of ours should arise, and the first steps be taken to the funding of the mightiest empire the world has known—next to [that of the gods]. The Vestal Virgin was raped and gave birth to twin boys.[2] Mars, she declared, was their father—perhaps she believed it, perhaps she was merely hoping by the pretence to palliate her guilt. Whatever the truth of the matter, neither gods nor men could save her or her babes from the savage hands of [King Amulius]. The mother was bound and flung into prison; the boys, by the king's order, were condemned to be drowned in the river. Destiny, however, intervened; the Tiber had overflowed its banks; because of the flooded ground it was impossible to get to the actual river, and the men entrusted to do the deed thought that the flood-water, sluggish though it was, would serve their purpose. Accordingly they made shift to carry out the king's orders by leaving the infants on the edge of the first flood-water they came to, at the spot where now stands the Ruminal fig-tree—said to have once been known as the fig-tree of Romulus. In those days the country thereabouts was all wild and uncultivated, and the story goes that when the basket

[1]Romulus was the legendary founder and first king of Rome in 753 B.C.; his mother claimed that his father was Mars (called Ares by the Greeks), god of war, gladiators, hunting, and other warlike pursuits. Mars was worshipped extensively in Rome as a patron god of the city.
[2]The Vestals were virgin priestesss selected from noble families for terms of thirty years; they were expected to remain chaste and to tend the sacred fire in the temple of Vesta (Roman goddess of the family hearth). Rhea Silvia, a Vestal Virgin and King Numitor's daughter, gave birth to twin boys, Romulus and Remus, supposedly after having been raped by Mars. Her uncle, King Amulius, usurper of his brother Numitor's crown, had consecrated Rhea Silvia to the service of Vesta so that she would not have children who might threaten his royal position.

in which the infants had been exposed was left high and dry by the receding water, a she-wolf, coming down from the neighbouring hills to quench her thirst, heard the children crying and made her way to where they were. She offered them her teats to suck and treated them with such gentleness that Faustulus, the king's herdsman, found her licking them with her tongue. Faustulus took them to his hut and gave them to his wife Larentia to nurse. Some think that the origin of this fable was the fact that Larentia was a common whore and was called Wolf by the shepherds.

Such, then, was the birth and upbringing of the twins. By the time they were grown boys, they employed themselves actively on the farm and with the flocks and began to go hunting in the woods; their strength grew with their resolution, until not content only with the chase they took to attacking robbers and sharing their stolen goods with their friends the shepherds. Other young fellows joined them, and they and the shepherds would fleet the time together, now in serious talk, now in jollity.

Even in that remote age the Palatine hill[3] (which got its name from the Arcadian settlement Pallanteum) is supposed to have been the scene of the gay festival of the Lupercalia. The Arcadian Evander,[4] who many years before held that region, is said to have instituted there the old Arcadian practice of holding an annual festival in honour of Lycean Pan (afterwards called Inuus by the Romans), in which young men ran about naked and disported themselves in various pranks and fooleries. The day of the festival was common knowledge, and on one occasion when it was in full swing some brigands, incensed at the loss of their ill-gotten gains, laid a trap for Romulus and Remus. Romulus successfully defended himself, but Remus was caught and handed over to Amulius. The brigands laid a complaint against their prisoner, the main charge being that he and his brother were in the habit of raiding Numitor's land with an organized gang of ruffians and stealing the cattle. Thereupon Remus was handed over for punishment to Numitor.

Now Faustulus had suspected all along that the boys he was bringing up were of royal blood. He knew that two infants had been exposed by the king's orders, and the rescue of his own two fitted perfectly in point of time. Hitherto, however, he had been unwilling to declare what he knew, until either a suitable opportunity occurred or circumstances compelled him. Now the truth could no longer be concealed, so in his alarm he told Romulus the whole story; Numitor, too, when he had Remus in custody and was told that the two brothers were twins, was set thinking about his grandsons; the young men's age and character, so different from the lowly born, confirmed his supicions; and further inquiries led him to the same conclusion, until he was on the point of acknowledging Remus. The net was closing in, and Romulus acted. He was not strong enough for open hostilities, so he instructed a number of the herdsmen to meet at the king's house by different routes at a preordained time; this was done, and with the help of Remus, at the head of another body of men, the king [Amulius] was surprised and killed. Before the first blows were struck, Numitor gave it out that an enemy had broken into the town and attacked the palace; he then drew off all the men of military age to garrison the inner fortress, and, as soon as he saw Romulus and Remus, their purpose accomplished, coming to congratulate him, he summoned a meeting of the people and laid the facts before it: Amulius's crime against himself, the birth of his grandsons, and the circumstances attending it, how they were brought up and ultimately recognized, and, finally, the murder of the king [Amulius] for which he himself assumed responsibility. The two brothers marched through the crowd at the head of their men and saluted their grandfather as king, and by a shout of unanimous consent his royal title was confirmed.

Romulus and Remus, after the control of Alba had passed to Numitor in the way I have described, were suddenly seized by an urge to found a new settlement on the spot where they had been left to drown as infants and had been subsequently brought up. There was, in point of fact, already an excess of population at Alba, what with the Albans themselves, the Latins, and the addition of the herdsmen—enough, indeed, to justify the hope that Alba and Lavinium would one day be small places compared with the proposed new settlement. Unhappily the brothers' plans for the future were marred by the same curse which had divided their grandfather and Amulius—jealousy and ambition. A disgraceful quarrel arose from a matter in itself trivial. As the brothers were twins and all question of seniority was thereby precluded, they determined to ask the tutelary [guardian] gods of the countryside to declare by augury [prophecy] which of them should govern the new town once it was founded, and give his name to it. For this purpose Romulus took the Palatine hill and Remus the Aventine as their respective stations from

---

[3]One of the famed Seven Hills of Rome.

[4]Arcadia is in Greece; thus, one of the many legendary ways that the origin of Rome was connected to Greece was through the story of Evander, who transmitted the worship of the Greek woodland god Pan to the site that would become Rome.

which to observe the [bird signs]. Remus, the story goes, was the first to receive a sign—six vultures; and no sooner was this made known to the people than double the number of birds appeared to Romulus. The followers of each promptly saluted their master as king, one side basing its claim upon priority, the other upon number. Angry words ensued, followed all too soon by blows, and in the course of the affray Remus was killed. There is another story, a commoner one, according to which Remus, by way of jeering at his brother, jumped over the half-built walls of the new settlement, where upon Romulus killed him in a fit of rage, adding the threat, 'So perish whoever else shall overleap my battlements.'

This, then, was how Romulus obtained the sole power. The newly built city was called by its founder's name.

•   •   •

Meanwhile Rome was growing. More and more ground was coming within the circuit of its walls. Indeed, the rapid expansion of the enclosed area was out of proportion to the actual population, and evidently indicated an eye to the future. In antiquity the founder of a new settlement, in order to increase its population, would as a matter of course shark up a lot of homeless and destitute folk and pretend that they were 'born of earth' to be his progeny [descendants]; Romulus now followed a similar course: to help fill his big new town, he threw open, in the ground—now enclosed—between the two copses as you go up the Capitoline hill, a place of asylum for fugitives. Hither fled for refuge all the rag-tag-and-bobtail from the neighbouring peoples: some free, some slaves, and all of them wanting nothing but a fresh start. That mob was the first real addition to the City's strength, the first step to her future greatness.

Having now adequate numbers, Romulus proceeded to temper strength with policy and turned his attention to social organization. He created a hundred senators—fixing that number either because it was enough for his purpose, or because there were no more than a hundred who were in a position to be made 'Fathers,' as they were called, or Heads of Clans. The title of 'fathers' (*patres*) undoubtedly was derived from their rank, and their descendants were called 'patricians.'

Rome was now strong enough to challenge any of her neighbours; but, great though she was, her greatness seemed likely to last only for a single generation. There were not enough women, and that, added to the fact that there was no intermarriage with neighbouring communities, ruled out any hope of maintaining the level of population. Romulus accordingly, on the advice of his senators, sent representatives to the various peoples across his borders to negotiate alliances and the right of intermarriage for the newly established state. The envoys were instructed to point out that cities, like everything else, have to begin small; in course of time, helped by their own worth and the favour of heaven, some, at least, grow rich and famous, and of these Rome would assuredly be one. Gods had blessed her birth, and the valour of her people would not fail in the days to come. The Romans were men, as they were; why, then, be reluctant to intermarry with them?

Romulus's overtures were nowhere favourably received; it was clear that everyone despised the new community, and at the same time feared, both for themselves and for posterity, the growth of this new power in their midst. More often than not his envoys were dismissed with the question of whether Rome had thrown open her doors to female, as well as to male, runaways and vagabonds, as that would evidently be the most suitable way for Romans to get wives. The young Romans naturally resented this jibe, and a clash seemed inevitable. Romulus, seeing it must come, set the scene for it with elaborate care. Deliberately hiding his resentment, he prepared to celebrate the Consualia, a solemn festival in honour of Neptune,[5] patron of the horse, and sent notice of his intention all over the neighbouring countryside. The better to advertise it, his people lavished upon their preparations for the spectacle all the resources—such as they were in those days—at their command. On the appointed day crowds flocked to Rome, partly, no doubt, out of sheer curiosity to see the new town. The majority were from the neighbouring settlements of Caenina, Crustumium, and Antemnae, but all the Sabines were there too, with their wives and children. Many houses offered hospitable entertainment to the visitors; they were invited to inspect the fortifications, layout, and numerous buildings of the town, and expressed their surprise at the rapidity of its growth. Then the great moment came; the show began, and nobody had eyes or thoughts for anything else. This was the Romans' opportunity: at a given signal all the able-bodied men burst through the crowd and seized the young women. Most of the girls were the

[5]Neptune (Poseidon to the Greeks) was also god of the sea.

prize of whoever got hold of them first, but a few conspicuously handsome ones had been previously marked down for leading senators, and these were brought to their houses by special gangs. . . .

By this act of violence the fun of the festival broke up in panic, The girls' unfortunate parents made good their escape, not without bitter comments on the treachery of their hosts and heartfelt prayers to the God to whose festival they had come in all good faith in the solemnity of the occasion, only to be grossly deceived. The young women were no less indignant and as full of foreboding for the future.

Romulus, however, reassured them. Going from one to another he declared that their own parents were really to blame, in that they had been too proud to allow intermarriage with their neighbours; nevertheless, they need not fear; as married women they would share all the fortunes of Rome, all the privileges of the community, and they would be bound to their husbands by the dearest bond of all, their children. He urged them to forget their wrath and give their hearts to those to whom chance had given their bodies. Often, he said, a sense of injury yields in the end to affection, and their husbands would treat them all the more kindly in that they would try, each one of them, not only to fulfill their own part of the bargain but also to make up to their wives for the homes and parents they had lost. The men, too, played their part; they spoke honied words and vowed that it was passionate love which had prompted their offence. No plea can better touch a woman's heart.

•   •   •

Now began the reign of [Lucius] Tarquinius Superbus—Tarquin the Proud.[6] His conduct merited the name. . . . He executed the leading senators who he thought had supported Servius.[7] Well aware that his treachery and violence might form a precedent to his own disadvantage, he employed a bodyguard. His anxiety was justified; for he had usurped by force the throne to which he had no title whatever; the people had not elected him, the Senate had not sanctioned his accession. Without hope of his subjects' affection, he could rule only by fear; and to make himself feared as widely as possible he began the practice of trying capital causes without consultation and by his own sole authority. He was thus enabled to punish with death, exile, or confiscation of property not only such men as he happened to suspect or dislike, but also innocent people from whose conviction he had nothing to gain but their money. Those of senatorial rank were the worst sufferers from this procedure; their numbers were reduced, and no new appointments made, in the hope, no doubt, that sheer numerical weakness might bring the [senatorial] order into contempt, and the surviving members be readier to acquiesce in political impotence. Tarquin was the first king to break the established tradition of consulting the Senate on all matters of public business, and to govern by the mere authority of himself and his household. In questions of war and peace he was his own sole master; he made and unmade treaties and alliances whom he pleased without any reference whatever either to the [people] or to the Senate. He made particular efforts to win the friendship of the Latins,[8] in the hope that any power or influence he could obtain abroad might give him greater security at home. With this in view he went beyond mere official friendly relations with the Latin nobility, and married his daughter to Octavius Mamilius of Tusculum [a town in Latium], by far the most distinguished bearer of the Latin name. . . . By this marriage he attached to his interest Mamilius's numerous relatives and friends.

•   •   •

Tarquin next turned his attention to home affairs. His first concern was the temple of Jupiter[9] on the Capitoline,[10] which he hoped to leave as a memorial of the royal house of the Tarquins—of the father who had made the vow, and of the son who had fulfilled it. . . . The new work was hardly begun, when, we are told, heaven itself was moved to give a sign of the future greatness of Rome's dominion. . . . A man's head with the features intact was discovered by the workmen who were digging the foundations of the temple [of Jupiter]. This meant without any doubt that on this spot would stand the imperial citadel of the capital city of the world. Nothing could be plainer—and such was the interpretation put upon the discovery not only by the Roman soothsayers but also by those who were specially brought from Etruria[11] for consultation.

[6]The last king of Rome. After the citizens expelled him in 510 B.C., they formed a republic.
[7]Servius Tullius was the previous mild and moderate king, Tarquin's father-in-law. According to Livy he was murdered by the plotting of his own daughter, Tullia, and her husband, Tarquin.
[8]Inhabitants of Latium, a coastal strip extending south of Rome.
[9]The most powerful of the ancient gods (known to the Greeks as Zeus).
[10]Chief of the Seven Hills of Rome.
[11]An area of Italy north of Rome, occupied by the once-dominating Etruscans.

In view of all this, Tarquin became more extravagant in his ideas. . . . Tarquin's chief interest was now the completion of the temple. Builders and engineers were brought in from all over Etruria, and the project involved the use not only of public funds but also of a large number of labourers from the poorer classes. The work was hard in itself, and came as an addition to their regular military duties; but it was an honourable burden with a solemn and religious significance, and they were not, on the whole, unwilling to bear it; but it was a very different matter when they were put on to other tasks less spectacular but more laborious still, such as the construction of the tiers of seats in the Circus[12] and the excavation of the . . . Great Sewer, designed to carry off the sewage of the entire city by an underground pipe-line. The magnitude of both these projects could hardly be equalled by any work even of modern times. It was Tarquin's view that an idle proletariat was a burden on the state, so in addition to the major works I have mentioned he made use of some of the surplus population by sending settlers out to [nearby towns]. This had the further advantages of increasing the extent of Roman territory and of providing points of resistance against future attack either by land or sea.

About this time an alarming and ominous event occurred: a snake slid out from a crack in a wooden pillar in the palace. Everyone ran from it in fright; even the king was scared, though in his case it was not fear so much as foreboding. About signs and omens of public import the custom had always been to consult only Etruscan soothsayers; this, however, was a different matter. It was in the king's own house that the portentous sight had been seen; and that, Tarquin felt, justified the unusual step of sending to Delphi, to consult the most famous oracle in the world. Unwilling to entrust the answer of the oracle to anybody else, he sent on the mission two of his sons, Titus and Arruns, who accordingly set out for Greece through country which Roman feet had seldom trod and over seas which Roman ships had never sailed. With them went Lucius Junius Brutus, son of the king's sister Tarquinia.

Now Brutus had deliberately assumed a mask to hide his true character. When he learned of the murder by Tarquin of the Roman aristocrats, one of the victims being his own brother, he had come to the conclusion that the only way of saving himself was to appear in the king's eyes as a person of no account. If there were nothing in his character for Tarquin to fear, and nothing in his fortune to covet, then the sheer contempt in which he was held would be a better protection than his own rights could ever be. Accordingly he pretended to be a half-wit and made no protest at the seizure by Tarquin of everything he possessed. He even submitted to being known publicly as the 'Dullard' (which is what his name signifies), that under cover of that [degrading] title the great spirit which gave Rome her freedom might be able to bide its time. On this occasion he was taken by Arruns and Titus to Delphi less as a companion than as a butt for their amusement; and he is said to have carried with him, as his gift to Apollo, a rod of gold inserted into a hollow stick of cornel-wood—symbolic, it may be of his own character.

The three young men reached Delphi, and carried out the king's instructions. That done, Titus and Arruns found themselves unable to resist putting a further question to the oracle. Which of them, they asked, would be the next king of Rome? From the depths of the cavern came the mysterious answer: 'He who shall be the first to kiss his mother shall hold in Rome supreme authority.' Titus and Arruns were determined to keep the prophecy absolutely secret, to prevent their other brother, Tarquin, who had been left in Rome, from knowing anything about it. Thus he, at any rate, would be out of the running. For themselves, they drew lots to determine which of them, on their return, should kiss his mother first.

Brutus, however, interpreted the words of Apollo's priestess in a different way. Pretending to trip, he fell flat on his face, and his lips touched the Earth—the mother of all living things.

Back in Rome, they found vigorous preparations in progress for war with the Rutuli.[13] The chief town of the Rutuli was Ardea, and they were a people, for that place and period, of very considerable wealth. Their wealth was, indeed, the reason for Tarquin's preparations; he needed money to repair the drain on his resources resulting from his ambitious schemes of public building and he knew, moreover, that the [common people] were growing ever more restive, not only in view of his tyrannical behaviour generally but also, and especially, because they had been

[12]A circular, open-air arena, for races and other spectacles.
[13]Close neighbors of the Romans.

so long employed in manual labour such as belonged properly to slaves, and the distribution of plunder from a captured town would do much to soften their resentment.

The attempt was made to take Ardea by assault. It failed; siege operations were begun, and the army settled down into permanent quarters. With little prospect of any decisive action, the war looked like being a long one, and in these circumstances leave was granted, quite naturally, with considerable freedom, especially to officers. Indeed, the young princes, at any rate, spent most of their leisure enjoying themselves in entertainments on the most lavish scale. They were drinking one day in the quarters of Sextus Tarquinius[14]—Collatinus, son of Egerius, was also present—when someone chanced to mention the subject of wives. Each of them, of course, extravagantly praised his own; and the rivalry got hotter and hotter, until Collatinus suddenly cried: 'Stop! What need is there of words, when in a few hours we can prove beyond doubt the incomparable superiority of my Lucretia? We are all young and strong: why shouldn't we ride to Rome and see with our own eyes what kind of women our wives are? There is no better evidence, I assure you, than what a man finds when he enters his wife's room unexpectedly.'

They had all drunk a good deal, and the proposal appealed to them; so they mounted their horses and galloped off to Rome. They reached the city as dusk was falling; and there the wives of the royal princes were found enjoying themselves with a group of young friends at a dinner-party, in the greatest of luxury. The riders then went on to Collatia, where they found Lucretia very differently employed: it was already late at night, but there, in the hall of her house, surrounded by her busy maid-servants, she was still hard at work by lamplight upon her spinning. Which wife had won the contest in womanly virtue was no longer in doubt.

With all courtesy Lucretia rose to bid her husband and the princes welcome, and Collatinus, pleased with his success, invited his friends to sup with him. It was at that fatal supper that Lucretia's beauty, and proven chastity, kindled in Sextus Tarquinius the flame of lust, and determined him to [degrade] her.

Nothing further occurred that night. The little jaunt was over, and the young men rode back to camp.

A few days later Sextus, without Collatinus's knowledge, returned with one companion to Collatia, where he was hospitably welcomed in Lucretia's house, and, after supper, escorted, like the honoured visitor he was thought to be, to the guest-chamber. Here he waited till the house was asleep, and then, when all was quiet, he drew his sword and made his way to Lucretia's room determined to rape her. She was sleep. Laying his left hand on her breast, 'Lucretia,' he whispered, 'not a sound! I am Sextus Tarquinius. I am armed—if you utter a word, will kill you.' Lucretia opened her eyes in terror; death was imminent, no help at hand. Sextus urged his love, begged her to submit, pleaded, threatened, used every weapon that might conquer a woman's heart. But all in vain; not even the fear of death could bend her will. 'If death will not move you,' Sextus cried, 'dishonour shall. I will kill you first, then cut the throat of a slave and lay his naked body by your side. Will they not believe that you have been caught in adultery with a servant—and paid the price?' Even the most resolute chastity could not have stood against this dreadful threat.

Lucretia yielded. Sextus enjoyed her, and rode away, proud of his success.

The unhappy girl wrote to her father in Rome and to her husband in Ardea, urging them both to come at once with a trusted friend—and quickly, for a frightful thing had happened. Her father came with Valerius, Volesus's son, her husband with Brutus, with whom he was returning to Rome when he was met by the messenger. They found Lucretia sitting in her room, in deep distress. Tears rose to her eyes as they entered, and to her husband's question, 'Is it well with you?' she answered, 'No. What can be well with a woman who has lost her honour? In your bed, Collatinus, is the impress of another man. My body only has been violated. My heart is innocent, and death will be my witness. Give me your solemn promise that the adulterer shall be punished—he is Sextus Tarquinius. He it is who last night came as my enemy disguised as my guest, and took his pleasure of me. That pleasure will be my death—and his, too, if you are men.'

The promise was given. One after another they tried to comfort her. They told her she was helpless, and therefore innocent; that he alone was guilty. It was the mind, they said, that sinned, not the body; without intention there could never be guilt.

'What is due to *him*,' Lucretia said, 'is for you to decide. As for me I am innocent of fault, but I will take my punishment. Never shall Lucretia provide a precedent for unchaste women to escape what they deserve.' With these words she drew a knife from under her robe, drove it into her heart, and fell forward, dead.

[14]Son of King Tarquin.

Her father and husband were overwhelmed with grief. While they stood weeping helplessly, Brutus drew the bloody knife from Lucretia's body, and holding it before him cried: 'By this girl's blood—none more chaste till a tyrant wronged her—and by the gods, I swear that with sword and fire, and whatever else can lend strength to my arm, I will pursue Lucius Tarquinius the Proud, his wicked wife, and all his children, and never again will I let them or any other man be King in Rome.'

He put the knife into Collatinus's hands, then passed it to Lucretius,[15] then to Valerius. All looked at him in astonishment: a miracle had happened—he was a changed man. Obedient to his command, they swore their oath. Grief was forgotten in the sudden surge of anger, and when Brutus called upon them to make war, from that instant, upon the tyrant's throne, they took him for their leader.

Lucretia's body was carried from the house into the public square. Crowds gathered, as crowds will, to gape and wonder—and the sight was unexpected enough, and horrible enough, to attract them. Anger at the criminal brutality of the king's son and sympathy with the father's grief stirred every heart; and when Brutus cried out that it was time for deeds not tears, and urged them, like true Romans, to take up arms against the tyrants who had dared to treat them as a vanquished enemy, not a man amongst them could resist the call. The boldest spirits offered themselves at once for service; the rest soon followed their lead. Lucretia's father was left to hold Collatia; guards were posted to prevent news of the rising from reaching the palace, and with Brutus in command the armed populace began their march on Rome.

In the city the first effect of their appearance was alarm and confusion, but the sight of Brutus, and others of equal distinction, at the head of the mob, soon convinced people that this was, at least, no mere popular demonstration. Moreover the horrible story of Lucretia had had hardly less effect in Rome than in Collatia. In a moment the Forum[16] was packed, and the crowds, by Brutus's order, were immediately summoned to attend the Tribune of Knights—an office held at the time by Brutus himself. There, publicly throwing off the mask under which he had hitherto concealed his real character and feelings, he made a speech painting in vivid colours the brutal and unbridled lust of Sextus Tarquinius, the hideous rape of the innocent Lucretia and her pitiful death, and the bereavement of her father, for whom the cause of her death was an even bitterer and more dreadful thing than the death itself. He went on to speak of the king's arrogant and tyrannical behaviour; of the sufferings of the [common people] condemned to labour underground clearing or constructing ditches and sewers; of gallant Romans—soldiers who had beaten in battle all neighbouring peoples—robbed of their swords and turned into stone-cutters and artisans. . . . Doubtless he told them of other, and worse, things, brought to his mind in the heat of the moment and by the sense of this latest outrage, which still lived in his eye and pressed upon his heart; but a mere historian can hardly record them.

The effect of his words was immediate: the populace took fire, and were brought to demand the [removal] of the king's authority and the exile of himself and his family.

With an armed body of volunteers Brutus then marched for Ardea to rouse the army to revolt. Lucretius, who some time previously had been appointed by the king Prefect of the City, was left in command in Rome. [Queen] Tullia fled from the palace during the disturbances; wherever she went she was met with curses; everyone, men and women alike, called down upon her head the vengeance of the furies who punish sinners against the sacred ties of blood.

When news of the rebellion reached Ardea, the king immediately started for Rome, to restore order. Brutus got wind of his approach, and changed his route to avoid meeting him, finally reaching Ardea almost at the same moment as Tarquin arrived at Rome. Tarquin found the city gates shut against him and his exile decreed. Brutus the Liberator was enthusiastically welcomed by the troops, and Tarquin's sons were expelled from the camp. Two of them followed their father into exile at Caere in Etruria. Sextus Tarquinius went to Gabii—his own territory, as he doubtless hoped; but his previous record there of robbery and violence had made him many enemies, who now took their revenge and assassinated him.

Tarquin the Proud reigned for twenty-five years. The whole period of monarchical government, from the founding of Rome to its liberation, was 244 years. After the liberation two consuls were elected by popular vote. . . . The two consuls were Lucius Junius Brutus and Lucius Tarquinius Callatinus.

•   •   •

[15]Father of Lucretia.
[16]The chief public square of the city.

It was argued in the council that if ever at any time a war had been conducted under strict command, now was the moment to recall military discipline to its former ways.[17] Their anxiety was more acute because they had to make war on Latins, who were the same as themselves in language, customs, type of arms, and above all in military institutions; soldiers had intermingled with soldiers, centurions [officers] with centurions, tribunes with tribunes as equals and colleagues in the same garrisons and often in the same maniples.[18] To prevent the men committing some blunder on account of this, the consuls issued the order that no one was to leave his position to fight the enemy.

It happened that among the squadron leaders in the cavalry, who had been sent off to reconnoitre in all directions, was the consul's son, Titus Manlius.[19] He had managed to ride with his cavalry beyond the enemy's camp until he was hardly a spear throw from their nearest outpost. There the Tusculan [Latin] cavalry were stationed under the command of Geminus Maecius, whose reputation was high amongst his fellows for his exploits as much as for his noble birth. He recognized the Roman cavalry, and amongst them the conspicuous figure of the consul's son, riding at their head (for they were all known to each other, especially the nobility). 'Do you Romans,' he cried, 'intend to make war on the Latins and their allies with a single squadron? What will your consuls and your two consular armies be doing meanwhile? 'They'll be here in good time,' replied Manlius, 'and with them will be Jupiter himself, who has more power and might than they, as witness of the treaties violated by you. If we gave you your fill of fighting at Lake Regillus, here too we shall certainly see that you get little joy out of our fighting force and a clash with us.' At this Geminus rode out a little in front of his men: 'Then will you fight me yourself, while waiting for that great day to come when you all make a mighty effort to get your armies moving? The outcome of a duel between you and me will show how much better a Latin cavalryman is than a Roman.'

The young man's bold spirit was roused, whether by anger, by shame at the thought of refusing the challenge, or through the invincible power of destiny. And so, forgetting his father's supreme authority and the consuls' order, he threw himself headlong into a fight where it mattered little whether he won or lost. The rest of the cavalry were made to stand back, as if to watch a riding display, and the two men rode their horses hard at each other across the empty space between them. But when they met with spears levelled for attack, Manlius's spear glanced off his enemy's helmet, while Maecius's passed over the neck of the other's horse. Then when they wheeled their horses round, Manlius was the first to collect himself for a second blow and pricked Maecius's horse between the ears with his spear-point. The horse reared when it felt the wound and shook its head so violently that it threw its rider; and as Maecius was trying to get up after the heavy fall, leaning on his spear and shield, Manlius ran through his throat so that the spear came out between his ribs and pinned him to the ground. Gathering up the spoils, Manlius rode back to his men, and then made for the camp, accompanied by their shouts of triumph. He went straight to his father's headquarters, not knowing what fate and future waited him, or whether praise or punishment were to be his desert.

'Father,' he said, 'so that all men may proclaim me your true son, I am bringing you these cavalryman's spoils, taken from the enemy I killed after accepting his challenge.' On hearing this, the consul promptly turned away from his son and gave orders for a trumpet to summon an assembly. When this had filled up, he spoke as follows: 'Titus Manlius, you have respected neither consular authority nor your father's dignity; you have left your position to fight the enemy in defiance of my order, and, as far as was in your power, have subverted military discipline, on which the fortune of Rome has rested up to this day; you have made it necessary for me to forget either the republic or myself. We would therefore rather be punished for our own wrong-doing than allow our country to [suffer] our sins at so great a cost to itself; it is a harsh example we shall set, but a salutary one for the young men of the future. As far as my own feelings are concerned, they are stirred by a man's natural love for his children, as well as by the example you have given of your courage, even though this was marred by a false conception of glory. But since consular authority must either be confirmed by your death or annulled for ever by your going unpunished, I believe that you yourself, if you have any drop of my blood in you, would agree that the military discipline which you undermined by your error must be restored by your punishment. Go, lector,[20] bind him to the stake.'

All were transfixed with horror by this dreadful command; every man saw the axe as if raised against himself, and it was fear, not obedience, which held them in check. So they stood rooted to the spot in silence, as if lost in amazement; then when the blood gushed from the severed neck, suddenly their voices broke out in agonized complaint so unrestrained that they spared neither laments nor curses. They covered the young man's body with his

---

[17]The following episode occurred, calculating from Livy's chronology, around 340 B.C.
[18]A maniple was a subdivision of a Roman legion, consisting of 60 or 120 heavily armed foot-soldiers.
[19]The consul's (father's) name was also Titus Manlius.
[20]An attendant who walked before certain high Roman officials carrying the *fasces*, bundle of wooden rods enclosing an axe, a symbol of Roman authority.

spoils, built a pyre outside the earthworks, and burnt it with all the honours that can attend any military funeral. The 'commands of Manlius' not only caused a shudder at the time but were a grim warning in the future. However, the brutality of the punishment made the soldiers more obedient to their commander, and not only was better attention given everywhere to guard-duties, night watches, and picket-stationing, but in the final struggle too, when the army went into battle, that stern act of discipline did them good.

Plutarch

LIVES: MARCUS CATO

The most famous biographer of classical antiquity was Lucius Mestrius Plutarchus, better known today as Plutarch (ca. A.D. 46-124), a native of the small city of Chaeronea in central Greece. The glorious days of the ancient Greek city-states were by then only a revered memory and Greece was now firmly under Roman rule. Born from an aristocratic and wealthy family, Plutarch was educated at the Academy in Athens and obtained Roman citizenship. He was active in the local politics of his native city as well as a prolific writer. In his later life he served as a priest at the famous Oracle of Apollo at the temple at Delphi, only a few miles from his hometown.

Among his many literary works was the **Parallel Lives,** *twenty-three pairs of biographies matching a famous Greek general or politician with a famous Roman commander or statesman. Although written in Greek, the* **Lives** *were clearly intended for both Greek and Roman audiences as many educated Romans were by then literate in Greek. Plutarch's main focus in these biographies aimed primarily to describe their moral character and personality rather than a strictly narrative account of their lives. These biographies would be widely read and highly influential for subsequent Western literature. For example they were extensively exploited by Shakespeare for his plays about famous Greeks and Romans.*

The following excerpt is from Plutarch's biography of Marcus Porcius Cato (234-149 B.C.), more commonly called Cato the Elder or Cato the Censor. It traces the rise of a **novus homo** *("new man") who rose from fairly humble origins to the highest political offices in the Roman Republic. Cato in many ways epitomized the ideal Roman of the Republic because he espoused so many of the traditional virtues that many Romans believed had made them great. Although Plutarch clearly shares this admiration he also does not hesitate to offer some criticism of Cato when warranted. A traditional conservative, Cato also waged an ultimately losing battle against the rising intrusion of Greek culture into Roman society in the 2nd century B.C. In fact, nothing better illustrates the ultimate futility of Cato's opposition to the Roman embrace of things Greek than the later popularity of Plutarch himself!*

Marcus Cato

The family of Marcus Cato, it is said, was of Tusculan[1] origin, though he lived, previous to his career as soldier and statesman, on an inherited estate in the country of the Sabines.[2] His ancestors commonly passed for men of no note whatever, but Cato himself extols his father, Marcus, as a brave man and good soldier. He also says that his grandfather, Cato, often won prizes for soldierly valour, and received from the state treasury, because of his bravery, the price of five horses which had been killed under him in battle. The Romans used to call men who had no family distinction, but were coming into public notice through their own achievements, "new men," and such they called Cato. But he himself used to say that as far as office and distinction went, he was indeed new, but having regard to

[1]Tusculum was an ancient town about ten miles southeast of Rome.
[2]The Sabines were a tribal group living northeast of Rome in its earliest days. (See the legendary rape of the Sabine women described by Livy, pp. 390–92.) By 268 B.C. the Sabines had become fully Romanized and ceased to be a separate people.

ancestral deeds of valour, he was oldest of the old. His third name[3] was not Cato at first, but Priscus. Afterwards he got the surname of Cato for his great abilities. The Romans call a man who is wise and prudent, *catus.*

As for his outward appearance, he had reddish hair, and keen grey eyes, as the author of the well-known epigram ill-naturedly gives us to understand:

> Red-haired, snapper and snarler, his grey eyes flashing defiance,
>
> Cato, come to Hades, will be thrust back by their Queen.[4]

His physical body—since he laboured from the very first with his own hands, held to a temperate way of life, and performed military duties—was very serviceable, vigorous, and healthy. His eloquence—a second body, as it were, and an instrument with which to perform not only necessary, but also high and noble services—he developed and perfected in the villages and towns about Rome. There he served as advocate for all who needed him, and got the reputation of being, first a zealous pleader, and then a capable orator. Thenceforth the weight and dignity of his character revealed themselves more and more to those who had dealings with him; they saw that he was bound to be a man of great affairs, and have a leading place in the state. For he not only gave his services in legal contests without fee of any sort, but did not appear to cherish even the reputation won in such contests. For he was more desirous of high reputation in battles and campaigns against the enemy, and while he was yet a mere youth had his breast covered with honourable wounds. He says himself that he made his first campaign when he was seventeen years old, at the time when Hannibal was consuming Italy with the flames of his successes.[5]

In battle, he showed himself effective in hand combat, sure and steadfast of foot, and with a fierce expression. With threatening speech and harsh cries he would advance upon the foe, for he rightly thought, and tried to show others, that often-times such action terrifies the enemy more than does the sword. On the march, he carried his own armour on foot, while a single servant followed in charge of his camp provisions. With this man, it is said, he was never angry, and never scolded him when he served up a meal; he actually assisted in most of such preparations, provided he was free from his military duties. Water was what he drank on his campaigns, except that once in a while, in a raging thirst, he would call for vinegar, or, when his strength was failing, would add a little wine.

Near his fields was the cottage which had once belonged to Manius Curius, a hero of three triumphs.[6] To this he would often go, and the sight of the small farm and the simple dwelling led him to think of their former owner, who, though he had become the greatest of the Romans, had subdued the most warlike nations, and driven Pyrrhus[7] out of Italy. Nevertheless, he tilled this little patch of ground with his own hands and occupied this cottage, after three triumphs. Here it was that the ambassadors of the Samnites once found him seated at his hearth cooking turnips, and offered him much gold; but he dismissed them, saying that a man whom such a meal satisfied had no need of gold, and for his part he thought that a more honourable thing than the possession of gold was the conquest of its possessors. Cato would go away with his mind full of these things, and on viewing again his own house and lands and servants and way of life, would increase the labours of his hands and reduce his extravagances.

• • •

The influence which Cato's oratory won for him increased, and men called him a Roman Demosthenes;[8] but his manner of life was even more talked about and carried abroad. For his oratorical ability set before young men not only a goal which many already were striving eagerly to attain, but a man who worked with his own hands, as his fathers did, and was contented with a cold breakfast, a frugal dinner, simple clothing, and

---

[3]Roman men normally had a first, second, and third name.

[4]That is, according to this writer, Cato is so ill-tempered that even the queen of the underworld will not admit him.

[5]Hannibal, pledged to undying hatred of Rome, was the most brilliant general of Carthage in its wars against Rome. His army devastated much of Italy, although he never succeeded in capturing Rome itself. The year was 217 B.C. when Cato fought against Hannibal's army.

[6]When a Roman general had won a great victory against foreign enemies, he was rewarded with a triumphal procession, by the authority of the Senate, at Rome. This elaborate celebration was the highest Roman military honor.

[7]A king of Epirus, northwest of Greece, distant cousin of Alexander the Great. Pyrrhus invaded Italy in 280 B.C.

[8]An Athenian (383–322 B.C.), the most famous Greek orator.

a humble dwelling—one who thought more of rejecting the extras of life than of possessing them. The Roman common wealth had now grown too large to keep its earlier integrity. The conquest of many kingdoms and peoples had brought a large mixture customs, and the adoption of ways of life of every sort. It was natural, therefore, that men should admire Cato, when they saw that, whereas other men were broken down by labors and weakened by pleasures, he was victor over both. And this too, not only while he was still young and ambitious, but even in his old age, after consulship[9] and triumph. Then, like some victorious athlete, he persisted in the regimen of his training, and kept his mind unaltered to the last.

He tells us that he never wore expensive clothing; that he drank the same wine as his slaves; that as for fish and meats, he would buy enough for his dinner from the public stalls—and even this for Rome's sake, that he might strengthen his body for military service. He once inherited an embroidered Babylonian robe, but sold it at once; not a single one of his farm-houses had plastered walls; he never paid much for a slave, since he did not want them to be delicately beautiful, but sturdy workers, such as grooms and herdsmen. And these he thought it his duty to sell when they got old, instead of feeding them when they were useless; and that in general, he thought nothing cheap that one could do without. He said also that he bought lands where crops were raised and cattle herded, not those where lawns were sprinkled and paths swept for pleasure.

These things were thought by some to be the result of the man's stinginess; but others excused them in the belief that he lived in this way only to correct and moderate the extravagance of others. However, for my part, I regard his treatment of his slaves like beasts of burden, using them to the utmost, and then, when they were old, driving them off and selling them, as the mark of a very mean nature, which recognizes no tie between man and man but that of profit. . . . A kindly man will take good care even of his horses when they are worn out with age, and of his dogs, too, not only in their puppyhood, but when their old age needs nursing. . . .

We should not treat living creatures like shoes or pots and pans, casting them aside when they are bruised and worn out with service; but, if for no other reason, than for the sake of practice in kindness to our fellow men, we should accustom ourselves to mildness and gentleness in our dealings with other creatures. I certainly would not sell even an ox that had worked for me, just because he was old, much less an elderly man, removing him from his habitual place and customary life, as it were from his native land, for a paltry price, useless as he is to those who sell him and as he will be to those who buy him. But which had carried him through his military campaign, that he might not tax the city with the cost of its transportation home. Whether these things should be set down to greatness of spirit or littleness of mind, is an open question.

But in other matters, his self-restraint was beyond measure admirable. For instance, when he was in command of an army, he took for himself and his staff not more than three bushels of wheat a month, and for his beasts of burden, less than a bushel and a half of barley a day. He received Sardinia to govern as his province; and whereas his predecessors used to charge the public treasury for their tents, couches, and clothing, . . . his simple economy stood out in an incredible contrast. He made no demands whatever upon the public treasury, and made his circuit of the cities on foot, followed by a single public office, who carried his robe and cup for libations to the gods. And yet, though in such matters he showed himself mild and lenient to those under his authority, in other ways he displayed a dignity and severity proper to the administration of justice. He carried out the edicts of the government in a direct and masterful way so that the Roman power never inspired its subjects with greater fear or affection.

•　　•　　•

He dealt with the Athenians through an interpreter. He could have spoken to them directly, but he always clung to his native ways, and mocked at those who were lost in admiration of anything that was Greek.

•　　•　　•

Ten years after his consulship, Cato was a candidate for the censorship. This office towered, as it were, above every other civic honour, and was, in a way, the high point of a political career. The variety of its powers was great,

[9]During the time of the Roman Republic, when Cato lived, two consuls were elected annually by the male citizens. They carried the judicial and military authority that had formerly been wielded by the kings. The Romans of that period even dated the years by the names of their consuls. (Cato was consul in 195 B.C.)

including that examining into the lives and manners of the citizens. Its creators thought that no one should be left to his own ways and desires, without inspection and review, either in his marrying, having children, ordering his daily life, or in the entertainment of his friends. Thinking that these things revealed a man's real character more than did his public and political career, they set men in office to watch, warn, and chastise, that no one should turn to vices and give up his native and customary way of life. They chose to this office one of the so-called patricians,[10] and one of the plebeians.[11] These officers were called censors, and they had authority to degrade a knight, or to expel a senator who led a wild and disorderly life. They also revised the assessments of property, and arranged the citizens in lists [for military service] according to their social and political classes. There were other great powers also connected with the office.

Therefore, when Cato became a candidate, nearly all the best known and most influential men of the senatorial party united to oppose him. The men of noble parentage among them were moved by jealousy, thinking that nobility of birth would be trampled if men of lowly origin forced their way up to the summits of honour and power; while those who were conscious of base practices and of a departure from ancestral customs, feared the severity of the man, which was sure to be harsh and unyielding in the exercise of power. Therefore, after due consultation and preparation, they put up in opposition to Cato seven candidates for the office, who sought the favour of the people with promises of mild conduct in office, supposing that they wanted to be ruled with a lax and indulgent hand. Cato, on the contrary, showed no inclination to be agreeable whatever, but plainly threatened wrongdoers in his speeches, and loudly cried that the city had need of a great purification. He urged the people, if they were wise, not to choose the most agreeable physician, but the one who was most in earnest. He himself, he said, was such a physician, and so was Valerius Flaccus, of the patricians. With him as colleague, and him alone, he thought he could cut the excessive luxury and effeminacy of the time. As for the rest of the candidates, he saw that they were all trying to force their way into the office in order to administer it badly, since they feared those who would administer it well. And so truly great were the Roman voters, and so worthy of great leaders, that they did not fear Cato's rigour and haughty independence, but rejected those candidates who, it was believed, would do every thing to please them, and elected Flaccus to the office along with Cato.[12]

• • •

As censor, Cato paid not the slightest heed to his accusers, but grew still more strict. He cut off the pipes by which people conveyed part of the public water supply into their private houses and gardens; he upset and demolished all buildings that encroached on public land; he reduced the cost of public works to the lowest, and forced the rent of public lands to the highest possible figure. All these things brought much hatred upon him. Titus Flamininus headed a party against him which induced the Senate to annul as useless the outlays and payments which he had authorised for temples and public works, and incited the boldest of the tribunes to call him to account before the people and fine him two talents. The Senate also strongly opposed the erection of the basilica [large rectangular public hall] which he built at the public cost below the council-house in the Forum, and which was called the Basilica Porcia.

Still, it appears that the people approved of his censorship to an amazing extent. At any rate, after erecting a statue to his honour in the temple of Health, they commemorated in the inscription upon it, not the military commands nor the triumph of Cato, but, as the inscription may be translated, the fact "that when the Roman state was tottering to its fall, he was made censor, and by helpful guidance, wise restraints and sound teachings, restored it again." . . .

He heaped high praise upon himself. He tells us that men of self-indulgent lives, when rebuked for it, used to say: "We ought not to be blamed; we are no Catos." Also that those who imitated some of his practices and did it clumsily, were called "left-handed Catos." Also that the Senate looked to him in the most dangerous crises as seafarers to their helmsman, and often, if he was not present, postponed its most serious business. These boasts of his are confirmed by other witnesses, for he had great authority in the city, alike for his life, his eloquence, and his age.

---

[10]Members of the Roman aristocratic, privileged class.
[11]The majority of citizens, like Cato, who were not patricians.
[12]In 184 B.C.

He was also a good father, a considerate husband, and a household manager of no little talent; nor did he give only a fitful attention to his, a matter of little or no importance. Therefore, I think I ought to give suitable instances of his conduct in these relations. He married a wife who was of higher birth than she was rich, thinking that, although the rich and the high-born may be alike given to pride, still, women of high birth have such a horror of what is disgraceful that they are more obedient to their husbands in all that is honourable. He used to say that the man who struck his wife or child, laid violent hands on the holiest of holy things. Also that he thought it more praiseworthy to be a good husband than a great senator, and there was nothing more to admire in Socrates of old than that he was always kind and gentle with his shrewish wife and stupid sons. After the birth of his own son, no business could be so urgent, unless it had a public character, as to prevent him from being present when his wife bathed and wrapped the babe. For the mother nursed it herself, and often gave her breast also to the infants of her slaves, that so they might come to cherish a brotherly affection for her son. As soon as the boy showed signs of understanding, his father took him under his own charge and taught him to read, although he had an accomplished slave, Chilo by name, who was a school-teacher, and taught many boys. Still, Cato thought it not right, as he tells us himself, that his son should be scolded by a slave, or have his ears tweaked when he was slow to learn, still less that he should be indebted to his slave for such a priceless thing as education. He was therefore himself not only the boy's reading-teacher, but his tutor in law, and his athletic trainer, and he taught his son not merely to hurl the javelin and fight in armour and ride the horse, but also to box, to endure heat and cold, and to swim strongly through the eddies and billows of the Tiber. His "History of Rome," as he tells us himself, he wrote out with his own hand and in large characters, that his son might have in his own home an aid to acquaintance with his country's ancient traditions. He declares that his son's presence put him on guard against making indecencies of speech as if in the presence of the Vestal Virgins,[13] and that he never bathed with him. This, indeed, would seem to have been a general taboo with the Romans, for even fathers-in-law avoided bathing with their sons-in-law, because they were ashamed to uncover their nakedness. Afterwards, however, when they had learned from the Greeks their freedom in going naked before men, they in their turn infected the Greeks with the practice of doing so even before women.

So Cato worked at the task of molding his son to virtue. But since his body was rather too frail to endure much hardship, he relaxed somewhat the excessive rigidity and austerity of his own way of life. But his son, although frail, made a sturdy soldier, and fought brilliantly under Aemilius Paulus in the battle against Perseus.[14] On that occasion his sword either was knocked from his hand or slipped from his moist grasp. Distressed by this mishap, he turned to some of his companions for aid, and supported by them rushed again into the thick of the enemy. After a long and furious struggle, he succeeded in clearing the place, and found the sword at last among the many heaps of arms and dead bodies where friends and foes alike lay piled upon one another. Paulus, his commander, admired the young man's exploit, and there is still in existence a letter written by Cato himself to his son, in which he heaps extravagant praise upon him for this honourable zeal in recovering his sword. The son afterwards married Tertia, a daughter of Paulus and a sister of Scipio the Younger;[15] his admission into such a family was due no less to himself than to his father. Thus Cato's careful attention to the education of his son bore worthy fruit.

He owned many slaves, and usually bought those prisoners of war who were young and still capable of being reared and trained. Not one of his slaves ever entered another man's house unless sent there by Cato or his wife, and when any of them was asked what Cato was doing, he always answered that he did not know. A slave of his was expected either to be busy about the house, or to be asleep, and he preferred the sleepy ones. He thought these gentler than the wakeful ones, and that those who had enjoyed the gift of sleep were better for any kind of service than those who lacked it. In the belief that his slaves were led into most mischief by their sexual passions, he required that the males should have sex with the female slaves of the house at a fixed price, but should never approach any other woman.

At the outset, when Cato was still poor and in military service, he found no fault at all with what was served up to him, declaring that it was shameful for a man to quarrel with a servant over food and drink. But afterwards, when his circumstances were improved and he used to entertain his friends and colleagues at table, no sooner was the

[13]The Vestals were virgin priestesses selected from noble families for terms of thirty years; they were expected to remain chaste and to tend the sacred fire in the temple of Vesta (Roman goddess of the family hearth).

[14]Aemilius Paulus was a consul who totally defeated Perseus, the last king of Macedonia, at the battle of Pydna in 168 B.C. Twenty years after that decisive battle, Macedonia became a Roman province.

[15]This Scipio was adopted into the distinguished family of Scipio Africanus, conqueror of Hannibal the Carthaginian general. Scipio the Younger later (146 B.C.) won the *final* victory for Rome against Carthage.

dinner over than he would flog those slaves who had been unsatisfactory in preparing or serving it. He was always arranging that his slaves should have feuds and disagreements among themselves; harmony among them made him suspicious and fearful of them. He had those who were suspected of some capital offence brought to trial before all their fellow servants, and, if convicted, put to death.

However, as he applied himself more strenuously to money-getting, he came to regard agriculture as more entertaining than profitable, and invested his money in business that was safe and sure. He bought ponds, hot springs, districts given over to fullers,[16] pitch factories, land with natural pasture and forest, all of which brought him large profits. He used to loan money also on ships, and his method was as follows. He required his borrowers to form a large company, and when there were fifty partners and as many ships for his security, he took one share in the company himself, and was represented by Quintio, a freedman of his, who accompanied his clients in all their ventures. In this way his entire security was not risked, but only a small part of it, and his profits were large. He used to lend money also to those of his slaves who wished it, and they would buy boys with it, and after training and teaching them for a year, at Cato's expense, would sell them again. Many of these boys Cato would retain for himself, counting to the credit of the slave the highest price bid for his boy by outsiders. He tried to persuade his son also to such investments, by saying that it was not the part of a man, but of a widow woman, to lessen his property. But surely Cato was going too far when he said that a man should be admired and glorified like a god if the final inventory of his property showed that he had added to it more than he had inherited.

When he was now well on in years, there came as delegates from Athens to Rome, Carneades the Academic, and Diogenes the Stoic philosopher,[17] to beg the reversal of a certain decision against the Athenian people, which imposed upon them a heavy fine. Upon the arrival of these philosophers, the most studious of the city's youth hastened to wait upon them, and became their devoted and admiring listeners. The charm of Carneades especially, which had boundless power, and a fame not inferior to its power, won large and sympathetic audiences and filled the city, like a rushing mighty wind, with the noise of his praises. Report spread far and wide that a Greek of amazing talent who disarmed all opposition by the magic of his eloquence, had infused a tremendous passion into the youth of the city— in consequence of which they gave up their other pleasures and pursuits and were "possessed" about philosophy. The other Romans were pleased at this and glad to see their young men lay hold of Greek culture and associate with such admirable men. But Cato, at the very outset, when this zeal for discussion came into the city, was distressed—fearing that the young men, by giving this direction to their ambition, should come to love a reputation based on mere words more than one achieved by military deeds. And when the fame of the visiting philosophers rose yet higher in the city, and their first speeches before the Senate were interpreted, at his own instance and request, by so conspicuous a man as Gaius Acilius, Cato determined, on some excuse or other, to rid the city of them all. So he rose in the Senate and condemned the city officials for keeping for so long a time a delegation composed of men who could easily secure anything they wished, so persuasive were they, "We ought," he said, "to make up our minds one way or another, and vote on what the delegation proposes, in order that these men may return to their schools and lecture to the sons of Greece, while the youth of Rome give ear to their laws and officials, as before."

This he did, not, as some think, out of personal hostility to Carneades, but because he was wholly opposed to philosophy, and made mock of all Greek culture and training, out of patriotic Roman zeal. He says, for instance, that Socrates was a mighty talker, who attempted, as best he could, to be his country's tyrant, by abolishing its customs, and by enticing his fellow citizens into opinions contrary to the laws. He made fun of the school of Isocrates,[18] declaring that his pupils kept on studying with him till they were old men, as if they were to practise their arts and plead their cases before Minos[19] in Hades. And seeking to prejudice his son against Greek culture, he declared, in the tone of a prophet or a seer, that Rome would lose her empire when she had become infected with Greek literature. But time has certainly shown the emptiness of this pessimistic declaration, for while the city was at the height of its empire, she made every form of Greek learning and culture her own.

It was not only Greek philosophers that he hated, but he was also suspicious of Greeks who practised medicine at Rome. He had heard, it would seem, of Hippocrates'[20] reply when the Great King of Persia sent for him, with the

---

[16]Fuller's earth is an absorbent clay, used especially for removing grease from fabrics, as a filter, and as a dusting powder.

[17]This visit in 155 B.C. became quite famous as it drew the attention of many Romans to the Greek schools of philosophy. Carneades was called "the Academic" because he was head of the Academy founded by Plato. (See introduction to selection 10.) Diogenes was the head of the Stoic school of philosophy.

[18]A student of Socrates (see selections 8 and 9) and a famous orator, who established his own school in Athens.

[19]In Greco-Roman mythology, the judge of dead souls in the underworld.

[20]A famous Greek physician of the fifth century B.C.

promise of a large fee, that he would never put his skill at the service of non-Greeks who were enemies of Greece. He said all Greek physicians had taken a similar oath, and urged his son to beware of them all. He himself, he said, had written a book of recipes, which he followed in the treatment of any who were sick in his family. He never required his patients to fast, but fed them on greens, or bits of duck, pigeon, or hare. Such a diet, he said, was light and good for sick people, except that it often causes dreams. By following such treatment he said he had good health himself, and kept his family in good health.

•   •   •

The last of his public services is supposed to have been the destruction of Carthage.[21] It was Scipio the Younger who actually brought the task to completion, but it was largely in consequence of the advice and counsel of Cato that the Romans undertook the war. Cato first became involved when sent on a mission to the Carthaginians and Masinissa the Numidian,[22] who were at war with one another, to inquire into the grounds of their quarrel. Masinissa had been a friend of the Roman people from the first, and the Carthaginians had entered into treaty relations with Rome only after the defeat which the elder Scipio [Africanus] had given them. The treaty deprived them of their empire, and imposed a heavy money tribute upon them. Cato, however, found the city by no means in a poor and lowly state, as the Romans supposed, but rather teeming with vigorous fighting men overflowing with enormous wealth, filled with arms of every sort and with military supplies, and not a little puffed up by all this. He therefore thought it no time for the Romans to be straightening out the affairs of Masinissa and the Numidians, but that they should repress the power of Carthage, which was becoming once again a deadly danger. Accordingly, he returned speedily to Rome, and advised the Senate that the former defeats of the Carthaginians had diminished not so much their power as their foolhardiness, and were likely to make them in the end not weaker, but more expert in war. He declared that their present contest with Numidia was but a prelude to a contest with Rome, while peace and treaty were mere names wherewith to cover their postponement of war till a proper occasion arose.

In addition to this, it is said that Cato purposely dropped an African fig in the Senate, as he shook out the folds of his toga; and then, as the senators admired its size and beauty, he said that the country where it grew was only three days' sail from Rome. And in one thing he was even more savage, namely, in adding to any speech of his whatsoever these words: "And, in my opinion, Carthage must be destroyed." . . . He saw, probably, that the Roman public, in its recklessness, was already guilty of many excesses—and in the pride of its prosperity, spurned the control of the Senate, and dragged the whole state with it, wherever its mad desires led it. He wished, therefore, that the fear of Carthage should continue to curb the public, like a bridle, believing Carthage not strong enough to conquer Rome, nor yet weak enough to be despised. What Cato dreaded was that the Roman people, sunk in their follies and excesses, faced a growing and sober external power that had always threatened them. That power ought to be done away with altogether, he thought, so that the Romans might be free to concentrate on a cure for their internal failings.

In this way Cato is said to have brought to pass the third and last war against Carthage. . . .

---

[21]The powerful city on the African coast that rivalled Rome for control of the Mediterranean world. The Roman Republic fought three major wars against Carthage, ending in its capture and total destruction by Scipio the Younger in 146 B.C., three years after Cato's death.
[22]Numidia was a country of the African nomads lying immediately west and south of Carthage. Masinissa was the head of one of their tribal alliances.

Suetonius

THE LIVES OF THE TWELVE CAESARS: AUGUSTUS

*Little is known about Gaius Suetonius Tranquillus, better known today as Suetonius (ca. A.D. 69-ca. 130?). A native of the Roman province of Africa, Suetonius was born into an equestrian family (the **equites**, who comprised the second tier of the Roman elite under the senatorial class) and his father served as a staff officer in the Roman army. Suetonius was educated in Rome and served in several high ranking administrative posts in the imperial bureaucracy. This gave him extraordinary access to the imperial archives as primary sources for his imperial biographies and other literary works.*

*Suetonius was a prolific writer judging from the number of his works known from their titles, although many of these have subsequently been lost. His most important work was **The Twelve Caesars**, probably published about 120. This collection of imperial biographies begins with Julius Caesar and extends through each of his successors, ending with Domitian (reigned A.D. 81-96). Each of these biographies follows a fairly predictable but not strictly chronological model, beginning with an account of the ancestry and early life of the future emperor up to the beginning of his reign. But Suetonius approaches the reign itself from a thematic rather than a chronological perspective, usually employing anecdotes to illustrate the general characteristics of each ruler. Although he sometimes employs precious primary sources (such as personal letters) he also often reproduces sensational and lurid details about an emperor's personal life, such as his alleged sexual proclivities, that may have been little more than rumors.*

The excerpt presented here is drawn from the biography of Octavian, later styled Augustus (63 B.C. - A.D. 14), who was the first emperor of Rome and arguably the single most important individual in Roman history. Although the biography contains much key evidence, its value is limited in some ways by Suetonius' organization of his material as described above. For example, it is difficult at times to place specific actions or events within a narrow chronological timeframe over the forty-four year reign of Augustus (30 B.C. – A.D.14), longer than any other emperor. Despite these shortcomings, Suetonius still presents a picture of a cunning political leader who, although at times completely ruthless, brought back peace, prosperity, and rule of law to a Roman world that had experienced increasing political disorder and several bouts of civil was during the death throes of the Republic.

He lost his father when he was only four years of age; and, in his twelfth year, pronounced a funeral oration in praise of his grandmother Julia. Four years afterwards, having assumed the robe of manhood, he was honoured with several military rewards by Caesar in his African triumph, although he took no part in the war on account of his youth. Upon his uncle's[1] expedition to Spain against the sons of Pompey, he was followed by his nephew, although he was scarcely recovered from a dangerous sickness: and after being shipwrecked at sea, and travelling with very few attendants through roads that were infested with the enemy, he at last came up with him. This activity gave great

[1] His "uncle" was Julius Caesar (actually, his great-uncle)

satisfaction to his uncle, who soon conceived an increasing affection for him, on account of such indications of character. After the subjugation of Spain, while Caesar was planning an expedition against the Dacians and Parthians, he was sent before him to Apollonia, where he applied himself to his studies; until receiving intelligence that his uncle was murdered, and that he was appointed his heir, he hesitated for some time whether he should call to his and the legions stationed in the neighbourhood, but he abandoned the design as rash and premature. However, returning to Rome, he took possession of his inheritance. Although his mother was apprehensive that such a measure might be attended with danger, and his step-father, Marcius Philippus, a man of consular rank, very earnestly dissuaded him from it. From this time, collecting together a strong military force, he first held the government in conjunction with Mark Antony and Marcus Lepidus, then with Antony only for nearly twelve years, and at last in his own hands during a period of four and forty.

Having thus given a very short summary of his life, I shall prosecute the several parts of it, not in order of time, but arranging his acts into distinct classes, for the sake of perspicuity. He was engaged in five civil wars, namely those of Modena, Philippi, Perugia, Sicily, and Actium; the first and last of which were against Antony, and the second against Brutus and Cassius; the third against Lucius Antonius, the triumvir's brother, and the fourth against Sextus Pompeius, the son of Gnaeus Pompeius.

The motive which gave rise to all these wars was the opinion he entertained that both his honour and interest were concerned in revenging the murder of his uncle, and maintaining the state of affairs he had established.

•   •   •

The alliance between him and Antony, which had always been precarious, often interrupted, and ill cemented by repeated reconciliations, he at last entirely dissolved. And to make it known to the world how far Antony had degenerated from patriotic feelings, he caused a will of his, which had been left at Rome, and in which he had nominated Cleopatra's children, amongst others, as his heirs, to be opened and read in an assembly of the people . . . And not long afterwards he defeated him in a naval engagement near Actium, which was prolonged to so late an hour, that, after the victory, he was obliged to sleep on board his ship.

From Actium he went to the isle of Samos to winter, but being alarmed with the accounts of a mutiny amongst the soldiers he had selected from the main body of his army sent to Brundisium after the victory, who insisted on their being rewarded for their service and discharged, he returned to Italy. . . .

He remained only twenty-seven days at Brundisium, until the demands of the soldiers were settled, and then went, by way of Asia[2] and Syria, to Egypt, where laying siege to Alexandria, whether Antony had fled with Cleopatra, he made himself master of it in a short time. He drove Antony to kill himself, after he had used every effort to obtain conditions of peace, and he saw his corpse. Cleopatra he anxiously wished to save for his triumph; and when she was supposed to have been bit to death by an asp, he sent for the Psylli to endeavor to suck out the poison. He allowed them to be buried together in the same grave, and ordered a mausoleum, begun by themselves, to be completed. The eldest of Antony's two sons by Fulvia he commanded to be taken by force from the statue of Julius Caesar, to which he had fled, after many fruitless supplications for his life, and put him to death. The same fate attended Caesarion, Cleopatra's son by Caesar, as he pretended, who had fled for his life, but was retaken. The children which Antony had by Cleopatra he saved, and brought up and cherished in a manner suitable to their rank, just as if they had been his own relations.

•   •   •

He conducted in person only two foreign wars; the Dalmatian, whilst he was yet but a youth; and, after Antony's final defeat, the Cantabrian. He was wounded in the former of these wars; in one battle he received a contusion in the right knee from a stone—and in another, he was much hurt in one leg and both arms, by the fall of a bridge. His other wars he carried on by his lieutenants; but occasionally visited the army, in some of the wars of Pannonia and Germany, or remained at no great distance, proceeding from Rome as far as Ravenna, Milan, or Aquileia.

He conquered, however, partly in person, and partly by his lieutenants, Cantabria, Aquitania and Pannonia, Dalmatia, with all Illyricum and Rhaetia, besides the two Alpine nations, the Vindelici and the Salassii. He also checked the incursions of the Dacians, by cutting off three of their generals with vast armies, and drove the Germans

---

[2]The Roman province located in the western portion of Asia Minor

beyond the river Elbe; removing two other tribes who submitted, the Ubii and Sicambri, into Gaul, and settling them in the country bordering on the Rhine. Other nations also, which broke into revolt, he reduced to submission. But he never made war upon any nation without just and necessary cause; and was so far from being ambitious either to extend the empire, or advance his own military glory, that he obliged the chiefs of some barbarous tribes to swear in the temple of Mars the Avenger, that they would faithfully observe their engagements, and not violate the peace which they had implored. Of some he demanded a new description of hostages, their women, having found from experience that they cared little for their men when given as hostages; but he always afforded them the means of getting back their hostages whenever they wished it.

Even those who engaged most frequently and with the greatest perfidy in their rebellion, he never punished more severely than by selling their captives, on the terms of their not serving in any neighbouring country, nor being released from their slavery before the expiration of thirty years. By the character which he thus acquired, for virtue and moderation, he induced even the Indians and Scythians,[3] nations before known to the Romans by report only, to solicit his friendship, and that of the Roman people, by ambassadors. The Parthians[4] readily allowed his claim to Armenia; restoring at his demand, the standards which they had taken from Marcus Crassus and Mark Antony, and offering him hostages besides. Afterwards, when a contest arose between several pretenders to the crown of that kingdom, they refused to acknowledge any one who was not chosen by him.

•   •   •

In military affairs he made many alterations, introducing some practices entirely new, and reviving others, which had become obsolete. He maintained the strictest discipline among the troops; and would not allow even his lieutenants the liberty to visit their wives, except reluctantly, and in the winter season only. A Roman knight having cut off the thumbs of his two young sons, to render them in-capable of serving in the wars, he exposed both him and his estate to public sale. But upon observing the farmers of the revenue very greedy for the purchase, he assigned him to a freedman of his own, that he might send him into the country, and suffer him to retain his freedom. The tenth legion becoming mutinous, he disbanded it with ignominy; and did the same by some others which petulantly demanded their discharge; withholding from them the rewards usually bestowed on those who had served their stated time in the wars. The cohorts which yielded their ground in time of action, he decimated, and fed with barley. Centurions, as well as common sentinels, who deserted their posts when on guard, he punished with death. For other misdemeanors he inflicted upon them various kinds of disgrace; such as obliging them to stand all day before the praetorium, sometimes in their tunics only, and without their belts, sometimes to carry poles ten feet long, or sods of turf.

•   •   •

He twice entertained thoughts of restoring the republic; first, immediately after he had crushed Antony, remembering that he had often charged him with being the obstacle to its restoration. The second was in consequence of a long illness, when he sent for the magistrates and the senate to his own house, and delivered them particular account of the state of the empire. But reflecting at the same time that it would be both hazardous to himself to return to the condition of a private person, and might be dangerous to the public to have the government placed again under the control of the people, he resolved to keep it in his own hands, whether with the better event or intention, is hard to say. His good intentions he often affirmed in private discourse, and also published an edict, in which it was declared in the following terms: "May it be permitted me to have the happiness of establishing the commonwealth on a safe and sound basis, and thus enjoy the reward of which I am ambitious, that of being celebrated for moulding it into the form best adapted to present circumstances; so that, on my leaving the world, I may carry with me the hope that the foundations which I have laid for its future government, will stand firm and stable."

The city, which was not built in a manner suitable to the grandeur to the empire, and was liable to inundations of the Tiber, as well as to fires, was so much improved under his administration, that he boasted, not without reason, that he "found it of brick, but left it of marble." He also rendered it secure for the time to come against such disasters, as far as could be effected by human foresight.

[3]Inhabitants of an area now called the Ukraine.
[4]Successors to the ancient Persians.

A great number of public buildings were erected by him, the most considerable of which were a forum, containing the temple of Mars the Avenger, the temple of Apollo on the Palatine hill, and the temple of Jupiter Tonans in the capitol. The reason of his building a new forum was the vast increase in the population, and the number of causes to be tried in the courts, for which, the two already existing not affording sufficient space, it was thought necessary to have a third. It was therefore opened for public use before the temple of Mars was completely finished; and a law was passed, that causes should be tried, and judges chosen by lot, in that place. The temple of Mars was built in fulfilment of a vow made during the war of Philippi, undertaken by him to avenge his father's murder. He ordained that the senate should always assemble there when they met to deliberate respecting wars and triumphs; that thence should be despatched all those who were sent into the provinces in the command of armies; and that in it those who returned victorious from the wars, should lodge the trophies of their triumphs. He erected the temple of Apollo in that part of his house on the Palatine hill which had been struck with lightning, and which, on that account, the soothsayers declared the God to have chosen. He added porticos to it, with a library of Latin and Greek authors; and when advanced in years, used frequently there to hold the senate, and examine the rolls of the judges.

He dedicated the temple to Apollo Tonans, in acknowledgment of his escape from a great danger in his Cantabrian expedition; when, as he was travelling in the night, his litter was struck by lightning, which killed the slave who carried a torch before him. He likewise constructed some public buildings in the name of others; for instance, his grandsons, his wife, and sister. Thus he built the portico and basilica of Lucius and Caius, and the porticos of Livia and Octavia, and the theatre of Marcellus. He also often exhorted other persons of rank to embellish the city by new buildings, or repairing and improving the old, according to their means. In consequence of this recommendation, many were raised; such as the temple of Hercules and the Muses, by Marcius Philippus; a temple of Diana by Lucius Cornificius; the Court of Freedom by Asinius Pollio; a temple of Saturn by Munatius Plancus; a theatre by Cornelius Balbus; an amphitheatre by Statilius Taurus; and several other noble edifices by Marcus Agrippa.

He divided the city into regions and districts, ordaining that the annual magistrates should take by lot the charge of the former; and that the latter should be superintended by wardens chosen out of the people of each neighbourhood. He appointed a nightly watch to be on their guard against accidents from fire; and, to prevent the frequent inundations, he widened and cleansed the bed of the Tiber, which had in the course of years been almost dammed up with rubbish, and the channel narrowed by the ruins of houses. To render the approaches to the city more commodious, he took upon himself the charge of repairing the Flaminian way as far as Ariminum, and distributed the repairs of the other roads amongst several persons who had obtained the honour of a triumph; to be defrayed out of the money arising from the spoils of war. Temples decayed by time, or destroyed by fire, he either repaired or rebuilt; and enriched them, as well as many others, with splendid offerings. On a single occasion, he deposited in the cell of the temple of Jupiter Capitolinus, sixteen thousand pounds of gold, with jewels and pearls to the amount of fifty millions of sesterces.

• • •

He restored the calendar, which had been corrected by Julius Caesar, but through negligence had again fallen into confusion, to its former regularity; and upon that occasion called the month Sextilis by his own name, August, rather than September, in which he was born; because in it he had obtained his first consulship, and all his most considerable victories. He increased the number, dignity, and revenues of the priests, and especially those of the Vestal Virgins.[5] And when, upon the death of one of them, a new one was to be taken, and many persons made interest that their daughters' names might be omitted in the lists for election, he replied with an oath, "If either of my own grand-daughters were old enough, I would have proposed her."

He likewise revived some old religious customs, which had become obsolete; as the augury of public health, the office of high priest of Jupiter, the religious solemnity of the Lupercalia, with the Secular, and Compitalian games. He prohibited young boys from running in the Lupercalia; and in respect of the Secular games, issued an order, that no young persons of either sex should appear at any public diversions in the night-time, unless in the company of some elderly relation. He ordered the household gods to be decked twice a year with spring and summer flowers, in the Compitalian festival.

Next to the immortal gods, he paid the highest honours to the memory of those generals who had raised the Roman state from its low origin to the highest pitch of grandeur. He accordingly repaired or rebuilt the public edifices

---

[5]Selected young women who devoted their lives to attending the flame in the temple of Vesta (goddess of the family hearth).

erected by them; preserving the former inscriptions, and placing statues of them all, with triumphal emblems, in both the porticos of his forum, issuing an edict on the occasion, in which he made the following declaration: "My design in so doing is, that the Roman people may require from me, and all succeeding princes, a conformity to those illustrious examples." He likewise removed the statue of Pompey from the senate-house, in which Caius Caesar had been killed, and placed it under a marble arch, fronting the palace attached to Pompey's theatre.

He corrected many ill practices, which, to the detriment of the public, had either survived the licentious habits of the late civil wars, or else originated in the long peace. Bands of robbers showed themselves openly, completely armed, under colour of self-defence; and in different parts of the country, travellers, freemen and slaves without distinction, were forcibly carried off, and kept to work in the houses of correction. Several associations were formed under the specious name of a new college, which banded together for the perpetration of all kinds of villany. The bandits he quelled by establishing posts of soldiers in suitable stations for the purpose; the houses of correction were subjected to a strict superintendance; all associations, those only excepted which were of ancient standing, and recognised by the laws, were dissolved.

He burnt all the notes of those who had been a long time in arrear with the treasury, as being the principal source of vexatious suits and prosecutions. Places in the city claimed by the public, where the right was doubtful, he adjudged to the actual possessors. He struck out of the list of criminals the names of those over whom prosecutions had been long impending, where nothing further was intended by the informers than to gratify their own malice, by seeing their enemies humiliated; laying it down as a rule, that if any one chose to renew a prosecution, he should incur the risk of the punishment which he sought to inflict. And that crimes might not escape punishment, nor business be neglected by delay, he ordered the courts to sit during the thirty days which were spent in celebrating honorary games. . . .

He was himself assiduous in his functions as a judge, and would sometimes prolong his sittings even into the night: if he were in disposed, his litter[6] was placed before the tribunal, or he administered justice reclining on his couch at home; displaying always not only the greatest attention, but extreme leniency. To save a culprit, who evidently appeared guilty of parricide, from the extreme penalty of being sewn up in a sack, because none were punished in that manner but such as confessed the fact, he is said to have interrogated him thus: "Surely you did not kill your father, did you?" And when, in a trial of a case about a forged will, all those who had signed it were liable to the penalty of the Cornelian law, he ordered that his colleagues on the tribunal should not only be furnished with the two tablets by which they decided, "guilty or not guilty," but with a third likewise, ignoring the offence of those who should appear to have given their signatures through any deception or mistake. All appeals in cases between inhabitants of Rome, he assigned every year to the praetor of the city; and where provincials were concerned, to men of consular rank, to one of whom the business of each province was referred.

Some laws he abrogated, and he made some new ones; such as the sumptuary law, that relating to adultery and the violation of chastity, the law against bribery in elections, and likewise that for the encouragement of marriage. Having been more severe in his reform of this law than the rest, he found the people utterly averse to submit to it, unless the penalties were abolished or mitigated, besides allowing an interval of three years after a wife's death, and increasing the premiums on marriage. . . . But finding that the force of the law was eluded by marrying girls under the age of puberty and by frequent change of wives, he limited the time for consummation after espousals, and imposed restrictions on divorce.

By two separate scrutinies[7] he reduced to their former number and splendour the senate, which had been swamped by a disorderly crowd; for they were now more than a thousand and some of them very mean persons, who, after Caesar's death, had been chosen by dint of interest and bribery, so that they had the nickname of Orcini among the people. The first of these scrutinies was left to themselves, each senator naming another; but the last was conducted by himself and Agrippa. On this occasion he is believed to have taken his seat as he presided, with a coat of mail under his tunic, and a sword by his side, and with ten of the stoutest men of senatorial rank, who were his friends, standing round his chair. Cordus Cremutius relates that no senator was suffered to approach him, except singly, and after having his bosom searched {for secreted daggers}. Some he obliged to have the grace of declining

---

[6]A portable couch.
[7]Reviews of the senate membership.

the office; these he allowed to retain the privileges of wearing the distinguishing dress, occupying the seats at the solemn spectacles, and of feasting publicly, reserved to the senatorial order.

That those who were chosen and approved of, might perform their functions under more solemn obligations, and with less inconvenience, he ordered that every senator, before he took his seat in the house, should pay his devotions, with an offering of frankincense and wine, at the altar of that God in whose temple the senate then assembled, and that their stated meetings, should be only twice in the month, namely, on the calends and ides;[8] and that in the months of September and October, a certain number only, chosen by lot, such as the law required to give validity to a decree, should be required to attend. For himself, he resolved to choose every six months a new council, with whom he might consult previously upon such affairs as he judged proper at any time to lay before the full senate. He also took the votes of the senators upon any subject of importance, not according to custom, nor in regular order, but as he pleased; that every one might hold himself ready to give his opinion, rather than a mere vote of assent.

• • •

Having thus regulated the city and its concerns, he augmented the population of Italy by planting in it no less than twenty-eight colonies, and greatly improved it by public works, and a beneficial application of the revenues. In rights and privileges, he rendered it in a measure equal to the city itself, by inventing a new kind of suffrage, which the principal officers and magistrates of the colonies might take at home, and forward under seal to the city, against the time of the elections. To increase the number of persons of condition, and of children among the lower ranks, he granted the petitions of all those who requested the honour of doing military service on horseback as knights, provided their demands were seconded by the recommendation of the town in which they lived; and when he visited the several districts of Italy, he distributed a thousand sesterces a head to such of the lower class as presented him with sons or daughters.

The more important provinces, which could not with ease or safety be entrusted to the government of annual magistrates, he reserved for his own administration: the rest he distributed by lot amongst the proconsuls: but sometimes he made exchanges, and frequently visited most of both kinds in person. Some cities in alliance with Rome, but which by their great licentiousness were hastening to ruin, he deprived of their independence. Others, which were much in debt, he relieved, and rebuilt such as had been destroyed by earthquakes. To those that could produce any instance of their having deserved well of the Roman people, he presented the freedom of Latium, or even that of the City. There is not, I believe, a province, except Africa and Sardinia, which he did not visit. . . .

Kingdoms, of which he had made himself master by the right of conquest, a few only excepted, he either restored to their former possessors, or conferred upon aliens. Between kings in alliance with Rome, he encouraged most intimate union; being always ready to promote or favour any proposal of marriage or friendship amongst them; and, indeed, treated them all with the same consideration, as if they were members and parts of the empire. To such of them as were minors or lunatics he appointed guardians, until they arrived at age, or recovered their senses; and the sons of many of them he brought up and educated with his own.

With respect to the army, he distributed the legions and auxiliary troops throughout the several provinces. He stationed a fleet at Misenum, and another at Ravenna, for the protection of the Upper and Lower Seas. A certain number of the forces were selected, to occupy the posts in the city, and partly for his own body-guard; but he dismissed the Spanish guard, which he retained about him till the fall of Antony; and also the Germans, whom he had amongst his guards, until the defeat of Varus. Yet he never permitted a greater force than three cohorts[9] in the city, and had no (praetorian) camps.[10] The rest he quartered in the neighbourhood of the nearest towns, in winter and summer camps.

All the troops throughout the empire he reduced to one fixed model with regard to their pay and their pensions; determining these according to their rank in the army, the time they had served, and their private means; so that after their discharge, they might not be tempted by age or necessities to join the agitators for a revolution. For the purpose of providing a fund always ready to meet their pay and pensions, he instituted a military exchequer, and appropriated new taxes to that object. In order to obtain the earliest intelligence of what was passing in the provinces, he established posts, consisting at first of young men stationed at moderate distances along the military roads, and afterwards of regular couriers with fast vehicles; which appeared to him the most commodious, because

[8]The first and the middle days of the month.
[9]Each cohort, a subdivision of a Roman "legion," included about 500 men.
[10]Praetorian troops were special guards for the chief magistrate of the city.

the persons who were the bearers of dispatches, written on the spot, might then be questioned about the business, as occasion occurred.

•   •   •

He always abhorred the title of *Lord*, as ill-omened and offensive. And when, in a play, performed at the theatre, at which he was present, these words were introduced, "O just and gracious lord," and the whole company, with joyful acclamations, testified their approbation of them, as applied to him, he instantly put a stop to their indecent flattery, by waving his hand, and frowning sternly, and the next day publicly declared his displeasure, in a proclamation. He never afterwards would suffer himself to be addressed in that manner, even by his own children or grand-children, either in jest or earnest and forbad them the use of all such complimentary expressions to one another.

He rarely entered any city or town, or departed from it, except in the evening or the night, to avoid giving any person the trouble of complimenting him. During his consulships, he commonly walked the streets on foot; but at other times, rode in a closed carriage. He admitted to court even plebeians, in common with people of the higher ranks; receiving the petitions of those who approached him with so much affability, that he once jocosely rebuked a man, by telling him, "You present your memorial with as much hesitation as if you were offering money to an elephant." On senate days, he used to pay his respects to the Conscript Fathers[11] only in the house, addressing them each by name as they sat, without any prompter; and on his departure, he bade each of them farewell, while they retained their seats. In the same manner, he maintained with many of them a constant intercourse of mutual civilities, giving them his company upon occasions of any particular festivity in their families; until he became advanced in years, and was incommoded by the crowd at a wedding.

•   •   •

How much he was beloved for his worthy conduct in all these respects, it is easy to imagine. I say nothing of the decrees of the senate in his honour, which may seem to have resulted from compulsion or deference. The Roman knights[12] voluntarily, and with one accord, always celebrated his birth for two days together; and all ranks of the people, yearly, in performance of a vow they had made, threw a piece of money into the Curtian lake, as an offering for his welfare. They likewise, on the calends [first] of January, presented for his acceptance new-year's gifts in the capitol, though he was not present: with which donations he purchased some costly images of the Gods, which he erected in several streets of the city; as that of Apollo Sandaliarius, Jupiter Tragoedus, and others.

When his house on the Palatine hill was accidentally destroyed by fire, the veteran soldiers, the judges, the tribes, and even the people, individually, contributed, according to the ability of each, for rebuilding it; but he would accept only of some small portion out of the several sums collected, and refused to take from any one person more than a single denarius. Upon his return home from any of the provinces, they attended him not only with joyful acclamations, but with songs. It is also remarked, that as often as he entered the city, the infliction of punishment was suspended for the time.

The whole body of the people, upon a sudden impulse, and with unanimous consent, offered him the title of Father of His Country. It was announced to him first at Antium, by a deputation from the people, and upon his declining the honour, they repeated their offer on his return to Rome, in a full theatre, when they were crowned with laurel. The senate soon afterwards adopted the proposal.

•   •   •

Having thus given an account of the manner in which he filled his public offices both civil and military, and his conduct in the government of the empire, both in peace and war; I shall now describe his private and domestic life.

•   •   •

He ate sparingly (for I must not omit even this), and commonly used a plain diet. He was particularly fond of coarse bread, small fishes, new cheese made of cow's milk, and green figs of the sort which bear fruit twice a year. He did not wait for supper, but took food at any time, and in any place, when he had an appetite. The following

---

[11]The senate.

[12]A class of wealthy citizens, next below the senatorial class in political influence. Originally a cavalry corps.

passages relative to this subject, I have transcribed from his letters. "I ate a little bread and some small dates, in my carriage." Again. "In returning home from the palace in my litter, I ate an ounce of bread, and a few raisins." Again. "No Jew, my dear Tiberius, ever keeps such strict fast upon the Sabbath, as I have to-day; for while in the bath, and after the first hour of the night, I only ate two biscuits, before I began to be rubbed with oil." From this great indifference about his diet, he sometimes supped by himself, before his company began, or after they had finished, and would not touch a morsel at table with his guests.

He was by nature extremely sparing in the use of wine. Cornelius Nepos says that he used to drink only three times at supper in the camp at Modena; and when he indulged himself the most, he never exceeded a pint; or if he did, his stomach rejected it. Of all wines, he gave the preference to the Rhaetian,[13] but scarcely ever drank any in the day-time. Instead of drinking, he used to take a piece of bread dipped in cold water, or a slice of cucumber, or some leaves of lettuce, or a green, sharp, juicy apple.

After a slight repast at noon, he used to seek repose, dressed as he was, and with his shoes on, his feet covered, and his hand held before his eyes. After supper he commonly withdrew to his study, a small closet, where he sat late, until he had put down in his diary all or most of the remaining transactions of the day, which he had not before registered. He would then go to bed, but never slept above seven hours at most, and that not without interruption; for he would wake three or four times during that time. If he could not again fall asleep, as sometimes happened, he called for some one to read or tell stories to him, until he became drowsy, and then his sleep was usually protracted till after day-break. He never liked to lie awake in the dark, without somebody to sit by him. Very early rising was apt to disagree with him. On which account, if he was sometimes obliged to rise, for any civil or religious functions, in order to guard as much as possible against the inconvenience resulting from it, he used to lodge in some apartment near the spot, belonging to any of his attendants. If at any time a fit of drowsiness seized him in passing along the streets, his litter was set down while he snatched a few moments' sleep.

In person he was handsome and graceful, through every period of his life. But he was negligent in his dress; and so careless about dressing his hair, that he usually had it done in great haste by several barbers at a time. His beard he sometimes clipped, and sometimes shaved; and either read or wrote during the operation. His countenance, either when discoursing or silent, was so calm and serene that a Gaul of the first rank declared amongst his friends that he was so softened by it, as to be restrained from throwing him down a precipice, in his passage over the Alps, when he had been admitted to approach him, under pretence of conferring with him. His eyes were bright and piercing; and he was willing it should be thought that there was something of a divine vigour in them. He was likewise not a little pleased to see people, upon his looking steadfastly at them, lower their countenances, as if the sun shone in their eyes. But in his old age, he saw very imperfectly with his left eye. His teeth were thin set, small and scaly, his hair a little curled, and inclining to a yellow colour. His eye-brows met; his ears were small, and he had an aquiline nose. His complexion was betwixt brown and fair; his stature but low; though Julius Marathus, his freedman, says he was five feet and nine inches in height. This, however, was so much concealed by the just proportion of his limbs, that it was only perceivable upon comparison with some taller person standing by him.

He is said to have been born with many spots upon his breast and belly, answering to the figure, order, and number of the stars in the constellation of the Bear. He had besides several callosities resembling scars, occasioned by an itching in his body, and the constant and violent use of the strigil in being rubbed. He had a weakness in his left hip, thigh, and leg, insomuch that he often halted on that side; but he received much benefit from the use of sand and reeds. He likewise sometimes found the fore-finger of his right hand so weak that, when it was benumbed and contracted with cold, to use it in writing he was obliged to have recourse to a circular piece of horn. He had occasionally a complaint in the bladder; but upon voiding some stones in his urine, he was relieved from that pain.

[13]Rhaetia was a Roman province that included areas now part of Switzerland and Austria.

Lucretius

ON THE NATURE OF THINGS

Western philosophy originated with the Greeks of the Ionian School in the sixth century B.C. These philosophers observed and then speculated about the world and the cosmos. Their most important contribution was the search for natural causation, i.e., to propose natural rather than supernatural or mythical explanations for their world. The great classical philosophers of fifth and fourth century B.C. Athens (e.g., Socrates, Plato, and Aristotle) shifted their focus to human societies, especially ethics and morality. Greek philosophy continued to develop in the Hellenistic era (323–30 B.C.). Athens remained the center of philosophy as it witnessed the emergence of several new philosophies.

One of these was Epicureanism, so-named from its founder Epicurus (341-270 B.C.), a native of Samos but who taught in Athens. This philosophy was based on the "atomic theory of matter" developed by Democritus. This theory held that all matter is composed of tiny indivisible particles (Greek "atoma") which can neither be created nor destroyed. These particles are in continual flux. Thus all events in the cosmos result from combinations of atoms coming together, coming apart, and recombining. In this atomic world, therefore, there is no creation, no end of time, no gods, no human soul, nor afterlife. In short, this was a philosophy that was or at least bordered on atheism. This still left the issue of how to obtain happiness during one's life. Epicurus argued that the best way to achieve happiness was to pursue moderate pleasures and avoid pain. One could best to do this by withdrawal from the many cares of the world, which would otherwise inevitably bring failure, disappointment, and pain.

The most famous adherent of Epicureanism in the Roman world was Titus Lucretius Carus (ca. 99-55 B.C), a high-born Roman aristocrat who spurned a potential career in public life for pursuit of philosophy. His only surviving work, **De rerum natura (On the Nature of Things)** *is a long poem that credits Epicurus with the discovery of truth that liberates humans from the irrational fears fostered by religion. The use of reason, Lucretius argues, allows one to free oneself from the shackles of religion, which originated from ignorance and superstition and has caused great and needless suffering in the world. This is one of the few surviving works of unabashed atheism from the ancient Mediterranean world, although it apparently attracted relatively few adherents.*

When human life, all too conspicuous,
Lay foully grovelling on earth, weighed down
By grim Religion looming from the skies,
Horribly threatening mortal men, a man,
A Greek,[1] first raised his mortal eyes
Bravely against this menace. No report
Of gods, no lightning-flash, no thunder-peal

---

[1] The materialist philosopher Epicurus (341–270 B.C.).

Made this man cower, but drove him all the more
With passionate manliness of mind and will
To be the first to spring the tight-barred gates
Of Nature's hold asunder. So his force,
His vital force of mind, a conqueror
Beyond the flaming ramparts of the world
Explored the vast immensities of space
With wit and wisdom, and came back to us
Triumphant, bringing news of what can be
And what cannot, limits and boundaries,
The borderline, the bench mark, set forever.
Religion, so, is trampled underfoot,
And by his victory we reach the stars.
I fear that, in these matters, you may think
You're entering upon a path of crime,
The ABC's of godlessness. Not so.
The opposite is true. Too many times
Religion mothers crime and wickedness.
Recall how once at Aulis, when the Greeks,
Those chosen peers, the very first of men,
Defiled, with a girl's blood, the altar-stone
Sacred to Artemis.[2] The princess stood
Wearing the sacred fillets or a veil,
And sensed but could not see the king her father,
Agamemnon, standing sorrowful
Beside the altar, and the priests near-by
Hiding the knife-blade, and the folk in tears
At what they saw. She knelt, she spoke no word,
She was afraid, poor thing. Much good it did her
At such a time to have been the very first
To give the king that other title, *Father*!
Raised by men's hands and trembling she was led
Toward the altar, not to join in song
After the ritual of sacrifice
To the bright god of marriage. No; she fell
A victim by the sacrificing stroke
Her father gave, to shed her virgin blood—
Not the way virgins shed it—but in death,
To bring the fleet a happy exodus!
A mighty counselor, Religion stood
With all that power for wickedness.

•   •   •

Our terrors and our darknesses of mind
Must be dispelled, not by the sunshine's rays,
Not by those shining arrows of the light,
But by insight into nature, and a scheme
Of systematic contemplation. So

[2]This story is recalled from the Greek legend of the Trojan War. The princess is Iphigeneia, a daughter of King Agamemnon, commander of the Greek forces at Troy (see Homer's *Iliad*). Before his expedition sailed from the port of Aulis, Agamemnon had offended the goddess Artemis; he was required to atone for this by sacrificing his daughter. Only then were favorable winds provided for the departure of Agamemnon's fleet toward Troy.

Our starting-point shall be this principle:
Nothing at all is ever born from nothing
By the gods' will. Ah, but men's minds are frightened
Because they see, on earth and in the heaven,
Many events whose causes are to them
Impossible to fix; so, they suppose,
The gods' will is the reason. As for us,
Once we have seen that *Nothing comes from nothing,*
We shall perceive with greater clarity
What we are looking for, whence each thing comes,
How things are caused, and no "gods' will" about it.

Now, if things come from nothing, all things could
Produce all kinds of things; nothing would need
Seed[3] of its own. Men would burst out of the sea,
And fish and birds from earth, and, wild or tame,
All kinds of beasts, of dubious origin,
Inhabit deserts and the greener fields,
Nor would the same trees bear, in constancy,
The same fruit always, but, as like as not,
Oranges would appear on apple-boughs.
If things were not produced after their kind,
Each from its own determined particles,
How could we trace the substance to the source?
But now, since all created things have come
From their own definite kinds of seed, they move
From their beginnings toward the shores of light
Out of their primal motes. Impossible
That all things issue everywhere; each kind
Of substance has its own inherent power,
Its own capacity. Does not the rose
Blossom in spring, the wheat come ripe in summer,
The grape burst forth at autumn's urge? There must be
A proper meeting of their seeds in time
For us to see them at maturity
Grown by their season's favor, living earth
Bringing them safely to the shores of light.
But if they came from nothing, they might spring
To birth at any unpropitious time,—
Who could predict?—since there would be no seeds
Whose character rules out untimely union.
Thirdly, if things could come from nothing, time
Would not be of the essence, for their growth,
Their ripening to full maturity.
Babies would be young men, in the blink of an eye,
And full-grown forests come leaping out from the ground.
Ridiculous! We know that all things grow
Little by little, as indeed they must
From their essential nature.

•　　•　　•

[3]*Seed, atom, more, firstling,* and *particle* are used by Lucretius interchangeably. They refer to his concept of the smallest, indestructible units of matter.

Our second axiom is this, that nature
Resolves each object to its basic atoms
But does not ever utterly destroy it.
If anything could perish absolutely,
It might be suddenly taken from our sight,
There would be no need of any force to smash it,
Disrupt and shatter all its fastenings,
But as it is, since everything coheres
Because of its eternal seed, its essence,
Until some force is strong enough to break it
By violent impact, or to penetrate
Its void interstices, and so dissolve it,
Nature permits no visible destruction
Of anything.

Besides, if time destroys
Completely what it banishes from sight
With the procession of the passing years,
Out of what source does Venus[4] bring again
The race of animals, each after its kind,
To the light of life? and how, being restored,
Is each thing fed, sustained and given increase
By your miraculous contriving earth?
And what supplies the seas, the native springs,
The far-off rivers? And what feeds the stars?
By rights, if things can perish, infinite time
And ages past should have consumed them all,
But if, throughout this history, there have been
Renewals, and the sum of things can stay,
Beyond all doubt, there must be things possessed
Of an immortal essence. Nothing can
Disintegrate entirely into nothing.

An indiscriminate common violence
Would finish everything, except for this—
Matter is indestructible; it holds
All things together, though the fastenings
Vary in tightness. Otherwise, a touch,
The merest touch, would be a cause of death,
A force sufficient to dissolve in air
 Textures of mortal substance. But here's the fact—
The elements are held, are bound together
In different degrees, but the basic stuff
Is indestructible, so things remain
Intact, unharmed, until a force is found
Proportionate to their texture, to effect
Reversion to their primal elements,
But never to complete annihilation.

Finally, when the fathering air has poured
His rainfall into mother earth, the drops
Seem to have gone, but look!—bright harvests rise,

[4]Roman name for the goddess of love.

Boughs on the trees bring greenery and growth
And are weighed down by fruit, by which, in turn,
Our race is fed, and so are animals,
And we see happy cities, flowering
With children, and we hear the music rise
As new birds sing all through the leafy woods.
Fat cows lie down to rest their weary sides
In welcome pastures, and the milk drops white
Out of distended udders; and the calves
Romp over the tender grass, or wobble, drunk
On that pure vintage, more than strong enough
For any such experience as theirs.
To sum it up: no visible object dies;
Nature from one thing brings another forth,
And out of death new life is born.

     •   •   •

But not all bodily matter is tightly-packed
By nature's law, for there's a void in things.
This knowledge will be useful to you often,
Will keep you from the path of doubt, from asking
Too many questions on the sum of things,
From losing confidence in what I tell you.
By *void* I mean vacant and empty space,
Something you cannot touch. Were this not so,
Things could not move. The property of matter,
Its most outstanding trait, is to stand firm,
Its office to oppose; and everything
Would always be immovable, since matter
Never gives way. But with our eyes we see
Many things moving, in their wondrous ways,
Their marvelous means, through sea and land and sky.
Were there no void, they would not only lack
This restlessness of motion altogether,
But more than that—they never could have been
Quickened to life from that tight-packed quiescence.

Besides, however solid things appear,
Let me show you proof that even these are porous:
In a cave of rocks the seep of moisture trickles
And the whole place weeps its fat blobs of tears.
Food is dispersed all through a creature's body;
Young trees grow tall and yield their fruit in season,
Drawing their sustenance from the lowest roots
Through trunks and branches; voices penetrate
Walls and closed doors; the seep of stiffening cold
Permeates bone. Phenomena like these
Would be impossible but for empty spaces
Where particles can pass. And finally,
Why do we see that some things outweigh others
Which are every bit as large? If a ball of wool
Has the same substance as a ball of lead,

(Assuming the dimensions are the same)
They both should weigh as much, since matter tends
To exercise a constant downward pressure.
But void lacks weight. So, when two objects bulk
The same, but one is obviously lighter,
It clearly states its greater share of void,
And, on the other hand, the heavier thing
Proclaims it has less void and greater substance.
Certainly, therefore, what we're looking for
By logical deduction, does exist,
Is mixed with solid, and we call it *void*.

      •   •   •

Bodies are partly basic elements
Of things, and partly compounds of the same.
The basic elements no force can shatter
Since, being solid, they resist destruction.
Yet it seems difficult to believe that objects
Are ever found to be completely solid.
A thunderbolt goes through the walls of houses,
As noise and voices do, and iron whitens
In fire, and steam at boiling point splits rocks,
Gold's hardnesses are pliant under heat,
The ice of bronze melts in the flame, and silver
Succumbs to warmth or chill, as our senses tell us
With the cup in our hands, and water, hot or cold,
Poured into the wine. No, there is nothing solid
In things, or so it seems; reason, however,
And science are compelling forces—therefore
Stay with me; it will not take many verses
For me to explain that there are things with bodies
Solid and everlasting; these we call
Seeds of things, firstlings, atoms, and in them lies
The sum of all created things.

To start with,
Since it has been established that the nature
Of things is different, dual, one being substance,
The other void, it follows that each one
Must, in its essence, be itself completely.
Where space exists, or what we call the void,
Matter cannot be found; what substance holds
Void cannot occupy. So atoms are
Solid and therefore voidless. Furthermore,
If there is void in things, there has to be
Solid material surrounding this.
Nothing, by logic, can be proved to hold
A void within its mass, unless you grant
It must itself be solid. There can be
Nothing except an organized composure
Of matter, which can hold a void within it.
And matter, therefore, being of solid substance,

Can last forever, while all else is shattered.
Then, were there nothing which we label *void,*
All would be solid substance; and again,
Were there no substance to fill up the spaces,
All would be void and emptiness. These, then,
Must alternate, substance and void, since neither
Exists to the exclusion of the other.
So there is substance, which marks off the limits
Between the full and the empty, and this substance
Cannot be broken if blows are struck against it
From anywhere outside it, not exploded
By dissolution from within, nor weakened
In any other way, as I have shown you.
It must be obvious that, lacking void,
Nothing can possibly be crushed or broken
Or split in two by cutting, or allow
Invasion by water, cold, or fire, those forces
Of dissolution. The more an object holds
Void space within it, the more easily
It weakens under stress and strain; and therefore,
As I have pointed out, when stuff is solid,
Without that void, it must be everlasting.
Were this not true of matter, long ago
Everything would have crumbled into nothing
And things we see today have been restored
From nothing; but remember, I have proved
Nothing can be created out of nothing.
Also, that nothing can be brought to nothing,
So basic elements must be immortal,
Impossible to dissolve in some last moment
Else there would be no matter for renewal.
They must be, then, completely singly solid,
For otherwise they could not through the ages
Be kept intact for restoration's work

●　　　●　　　●

There is no end,
No limit to the cosmos, above, below,
Around, about, stretching on every side.
This I have proven, but the fact itself
Cries loud in proclamation, nature's deep
Is luminous with proof. The universe
Is infinitely wide; its vastness holds
Innumerable seeds, beyond all count,
Beyond all possibility of number,
Flying along their everlasting ways.
So it must be unthinkable that our sky
And our round world are precious and unique
While all those other motes of matter flit
In idleness, achieve, accomplish nothing,
Especially since this world of ours was made

By natural process, as the atoms came
Together, willy-nilly, quite by chance,
Quite casually and quite intentionless
Knocking against each other, massed, or spaced
So as to colander [pass] others through, and cause
Such combinations and conglomerates
As form the origin of mighty things,
Earth, sea and sky, and animals and men.
Face up to this, acknowledge it. I tell you
Over and over—out beyond our world
There are, elsewhere, other assemblages
Of matter, making other worlds. Oh, ours
Is not the only one in air's embrace.

With infinite matter available, infinite space,
And infinite lack of any interference,
Things certainly ought to happen. If we have
More seeds, right now, than any man can count,
More than all men of all time past could reckon,
And if we have, in nature, the same power
To cast them anywhere at all, as once
They were cast here together, let's admit—
We really have to—there are other worlds,
More than one race of men, and many kinds
Of animal generations.

        •   •   •

Since I have taught how everything begins,
The nature of those first particles, their shape,
Their differences, their voluntary course,
Their everlasting motion, and the ways
Things are created from them, I must now
Make use of poetry to clarify
The nature of intelligence and spirit,
Of mind and soul. The fear of Acheron[5]
Must, first and foremost, be dismissed; this fear
Troubles the life of man from its lowest depths,
Stains everything with death's black darkness, leaves
No pleasure pure and clear; it drives a man
To violate honor, or to break the bonds
Of friendship, and, in general, overthrow
All of the decencies. Men have betrayed
Their country or their parents, desperate
To avoid the realms of Acheron.

        •   •   •

First,
The mind—the intellect, we sometimes call it—
The force that gives direction to a life
As well as understanding, is a part

---

[5]A river in the underworld (the Greek Hades).

Of a man's make-up, every bit as much
As are his hands and feet and seeing eyes.

•   •   •

Now pay heed,
I have more to say. To start with, I maintain
That mind and spirit are held close together,
Compose one unity, but the lord and master
Holding dominion over all the body
Is purpose, understanding—in our terms
Mind or intelligence, and this resides
In the region of the heart. Hence we derive
Terror and fear and panic and delight.
Here therefore dwell intelligence and mind.
The rest of spirit is dispersed all through
The entire frame, and it obeys the mind,
Moves, gains momentum, at its nod and beck,
And mind alone is sensible or wise
Or glad all by itself, when body and soul
Are quite unmoved by anything; and as an eye
Or head can hurt us, though we feel no pain
In any other part, so now and then
The mind can suffer or rejoice, while spirit
Is nowhere stirred in any part by strangeness;
But when the mind is deeply moved by fear
We see the spirit share that panic sense
All through the body: sweat breaks out, and pallor comes;
The tongue grows thick, the voice is choked, the eyes
Grow dark, ears ring, the limbs collapse. Men faint,
We have often seen, from a terror in the mind;
From this example all can recognize
That spirit and mind are closely bound together,
And spirit, struck by the impulse of the mind,
Propels and thrusts the body.

This same doctrine
Shows that the nature of both mind and spirit
Must be corporeal. We are bound to admit
That spirit and mind are properties of body
When they propel the limbs, arouse from sleep,
Change an expression, turn a man around,
Control him utterly, but none of this
Is possible without contact, nor is touch
Possible without body. Furthermore,
You see that mind can sympathize with body,
Share its emotions. If a weapon drives
Deep into bone and sinew, and yet fails
To shatter life entirely, still it brings
Weakness, collapse, and turbulence of mind
Within the fallen victim, a desire,
Half-hearted and confused, to rise again.
So mind, which suffers under wounds and blows,
Must have a bodily nature.

I'll explain,
At this point, what that body's like, what forms it;
First, it [mind] is very delicate indeed,
Made of the most diminutive particles.
That this is so requires no argument
Beyond the fact that nothing seems to move
With such velocity as mind intends
Or mind anticipates; mind acts, we know,
Quicker than anything natural we see.
But anything so mobile must consist
Of particles very round and smooth indeed,
And very small indeed, to be so stirred,
So set in motion by the slightest urge.
Water is moved in just this way, and flows
With almost no impulsion, being formed
Of tiny little round motes, adaptable
Most easily for rolling. Honey, though,
Is more cohesive, less disposed to flow,
More sluggish, for its whole supply of matter
Is more condensed; its motes are not as smooth,
As round, as delicate. The slightest stir
Of air disturbs a cone of poppy seeds,
Sends the top sliding downward; no such breath
Is adequate to disturb a pile of pebbles
Or even a heap of wheat-ears. Bodies move
With speed proportionate to their size and weight,
If small, then swift. The heavy or the rough
Are the more stable, solid, hard to move.
Now, since the nature of the mind appears
Mobile, extremely so, it must consist
Of particles which are small and smooth and round.
This knowledge, my good scholar, you will find
To your advantage in more ways than one.
Another fact gives evidence how frail,
How delicate spirit is, or soul, or mind,
How almost infinitesimal its compass
Even supposing it were massed together:
When death's calm reassurance takes a man,
And mind and spirit have left him, you perceive
Nothing at all subtracted from the body,
Nothing of weight, of semblance, gone. Death shows
All that was his except the vital sense,
The warming breath. And so the spirit must
Consist throughout of very tiny seeds,
All sown minutely in sinew, flesh, and veins—
So tenuous that when it leaves the body
There seems no difference, no diminution
Of outward contour nor of inward weight.
The same thing happens when the scent of wine,
Or nard's[6] aroma, or any effluence,

---

[6]An aromatic plant.

Vanishes into air, and still its source
Appears no less substantial to our eyes,
Especially since nothing of its weight
Is lost—so many and such tiny seeds
Imparting scent and flavor in all things.
Let me repeat: infinitesimal motes
Must form both mind and spirit, since we see
No loss of weight when these depart the body.

     •   •   •

How sweet it is, when whirlwinds roil great ocean,
To watch, from land, the danger of another,
Not that to see some other person suffer
Brings great enjoyment, but the sweetness lies
In watching evils you yourself are free from.
How sweet, again, to see the clash of battle
Across the plains, yourself immune to danger.
But nothing is more sweet than full possession
Of those calm heights, well built, well fortified
By wise men's teaching, to look down from here
At others wandering below, men lost,
Confused, in hectic search for the right road,
The strife of wits, the wars for precedence,
The everlasting struggle, night and day,
To win towards heights of wealth and power. O wretched,
O wretched minds of men! O hearts in darkness!
Under what shadows and among what dangers
Your lives are spent, such as they are. But look—
Your nature snarls, yaps, barks for nothing, really,
Except that pain be absent from the body
And mind enjoy delight, with fear dispelled,
Anxiety gone. We do not need so much
For bodily comfort, only loss of pain.
I grant you, luxuries are very pleasant,
But nature does not really care if houses
Lack golden statues in the halls, young men
Holding out fiery torches in their hands
To light the all-night revels. Let the house
Gleam silver and gold, the music waken echoes
In gilded panel and crossbeam—never mind.
Much poorer men are every bit as happy,
Are quite well-off, stretched out in groups together
On the soft grass beside a running brook,
Under a tall tree's shade, in lovely weather,
Where flowers star green meadows. Fever's heat
Departs no sooner if your bodies toss
On crimson sheets, or under figured covers,
Than if you have to lie on a poor blanket.
So, since our bodies find in wealth no profit,
And none in rank or power, it must be mind
Is no more profited. You may see your hosts

Make mimic wars, surging across the drill-ground,
Flanked by their cavalry and well-supported
By strong reserves, high in morale. You may
Behold your fleet churn wide across great seas—
And does all this frighten religious terror
In panic from your heart? does the great fear
Of death depart, and leave you comforted?
What vanity, what nonsense! If men's fears,
Anxieties, pursuing horrors, move,
Indifferent to any clash of arms,
Untroubled among lords and monarchs, bow
Before no gleam of gold, no crimson robe,
Why do you hesitate, why doubt that reason
Alone has absolute power? Our life is spent
In shadows, and it suffers in the dark.
As children tremble and fear everything
In their dark shadows, we, in the full light,
rear things that really are not one bit more awful
Than what poor babies shudder at in darkness,
The horrors they imagine to be coming.
Our terrors and our darknesses of mind
Must be dispelled, then, not by sunshine's rays,
Not by those shining arrows of the light,
But by insight into nature, and a scheme
Of systematic contemplation.

      •   •   •

Men seem to feel some burden on their souls,
Some heavy weariness; could they but know
Its origin, its cause, they'd never live
The way we see most of them do, each one
Ignorant of what he wants, except a change,
Some other place to lay his burden down.
One leaves his house to take a stroll outdoors
Because the household's such a deadly bore,
And then comes back, in six or seven minutes—
The street is every bit as bad. Now what?
He has his horses hitched up for him, drives,
Like a man going to a fire, full-speed,
Off to his country-place, and when he gets there
Is scarcely on the driveway, when he yawns,
Falls heavily asleep, oblivious
To everything, or promptly turns around,
Whips back to town again. So each man flees
Himself, or tries to, but of course that pest
Clings to him all the more ungraciously.
He hates himself because he does not know
The reason for his sickness; if he did,
He would leave all this foolishness behind,
Devote his study to the way things are,
The problem being his lot, not for an hour,

But for all time, the state in which all men
Must dwell forever and ever after death.

•   •   •

Death
Is nothing to us, has no relevance
To our condition, seeing that the mind
Is mortal. Just as, long ago, we felt
Not the least touch of trouble when the wars
Were raging all around the shaken earth
And from all sides the Carthaginian hordes[7]
Poured forth to battle, and no man ever knew
Whose subject he would be in life or death,
Which doom, by land or sea, would strike him down,
So, when we cease to be, and body and soul,
Which joined to make us one, have gone their ways,
Their separate ways, nothing at all can shake
Our feelings, not if earth were mixed with sea
Or sea with sky. Perhaps the mind or spirit,
After its separation from our body,
Has some sensation; what is that to us?
Nothing at all, for what we knew of being,
Essence, identity, oneness, was derived
From body's union with spirit, so, if time,
After our death, should some day reunite
All of our present particles, bring them back
To where they now reside, give us once more
The light of life, this still would have no meaning
For us, with our self-recollection gone.
As we are now, we lack all memory
Of what we were before, suffer no wound
From those old days. Look back on all that space
Of time's immensity, consider well
What infinite combinations there have been
In matter's ways and groupings. How easy, then,
For human beings to believe we are
Compounded of the very selfsame motes,
Arranged exactly in the selfsame ways
As once we were, our long-ago, our now
Being identical. And yet we keep
No memory of that once-upon-a-time,
Nor can we call it back; somewhere between
A break occurred, and all our atoms went
Wandering here and there and far away
From our sensations. If there lies ahead
Tough luck for any man, he must be there,
Himself, to feel its evil, but since death
Removes this chance, and by injunction stops
All rioting of woes against our state,

[7]The Carthaginians, holding an empire in North Africa, sought to conquer Rome in the third and second centuries B.C.

We may be reassured that in our death
We have no cause for fear, we cannot be
Wretched in nonexistence. Death alone
Has immortality, and takes away
Our mortal life. It does not matter a bit
If we once lived before.

So, seeing a man
Feel sorry for himself, that after death
He'll be a rotting corpse, laid in a tomb,
Succumb to fire, or predatory beasts,
You'll know he's insincere, just making noise,
With rancor in his heart, though he believes,
Or tries to make us think so, that death ends all.
And yet, I'd guess, he contradicts himself,
He does not really see himself as gone,
As utter nothingness, but does his best—
Not really understanding what he's doing—
To have himself survive, for, in his life,
He will project a future, a dark day
When beast or bird will lacerate his corpse.
So he feels sorry for himself; he fails
To make the real distinction that exists
Between his castoff body, and the man
Who stands beside it grieving, and imputes
Some of his sentimental feelings to it.
Resenting mortal fate, he cannot see
That in true death he'll not survive himself
To stand there as a mourner, stunned by grief
That he is burned or mangled.

         •   •   •

Hark! The voice of Nature
Is scolding us: "What ails you, little man,
Why this excess of self-indulgent grief,
This sickliness? Why weep and groan at death?
If you have any sense of gratitude
For a good life, if you can't claim her gifts
Were dealt you in some kind of riddled jar
So full of cracks and holes they leaked away
Before you touched them, why not take your leave
As men go from a banquet, fed to the full
On life's good feast, come home, and lie at ease,
Free from anxiety? Alas, poor fool,
If, on the other hand, all of your joys
Are gone, and life is only wretchedness,
Why try to add more to it? Why not make
A decent end? There's nothing, it would seem,
My powers can contrive for your delight.
The same old story, always. If the years
Don't wear your body, don't corrode your limbs
With lassitude [weariness], if you keep living on

For centuries, if you never die at all,
What's in it for you but the same old story
Always, and always?"

     •   •   •

Such a rebuke from Nature would be right,
For the old order yields before the new,
All things require refashioning from others.
No man goes down to Hell's black pit; we need
Matter for generations yet to come,
Who, in their turn, will follow you, as men
Have died before you and will die hereafter.
So one thing never ceases to arise
Out of another; life's a gift to no man
Only a loan to him. Look back at time—
How meaningless, how unreal!—before our birth.
In this way Nature holds before our eyes
The mirror of our future after death.
Is this so grim, so gloomy? Is it not
A rest more free from care than any sleep?

Marcus Aurelius

———◆———

THOUGHTS

Another of the major Hellenistic philosophies which arose in the Hellenistic Greek world was Stoicism, so called from the tradition that it was originally taught from a "stoa" (in Greek a "covered porch") by its founder, Zeno of Citium (ca. 334-262 B.C.). Although by birth a Phoenician from Cyprus, Zeno was thoroughly Hellenized in culture and came to Athens to teach his philosophy.

Whereas most Greeks were polytheists, Stoicism at least tended towards monotheism, based on belief in a Supreme Intelligence (the "Divine Reason" or "Divine Fire") which created all things and was imbued in all things. Some Stoics were strict monotheists while others accepted the existence of other deities as lesser manifestations of the one high God. Stoics believed that all humans share a spark of this Divine Fire as their soul which therefore makes all humans the brothers or sisters of all other humans. Upon physical death, the soul or spark of the divine will rejoin the Divine Reason and thus achieve a kind of immortality of the soul. Stoics also believed that happiness was best obtained through achieving virtue (goodness) and virtue could be acquired by performance of one's duty to God, family, state, and occupation. The emphasis on duty made this philosophy especially appealing to aristocratic Romans, among whom Stoicism was especially popular.

The most famous Stoic of the Roman Empire was the Emperor Marcus Aurelius, who ruled from A.D. 161-180 and was the last of the so-called "Five Good Emperors". His reign was marked by almost continuous warfare, particularly against German tribes on the upper Danube River in central Euope, where Marcus spent much of his reign. He wrote the Thoughts *(often called* The Meditations*) in Greek while in his camp on campaign, apparently jotting down a kind of philosophical diary from the perspective of Stoicism. Interestingly, just like Epicureanism, Marcus places the highest value on human reason. But in this case reason allows one to perform his or her duty based on self-discipline.*

On Nature

All things are connected with one another, and the bond is holy; and there is hardly anything unconnected with any other thing. For things have been co-ordinated, and they combine to form the same universe. For there is one universe made up of all things, one god who pervades all things, one substance, one law, one reason common to all intelligent beings, and one truth. . . .

•   •   •

The intelligence of the universe is social. Accordingly it has made the inferior things for the sake of the superior, and it has fitted the superior to one another. You see how it has subordinated, co-ordinated, and assigned to everything its proper portion, and has brought together into concord with one another the things which are the best.

On Lining in Harmony with Nature

Everything harmonizes with me, which is harmonious to you, O Universe. Nothing for me is too early nor too late, which is in due time for you. Everything is fruit to me which your seasons bring, O Nature: from you are all things, in you are all things, to you all things return. The poet says, Dear city of Cecrops;[1] and will you not say, Dear city of Zeus?

· · ·

Judge every word and deed which are according to nature to be fit for you; and be not diverted by the blame which follows from any people nor by their words, but if a thing is good to be done or said, do not consider it unworthy of you. For those persons have their own leading principle and follow their own movement; which things you must not regard, but go straight on, following your own nature and the common nature; and the way of both is one.

· · ·

No man will hinder you from living according to the reason of your own nature: nothing will happen to you contrary to the reason of the universal nature.

On Reason

Whatever this is that I am, it is a little flesh and breath, and the ruling part [reason].

· · ·

If our intellectual part is common, the reason also, because of which we are rational beings, is common: if this is so, common also is the reason which commands us what to do, and what not to do; if this is so, there is a common law also; if this is so, we are fellow-citizens; if this is so, we are members of some political community; if this is so, the world is in a manner a state. For of what other common political community will any one say that the whole human race are members?

And from that, from this common political community comes also our very intellectual faculty and reasoning faculty and our capacity for law; or from what place do they come?

· · ·

A man should always have these two rules in readiness; the one to do only what the reason of the ruling faculty may suggest for the use of men; the other, to change his opinion, if there is any one at hand who sets him right and moves him from any opinion. But this change of opinion must proceed only from a certain persuasion, as of what is just or of common advantage, and the like, not because it appears pleasant or brings reputation.

Have you reason? I have.—Why then not use it? For if this does its own work, what else do you wish?

· · ·

Remember that the ruling faculty is invincible; when self-collected it is satisfied with itself, if it does nothing which it does not choose to do, even if it resist from mere obstinacy. What then will it be when it forms a judgment about anything aided by deliberate reason? Therefore the mind which is free from passions is a fortress, for man has nothing more secure to which he can fly for refuge and for the future be invincible. He then who has not seen this is an ignorant man; but he who has seen it and does not fly to this refuge is unhappy.

On Duty and Responsibility

Every moment think steadily as a Roman and a man to do what you have in hand with perfect and simple dignity, and feeling of affection, and freedom, and justice, and to give yourself relief from all other thoughts. And you will

---

[1] The legendary first king of Athens. Here the distinction made by Marcus is, of course, between devotion to a mere city-state (Athens) and devotion to the order of nature (symbolized by the reference to Zeus, mythical lord of the universe).

give yourself relief if you do every act of your life as it if were the last, laying aside all carelessness and passionate opposition to the commands of reason, and all hypocrisy, and self-love, and discontent with the portion which has been given to you. You see how few the things are, which, if a man lays hold of, he is able to live a life which flows in quiet, and is like the existence of the gods; and the gods on their part will require nothing more from him who observes these things.

•   •   •

Do not disturb yourself by thinking of the whole of your life. Let not your thoughts at once embrace all the various troubles which you may expect to come, but on every occasion ask yourself, What is there in this which is intolerable and past bearing? for you will be ashamed to confess. In the next place remember that neither the future nor the past pains you, but only the present. And this is reduced to a very little, if you only limit it, and scold your mind if it is unable to hold out against even this.

•   •   •

If you work at that which is before you, following right reason seriously, vigorously, calmly, without allowing anything else to distract you, but keeping your divine part pure, as if you should be bound to give it back immediately; if you hold to this, expecting nothing, fearing nothing, but satisfied with your present activity according to nature, and with heroic truth in every word and sound which you utter, you will live happy. And there is no man who is able to prevent this.

On the Moral Life

If you find in human life anything better than justice, truth, temperance, fortitude, and, in a word, anything better than your own mind's self-satisfaction in the things which it enables you to do according to right reason; if, I say, you see anything better than this, turn to it with all your soul, and enjoy that which you have found to be the best. But if nothing appears to be better than the Deity [Reason] which is planted in you, which has subjected to itself all your appetites, and carefully examines all the impressions, and, as Socrates[2] said, has detached itself from the persuasions of sense, and has submitted itself to the gods, and cares for mankind; if you find everything else smaller and of less value than this, give place to nothing else, for if you once diverge and incline to it, you will no longer without distraction be able to give the preference to that good thing which is your proper possession; for it is not right that anything of any other kind, such as praise from the many, or power, or enjoyment of pleasure, should come into competition with that which is rationally and politically [or, practically] good. . . . I say, do simply and freely choose the better, and hold to it. . . .

Never value anything as profitable to you which shall compel you to break your promise, to lose your self-respect, to hate any man, to suspect, to curse, to act the hypocrite, to desire anything which needs walls and curtains. For he who has preferred to everything else his own intelligence and daemon[3] and the worship of its excellence, acts no tragic part, does not groan, will not need either solitude or much company; and, what is chief of all, he will live without either pursuing or flying from death, and whether for a longer or a shorter time he shall have the soul enclosed in the body, he cares not at all. For even if he must depart immediately, he will go as readily as if he were going to do anything else which can be done with decency and order; taking care of this alone all through life, that his thoughts turn not away from anything which belongs to an intelligent animal and a member of a civil community.

•   •   •

Occupy yourself with few things, says the philosopher, if you would be tranquil.—But consider if it would not be better to say, Do what is necessary, and whatever the reason of the animal, which is naturally social, requires. For this brings not only the tranquillity which comes from doing well, but also that which comes from doing few

[2]Athenian philosopher of the fifth century B.C.
[3]Inner spirit, or conscience.

things. For the greatest part of what we say and do being unnecessary, if a man takes this away, he will have more leisure and less uneasiness. Accordingly, on every occasion a man should ask himself, Is this one of the unnecessary things? Now a man should take away not only unnecessary acts, but also unnecessary thoughts, for thus superfluous acts will not follow after.

Try how the life of the good man suits you, the life of him who is satisfied with his portion out of the whole, and satisfied with his own just acts and benevolent feelings.

Have you seen those things? Look also at these. Do not disturb yourself. Make yourself all simplicity. Does any one do wrong? It is to himself that he does the wrong. Has anything happened to you? Well; out of the universe from the beginning everything which happens has been apportioned and spun out to you. In a word, your life is short. You must turn to profit the present by the aid of reason and justice.

On Humility and Patience

When you are offended with any man's shameless conduct, immediately ask yourself, Is it possible, then, that shameless men should not be in the world? It is not possible. Do not, then, require what is impossible. For this man also is one of those shameless men who must of necessity be in the world. Let the same considerations be remembered in the case of the dishonest man, the faithless man, and every man who does wrong in any way. For at the same time that you remind yourself that it is impossible that such sort of men should not exist, you will feel more kindly towards every one individually. It is useful to perceive, too, when the occasion arises, what power nature has given to man to oppose to every wrongful act. For she has given to man, as an antidote against the stupid man, mildness, and against another kind of man some other power. And in all cases it is possible for you to correct by teaching the man who is gone astray; for every man who errs misses his object and is gone astray. Besides, wherein have you been injured? For you will find that no one among those who have irritated you has done anything that could injure your mind, but that which is evil to you and harmful has its foundation only in the mind. And what harm is done or what is there strange, if the man who has not been instructed does the acts of an uninstructed man? Consider whether you should not rather blame yourself because you did not expect such a man to err in such a way. For you had means given you by your reason to suppose that it was likely that he would commit this error, and yet you have forgotten and are amazed that he has erred. But most of all when you blame a man as faithless or ungrateful, turn to yourself. For the fault is plainly your own, whether you did trust that a man who had such a disposition would keep his promise, or when conferring your kindness you did not confer it absolutely, nor yet in such a way as to have received from your very act all the profit. For what more do you want when you have done a man a service? Are you not content that you have done something conformable to your nature, and do you seek to be paid for it? just as if the eye demanded a payment for seeing, or the feet for walking. For as these members are formed for a particular purpose, and by working according to their several constitutions obtain what is their own; so also a man is formed by nature to acts of benevolence. When he has done anything benevolent or in any other way helpful to the common interest, he has acted comformably to his constitution, and he gets what is his own.

On Balance and Serenity

Hippocrates,[4] after curing many diseases, himself fell sick and died. The Chaldeans[5] foretold the deaths of many, and then fate caught them too. Alexander and Pompey and Julius Caesar, after so often completely destroying whole cities, and in battle cutting to pieces many ten thousands of cavalry and infantry, themselves too at last departed from life. Heraclitus,[6] after so many speculations on the conflagration of the universe, was filled with water internally and died smeared all over with mud. And lice destroyed Democritus;[7] and other lice[8] killed Socrates. What means all this? You have embarked, you have made the voyage, you have come to shore; get out. If indeed to another life, there is no lack of gods, not even there; but if to a state without sensation, you will cease to be held by pains and

[4]Famous Greek physician of the fifth century B.C.
[5]The ancient Chaldeans (of Mesopotamia) enjoyed a high reputation as astrologers and sorcerers—thus, the biblical phrase "Wise Men of the East."
[6]Greek "nature" philosopher of the sixth century B.C., who believed that all things are in a state of flux and originated in fire. He is alleged to have died of dropsy (marked by swelling from internal bodily fluids), while living on a dunghill.

pleasures, and to be a slave to the body, which is as much inferior as that which serves it is superior: for the one is intelligence and deity; the other is earth and corruption.

•   •   •

Labor not unwillingly, nor without regard to the common interest, nor without due consideration, nor with distraction; nor let fancy words set off your thoughts, and be not either a man of many words, or busy about too many things. And further, let the deity which is in you be the guardian of a living being, manly and of ripe age, and engaged in matter political. Be a Roman and a ruler, who has taken his post like a man waiting for the signal which summons him from life, and ready to go, having need neither of oath nor of any man's advice. Be cheerful also, and seek not external help nor the tranquillity which others give. A man, then, must stand erect, not be kept erect by others?

•   •   •

This is the chief thing: Be not agitated, for all things are according to the nature of the universal; and in a little time you will be nobody and nowhere, like Hadrian and Augustus.[9] In the next place, having fixed your eyes steadily on your business, look at it; and at the same time remembering that it is your duty to be a good man, and what man's nature demands, do that without turning aside; and speak as it seems to you most just, only let it be with a good disposition and with modesty and without hypocrisy.

•   •   •

Things themselves touch not the soul,[10] not in the least degree; nor have they admission to the soul, nor can they turn or move the soul. But the soul turns and moves itself alone, and whatever judgments it may think proper to make, such it makes for itself the things which present themselves to it.

•   •   •

Pain is either an evil to the body—then let the body say what it thinks of it—or to the soul; but it is in the power of the soul to maintain its own serenity and tranquillity, and not to think that pain is an evil. For every judgment and movement and desire and dislike is within, and no outside evil can force itself upon the soul.

On Retirement into One's Self

I have often wondered how it is that every man loves himself more than all the rest of men, but yet sets less value on his own opinion of himself than on the opinions of others.

•   •   •

Men seek retreats for themselves, houses in the country, seashores, and mountains; and you too are accustomed to desire such things very much. But this is altogether a mark of the most ordinary sort of men, for it is in your power whenever you choose to retire into *yourself.* For nowhere either with more quiet or more freedom from trouble does a man retire than into his own soul, particularly when he has within him such thoughts that can bring him immediate tranquillity; and I affirm that tranquillity is nothing else than the good ordering of the mind. Constantly, then, give yourself this retreat and renew yourself; and let your principles be brief and fundamental, which, as soon as you apply them, will cleanse the soul completely, and send you back free from all discontent with the things to which you return. For with what are you discontented? With the badness of men? Recall to your mind this conclusion, that rational animals exist for one another, and that to endure is a part of justice, and that men do wrong involuntarily; and consider how many already, after mutual suspicion, hatred, and fighting, have been stretched

[7]A Greek philosopher who conceived the "atomic" theory of matter, in the fifth century B.C. He chose, for the sake of his studies, to live in poverty. Thus, the legend arose that Democritus had been devoured by lice.
[8]A play on words; Marcus here refers to the mean-spirited men ("lice") who convicted Socrates on charges of inventing his own gods and corrupting the youth.
[9]Deceased Roman emperors.
[10]By "soul," Marcus means, essentially, the mind.

dead, reduced to ashes; and be quiet at last. But perhaps you are dissatisfied with that which is assigned to you out of the universe.—Recall to your recollection this alternative: either there is divine providence or atoms [chance concurrence of things]; or remember the arguments by which it has been proved that the world is a kind of political community. But perhaps bodily things will still fasten upon you.—Consider then further that the mind mingles not with the breath, whether moving gently or violently, when it has once drawn itself apart and discovered its own power, and think also of all that you have heard and assented to about pain and pleasure.—But perhaps the desire of the thing called fame will torment you.—See how soon everything is forgotten, and look at the chaos of infinite time on each side of the present and the emptiness of applause, and the changeableness and lack of judgment in those who pretend to give praise, and the narrowness of the space within its limits. For the whole earth is a point, and how small a nook in it is this your dwelling, and how few there are in it, and what kind of people they are who will praise you.

This then remains: Remember to retire into this little territory of your own, and above all do not distract or strain yourself. But be free, and look at things as a man, as a human being, as a citizen, as a mortal. But among the things readiest to your hand to which you will turn, let there be these two. One is that *things* do not touch the soul, for they are external and remain outside the soul; but our agitations come only from our perception, which is within. The other is that all these things, which you see, change immediately and will no longer be; and constantly bear in mind how many of these changes you have already witnessed. The universe is change; life is your perception of it.

The Gods

Since it is possible that you may depart from life this very moment, direct every act and thought accordingly. But to go away from among men, if there are gods, is not a thing to be afraid of, for the gods will not involve you in evil; and if indeed they do not exist, or if they have no concern about human affairs, what is it to me to live in a universe without gods or without providence? But in truth they do exist, and they do care for human things, and they have put all the means in man's power to enable him not to fall into real evils.

• • •

What do you wish,—to continue to exist? Well, do you wish to have sensation, movement, growth, and then cease to grow, to use your speech, to think? What is there of all these things which seems to you worth desiring? But if it is easy to set little value on all these things, turn to that which remains, which is to follow reason and the gods. But it is inconsistent with honoring reason and the gods if one is troubled because by death a man will be deprived of the other things.

• • •

As physicians have always their instruments and knives ready for cases which suddenly require their skill, so do you have principles ready for the understanding of things divine and human, and for doing everything, even the smallest, while remembering the bond which unites the divine and human to one another. For you will not do anything well affecting humans without at the same time referring to things, divine; or the contrary.

THE BIBLE: NEW TESTAMENT

Written in Greek during the late first and early second centuries A.D., the New Testament was seen by Christians as an addition to the Hebrew Bible (Old Testament) and a new covenant that in some ways superseded the Old Testament. Its twenty-seven books were culled from a much larger mass of Christian writings that circulated widely within the early Christian movement. There was naturally much debate among early Christians about which writings should be regarded as sacred and thus the word of God and which should be regarded as inauthentic or bogus. In fact, it was not until A.D. 367, or more than three centuries after the appearance of the new faith, that the church made its final choices about which books to include and which to exclude. Nevertheless, the twenty-seven "canonical" books (so-called because they were included in the "canon" of writings accepted as authentic) were still the products of different authors written over several decades and naturally reflect to some degree differing points of view.

The four canonical gospels reflect such changes in the presentation of Jesus of Nazareth. The Gospel of Mark, perhaps the earliest (ca. A.D. 70), focuses above all on the "Passion", i.e., the arrest, trial, and crucifixion of Jesus Christ. The Gospels of Matthew and Luke (ca. A.D. 80-90) possibly used Mark for their passion narrative but also exploited other sources, such as the collected sayings of Jesus and other unique material. This latter is best illustrated by comparing the infancy narratives of Matthew versus Luke, which differ widely in their details. The fact that all three Gospels seem to have some dependency on each other has led modern scholars to group them together as the Synoptic Gospels. All three focus on portraying Jesus as the Messiah. The Gospel of John, probably the latest in date (ca. A.D. 90-100), presents a rather different portrait of Jesus, as God incarnate, a theme not stressed in the Synoptic Gospels. The following excerpt from the 'Sermon on the Mount' in the Gospel of Matthew illustrates the ethical teaching of Jesus which often goes beyond the Law of Moses in the Hebrew Bible.

The Acts of the Apostles, the book which follows the four gospels, is a kind of history of the primitive church. It presents the message and activity of the earliest Christians, who were now seeking converts to the new faith.

Most of the remainder the New Testament is comprised of epistles, i.e. letters written to different Christian congregations scattered throughout the eastern Roman Empire. Most of these letters were written by the Apostle Paul (although the Pauline authorship of some has been questioned by scholars). The excerpt presented here is from his first letter to the Christian community at Corinth (i.e., First Corinthians), written in response to their questions about the practice of their new faith. Paul responds with advice about such matters as the proper conduct of worship services, the different roles of men and women in the church, and sexual morality. He also explains the nature of the resurrection and the meaning of the Lord's Supper. It also contains his famous passage about Christian love. Not surprisingly, Paul's views about such topics naturally reflect his own beliefs as a Jewish Christian convert of the Diaspora (he was from the city of Tarsus in southeastern Asia Minor). He was martyred in Rome in A.D. 64.

Such advice, it must be remembered, was critical to the survival of such Christian communities, because the New Testament did not yet exist. But Paul probably never dreamed that his advice to these small scattered Christian communities would later be collected for inclusion in the New Testament and thus henceforth be considered the word of God.

The Gospel According to Matthew[1]

The Sermon on the Mount[2]

4:23–7:29

And he went about all Galilee, teaching in their synagogues and preaching the gospel of the kingdom and healing every disease and every infirmity among the people. So his fame spread throughout all Syria, and they brought him all the sick, those afflicted with various diseases and pains, demoniacs, epileptics, and paralytics, and he healed them. And great crowds followed him from Galilee and the Decapolis[3] and Jerusalem and Judea and from beyond the Jordan.

Seeing the crowds, he went up on the mountain, and when he sat down[4] his disciples came to him. And he opened his mouth and taught them, saying:

"Blessed are the poor in spirit, for theirs is the kingdom of heaven.

"Blessed are those who mourn, for they shall be comforted.

"Blessed are the meek, for they shall inherit the earth.

"Blessed are those who hunger and thirst for righteousness, for they shall be satisfied.

"Blessed are the merciful, for they shall obtain mercy.

"Blessed are the pure in heart, for they shall see God.

"Blessed are the peacemakers, for they shall be called sons of God.

"Blessed are those who are persecuted for righteousness' sake, for theirs is the kingdom of heaven.

"Blessed are you when men revile you and persecute you and utter all kinds of evil against you falsely on my account. Rejoice and be glad, for your reward is great in heaven, for so men persecuted the prophets[5] who were before you.

"You are the salt of the earth; but if salt has lost its taste, how shall its saltness be restored? It is no longer good for anything except to be thrown out and trodden under foot by men.

"You are the light of the world. A city set on a hill cannot be hid. Nor do men light a lamp and put it under a bushel, but on a stand, and it gives light to all in the house. Let your light so shine before men, that they may see your good works and give glory to your Father who is in heaven.

"Think not that I have come to abolish the law and the prophets; I have come not to abolish them but to fulfil them.[6] For truly, I say to you, till heaven and earth pass away, not an iota, not a dot, will pass from the law until all is accomplished. Whoever then relaxes one of the least of these commandments and teaches men so, shall be called least in the kingdom of heaven; but he who does them and teaches them shall be called great in the kingdom of heaven. For I tell you, unless your righteousness exceeds that of the scribes and Pharisees,[7] you will never enter the kingdom of heaven.

"You have heard that it was said to the men of old,[8] 'You shall not kill; and whoever kills shall be liable to judgment.' But I say to you that every one who is angry with his brother shall be liable to judgment; whoever insults his brother shall be liable to the council, and whoever says, 'You fool!' shall be liable to the hell of fire. So if you are offering your gift at the altar, and there remember that your brother has something against you, leave your gift there before the altar and go; first be reconciled to your brother, and then come and offer your gift. Make friends quickly with your accuser, while you are going with him to court, lest your accuser hand you over to the

---

[1]Of unknown authorship, this gospel may have acquired its title because the writer possibly used, as one of his sources, a collection of Jesus' sayings prepared by the disciple Matthew. Like the other gospels it was written in Greek for a mainly non-Jewish audience after the Roman destruction of Jerusalem in A.D. 70. It attempts to distinguish the new religion of Christianity from its Jewish roots. Nevertheless, this gospel assumes the reader's knowledge of the Old Testament and of Jewish history and religious ideas. Many of Jesus' sayings are, in fact, quotations or adaptations of the older Hebrew scriptures.

[2]This passage is often described as the essence of Christian ethical teaching. The sermon's delivery on a mountain suggests Jesus' relationship to the Law of Moses, delivered on Mount Sinai.

[3]A region—also occupied by Rome—just east of the Jordan River.

[4]The usual posture of Jewish rabbis (religious leaders) while teaching.

[5]The Jewish prophets of the Old Testament. (See, for example, Amos and Isaiah.)

[6]The relation of Jesus' message to the Jewish Law (given at Mount Sinai) obviously was of great concern to his followers, who were mostly of Jewish heritage. Here he clearly states the enduring force of that law.

[7]The Pharisees, one of the main Jewish sects in Jesus' time, had become the principal interpreters of Judaism after the fall of Jerusalem. Their "scribes" (specialists in religious law) conducted prayers in the synagogues and explained the Hebrew bible.

[8]That is, the men who received the Law at Mount Sinai.

judge, and the judge to the guard, and you be put in prison; truly, I say to you, you will never get out till you have paid the last penny.

"You have heard that it was said, 'You shall not commit adultery.' But I say to you that every one who looks at a woman lustfully has already committed adultery with her in his heart. If your right eye causes you to sin, pluck it out and throw it away; it is better that you lose one of your members than that your whole body be thrown into hell. And if your right hand causes you to sin, cut it off and throw it away; it is better that you lose one of your members than that your whole body go into hell.

"It was also said, 'Whoever divorces his wife, let him give her a certificate of divorce.' But I say to you that every one who divorces his wife, except on the ground of unchastity, makes her an adulteress; and whoever marries a divorced woman commits adultery.

"Again you have heard that it was said to the men of old, 'You shall not swear falsely, but shall perform to the Lord what you have sworn.' But I say to you, Do not swear at all, either by heaven, for it is the throne of God, or by the earth, for it is his footstool, or by Jerusalem, for it is the city of the great King. And do not swear by your head, for you cannot make one hair white or black. Let what you say be simply 'Yes' or 'No'; anything more than this comes from evil.

"You have heard that it was said, 'An eye for an eye and a tooth for a tooth.' But I say to you, Do not resist one who is evil. But if any one strikes you on the right cheek, turn to him the other also; and if any one would sue you and take your coat, let him have your cloak as well; and if any one forces you to go one mile, go with him two miles. Give to him who begs from you, and do not refuse him who would borrow from you.

"You have heard that it was said, 'You shall love your neighbor and hate your enemy.' But I say to you, Love your enemies and pray for those who persecute you, so that you may be sons[9] of your Father who is in heaven; for he makes his sun rise on the evil and on the good, and sends rain on the just and on the unjust. For if you love those who love you, what reward have you? Do not even the tax collectors do the same? And if you salute only your brethren, what more are you doing than others? Do not even the Gentiles[10] do the same? You, therefore, must be perfect, as your heavenly Father is perfect.

"Beware of practicing your piety before men in order to be seen by them; for then you will have no reward from your Father who is in heaven.

"Thus, when you give alms, sound no trumpet before you, as the hypocrites do in the synagogues and in the streets, that they may be praised by men. Truly, I say to you, they have received their reward. But when you give alms, do not let your left hand know what your right hand is doing, so that your alms may be in secret; and your Father who sees in secret will reward you.

"And when you pray, you must not be like the hypocrites; for they love to stand and pray in the synagogues and at the street corners, that they may be seen by men. Truly, I say to you, they have received their reward. But when you pray, go into your room and shut the door and pray to your Father who is in secret; and your Father who sees in secret will reward you.

"And in praying do not heap up empty phrases as the Gentiles do; for they think that they will be heard for their many words. Do not be like them, for your Father knows what you need before you ask him. Pray then like this:

> Our Father who art in heaven,
> Hallowed be thy name.
> Thy kingdom come,
> Thy will be done,
> On earth as it is in heaven.
> Give us this day our daily bread;
> And forgive us our debts,
> As we also have forgiven our debtors;
> And lead us not into temptation,
> But deliver us from evil.

[9]That is, worthy followers of God's Law.
[10]Non-Jews, who did *not* receive the Law at Mount Sinai.

For if you forgive men their trespasses, your heavenly Father also will forgive you; but if you do not forgive men their trespasses, neither will your Father forgive your trespasses.

"And when you fast, do not look dismal, like the hypocrites, for they disfigure their faces that their fasting may be seen by men. Truly, I say to you, they have received their reward. But when you fast, anoint your head and wash your face, that your fasting may not be seen by men but by your Father who is in secret; and your Father who sees in secret will reward you.

"Do not lay up for yourselves treasures on earth, where moth and rust consume and where thieves break in and steal, but lay up for yourselves treasure in heaven, where neither moth nor rust consumes and where thieves do not break in and steal. For where your treasure is, there will your heart be also.

"The eye is the lamp of the body. So, if your eye is sound, your whole body will be full of light; but if your eye is not sound, your whole body will be full of darkness. If then the light in you is darkness, how great is the darkness!

"No one can serve two masters; for either he will hate the one and love the other, or he will be devoted to the one and despise the other. You cannot serve God and mammon.[11]

"Therefore I tell you, do not be anxious about your life, what you shall eat or what you shall drink, nor about your body, what you shall put on. Is not life more than food, and the body more than clothing? Look at the birds of the air: they neither sow nor reap nor gather into barns, and yet your heavenly Father feeds them. Are you not of more value than they? And which of you by being anxious can add one cubit[12] to his span of life? And why are you anxious about clothing? Consider the lilies of the field, how they grow; they neither toil nor spin; yet I tell you, even Solomon in all his glory was not arrayed like one of these. But if God so clothes the grass of the field, which today is alive and tomorrow is thrown into the oven, will he not much more clothe you, O men of little faith? Therefore do not be anxious, saying 'What shall we eat?' or 'What shall we drink?' or 'What shall we wear?' For the Gentiles seek all these things; and your heavenly Father knows that you need them all. But seek first his kingdom and his righteousness, and all these things shall be yours as well.

"Therefore do not be anxious about tomorrow, for tomorrow will be anxious for itself. Let the day's own trouble be sufficient for the day.

"Judge not, that you be not judged. For with the judgment you pronounce you will be judged, and the measure you give will be the measure you get. Why do you see the speck that is in your brother's eye, but do not notice the log that is in your own eye? Or how can you say to your brother, 'Let me take the speck out of your eye,' when there is the log in your own eye? You hypocrite, first take the log out of your own eye, and then you will see clearly to take the speck out of your brother's eye.

"Do not give dogs what is holy; and do not throw your pearls before swine, lest they trample them under foot and turn to attack you.

"Ask, and it will be given you; seek, and you will find; knock, and it will be opened to you. For every one who asks receives, and he who seeks finds, and to him who knocks it will be opened. Or what man of you, if his son asks him for bread, will give him a stone? Or if he asks for a fish, will give him a serpent? If you then, who are evil, know how to give good gifts to your children, how much more will your Father who is in heaven give good things to those who ask him! So whatever you wish that men would do to you, do so to them; for this is the law and the prophets.

"Enter by the narrow gate; for the gate is wide and the way is easy, that leads to destruction, and those who enter by it are many. For the gate is narrow and the way is hard, that leads to life, and those who find it are few.

"Beware of false prophets, who come to you in sheep's clothing but inwardly are ravenous wolves. You will know them by their fruits. Are grapes gathered from thorns, or figs from thistles? So, every sound tree bears good fruit, but the bad tree bears evil fruit. A sound tree cannot bear evil fruit, nor can a bad tree bear good fruit. Every tree that does not bear good fruit is cut down and thrown into the fire. Thus you will know them by their fruits.

"Not every one who says to me, 'Lord, Lord,' shall enter the kingdom of heaven, but he who does the will of my Father who is in heaven. On that day many will say to me, 'Lord, Lord, did we not prophesy in your name, and cast out demons in your name, and do many mighty works in your name?' And then will I declare to them, 'I never knew you; depart from me, you evildoers.'

[11]A Semitic word for money or material possessions.
[12]A measuring unit of about eighteen inches.

"Every one then who hears these words of mine and does them will be like a wise man who built his house upon the rock; and the rain fell, and the floods came, and the winds blew and beat upon that house, but it did not fall, because it had been founded on the rock. And every one who hears these words of mine and does not do them will be like a foolish man who built his house upon the sand; and the rain fell, and the floods came, and the winds blew and beat against that house, and it fell; and great was the fall of it."

And when Jesus finished these sayings, the crowds were astonished at his teaching, for he taught them as one who had authority, and not as their scribes.[13]

The Acts of the Apostles[14]

The Beginnings of the Church

1:1–2:47

In the first book,[15] O Theophilus,[16] I have dealt with all that Jesus began to do and teach, until the day when he was taken up, after he had given commandment through the Holy Spirit to the apostles whom he had chosen. To them he presented himself alive after his passion [death on the cross] by many proofs, appearing to them during forty days, and speaking of the kingdom of God. And while staying with them he charged them not to depart from Jerusalem, but to wait for the promise of the Father, which, he said, "you heard from me, for John baptized with water, but before many days you shall be baptized with the Holy Spirit."

So when they had come together, they asked him, "Lord will you at this time restore the kingdom to Israel?"[17] He said to them, "It is not for you to know times or seasons which the Father has fixed by his own authority. But you shall receive power when the Holy Spirit has come upon you; and you shall be my witnesses in Jerusalem and in all Judea and Samaria and to the end of the earth." And when he had said this, as they were looking on, he was lifted up, and a cloud took him out of their sight. And while they were gazing into heaven as he went, behold, two men stood by them in white robes, and said, "Men of Galilee, why do you stand looking into heaven? This Jesus, who was taken up from you into heaven, will come in the same way as you saw him go into heaven."

Then they returned to Jerusalem from the mount called Olivet, which is near Jerusalem, a sabbath day's journey away;[18] and when they had entered, they went up to the upper room, where they were staying, Peter and John and James and Andrew, Philip and Thomas, Bartholomew and Matthew, James the son of Alphaeus and Simon the Zealot and Judas the son of James. All these with one accord devoted themselves to prayer, together with the women and Mary the mother of Jesus, and with his brothers.[19]

In those days Peter stood up among the brethren (the company of persons was in all about a hundred and twenty), and said, "Brethren, the scripture had to be fulfilled, which the Holy Spirit spoke before-hand by the mouth of David, concerning Judas who was guide to those who arrested Jesus. For he was numbered among us, and was allotted his share in this ministry. (Now this man bought a field with the reward of his wickedness; and falling headlong he burst open in the middle and all his bowels gushed out. And it became known to all the inhabitants of Jerusalem, so that the field was called in their language Akeldama, that is, Field of Blood.)[20] For it is written in the book of Psalms [in the Old Testament],

---

[13]That is, as one who speaks on his own responsibility, as did the prophets—*not* as one who conforms to earlier authorities, as did the scribes.

[14]Written by the same person who had already written The Gospel According to Luke. This book traces the story of the Christian movement from the resurrection of Jesus to the time when the apostle Paul, as a prisoner, first travelled to Rome. We see in The Acts of the Apostles the broadening of the early Church from a small Jewish group centered in Jerusalem to a universal movement spreading throughout the Roman world. The time-span described is about A. D. 30–60.

[15]The Gospel According to Luke.

[16]Literally, in Greek, "lover of God," who might be any devout reader—or, possibly, an individual patron of the early Church.

[17]His followers are asking Jesus, since he had been promised the throne of his claimed ancestor, King David (tenth century B.C.), if he would restore the ancient kingdom of the Jews, now under Roman rule.

[18]The travel permitted Jews on the Sabbath, about a half-mile.

[19]Protestants believe that Mary had four sons—James, Joseph, Simon, and Judas—younger than Jesus. Catholic tradition regards them as relatives—but not blood brothers—of Jesus.

[20]The disciple Judas, who had betrayed Jesus to the Roman officials, had killed himself in this field. Now the sacred number of twelve disciples, corresponding to the ancient number of tribes among the Hebrews, must be restored.

'Let his habitation become desolate,
and let there be no one to live in it';

and

'His office let another take.'

So one of the men who have accompanied us during all the time that the Lord Jesus went in and out among us, beginning from the baptism of John until the day when he was taken up from us—one of these men must become with us a witness to his resurrection." And they put forward two, Joseph called Barsabbas, who was surnamed Justus, and Matthias. And they prayed and said, "Lord, who knowest the hearts of all men, show which one of these two thou hast chosen to take the place in this ministry and apostleship from which Judas turned aside, to go to his own place." And they cast lots for them, and the lot fell on Matthias; and he was enrolled with the eleven apostles.

When the day of Pentecost[21] had come, they were all together in one place. And suddenly a sound came from heaven like the rush of a mighty wind, and it filled all the house where they were sitting. And there appeared to them tongues as of fire, distributed and resting on each one of them. And they were all filled with the Holy Spirit and began to speak in other tongues,[22] as the Spirit gave them utterance.

Now there were dwelling in Jerusalem Jews, devout men from every nation under heaven. And at this sound the multitude came together, and they were bewildered, because each one heard them speaking in his own language. And they were amazed and wondered, saying, "Are not all these who are speaking Galileans? And how is it that we hear, each of us in his own native language? Parthians and Medes and Elamites and residents of Mesopotamia, Judea and Cappa-docia, Pontus and Asia, Phrygia and Pamphylia, Egypt and the parts of Libya belonging to Cyrene, and visitors from Rome, both Jews and proselytes, Cretans and Arabians, we hear them telling us in our own tongues the mighty works of God." And all were amazed and perplexed, saying to one another, "What does this mean?" But others mocking said, "They are filled with new wine."

But Peter, standing with the eleven, lifted up his voice and addressed them, "Men of Judea and all who dwell in Jerusalem, let this be known to you, and give ear to my words. For these men are not drunk, as you suppose, since it is only the third hour of the day;[23] but this is what was spoken by the prophet Joel:[24]

'And in the last days it shall be, God declares,
that I will pour out my Spirit upon all flesh,
and your sons and your daughters shall prophesy,
and your young men shall see visions,
and your old men shall dream dreams;
yea, and on my menservants and my maidservants in those days
I will pour out my Spirit; and they shall prophesy.
And I will show wonders in the heaven above
and signs on the earth beneath,
blood, and fire, and vapor of smoke;
the sun shall be turned into darkness
and the moon into blood,
before the day of the Lord comes, the great and manifest day.
And it shall be that whoever calls on the name of the Lord shall be saved.'

"Men of Israel, hear these words: Jesus of Nazareth, a man attested to you by God with mighty works and wonders and signs which God did through him in your midst, as you yourselves know—this Jesus, delivered up according to the definite plan and foreknowledge of God, you crucified and killed by the hands of lawless men. But God raised him up, having loosed the pangs of death, because it was not possible for him to be held by it. For David[25] says concerning him,

[21]Fifty days after Passover, the Jewish festival of Pentecost (Shavuot) celebrated the harvesting of the first fruits; at this time in Jewish history, Pentecost also celebrated the giving of the Law at Mount Sinai.

[22]That is, other languages. This ability is explained as a miracle from the Holy Spirit.

[23]About 9 a.m.

[24]Peter quotes the following passage from the Old Testament prophet Joel (2:28–32).

[25]Peter paraphrases from Psalm 16 in the Old Testament, credited to King David.

> 'I saw the Lord always before me,
> for he is at my right hand that I may not be shaken;
> therefore my heart was glad, and my tongue rejoiced;
> moreover my flesh will dwell in hope.
> For thou wilt not abandon my soul to Hades,
> nor let thy Holy One see corruption.
> Thou hast made known to me the ways of life;
> thou wilt make me full of gladness with thy presence.'

Brethren, I may say to you confidently of the patriarch David that he both died and was buried, and his tomb is with us to this day. Being therefore a prophet, and knowing that God had sworn with an oath to him that he would set one of his descendants upon his throne, he foresaw and spoke of the resurrection of the Christ, that he was not abandoned to Hades, nor did his flesh see corruption. This Jesus God raised up, and of that we all are witnesses. Being therefore exalted at the right hand of God, and having received from the Father the promise of the Holy Spirit, he has poured out this which you see and hear. For David did not ascend into the heavens; but he himself says,

> 'The Lord said to my Lord, Sit at my right hand,
> till I make [of] thy enemies a stool for thy feet.'[26]

Let all the house of Israel therefore know assuredly that God has made him both Lord and Christ, this Jesus whom you crucified."[27]

Now when they heard this they were cut to the heart, and said to Peter and the rest of the apostles, "Brethren, what shall we do?" And Peter said to them, "Repent, and be baptized every one of you in the name of Jesus Christ for the forgiveness of your sins; and you shall receive the gift of the Holy Spirit. For the promise is to you and to your children and to all that are far off, every one whom the Lord our God calls to him." And he testified with many other words and exhorted them, saying, "Save yourselves from this crooked generation." So those who received his word were baptized, and there were added that day about three thousand souls. And they devoted themselves to the apostles' teaching and fellowship, to the breaking of bread[28] and the prayers.

And fear came upon every soul; and many wonders and signs were done through the apostles. And all who believed were together and had all things in common; and they sold their possessions and goods and distributed them to all, as any had need. And day by day, attending the temple together and breaking bread in their homes, they partook of food with glad and generous hearts, praising God and having favor with all the people. And the Lord added to their number day by day those who were being saved.

•   •   •

The Conversion of Saul[29]

8:1–4; 9:1–20

And on that day a great persecution arose against the church in Jerusalem; and they were all scattered throughout the region of Judea and Samaria, except the apostles. Devout men buried Stephen,[30] and made great lamentation over him. But Saul laid waste the church, and entering house after house, he dragged off men and women and committed them to prison.

Now those who were scattered went about preaching the word. . . .

But Saul, still breathing threats and murder against the disciples of the Lord, went to the high priest and asked him for letters to the synagogues at Damascus, so that if he found any belonging to the Way, men or women, he

---

[26]From Psalm 110.

[27]That is, the human Jesus was not only Christ the Messiah ("anointed" savior who will rule Israel on earth), but also the heavenly Lord.

[28]Apparently, a common meal which included the Lord's Supper (see Paul's First Letter to the Corinthians).

[29]Saul was a Greek-speaking Jew from Tarsus in Asia Minor. Originally employed as a persecutor of the Christians in Jerusalem and Damascus, *ca.* A.D. 36, he was converted on the road to Damascus by the blinding vision described here. After the conversion he was usually known by his Greek name, Paul. Most of The Acts of the Apostles concerns Paul's travels to organize local congregations of Christians.

[30]The first Christian martyr, Stephen, had been stoned to death while Saul looked on.

might bring them bound to Jerusalem. Now as he journeyed he approached Damascus, and suddenly a light from heaven flashed about him. And he fell to the ground and heard a voice saying to him, "Saul, Saul, why do you persecute me?" And he said, "Who are you, Lord?" And he said, "I am Jesus, whom you are persecuting; but rise and enter the city, and you will be told what you are to do." The men who were travelling with him stood speechless, hearing the voice but seeing no one. Saul arose from the ground; and when his eyes were opened, he could see nothing; so they led him by the hand and brought him into Damascus. And for three days he was without sight, and neither ate nor drank.

Now there was a disciple at Damascus named Ananias. The Lord said to him in a vision, "Ananias." And he said, "Here I am, Lord." And the Lord said to him, "Rise and go to the street called Straight, and inquire in the house of Judas for a man of Tarsus named Saul; for behold, he is praying, and he has seen a man named Ananias come in and lay his hands on him so that he might regain his sight." But Ananias answered, "Lord, I have heard from many about this man, how much evil he has done to thy saints at Jerusalem; and here he has authority from the chief priests to bind all who call upon thy name." But the Lord said to him, "Go, for he is a chosen instrument of mine to carry my name before the Gentiles and kings and the sons of Israel; for I will show him how much he must suffer for the sake of my name." So Ananias departed and entered the house. And laying his hands on him he said, "Brother Saul, the Lord Jesus who appeared to you on the road by which you came, has sent me that you may regain your sight and be filled with the Holy Spirit." And immediately something like scales fell from his eyes and he regained his sight. Then he rose and was baptized, and took food and was strengthened.

For several days he was with the disciples at Damascus. And in the synagogues immediately he proclaimed Jesus, saying, "He is the Son of God."

The First Letter of Paul to the Corinthians[31]

Salutation {Greeting}

1:1–3

Paul, called by the will of God to be an apostle of Christ Jesus. . . .

To the Church of God which is at Corinth, to those sanctified in Christ Jesus, called to be saints together with all those who in every place call on the name of our Lord Jesus Christ, both their Lord and ours:

Grace to you and peace from God our Father and the Lord Jesus Christy.

On Sexual Morality and Marriage

5:1–2; 7:1–11

It is actually reported that there is immorality among you, and of a kind that is not found even among pagans; for a man is living with his father's wife. And you are arrogant! Ought you not rather to mourn? Let him who has done this be removed from among you.

• • •

Now concerning the matters about which you wrote. It is well for a man not to touch a woman. But because of the temptation to immorality, each man should have his own wife and each woman her own husband. The husband should give to his wife her conjugal rights, and likewise the wife to her husband. For the wife does not rule over her own body, but the husband does; likewise the husband does not rule over his own body, but the wife does. Do not refuse one another except perhaps by agreement for a season, that you may devote yourselves to prayer; but then come

[31]After his conversion Paul travelled untiringly throughout the eastern part of the Roman-controlled Mediterranean world, spreading the Christian message (mainly to non-Jews). This letter, written about A.D. 55, shows Paul in his typical stern role as the sender of doctrinal and moral advice to the backsliding Christian congregation at Corinth in Greece. Many of its new believers were illiterate slaves or freedmen, the lowest elements of a city noted for its vices, hostile factions, and a great variety of gods. (Corinth was the city where Lucius was transformed and became a worshipper of the pagan goddess Isis; see *The Golden Ass.*)

together again, lest Satan tempt you through lack of self-control. I say this by way of concession, not of command. I wish that all were as I myself am.[32] But each has his own special gift from God, one of one kind and one of another.

To the unmarried and the widows I say that it is well for them to remain single as I do. But if they cannot exercise self-control, they should marry. For it is better to marry than to be aflame with passion.

To the married I give charge, not I but the Lord, that the wife should not separate from her husband (but if she does, let her remain single or else be reconciled to her husband)—and that the husband should not divorce his wife.

On Roles of Men and Women

11:2–12; 14:34–35

I commend you because you remember me in everything and maintain the traditions even as I have delivered them to you. But I want you to understand that the head of every man is Christ, the head of a woman is her husband, and the head of Christ is God. Any man who prays or prophesies with his head covered dishonors his head, but any woman who prays or prophesies with her head unveiled dishonors her head—it is the same as if her head were shaven. For if a woman will not veil herself, then she should cut off her hair; but if it is disgraceful for a woman to be shorn or shaven, let her wear a veil. For a man ought not to cover his head, since he is the image and glory of God; but woman is the glory of man. (For man was not made from woman, but woman from man. Neither was man created for woman, but woman for man.) That is why a woman ought to have a veil on her head, because of the angels.[33] (Nevertheless, in the Lord woman is not independent of man nor man of woman; for as woman was made from man, so man is now born of woman. And all things are from God.)

• • •

As in all the churches of the saints, the women should keep silence in the churches. For they are not permitted to speak, but should be subordinate, as even the law says. If there is anything they desire to know, let them ask their husbands at home. For it is shameful for a woman to speak in church.

The Lord's Supper

10:1–5, 14–22; 11:17–27

I want you to know, brethren, that our fathers were all under the cloud, and all passed through the sea,[34] and all were baptized into Moses in the cloud and in the sea, and all ate the same supernatural food and all drank the same supernatural drink. For they drank from the supernatural Rock which followed them, and the Rock was Christ.[35] Nevertheless with most of them God was not pleased; for they were overthrown in the wilderness.[36] . . . Therefore, my beloved, shun the worship of idols. I speak as to sensible men; judge for yourselves what I say. The cup of blessing which we bless, is it not a participation in the blood of Christ? The bread which we break, is it not a participation in the body of Christ? Because there is one bread, we who are many are one body, for we all partake of the one bread. Consider the people of Israel; are not those who eat the sacrifices partners in the altar? What do I imply then? That food offered to idols is anything, or that an idol is anything? No, I imply that what pagans sacrifice they offer to demons and not to God.[37] I do not want you to be partners with demons. You cannot drink the cup of the Lord and the cup of demons. You cannot partake of the table of the Lord and the table of demons. Shall we provoke the Lord to jealousy? Are we stronger than he?

• • •

[32]That is, unmarried.
[33]The angels were thought to carry out God's law.
[34]In Exodus the Jews were led by Moses away from Egypt; God guided them by day with a "pillar of cloud" and divided the water of the Red Sea so they could cross over to the Sinai desert.
[35]According to a Hebrew legend, the Rock had followed the Jews in the desert; Paul asserts that the source of this life-giving water was the pre-existent Christ.
[36]That is, baptism and taking of the Lord's Supper are, by themselves, not enough to guarantee salvation, any more than similar acts provided salvation for most of the Jews of Exodus.
[37]That is, carved idols are nothing, but demons (pagan gods) use them as camouflage. Thus, eating food consecrated to demons is defiance of God.

But in the following instructions I do not commend you, because when you come together it is not for the better but for the worse. For, in the first place, when you assemble as a church, I hear that there are divisions among you; and I partly believe it, for there must be factions[38] among you in order that those who are genuine among you may be recognized. When you meet together, it is not the Lord's supper that you eat. For in eating, each one goes ahead with his own meal, and one is hungry and another is drunk. What! Do you not have houses to eat and drink in? Or do you despise the church of God and humiliate those who have nothing? What shall I say to you? Shall I commend you in this? No, I will not.

For I received from the Lord what I also delivered to you, that the Lord Jesus on the night when he was betrayed took bread, and when he had given thanks, he broke it, and said, "This is my body which is for you. Do this in remembrance of me." In the same way also the cup, after supper, saying, "This cup is the new covenant in my blood.[39] Do this, as often as you drink it, in remembrance of me." For as often as you eat this bread and drink the cup, you proclaim the Lord's death until he comes.

Whoever, therefore, eats the bread or drinks the cup of the Lord in an unworthy manner will be guilty of profaning the body and blood of the Lord.

On Love

13:1–13

If I speak in the tongues of men and of angels, but have not love, I am a noisy gong or a clanging cymbal. And if I have prophetic powers, and understand all mysteries and all knowledge, and if I have all faith, so as to remove mountains, but have not love, I am nothing. If I give away all I have, and if I deliver my body to be burned, but have not love, I gain nothing.

Love is patient and kind; love is not jealous or boastful; it is not arrogant or rude. Love does not insist on its own way; it is not irritable or resentful; it does not rejoice at wrong, but rejoices in the right. Love bears all things, believes all things, hopes all things, endures all things.

Love never ends; as for prophecies, they will pass away; as for tongues, they will cease; as for knowledge, it will pass away. For our knowledge is imperfect and our prophecy is imperfect; but when the perfect comes, the imperfect will pass away. When I was a child, I spoke like a child, I thought like a child, I reasoned like a child; when I became a man, I gave up childish ways. For now we see in a mirror dimly, but then face to face. Now I know in part; then I shall understand fully, even as I have been fully understood. So faith, hope, love abide, these three; but the greatest of these is love.

Life After Death

15:1–58

Now I would remind you, brethren, in what terms I preached to you the gospel, which you received, in which you stand, by which you are saved, if you hold it fast—unless you believed in vain.

For I delivered to you as of first importance what I also received, that Christ died for our sins in accordance with the scriptures,[40] that he was buried, that he was raised on the third day in accordance with the scriptures and that he appeared to Cephas, then to the twelve. Then he appeared to more than five hundred brethren at one time, most of whom are still alive, though some have fallen asleep. Then he appeared to James, then to all the apostles. Last of all, as to one untimely born he appeared also to me. For I am the least of the apostles, unfit to be called an apostle, because I persecuted the church of God. But by the grace of God I am what I am, and his grace toward me was not in vain. On the contrary, I worked harder than any of them, though it was not I, but the grace of God which is with me. Whether then it was I or they, so we preach and so you believed.

---

[38]Rival cliques, perhaps corresponding to the differing social classes at the common meal that took place in connection with the Lord's Supper.

[39]The old covenant with God at Mount Sinai had also been sealed with blood—from the sacrificed animals of the burnt offerings (Exodus 24:8).

[40]Probably Paul means the Old Testament in general when he refers to "the scriptures." However, later tradition specifically cited The Song of the Suffering Servant from Isaiah (pp. 571–72) as an Old Testament prophecy of Jesus' death—and Psalm 16:10 for prophecy of his resurrection ("For thou dost not give me up to Sheol [the underworld of the dead], or let thy godly one see the Pit").

Now if Christ is preached as raised from the dead, how can some of you say that there is no resurrection of the dead? But if there is no resurrection of the dead, then Christ has not been raised; if Christ has not been raised, then our preaching is in vain and your faith is in vain. We are even found to be misrepresenting God, because we testified of God that he raised Christ, whom he did not raise if it is true that the dead are not raised. For if the dead are not raised, then Christ has not been raised. If Christ has not been raised, your faith is futile and you are still in your sins. Then those also who have fallen asleep in Christ have perished.[41] If for this life only we have hoped in Christ, we are of all men most to be pitied.

But in fact Christ has been raised from the dead, the first fruits of those who have fallen asleep. For as by a man came death, by a man has come also the resurrection of the dead. For as in Adam all die, so also in Christ shall all be made alive. But each in his own order: Christ the first fruits, then at his coming[42] those who belong to Christ. Then comes the end, when he delivers the kingdom to God the Father after destroying every rule and every authority and power. For he must reign until he has put all his enemies under his feet. The last enemy to be destroyed is death. "For God has put all things in subjection under his feet." But when it says, "All things are put in subjection under him," it is plain that he is excepted who put all things under him. When all things are subjected to him, then the Son himself will also be subjected to him who put all things under him, that God may be everything to every one.

Otherwise, what do people mean by being baptized on behalf of the dead?[43] If the dead are not raised at all, why are people baptized on their behalf? Why am I in peril every hour? I protest, brethren, by my pride in you which I have in Christ Jesus our Lord, I die every day![44] What do I gain if, humanly speaking, I fought with beasts at Ephesus? If the dead are not raised, "Let us eat and drink, for tomorrow we die." Do not be deceived: "Bad company ruins good morals." Come to your right mind, and sin no more. For some have no knowledge of God. I say this to your shame.

But some one will ask, "How are the dead raised? With what kind of body do they come?" You foolish man! What you sow does not come to life unless it dies. And what you sow is not the body which is to be, but a bare kernel, perhaps of wheat or of some other grain. But God gives it a body as he has chosen, and to each kind of seed its own body. For not all flesh is alike, but there is one kind for men, another for animals, another for birds, and another for fish. There are celestial bodies and there are terrestrial bodies; but the glory of the celestial is one, and the glory of the terrestrial is another. There is one glory of the sun, and another glory of the moon, and another glory of the stars; for star differs from star in glory.

So is it with the resurrection of the dead. What is sown is perishable, what is raised is imperishable. It is sown in dishonour, it is raised in glory. It is sown in weakness, it is raised in power. It is sown a physical body, it is raised a spiritual body. If there is a physical body, there is also a spiritual body. Thus it is written, "The first man Adam became a living being";[45] the last Adam became a life-giving spirit. But it is not the spiritual which is first but the physical, and then the spiritual. The first man was from the earth, a man of dust; the second man is from heaven. As was the man of dust, so are those who are of the dust; and as is the man of heaven, so are those who are of heaven. Just as we have born the image of the man of dust, we shall also bear the image of the man of heaven. I tell you this, brethren: flesh and blood cannot inherit the kingdom of God, nor does the perishable inherit the imperishable.

Lo! I tell you a mystery. We shall not all sleep, but we shall all be changed, in a moment, in the twinkling of an eye, at the last trumpet.[46] For the trumpet will sound, and the dead will be raised imperishable, and we shall be changed. For this perishable nature must put on the imperishable, and this mortal nature must put on immortality. When the perishable puts on the imperishable, and the mortal puts on immortality, then shall come to pass the saying that is written:

> "Death is swallowed up in victory."
> "O death, where is thy victory?
> O death, where is thy sting?"

[41]That is, those who have died as Christians are utterly lost unless Christ was raised from the dead.

[42]The *second* coming of Christ, which will end the present age of humankind and establish his kingdom after a great struggle.

[43]Apparently, some of the early Christians accepted baptism in the names of their loved ones who had died without being baptized, in order to insure their loved ones' resurrection.

[44]That is, I risk death every day.

[45]See the second version of creation in Genesis.

[46]That is, many Christians, alive now, will survive until Christ returns, but all—whether living or dead—will receive spiritual bodies.

The sting of death is sin, and the power of sin is the law.[47] But thanks be to God, who gives us the victory through our Lord Jesus Christ.

Therefore, my beloved brethren, be steadfast, immovable, always abounding in the work of the Lord, knowing that in the Lord your labor is not in vain.

The Letter of Paul to the Romans[48]

Salutation

1:1–7

Paul, a servant of Jesus Christ, called to be an apostle, set apart for the gospel of God which he promised beforehand through his prophets in the holy scriptures, the gospel concerning his Son, who was descended from David according to the flesh and designated Son of God in power according to the Spirit of holiness by his resurrection from the dead, Jesus Christ our Lord, through whom we have received grace[49] and apostleship to bring about the obedience of faith for the sake of his name among all the nations, including yourselves who are called to belong to Jesus Christ;

To all God's beloved in Rome, who are called to be saints:

Grace to you and peace from God our Father and the Lord Jesus Christ.

Salvation Through Faith Alone

1:16–25

For I am not ashamed of the gospel: it is the power of God for salvation to every one who has faith, to the Jew first and also to the Greek.[50] For in it the righteousness of God is revealed through faith for faith; as it is written, "He who through faith is righteous shall live."

For the wrath of God is revealed from heaven against all ungodliness and wickedness of men who by their wickedness suppress the truth. For what can be known about God is plain to them, because God has shown it to them. Ever since the creation of the world his invisible nature, namely, his eternal power and deity, has been clearly perceived in the things that have been made. So they are without excuse; for although they knew God they did not honor him as God or give thanks to him, but they became futile in their thinking and their senseless minds were darkened. Claiming to be wise, they became fools, and exchanged the glory of the immortal God for images resembling mortal man or birds or animals or reptiles.

Therefore God gave them up in the lusts of their hearts to impurity, to the dishonoring of their bodies among themselves, because they exchanged the truth about God for a lie and worshiped and served the creature rather than the Creator, who is blessed for ever! Amen.

God Is For Every Person, Without Partiality

2:1–3:9

Therefore you have no excuse, O man, whoever you are, when you judge another; for in passing judgment upon him you condemn yourself, because you, the judge, are doing the very same things. We know that the judgment of God rightly falls upon those who do such things. Do you suppose, O man, that when you judge those who do such things and yet do them yourself, you will escape the judgment of God? Or do you presume upon the riches of his kindness

---

[47]That is, although the Law reflects God's intentions, in practice it is often powerless against sin and even encourages it by focusing a person's thoughts on sin.

[48]This letter, probably written from Corinth early in 57, tells of Paul's intention to visit Rome on his way to begin a new mission in Spain. In Rome there was a Christian community Paul had not founded or even seen. Paul's religious thinking is here clearly set forth. He argues for the doctrine of "justification": that forgiveness from the penalty of sin comes only through *faith in Christ*. Paul also deals with the role in the *new* covenant of his Jewish kindred, for justification applies equally to Jew and Gentile.

[49]The freely given, undeserved favor and love of God.

[50]Non-Jews in general; the eastern end of the Mediterranean was culturally Hellenistic (Greek). Thus, the entire New Testament was written in the Greek language.

and forbearance and patience? Do you not know that God's kindness is meant to lead you to repentance? But by your hard and impenitent heart you are storing up wrath for yourself on the day of wrath when God's righteous judgment will be revealed. For he will render to every man according to his works: to those who by patience in well-doing seek for glory and honor and immortality, he will give eternal life; but for those who are factious and do not obey the truth, but obey wickedness, there will be wrath and fury. There will be tribulation and distress for every human being who does evil, the Jew first and also the Greek,[51] but glory and honor and peace for every one who does good, the Jew first and also the Greek. For God shows no partiality.

All who have sinned without the law will also perish without the law, and all who have sinned under the law will be judged by the law. For it is not the hearers of the law who are righteous before God, but the doers of the law who will be justified. When Gentiles who have not the law do by nature what the law requires, they are a law to themselves, even though they do not have the law. They show that what the law requires is written on their hearts, while their conscience also bears witness and their conflicting thoughts accuse or perhaps excuse them on that day when, according to my gospel, God judges the secrets of men by Christ Jesus.

But if you call yourself a Jew and rely upon the law and boast of your relation to God and know his will and approve what is excellent, because you are instructed in the law, and if you are sure that you are a guide to the blind, a light to those who are in darkness, a corrector of the foolish, a teacher of children, having in the law the embodiment of knowledge and truth—you then who teach others, will you not teach yourself? While you preach against stealing, do you steal? You who say that one must not commit adultery, do you commit adultery? You who abhor idols, do you rob temples? You who boast in the law, do you dishonor God by breaking the law? For, as it is written, "The name of God is blasphemed among the Gentiles because of you."

Circumcision indeed is of value if you obey the law; but if you break the law, your circumcision becomes uncircumcision.[52] So, if a man who is uncircumcised keeps the precepts of the law, will not his uncircumcision be regarded as circumcision? Then those who are physically uncircumcised but keep the law will condemn you who have the written code and circumcision but break the law. For he is not a real Jew who is one outwardly, nor is true circumcision something external and physical. He is a Jew who is one inwardly, and real circumcision is a matter of the heart, spiritual and not literal. His praise is not from men but from God.

Then what advantage has the Jew? Or what is the value of circumcision? Much in every way. To begin with, the Jews are entrusted with the oracles of God. What if some were unfaithful? Does their faithlessness nullify the faithfulness of God? By no means! Let God be true though every man be false, as it is written,[53]

> "That thou mayest be justified in thy words,
> and prevail when thou art judged."

But if our wickedness serves to show the justice of God, what shall we say? That God is unjust to inflict wrath on us? (I speak in a human way.) By no means! For then how could God judge the world? But if through my falsehood God's truthfulness abounds to his glory, why am I still being condemned as a sinner? And why not do evil that good may come?—as some people slanderously charge us with saying. Their condemnation is just.

What then? Are we Jews any better off? No, not at all; for I have already charged that all men, both Jews and Greeks, are under the power of sin. . . .

Justification[54] through Faith by God's Grace—Not Through Works

3:21–31

But now the righteousness of God has been manifested apart from law, although the law and the prophets bear witness to it, the righteousness of God through faith in Jesus Christ for all who believe. For there is no distinction; since all have sinned and fall short of the glory of God, they are justified by his grace as a gift, through the

---

[51]The Jew *first* because the special relationship granted to the people who had received the earlier covenant increased their responsibility. Both Jews and Gentiles, however, are *judged* equally by their actions, the Jews under the Law of Moses as found in the Old Testament, the Gentiles by the same standard as "written on their hearts."

[52]That is, the Jewish violator of the Law stands before God precisely where the pagan violator stands. (Circumcision is the physical symbol of God's covenant with the Hebrews, Genesis 17.)

[53]In Psalm 51.

[54]Pardon, forgiveness by God of humans' sinful guilt—necessary for individual salvation.

redemption[55] which is in Christ Jesus, whom God put forward as an expiation by his blood,[56] to be received by faith. This was to show God's righteousness, because in his divine forbearance he had passed over former sins; it was to prove at the present time that he himself is righteous and that he justifies him who has faith in Jesus.

Then what becomes of our boasting? It is excluded. On what principle? On the principle of works? No, but on the principle of faith.[57] For we hold that a man is justified by faith apart from works of law. Or is God the God of Jews only? Is he not the God of Gentiles also? Yes, of Gentiles also, since God is one; and he will justify the circumcised on the ground of their faith and the uncircumcised through their faith. Do we then overthrow the law by this faith? By no means! On the contrary, we uphold the law.

[55]Payment (for sin), liberation, deliverance.

[56]Christ's death is a sacrificial atonement (expiation) for human sin; it is God's way of cleansing away the sins of the faithful.

[57]That is, if salvation could be achieved by human "works" (deeds), there might be a reason for boasting; but since salvation is through *faith*, there is no reason for pride.